Literatures of the Americas

Series Editor
Norma E. Cantú
San Antonio, TX, USA

The Literature of the Americas series seeks to establish a conversation between and among scholars working in different Latina/o/x and Latin American cultural contexts across historical and geographical boundaries. Designed to explore key questions confronting contemporary issues of literary and cultural transfers, the series, rooted in traditional frameworks to literary criticism, includes cutting-edge scholarly work using theories such as postcolonial, critical race, or ecofeminist approaches. With a particular focus on Latina/o/x realities in the United States, the books in the series support an inclusive and all-encompassing vision of what constitutes literary and textual studies that includes film, arts, popular culture, and traditional and avant-garde cultural expressions.

Editorial Board:
Larissa M. Mercado-López, California State University, Fresno, USA
Ricardo Ortiz, Georgetown University, USA
Romana Radlwimmer, Goethe-University of Frankfurt, Germany
Ana Maria Manzanas, University of Salamanca, Spain

Krzysztof A. Kulawik

Visions of Transmerica

Neobaroque Strategies of Nomadic Transgression

Krzysztof A. Kulawik
History, World Languages and Cultures
Central Michigan University
Michigan, United States Minor Outlying Islands

ISSN 2634-601X   ISSN 2634-6028   (electronic)
Literatures of the Americas
ISBN 978-3-031-42013-9   ISBN 978-3-031-42014-6   (eBook)
https://doi.org/10.1007/978-3-031-42014-6

© The Editor(s) (if applicable) and The Author(s), under exclusive licence to Springer Nature Switzerland AG 2024
This work is subject to copyright. All rights are solely and exclusively licensed by the Publisher, whether the whole or part of the material is concerned, specifically the rights of translation, reprinting, reuse of illustrations, recitation, broadcasting, reproduction on microfilms or in any other physical way, and transmission or information storage and retrieval, electronic adaptation, computer software, or by similar or dissimilar methodology now known or hereafter developed.
The use of general descriptive names, registered names, trademarks, service marks, etc. in this publication does not imply, even in the absence of a specific statement, that such names are exempt from the relevant protective laws and regulations and therefore free for general use.
The publisher, the authors, and the editors are safe to assume that the advice and information in this book are believed to be true and accurate at the date of publication. Neither the publisher nor the authors or the editors give a warranty, expressed or implied, with respect to the material contained herein or for any errors or omissions that may have been made. The publisher remains neutral with regard to jurisdictional claims in published maps and institutional affiliations.

This Palgrave Macmillan imprint is published by the registered company Springer Nature Switzerland AG.
The registered company address is: Gewerbestrasse 11, 6330 Cham, Switzerland

Paper in this product is recyclable.

In memoriam
Andrzej Kulawik
(1947–1998)
My dear father who instilled in me the spirit of discovery of New Worlds

Foreword to *Transmerica*

Logical identity, A=A, has no relevance in life nor in the enlightened use of language. The poetics of the baroque elaborates the "concept" (as Baltasar Gracián called it in *Agudeza y arte de ingenio*, 1642). The "concept" dismantles the notion of identity through the privileged figures of oxymoron and paradox. Identity, in logic, is only understood in opposition to contradiction, while for baroque thought there is neither identity nor contradiction, but a play of differences. Paradox is an apparent contradiction that is resolved through a careful examination of the problem at hand.

From an epistemological point of view, it is necessary to remember that since the end of the sixteenth century the Greek skeptical philosophers of late antiquity, in particular Sextus Empiricus, were translated into Latin and produced a decisive impact on baroque thought. The first to take up this skeptical questioning, which demolished the walls of scholastic philosophy, was Francisco Sánchez in his work *Que nada se sabe* (1580). He was followed by Michel de Montaigne in "Apologie de Raimond Sebond" (1582). Thomas Hobbes refutes, in his "Objections," the argumentation of Descartes' *Metaphysical Meditations* (1641). John Locke, in his *Essay Concerning Human Understanding* (1690), rejects the so-called innate ideas of the same philosopher (1688). The skeptical/empiricist tradition culminated in David Hume's *Treatise on Human Nature* (1740) which, as Immanuel Kant admitted referring to himself, awakened him from his "dogmatic dream."

In the second half of the twentieth century, the poetics that has come to be called neobaroque confronts two traditions of thought: (a) the

viii FOREWORD TO *TRANSMERICA*

theological/religious one does not recognize the variables of historical change and defends "traditional values" as if they were eternal, defined once and for all; (b) the metaphysical and totalizing tradition of Hegel, which passing on to Marx, operates in terms of identity and contradiction. According to Marx, one class must eliminate another: the "workers" must eliminate the "bourgeois," without considering the sociological fabric in its concrete complexity, which also includes the peasants, who have been an uncomfortable problem for Marxist doctrine. The "real socialism" of the Soviet Union sought to reduce and subjugate the peasants through deliberate, artificially introduced famines, causing the starvation of five million under Lenin and almost ten million under Stalin. The parliament of independent Ukraine declared Leninist-Stalinist policies as genocide.

Both the religious theological tradition and the Hegelian-Marxist tradition move on the basis of totalizations, be it the religious dogma that admits of no discussion or the vision of history from a single point of view that also admits of no discussion. Marx elaborates a new metaphysical formula of redemption on the way to a utopian paradise. Christianity places it outside of life, while the new formula (Marxism-Leninism) places it on Earth, in a future always postponed. In both cases, it is a vision of the afterlife. Marxist tradition has tended to replace the Christian tradition. In the twentieth century, the totalizing formula reached its apogee with the totalitarianism of Lenin, Hitler, and Stalin. Today, we are confronted by Putin's imperial fascism.

By contrast, neobaroque thought has taken up the thread of seventeenth-century baroque "sharpness," from which it developed a dissident politics and aesthetics. The events of the French May of 1968 determined a fundamental change in the understanding of the artistic, of the political, and of their boundaries. While the Marxist strategy was aimed at the seizure of a central locus of power to install dictatorship, from which all the supposed utopian benefits would derive, Michel Foucault introduced the notion of micropolitics, of wars of style, not aimed at the macro purpose of the seizure of a central power, but to the derailment of the very idea of the political, implying the change of lifestyles, an always differential plurality of minorities in the field of relations involving coexistence, sex, art, environmental problems, biopolitics, hot values of diversity. In any case, it is an attempt to recover and give value to bodily intensities.

Foucault writes:

FOREWORD TO *TRANSMERICA*   ix

In the development of a political process—I do not know if revolutionary—there has appeared, with increasing insistence, the problem of the body. It can be said that what happened in May '68—and, probably, what prepared it—was profoundly anti-Marxist. How are revolutionary movements going to be able to free themselves from the 'Marx effect', from the institutions proper to the Marxism of the nineteenth and twentieth centuries? Such was the orientation of this movement. In the critique of the identity of Marxism-as-revolutionary process, an identity that constituted a kind of dogma, the importance of the body is one of the decisive or essential pieces.[1]

So, problems that Marxism avoided, sidestepped, or ignored arise with increasing urgency. Marx and Engels considered heterosexuality a datum of nature; heterosexuality could not be questioned at all. Consequently, the division of labor between men and women was even, in greater part, a natural fact. They posed no problem that would not be defined in terms of economic conflict of interests. The Marxist standardization, the equivalence of "to each according to his needs," reveals that these "needs" were considered by Marx abstractly, just like labor. Everyone's needs vary all the time; they depend on circumstances in a plurivocal game of affirmations of difference; they are not to be decided and imposed from above by a command economy on the basis of a supposed consensus, nor hypostasized into a "collective will" or utopian transparency in which all would agree. Lifestyles, states altered by the experience of drugs, the exploration of new forms of family, music and art as primary factors of a desiring drift, gauged by intense moments, were dismissed by Marxists as epiphenomena of the bourgeoisie. In the tradition of Marxist governments, identity, as "class origin," became destiny.

Foucault considers identity an imposture that prevents participation in the being of others. He agrees with the following words of Gilles Deleuze:

There is no identity of a represented thing, nor of an author, nor of a character on the stage; nor any representation that can be the object of a final recognition, but only a theater of problems and of always open questions that drag the spectator, the scene, and the characters in the real movement of an apprenticeship.[2]

---

[1] Foucault, Michel, *Microfísica del poder*, Madrid, La Piqueta, 1980, p. 105.
[2] Deleuze, Gilles, *Diferencia y repetición*, Buenos Aires, Amorrortu, 2002, p. 291.

x FOREWORD TO *TRANSMERICA*

Foucault is anti-Hegelian "insofar as he does not expect from the dynamics of the subject of history the possibility of change. Change is political, at the level of forces, and not logical at the level of essences."[3] The possibility of change does not expect anything from any dialectical dynamics, nor does it expect anything from any prophecy. History does not have a unique explanation, which does not mean that it is absurd or incoherent. We wonder in what sense contradiction functions as the logical relation privileged by Hegel and by Marx: "Only in one: in relation to identity."[4]

Contradiction establishes fixed identities according to the categories of totalization (class struggle, economic interest, dictatorship of the proletariat). However, except in the case of tyranny, contradiction is not the appropriate logical form for conceiving relations between individuals and groups. Foucault does not think according to the mode of contradiction—frontal contradictions in the manner of Hegel's idealist dialectic or Marx's materialist one—but through difference. He admits flows, displacements, a play of truths and powers to a certain extent reciprocal, multilateral, in war, resistance, negotiation, stimulation, and pleasure. He abjures the nineteenth-century intellectual who "understood" his century and pontificated. By connecting historical research and present event in a strategy of struggle, Foucault collaborated with the rising winds of his time. How does will work there? How are power relations configured?

> In reality it is a matter of bringing into play local, discontinuous, unqualified, unlegitimized knowledge against the unitary theoretical instance that pretends to filter, hierarchize, order them in the name of true knowledge and the privileges of a science that is held by few.[5]

In my task as a writer, I have followed these guidelines, aware that the poetic game is a game of freedom that seeks to use the resources of language to articulate an unconditioned thought. In my research, I have tried to find the neobaroque symptoms of a new free thought in Latin America. Together with the Cuban poet José Kozer, I compiled a sample of Spanish

---

[3] Pompei, Marcelo, "Algún día Foucault será deleuziano." In: Abraham, Tomás, compiler, *La máquina Deleuze*. Buenos Aires: Sudamericana, 2006, p. 222.

[4] Pompei, ibid., p. 222.

[5] Foucault, Michel, *Microfísica del poder*, Madrid, La Piqueta, 1980, pp. 179–180.

American and Brazilian poetry, *Medusario*, which merges multiple voices of the neobaroque.[6]

I believe that this multifaceted trend draws its inspiration as much from the poetics of the "concept" of the Golden Age, for which the figures of oxymoron and paradox testify to a critical awareness of language, as from the emancipatory movements, both social and aesthetic, of the second half of the twentieth century.

Visions of Transmerica: Neobaroque Strategies of Nomadic Transgression presents a comprehensive mapping of neobaroque aesthetics and thought in Latin America. It describes new possibilities of conceiving selfhood as a process of becoming and of crossing the borders of previously prescribed traditions and ideology. It is devoted to registering new experiences—the bodily, literary, artistic, and the critical. It proposes to evade identity, as a non-concept, unable to describe or characterize our experiences in a changing society and cultural environment. It opens, one could say, "the doors of perception" toward new artistic objects and libidinal processes. There are two lines of change going hand in hand—one a political social process, the other an aesthetic process of artistic creation—that are not independent from one another. The crisis of authoritarian models, be they from the right or the left, be they military dictatorships (in Argentina, Uruguay, Chile) or the so-called revolutionary dictatorships (as in Cuba, Venezuela, Nicaragua), pivots around the notion of identity as such. The notion of identity is in crisis with the ongoing practice of difference that affords for a new visibility of previously censored ethnic and sexual minorities. Michel Foucault replaces the notion of identity with the notion of fight, the notion of macropolitics with the notion of micropolitics. All social relations of power are challenged now, be it inside the family, inside the institutions of learning, or in working relationships. *Transmerica* proposes a discourse of experiencing life "other"-wise. The foundations for this new outlook have been laid by previous events and research. Dr. Magnus Hirschfeld created The Institute for Social Research in Berlin at the beginning of the twentieth century. He coined a new term in his book *Transvestites* of 1912. This early effort was erased by the dictatorship of Hitler, a period during which homosexuals were killed or sent to concentration camps.

---

[6] Echavarren, Roberto y Kozer, José, *Medusario*, México, Fondo de Cultura, 1996, Buenos Aires, Mansalva, 2010, Santiago de Chile, Ril Editores, 2016.

xii FOREWORD TO *TRANSMERICA*

Crossing borders and pushing boundaries is a process that takes time and is subject to violent reversals. It doesn't need to be invested in a political party. It is rather an opposition articulated by the multiple voices and tendencies of civil society. Same-sex marriages, experiences with drugs, and otherwise institutional change come slowly, altering the limits of social tolerance. In Latin America, political change is shaped by multiple forces incarnated by activists, artists, and writers. Identity becomes alterity: plural, revolutionized, and nomadic, through style, through the elaboration of different lifestyles. By presenting a map of intersectional counter-discourses, *Transmerica* is an invitation for the interdisciplinary reader to experience the rich manifestations of becoming neobaroque.

Montevideo, Uruguay   Roberto Echavarren

PREFACE

This book is about identity. It is about plural, changeable, nomadic identities. It traces the concept of selfhood from a standpoint of cultural nomadism. It is also about (a hybrid) America—*the* Americas—and a style called the Neobaroque. Its ultimate objective is to develop an alternative discourse on transitive forms of selfhood embodied in the nomadic and transgressive identity of a *trans-self.* This "trans-identity" is modeled on ambiguous characters that appear in a series of Latin American literary and visual works characterized by an opulent and experimental style—the Neobaroque. These subjects are both literal and figurative border-crossers: migrants, exiles, social outsiders, and queer dissidents. They cross politically established borders of nations, races, and ethnicities. They break the boundaries of socio-culturally established categorizations of gender, sexuality, race, class, and humanity.

Visions of Transmerica comes as a call for an inclusive reckoning of selfhood and acceptance of "otherness" in times of increasing intercultural migration, interaction, and mixing with "difference." Yet, this happens in a time of bigotry, xenophobic intolerance, categorical labeling, and continuing neocolonial(-ist) hegemony. An analysis of select and distinctly "neobaroque" works of contemporary fiction, essay, and poetry as well as performance and visual pieces from Latin America and the United States will offer the possibility to transcend the bounds of established (and imposed) identity categorizations and adopt a more fluid and flexible position on selfhood—on who we are or want to be (and not ought to be). The questions raised in these literary and visual works go beyond identity politics, as they allow to see from a linguistic and cultural perspective how

xiii

identity and selfhood are construed when gender, race, ethnicity, nation-hood, and even (post)humanity are arbitrary—thus relative—categories and cultural indicators established by a heteronormative patriarchal system of colonialism. Like exiles in flight, the mobile signs of identity of the *trans-self* are in perpetual motion, in a state of "cultural nomadism." The works engaged in this book provide examples of such cultural migrations and border transgressions. They offer possibilities for reflection and theoretical speculation.

One common feature linking the works in question is the use of a style increasingly recognized as the Neobaroque, given its linguistic sumptuousness and experimental techniques. Such extravagantly "neobaroque" forms of expression constitute a textual-discursive and aesthetic platform for a post- and decolonial decentering of cultural categories and a subsequent disarticulation of normative identity. Combining the inclusiveness, dynamism, theatricality, and conceptualism of historical European Baroque with culturally diverse forms of American Colonial Baroque, today's Neobaroque is most fit to represent miscegenation, hybridity, and (di) fusion of cultural identifications. Its energetic expressivity has been adapted to contemporary literature and performance as a mode of anti-metropolitan resistance to the same entrenched power structures of discourse that created these categories of selfhood as prescribed forms of cultural belonging. Neobaroque discursive mechanisms destabilize old concepts and articulate selfhood in intersectional terms of mobile gender, racial, ethnic, and social forms of identity.

The conceptual framework of this analysis combines Neobaroque Studies with Queer and Gender Theories, as well as Chicana Feminist and Border Theories with Latin American Cultural Studies to explain how neobaroque aesthetics constitute a radical rendition of cultural hybridity and nomadism. The studied works exemplify eccentric and sexually ambiguous as well as ethnically, racially, and nationally displaced, undefined, changeable, and metamorphous subjects who are usually cross-dressers, androgynes, mutants, or cyborgs. Their unsettling presence in the multi-dimensionally exuberant neobaroque discourse allows to surpass the traditional notion of identity and envision trans-identity (or "transentity") as a fluid form of selfhood founded on nomadism.

Any individual potentially carries within themself elements of "otherness" that are activated while crossing pre-established boundaries, barriers, or limitations by adopting external-internal marks of otherness and "cross-dressing" the cultural labels defined by patriarchal discourse of post/neocolonialism. While this can be perceived as a form of transgression and subversion of an established order, the Neobaroque text/work of art becomes a disruptive space, an antihegemonic voice of anticolonial and anti-neoliberal cultural dissidence, part of an attitude of resistance that Bolívar Echeverría called the "baroque ethos." Using transgressive neobaroque discourse as reference, *Transmerica*'s attempt to reconceptualize the notion of identity does not suppose the (absolute) death of categories of gender, race, ethnicity, or nationality. It rather proposes a deconstructive change in thinking about the very notion of "category" as a reflection of institutionalized hegemony. It suggests only a partial, "clinical" death of category (as a stagnant parameter of an imposed normativity) and the elimination of any purity that it may imply. This approach presumes that identity is not a category but a process. Categorical belonging is substituted by becoming, being by process, and purity by hybridity. Neobaroque works provide the conceptual mechanisms to accomplish this shift in thinking.

Transmerica is a continuation and expansion of research on the role of Latin American Neobaroque in the process of cultural hybridization contained in *Travestismo lingüístico: el enmascaramiento de la identidad sexual en la narrativa latinoamericana neobarroca* [Linguistic Cross-Dressing: The Disguising of Sexual Identity in Neobaroque Latin American Narrative, n.t.] (Iberoamericana-Vervuert, 2009). It continues the topic where the previous book left off and expands it in terms of scope and approach. In addition to being in English, this book encompasses a broader range of works (including performance and visual arts) and touches on a fuller spectrum of borderland identities through the lens of queer theory. The book's originality lies in the combination of perspectives deriving from (Latin) American Cultural and Literary Studies (of the Neobaroque) with Gender, Queer, and Border Theories applied, with the aid of Discourse Theory, to the philosophy of identity.

A discussion of the decentering and dissolution of identity and its subsequent rearticulation in nomadic transitivity should contribute to available theoretical resources for the study of the changing notions of gender, race, ethnicity, nationhood, and (post)humanity not only in Latin America but also in the United States and other parts of the world where cultures interact and mix, and where cross-cultural hybridization takes place. *Transmerica*'s approach to identity as a process of nomadic *becoming* should benefit the promotion of tolerance and understanding of difference through intercultural contact and the study of languages. It should

xvi PREFACE

also aid the reader who reflects on the relationship of identity and community in Latin American culture and who, being critical of modern ideologies of individualism, directs their research toward collective forms of identity and identification. An example of such approach may be Lois Parkinson Zamora's current work on the "insubstantial self" and communal selfhood in Latin American fiction. Engaging Neobaroque literature, art, and theory may prove to be useful in such an undertaking.

This book is intended to be particularly helpful to scholars interested in non-heteronormative modes of sexuality, such as cross-dressing and androgyny, and in transformative conceptions of cultural identity, such as hybridity, migration, and border crossing, appearing in contemporary Latin American fiction and art. It may also be useful to any reader interested in cultural transformations of the late twentieth and early twenty-first centuries, and their expression in postmodernist, neoavant-garde literature and art. The motivation for this book comes from a life-long experience of studying and crossing borders—geographical, political, and conceptual boundaries of selfhood—that are not limited to the physical and cultural borderland of my origin: the Central European crossroads of Polish Silesia, nor to the multiple borders crossed while living in the Americas. Other boundaries have appeared in the diverse discourses and languages that voice other views of the world, avatars of being, and possibilities of becoming. One such discourse found along the long and winding road is the American Neobaroque. *Transmerica* is the result of its reading from a "borderland" perspective and with a migratory state of mind that corresponds to a life experience that has allowed me to utilize a combination of multilingualism and multiculturalism to experiment with a pluralized, mobile, nomadic, and transitive sense of self. This reading has also led me to reflect upon the aesthetic possibilities that Latin American literary and artistic discourse presents in conceiving transitive forms of identity. They are founded on crossing not only politically determined borders but also the socially arbitrated cultural boundaries of hegemonically defined categories of sexuality, gender, race, ethnic and social belonging, and the anthropocentrically limited bounds of humanity.

The book's scope is manifold: it constitutes a philosophical search of selfhood, an exercise in theoretical speculation in literary and cultural studies, an adventure in neobaroque textuality, an expression of political resistance to heteronormative (neo)colonial-ist/-izing discourse, and a personal—both intellectual and spiritual—quest of self-discovery in terms of identity, seen as a derivative of multiculturalism defined by multilingualism and polyglossia. By focusing on hybrid cultural and literary contexts of Latin America (Brazil, Uruguay, Argentina, Chile, Bolivia, Cuba, Mexico, and the US-Mexican border), this work reconsiders the essentialist concepts making up a unitary identity bound by binary distinctions of male/female, straight/queer, White/Colored, Anglo/Latine, and human/cyborg, in order to present a kaleidoscopic vision of nomadic transitivity in a process of becoming of the multi-trans-self. It also aspires to demonstrate the conceptual and expressive potential of the Neobaroque, whose works populate the American continent with eccentric characters and transitive identities. Its unique discursive capacity goes beyond the Self to open the way for the nomadic vagrancies of the trans-self.

Ultimately, this book presents a transformative mode(l) of thought about difference and otherness based on ground-breaking neobaroque aesthetics. It opens possibilities for conceiving selfhood as a process of becoming in crossing borders and pushing boundaries, interchangeably assuming traits from "the other side." *Transmerica* proposes a discourse of experiencing identity and life "other"-wise.

Mt. Pleasant, MI, USA   Krzysztof A. Kulawik

Acknowledgments

The writing of this book would not have been possible without the invaluable advice, example, and inspiration from professors, colleagues, and mentors around the world whose teaching and ideas guided me in the process of research and academic writing. They showed me the paths of (not only) Latin American literature with its Neobaroque alleys and postmodern dead ends. In the United States they include Andrés Avellaneda, Diane Marting, Elizabeth Ginway, and Lois Parkinson Zamora; in Colombia, Diógenes Fajardo Valenzuela and Luis Alfonso Ramírez; in Poland, Jerzy Sławomirski and Ewa Nawrocka. I thank them all for teaching me so much.

My recognition goes out to Central Michigan University (CMU), whose sabbatical program, together with the Office of Research and Graduate Studies' FRCE Research Grants program, offered me release time and financial support with a generous grant. Without them, my work would not have taken the direction that it took. And it took me to South America, where in Chile, I had the privilege to meet and work with writers Eugenia Prado, Juan Pablo Sutherland, and Diamela Eltit; with artists, writers, and activists Felipe Rivas, Claudia Rodríguez, and Débora Fernández; in Brazil, with Alcir Pécora (UNICAMP), Olga Bilenky (Instituto Hilda Hilst), and Eliane Robert Moraes (USP); and in Bolivia with artists David Aruquipa and Alfredo Muller. I am most sincerely thankful to all of them for granting me their time, wisdom, and friendship. To Eugenia Prado, I am especially indebted for offering me invaluable materials and contacting me with other writers, artists, and activists whose work shaped the outcome of this book. Likewise, my thanks go out to

xix

CMU students in my Spanish language, culture, and literature courses, especially in the Spring 2023 semester, who accompanied me in the final stages of writing this book with their valuable input, feedback, and patience.

I express my deep gratitude to Luz Marcela Hurtado, my wife, friend, colleague, and faithful companion in this and many other projects of a life full of journeys and adventures, not only academic. I thank her for her unwavering critical, intellectual, spiritual, and material support (and patience!) during the long process of putting together this book. I extend my thanks to my mother Maria and brother Zbigniew for their love and continuing support. To my mother and late father, Andrzej, I shall remain forever grateful for being my first teachers of foreign languages, for providing me the most desirable conditions for growth, and for instilling in me the passion for reading, writing, traveling, crossing borders, and discovering new worlds.

Thank you.

No wo-man is an island.

Praise for *Visions of Transmerica*

"Prof. Kris Kulawik's *Visions of Transamerica* brilliantly interprets Neobaroque prose and art, plus the identity theories they represent. Clearly and cogently, Kulawik's writing informs readers about how these works can increase tolerance by building a conceptual community. The tremendous creativity regarding identity in this literature and art becomes more comprehensible via the ideas of queer and gender identity. Essential reading."
—Diane E. Marting, Ph.D., *Professor of Spanish, Graduate Program Coordinator for the MA in Modern Languages for specializations in French, German, and Spanish. University of Mississippi, Modern Languages Department. Recent publication: "State Terror and the Destruction of Families for Reproductive 'Management' in Three Argentine Films,"* The Palgrave Handbook on Reproductive Justice in Literature and Culture, *ed. Beth Widmaier Capo & Laura Lazzari, Palgrave Macmillan, September 2022, pp. 490–511*

"*Visions of Transamerica* addresses Neobaroque ideology and aesthetics in a number of potential contexts: personal, social, cultural, political and sexual. Kulawik analyzes current transgressions of social norms to describe new forms of identity in fiction, theatre, film, and other modes of performance. He embeds these aesthetic practices in social contexts in order to show how artistic genres reflect "trans*" practices, and vice versa: how actual practices react to their representation. Professor Kulawik's focus is on Latin America, but his discussion is useful in all cultural and artistic contexts where new modes of identities are sought and desired."
—Lois Parkinson Zamora, *University of Houston. Author of* The Inordinate Eye: New World Baroque and Latin American Fiction. *University of Chicago Press, 2006, and coeditor of* Baroque New Worlds: Representation, Transculturation, Counterconquest. *Duke University Press, 2010*

"Kulawik's informed and insightful discussion of the neobaroque, gender, and the body broadens the understanding of performativity among artists and writers from the US borderlands and Latin America. As one of the few studies in English on the complex topic of destabilized gender identities, Kulawik's study makes a significant contribution to the wider field of global gender studies."
—M. Elizabeth Ginway, *Professor of Spanish and Portuguese Studies, University of Florida, USA and author of* Cyborgs, Sexuality, and the Undead: The Body in Mexican and Brazilian Speculative Fiction

CONTENTS

1 Introduction   1
    1.1 Boundaries and Transgressions: Presentation of Topic with Objectives   1
    1.2 Identit-y/-ies in Motion: Hypotheses, Claims, and Other Aims   5
    1.3 Why and Which America? Why the Neobaroque?   8
    1.4 (Un-)Situating Identity: A Discursive Process of Neobaroque Transgression   11
    1.5 Chapter Sequence and Methodology   18
    1.6 Why Experience the Neobaroque? Relevance and Scope of the Matter   23
    Works Cited   30

2 Neobaroque as Transgression: The Latin American Paradigm   33
    2.1 Latin America: Hybrid Contexts of Deterritorialization   35
       2.1.1 From Sameness to Otherness   35
       2.1.2 Heterogeneity, Transculturation, Mestizaje, Hybridity, and Simultaneity   45
    2.2 Neobaroque Literary and Artistic Transgressions   53
    2.3 Identity on the Borders: An Intersectional Approach to Nomadic Transits   68
       2.3.1 Intersectional Theorizations of Borders and Boundaries   69
       2.3.2 Borderland Identities and Nomadic Transits: Perspectives on Crossing Borders   75

xxiv CONTENTS

	2.3.3	*Queer Becomings in Trans(-itive) Genders*	87
2.4	2.3.4	*Eroticism as Deterritorialization Through Excess*	93
	Writing the Body and the Body of Writing: Neobaroque Enactment of Identity		98
	2.4.1	*Body, Text, and Performance as Spaces of Transgression and Embodiment of Selfhood*	99
	2.4.2	*Writing-Performing the Nomadic Body: A Material and Symbolic Relationship*	106
	2.4.3	*Performative Transits of Selfhood: Unwriting Genders and Genres*	111
Works Cited			119

3 Subversions of Selfhood: Transgressive CharACTerS of the Neobaroque 125

3.1	*Historical Determinants and Literary Environments*		126
3.2	*Nomadic Transgressions of Identity in Latin American Fiction, Performance, and Painting*		136
	3.2.1	*Cross-dressing*	136
	3.2.2	*Androgyny, Queerness, and Ambiguity*	189
	3.2.3	*Metamorphosis and the Posthuman*	203
	3.2.4	*Borderland Nomads of In-Between Spaces*	215
Works Cited			236

4 One-T(w)o-Many: Neobaroque Articulations of Nomadic Identity 241

4.1	*The Neobaroque as a Style of Instability and Excess: In the Footsteps of Sarduy and Bataille*		242
	4.1.1	*Techniques of Transgression: Artifice, Parody, and Simulation*	245
	4.1.2	*Nomadic Deterritorialization as a Neobaroque Semiosis*	258
	4.1.3	*Eroticism and the Exuberant Word*	261
4.2	*Articulation of Trans-Identity and the Mechanisms of Nomadism: From Peirce to Deleuze and Beyond*		266
	4.2.1	*The Open Sign: A Semiotics of Transgression*	267
	4.2.2	Devenir *or the Rhizomatic Subject-as-Becoming*	272
	4.2.3	*Queering Identity: Trans*,* Travesti, *and Disidentification*	276

	4.2.4	Transgressing Normative Categories: Transvestism, Androgyny, Metamorphosis, and Posthuman Cyborgs	285
4.3		On the Borders of Identity: In-Between Flows of the Trans-Self	309
	4.3.1	Borderland Spaces of In-Between: From Nepantla to Ch'ixi, from "dangerous beasts" to Border Crossers	310
	4.3.2	Santiago's entre-lugar and Perlongher's puntos de pasaje	320
	4.3.3	Nomadism as Transformative Flows of Identity: Braidotti's Point	324
4.4		The Neobaroque Strategy: From Self to Other, from Seduction to Sedition	328
	4.4.1	Politics of the Neobaroque	329
	4.4.2	Cross-Dressing and Androgyny as Destabilization of Heterosexual Hegemony	334
	4.4.3	Transformative Impact of Nomadic Subject Positions and the "Baroque Ethos"	337
	Works Cited		344

5 Conclusions: At the Crossroads of *Nepantla* — 353

5.1	Latin America and the Transformative Potential of Neobaroque Nomadism	353
5.2	From Identity to Alterity: Mappings of the Trans-Self in a Nomadic Cultural Theory	359
5.3	Political Implications: The Subversive Effect of the Neobaroque	364
5.4	Philosophical Openings for a Theory of Cultural Nomadism	368
Works Cited		371

Index — 373

About the Author

Krzysztof A. Kulawik is Professor of Spanish Language and Latin American Literature at Central Michigan University, USA. He received his first Master's Degree in Hispanic Philology from Uniwersytet Jagielloński in Kraków, Poland, and a second Master's Degree in Spanish American Literature from Instituto Caro y Cuervo in Bogotá, Colombia. He obtained his Ph.D. in Spanish and in Latin American Studies from the University of Florida in 2001. He also completed studies in Portuguese language and literature at Universidade de Coimbra, Portugal. His publications include the book *Travestismo lingüístico: el enmascaramiento de la identidad sexual en la narrativa latinoamericana neobarroca* (Iberoamericana-Vervuert, Frankfurt-Madrid, 2009), chapters in edited volumes *Latinoamérica en la globalización y el tercer milenio* (ed. Leopoldo Zea, Fondo de Cultura Económica, Mexico, 2002), *Fiestas infinitas de máscara: actos performativos de feminidad y masculinidad en México* (Georg Olms Verlag, Hildesheim, 2012), *México en el siglo XXI. Miradas desde Asia* (Institute of Iberoamerican Studies—Aleph, South Korea, 2020), and *Barroco latinoamericano y crisis contemporánea* (ed. Borja García, De Gruyter, Berlin, 2023), as well as articles in the areas of Latin American literature and cultural studies, the Neobaroque, gender and sexuality, performance, and discourse theory in scholarly journals in the United States (*Revista Iberoamericana, Revista de Estudios Hispánicos, Chasqui*), Colombia (*Literatura: teoría, historia, crítica*), Chile (*Nomadías, Alpha*), and France (*Amerika*).

LIST OF FIGURES

Fig. 2.1	Colonial baroque façade of San Lorenzo Church in Potosí, Bolivia. (Photo by author)	64
Fig. 2.2	Stages of the literary-semiotic process of identity formation	110
Fig. 2.3	Dispersion of unitary Subject/Identity (S1) into plural-transitive subjects/identities (Sn > a–c)	118
Fig. 3.1	Cover of Severo Sarduy's *Cobra and Maitreya*. Dalkey Archive Press, 1995. (Courtesy of Deep Vellum Eds.)	141
Fig. 3.2	*Sin título* [*No title*], Pedro Lemebel, 1990. (Photo by Pedro Marinello. Courtesy of Archivo Pedro Lemebel)	155
Fig. 3.3	*Las dos Fridas* [*The Two Fridas*], performance by Pedro Lemebel and Francisco Casas, 1990. (Photo by Pedro Marinello. Courtesy of photographer)	156
Fig. 3.4	*Refundación de la Universidad de Chile* [*Refounding of the University of Chile*], Las Yeguas del Apocalipsis, 1988. (Photo by Ulises Nilo. Courtesy of Archivo Yeguas del Apocalipsis)	160
Fig. 3.5	Pedro Lemebel (in red feathers). (Photo by Joanna Reposi Garibaldi. Courtesy of photographer)	161
Fig. 3.6	Naty Menstrual at a reading in Buenos Aires, 2020. (Photo by Augusto Starita, Ministerio de Cultura de la Nación. Source: Wikimedia Creative Commons)	167
Fig. 3.7	La Familia Galán, "Una historia sobre zancos" ["A Story on High Heels"]. (Photo by Antonio Suárez, published in *Zona Trans*. Courtesy of Comunidad Diversidad)	175
Fig. 3.8	La Familia Galán in La Paz, Bolivia, with Mt. Illimani in the background. (Courtesy of Comunidad Diversidad)	176
Fig. 3.9	Danna Galán as Waphuri, Oruro Carnival, 2012. (Photo by Pablo Céspedes. Courtesy of Comunidad Diversidad)	178

xxx   LIST OF FIGURES

Fig. 3.10   *Estéticas Galán 1* (Danna in yellow). Oil on canvas by Alfredo
Muller. (Courtesy of artist)   179

Fig. 3.11   *Andrómeda 1* (Miki). Oil on canvas by Alfredo Muller.
(Courtesy of artist)   183

Fig. 3.12   *Andrómeda 2* (Miki). Oil on canvas by Alfredo Muller.
(Courtesy of artist)   184

Fig. 3.13   *Estéticas Galán 2* (Danna in blue). Oil on canvas by Alfredo
Muller. (Courtesy of artist)   185

Fig. 3.14   Muller (right) and Miki (left) in the artist's studio in Santa
Cruz, Bolivia in 2022, with Muller's portraiture in the
background. (Photo by author)   186

Fig. 3.15   *El Libertador Simón Bolívar* [*The Liberator Simón Bolívar*] by
Juan Dávila, 1994. Oil on canvas on metal. (Photo by Mark
Ashkanasy, © Juan Davila. Courtesy of Kalli Rolfe
Contemporary Art, Melbourne)   187

Fig. 3.16   The Doors. Promotional photo of Jim Morrison about 1970.
(Photographer: Pictorial Press. Reproduced under license from
Alamy, Inc.)   192

Fig. 3.17   Jim Morrison 1969, author: Elektra Records. (Source:
Wikimedia Creative Commons)   196

Fig. 3.18   *Zona de dolor: Diamela Eltit* [*Area of Pain*]. (Photograph by
Lotty Rosenfeld, 1980. Courtesy of Diamela Eltit)   202

Fig. 3.19   Hembro levantándose [Hembro arising]. Scene from the
staging of Eugenia Prado's Hembros, 2004. Screenshot
from video clip by Marcelo Vega, CAIN. (Courtesy of
Eugenia Prado)   210

Fig. 3.20   Novia freak [Freaky Fiancée]. Scene from the staging of
Eugenia Prado's Hembros, 2004. Screenshot from video clip
by Marcelo Vega, CAIN. (Courtesy of Eugenia Prado)   211

Fig. 3.21   Coatlicue (sculpted figure), Mexica, central Mexico. National
Museum of Anthropology, Mexico City. (Source: Wikimedia
Creative Commons)   221

Fig. 3.22   *La Loca* [*The Drag Queen*], classic photo portrait of
Guillermo Gómez-Peña by Juan Carlos Ruiz Vargas, Mexico
City, 2019. (Courtesy of La Pocha Nostra Living Archives)   231

Fig. 3.23   Guillermo Gómez-Peña as "Naftazteca." (Photograph
by Lori Eanes, 2004. Source: Wikimedia Creative Commons)   232

Fig. 4.1   The triadic sign according to Peirce with the addition of
displaced meaning—SGFied-B   270

Fig. 4.2   Lego DNA. (Source: Wikimedia Creative Commons)   279

Fig. 4.3	Arturo Pozo, an androgynous emo. (Photo by José Miguel Serrano, Ecuador, 2007. Source: Wikimedia Creative Commons)	297
Fig. 4.4	*Nepantlera* by Celia Herrera Rodríguez. "Drawings from *A Xicana Codex of Changing Consciousness*." Handprinted screen-print on Mohawk birch archival paper, 2011. (Courtesy of the artist)	314

CHAPTER 1

Introduction

Visions of Transmerica deals with neobaroque aesthetic forms in the service of a Latin American discourse of cultural heterogeneity and hybridity as it pertains to questions of identity. This book intends to explain how literary and artistic works that use the extravagant techniques of neobaroque style decenter and destabilize normative categories of identity with ambiguous nomadic subjects. Transgressing culturally and politically established borders and boundaries, these works displace the idea of selfhood within fluctuating territories of gender, race, ethnicity, nationality, social group, and (post)humanity. Examples of Latin American and US-Latine fiction, performance, and visual works characterized by exuberant language and transgressive characters lead us to propose an alternative discourse of identity based on the concepts of "alterity" and "trans-identity." The nomadic figure appears in these works as the embodiment of a transitive identity or the "transentity" of a "trans-self." Subsequently, this study demonstrates the subversive political implications of nomadic migration, understood as physical cross-border transit as well as cultural boundary transgression.

1.1 Boundaries and Transgressions: Presentation of Topic with Objectives

An exuberant style of eccentric aesthetic forms af-/in-fects Latin American fiction—both narrative and poetic—as well as essay, performance, and other visual arts of the last six decades. Referred to by critics as the

© The Author(s), under exclusive license to Springer Nature Switzerland AG 2024
K. A. Kulawik, *Visions of Transmerica*, Literatures of the Americas, https://doi.org/10.1007/978-3-031-42014-6_1

1

Neobaroque, this aesthetic modality builds on a discourse of artifice, parody, and e(x/r)otic exuberance. Its stylistic techniques are formal expressions of hybridizing transformations taking place in Western, but particularly Latin American culture. Neobaroque experimentation and artistry represent a destabilizing figuration of a fluid and mobile identity that is not fixed in determined cultural categorizations. Neobaroque exuberance also uncovers the discursive process that governs selfhood. By means of mutant and ambiguous characters, a series of works illustrates personal, gender, racial, social, national, and (post)human identity as nomadic transformation. An example of such neobaroque decentering and queering is the figure of Cobra in Severo Sarduy's novel of the same title. This cross-dresser's transformative saga, originating in the cabarets of Havana and transiting Paris, Morocco, and Tibet, depicts the intricacies of the protagonist's sex-altering surgeries, identity changes, kidnappings, and ultimately *hir* death as victim of trans-homophobic hate. It is a story narrated with elaborate and figurative language, as shifting (meta)narrative voices and actions relocate in changing multicultural spaces. Another example is Guillermo Gómez-Peña's cross-dressed Performero-Border Brujo figure. S/he uses a polyphony of layered voices of a transnational and transgendered multiethnic shaman who represents simultaneously Hispanic, Native, and Anglo-American identities that escape any categorization of race, nationality, and gender, while using a profuse language (and code-switching) in a *Spanglish* fusion of English and Spanish. These figures are two examples amidst a multitude of cross-dressed, androgynous, and mutant characters populating Latin American and US-Latin*e* narrative fiction, criticism, and visual arts that resort to experimental, parodic, and eccentric techniques. They are part of a broader tendency of decentering and destabilizing cultural categories observable in Latin American aesthetic production since the 1960s.

The decentering of identity in neobaroque works can be interpreted using concepts from contemporary cultural studies. These include "nomadism" (Rosi Braidotti) as moving and transitioning of subject positions between categories, "rhizome" (Gilles Deleuze) as interconnectedness and transferability of movable traits, "points of passage" (Néstor Perlongher) as interconnecting "ports" and "plug-ins" of subjectivity, and "trans*" (Jack Halberstam) as fluid and inconclusive openness of self-identification within a "space of in-between" (Silviano Santiago), "contact zone" (Mary Louise Pratt), and two Native-American concepts (Nahuatl and Aymara, respectively): "nepantlism" (critically introduced by Gloria

Anzaldúa) as shape shifting of subjects in transitional borderland zones of in-betweenness, and *ch'ixi* (introduced by Silvia Rivera Cusicanqui) as the motley mix of being something and something else at the same time in a logic of the included third, of undifferentiation that joins opposites. The application of these terms to the study of Latin American culture and identity can be substantiated in the new expansive definitions of gender transitivity and variability coming from queer, trans, and feminist theory, as well as Chicana border studies. Their usefulness in assessing the decentering and fragmentation of categories taking place in the extravagant realm of the Latin American Neobaroque allows to transcend identity and to replace it with the concept of a "transitive selfhood" based on itinerant flows of interchangeable cultural traits and nomadic subject positions. They form an antihegemonic strategy of destabilization of categories that transit in simultaneous multiplicities.

Visions of Transmerica focuses specifically on *neobaroque*[1] literary and artistic forms that are transgressive: they cross boundaries of normative categories of identity (both individual and collective) and traditional literary-artistic genres. It examines a series of works that display such transgressions in Latin American fiction, performance, and visual arts from the last three decades of the twentieth century and the first two of the 2000s. Building on cultural and literary studies as well as on queer and border theory, our analysis centers on transgressive characters and (meta)narrative voices appearing in fiction, poetry, essay, and performance by contemporary Latin American and US-Latino creators whose works fall under the rubric of what has increasingly been recognized as the Neobaroque style. It intends to reveal that, apart from being a hidden commonality that underlies the American continent's national and regional differences, this exuberant and experimental aesthetic modality becomes an effective discursive strategy of decentering identity and suggesting nomadic "transidentity" instead. This neobaroque strategy is carried out with sexually ambiguous (in terms of heteronormative binarism), multiethnic, interracial, transcultural, metamorphous, or simply uncategorizable equivocal subjects that appear as fictional and artistic characters, metafictional

---

[1] Throughout this book, we will use the lowercase form of "neobaroque" as an adjective describing quality of a style or technique. We will apply the capitalized version, "Neobaroque," as a noun to refer to that style or poetics, or the critically defined aesthetic tendency with its determined period of incidence in Latin American and Western art and literature—the second half of the twentieth and early twenty-first centuries.

narrators and implicit authors, the empirical writers, or performers of the works. In their interchangeability and transitivity, these mutant subjects transcend any exclusive (and binary) categorizations.

More than a revivalist discourse originated in colonial tradition, the Neobaroque represents a transcultural stylization of techniques inherited from the seventeenth- and eighteenth-century European and American Baroque. It is a disruption of language and thought based on hegemonic schemes of Logo- and Euro-centric heteronormative thought. In the revived form, what its Cuban theorist and practitioner José Lezama Lima called *lepra creadora* [creative plague], the Neobaroque facilitates new, non-hackneyed meanings of heteronormative categories and cultural labels and, without totally rejecting them, it assimilates and transforms them in the hybrid context of the Americas (1957: 54).

Using as primary sources contemporary literary, performative, and visual works from various parts of Latin America, including the US-Mexican border, by authors and artists ranging from Severo Sarduy, Mario Bellatin, Pedro Lemebel, Diamela Eltit, Eugenia Prado, Hilda Hilst to Susy Shock, Naty Menstrual, La Familia Galán, Guillermo Gómez-Peña, and Gloria Anzaldúa, this study specifically addresses the topic of cultural transformation resulting from crossing borders and boundaries, and the ensuing emergence of a nomadic and fluid "trans-entity." Reaching beyond but also including the physical sense of the word "border," this analysis questions boundaries that determine and separate categorical, (hetero)normative, and, in many cases, binary definitions of identity. The concept acquires a mobile, nomadic, and transformative dimension that is best exemplified in queerness. Our objective is to present the discursive (aesthetic and expressive) potential of neobaroque literary and artistic forms in decentering the idea of a unitary identity based on arbitrary, logocentric, and hegemonically imposed categorizations of selfhood. This book intends to explore the literary, performative, and aesthetic possibilities of altering the very concept of Identity, understood as a discursively determined cultural formation. It achieves this by applying gender, queer, trans, feminist, and Chicana border theories to the analysis of transgressive fictional and empirical characters, narrative voices as well as performers in formally eccentric literary and visual works that can be characterized as *neobaroque*.

Utilizing the critical terms of "borderland identity," "cultural nomadism," and "transitivity," this study demonstrates how neobaroque discourse supports the idea of selfhood embodied in a "nomadic trans-self." This plural "trans-identity" is not a total rejection of existing identity markers, but rather a reconceptualization of "category" as hegemonic exercise of power, as explained by Michel Foucault (1972, 1980), Michel de Certeau (1974), Ernesto Laclau (1996), Rosi Braidotti (2006), and Silvia Rivera Cusicanqui (2010). This decentered notion of identity is based on a temporary and arbitrary adoption of culturally categorized (heterosexually, racially, ethnically, and socially determined) traits that are transitive and exchangeable. The decategorized—because mobile and shifting—trans-self becomes representative of the end-of-the-century (allegedly postmodern) phenomenon of cultural decolonization—destabilization, hybridization, and nomadism—as explained by Néstor García Canclini, Antonio Benítez Rojo, Antonio Cornejo Polar, Gloria Anzaldúa, Silvia Rivera Cusicanqui, and Rosi Braidotti. The "transitive self" is conceivable in the discursive dimension of the Neobaroque. The heterogeneity of the Americas, particularly Latin America, with its sumptuously hybrid literary-artistic discourse, resulting from what Benítez Rojo called "an interplay of supersyncretic signifiers" (1996: 21), is the catalyzer in this cultural and philosophical conversion.

In sum, this book is about discursive methods of destabilizing identity that result from hybridizations and transgressions observable in Latin and US-American culture molded by (not only) interracial and multiethnic encounters of differences. The aesthetic forms of instability have increasingly been recognized under the rubric of the Neobaroque. Its exuberant stylistic features lend themselves to the dissolution of the concepts of unity and purity. The Subject *becomes* a "subject-in-process," a "trans-self" in transitive multiplicity, simultaneity, and indeterminacy of categories. In a modern stylization of the historical Baroque, the Neobaroque takes language and discourse to their communicative limits, to the "borders" of representation, as it opens new spaces in cultural and philosophical thought on identity and selfhood.

1.2   Identit-y/-ies in Motion: Hypotheses, Claims, and Other Aims

Our claim is that the unstable eccentric characters in the works of art and literature, displaying ambiguous (androgynous), inverted (cross-dressed), or mutant identities, indicate new posthumanist and non-anthropocentric forms of subjectivity that characterize an epoch of cultural relativization and reformulation of categories, of questioning of what it means to be human. An additional caveat is that this relativization appears within a particularly heterogeneous cultural setting that is (Latin) America. A change in the mode of conceiving identity and perceiving selfhood in terms of mobility and fluidity leads us to envision an alternative epistemology of a post-/un-identity based on cultural nomadism and transitivity of variable subject positions. The examples presented by literary and artistic works originating from Latin America and the US-Mexican border allow us to perceive a plural multi-/trans-self, founded on coexistences and exchanges of traits, and on the shifting movement of gender, sexual, racial, ethnic, national, and social categories.

Another claim made is that the reformulation of identity into a nomadic "trans-identity" is the consequence of discursive aesthetic procedures taking place in literature, performance, painting, and film. Therefore, the Neobaroque becomes a *de facto* platform for deconstructing and rearticulating cultural categories with the use of deconstructive aesthetic devices of erotic exuberance, artifice, parody, and formal experimentation. Ultimately, neobaroque eccentricity denotes political resistance to and subversion of a patriarchal, logocentric, and postcolonial discursive order. Nomadic borderland identities can be perceived as forms of cultural endurance and critical interiorization of the colonializing capitalist project of Modernity within an existential attitude of resistance that Bolívar Echeverría defined as the "baroque ethos" (1994). We explain this concept in general terms in Sect. 2.1 in Chap. 2, "Latin America: Hybrid Contexts of Deterritorialization" and in more detail in Sect. 4.4 in Chap. 4, "The Neobaroque Strategy: From Self to Other, from Seduction to Sedition," in which a fuller explanation of the baroque ethos is related to Louis Althusser's concept of "interpellation" (1970).

The notion of "border" denotes the intermediate but also dividing space of contact, ambiguity, and transgression in its broader sense of "boundary," a hinge space situated in a transition zone between mobile categories of gender, ethnicity, race, nationality, social class, and posthuman (cyborg) identity. We will detail on the crossings and overlapping of these categories in Chap. 2 (Sect. 2.3.2 "Borderland Identities and Nomadic Transits") in which we will provide a detailed review of the term "intersectionality" and its theoretical as well as methodological impact on our analysis. Likewise, our approach pivots on interdisciplinary thresholds of Latin American literary and cultural studies, intersecting with women and gender studies as well as identity, feminist, and queer theory, Chicana border studies, literary semiotics, and narrative theory, without precluding

Neobaroque theory. The literary, performance, and visual works of "neo-baroque" authors from Latin America and the United States provide us the empirical basis for establishing a theoretical and methodological discourse on alternative, mobile, and transitive forms of selfhood epitomized in the idea of "nomadism."

In their representation of decentered and hybrid cultural subjects, the mentioned writers and artists offer the reader options for philosophical reflection on selfhood when gender, race, ethnicity, and nationality become fluid categories in perpetual motion. Latin America provides a unique aesthetic-cultural ground for expressing such cultural mobility. It comprises a hybrid space of cultural coexistence and miscegenation that has impulsed a vivid literature and daring visual works marked by innovation and syncretism since the colonial beginnings of the seventeenth to eighteenth centuries to the twentieth- to twenty-first-century Neobaroque. The notable presence of subjects with ambiguous genders and multicultural identities ultimately leads to envisioning a cross-cultural model of nomadic trans-identity founded on movement, transformation, and transitivity.

The stylized forms of the Baroque lend themselves as particularly adequate forms of cultural representation of the heterogeneous space of Latin America. Colonial Baroque's mixed artistic forms, incorporating varied cultural ideologies and practices of resistance to Iberian imperial hegemony, become the foundation for Neobaroque's expressive possibilities in the service of new models of cultural mobility in the Americas at the demise of Modernity's colonial metanarratives. More notably, Neobaroque stylization of the historical Baroque provides new forms of articulating American cultural heterogeneity and categorical transgression.

The recurrent theme of *cross-dressing* and *androgyny*, understood as either inversion or ambiguous combination of male/female traits, represents the mainstay of our approach. The cross-dresser's and androgyne's transgressive venturing into normatively (or officially) delimited territories of otherness symbolizes the leading question of our considerations: the decentering of *Identity*. Hegemonically defined categories of belonging become destabilized by narrative and performative characters who undergo new experiences of subjectivity as they cross normative marks of gender, sexual, ethnic, national, social, and human identity, the "legal" boundaries of selfhood, in their nomadic transits through "alterity." In this approach, identity becomes an obsolete term of instituted Modernity, giving way to what I propose to call a *Transmerican transentity*. This concept illustrates how, in the hybrid American context, identity becomes transitive, becomes trans-identity. It is allegorized in the figure of the nomadic trans-self: the cross-dresser, the androgyne, the racially, ethnically, and technologically undefined mutant.

The final objective of this study is to demonstrate *how* these (not only sexually) transgressive characters encourage the formulation of a *mobile cultural trans-identity* based on the embodiment and performance of transient identity roles that are taken on by the subject interchangeably from an array of cultural categories. Such transgressive nomadic identities are represented by Millennial or Generation Z mutants (often identifying with urban cliques), the Chican*es*, the Native-American, Black, and Brown minorities making part of Anglo-Euro-Hispano-White neocolonial societies of the United States and Latin America, alongside LGBTQ-I communities accompanied by the ever-increasing presence of Trans-American immigrants, nomadic subjects inhabiting or transiting the transnational borderland spaces of Hybrid America. Regardless of identifying with or disidentifying from any one defined nationality, ethnic group, race, or sexual orientation, these fictional and non-fictional individuals are carriers of "otherness" (or "alterity") within themselves. They deploy an internally fragmented and collectively dialogic mode of being that can be defined as *nomadic*. The hereby presented Neobaroque literary and artistic works provide the empirical support for conceptualizing American "transentity" as the embodiment of intercultural migration and nomadism, hybridity, and genuine American diversity.

1.3   WHY AND WHICH AMERICA? WHY THE NEOBAROQUE?

Culturally speaking and in broad terms, the Americas—the compound of Latin America, the Caribbean, the United States, and Canada—conform a space of liminality where the encounter of all the world's populations and races has resulted in interactions of Old World nations with Indigenous cultures on a level of intersecting ethnic, racial, geographic, national, political, social, and economic borders. Angel Rama explained this in *Transculturación narrativa en América Latina* (1982) [*Writing across Cultures...* 2012] as the interplay of at least three cultural macro-regions crossed by subsets of three to nine "microregions" (depending on the type of classification taken into account), spanning the more than twenty countries that form Latin America, and corresponding to the cultural systems formed by their physical and cultural environments, ethnic composition, and social systems (2012: 38–39). To this, we should add the inherent diversity of the United States, in most part the outcome of immigration, and the demographic variety of the rest of Anglo-America. The Americas, as a continent of encounters of Indigenous inhabitants with foreigners—invaders, settlers, exiles, and immigrants, both forced and voluntary—constitutes perhaps the largest mixture of humans on Earth, and can be seen as a confluence of borderlands between mixed and hybrid cultural formations, a unique space of distinct but coexistent, intersectionally interacting groups with their varying cultural traits.

When dealing with a broad topic such as cultural identity, the term "Latin America" becomes questionable as it risks nullifying its own validity, remitting to an empty signifier, a virtually void category. However, I propose to keep its generalizing usage here, along with the words "America" or "the Americas," although they are cultural and political abstractions. Their use is justified in analyzing works originated in countries so distant and distinct as Cuba, Mexico, Bolivia, Brazil, Argentina, and the United States because of the presence of neobaroque aesthetic forms in the representation of transgressive characters/subjects. In terms of scope, "although 'Latin America' is too large and diverse to be a useful category for many sorts of analysis [...]" (Chasteen, "Introduction" to Rama 1996: xiii), my reference to Latin America and the Americas is established with regard to the place of origin of the analyzed works in terms of the Inter-American cultural area that encompasses the use of the two major Neo-Latin languages—Spanish and Portuguese—in which most of the works were written or performed. This, without any claim to contain or define any totality of a single "Latin America." Neither does this study attempt to include all of Latin America in its variety or create a unified generalization of this concept. Nonetheless, it pinpoints cultural areas of (neobaroque) commonality. We shall let (Latin) America stand no more than as an introductory and conclusive generalization to the hemispheric origin of the analyzed works. What is more, any meaning of (Latin) America is subject to a categorical deconstruction in the same way as the concept of any unitary identity of gender, race, or nation. In its place is our vision of a nomadic "Transmerica."

Renowned critics have used various denominators, or macro-concepts, to describe the vast cultural entity referred to as Latin America: Antonio Cornejo Polar as a "radically heterogeneous space" defined by "heteroclite plurality" (2003: 6), Angel Rama—following Fernando Ortiz—a "transcultural narrative space" (1996), Antonio Benítez Rojo—referring to the Caribbean as an area of "disorderly polyrhythms," "a repeating island" in a *Chaos* of "dynamic states of regularities that repeat themselves globally" (1996: 1, 16–19, 2–3, 10), Néstor García Canclini as a "hybrid culture" (1990), and René Zavaleta as a "jumbled society" (*sociedad abigarrada*) (1986). By adopting these terms as denominators of the diversity of the American continent, we will attempt to puncture the borders and boundaries that divide and separate nations, races, ethnicities, and genders. In this sense, *Transmerica* is an attempt to transcend and subvert the meaning of not only the categories that try to define the collective American cultural space, but also of the very notion of Identity. The idea of an undefinable (Trans) American space allows to reconsider the notions of physical borders and categorical-cultural boundaries, not as dividing lines of separation, limitation, and exclusion, but rather as intermediate and transformative spaces of co-presence, and more importantly, of transition and exchange in a nomadic transit of categories.

Latin American heterogeneity—a "heteroclite plurality" defined by Cornejo Polar in the Andean zone (2003: vii, 6), "a *mestizo* text, but also a stream of texts in flight, in intense differentiation among themselves" situated by Benítez Rojo (1998: 43) in the Caribbean—is the result of the colonial legacy of multilayered encounters (or clashes) of races, civilizations, and not always common interests. On a world scale, it is a most unique cultural space of crossings in which it becomes virtually unavoidable to question and reconceptualize "Old World" Anglo-American cultural categories, established by the traditional discourse on identity. We refer to identity both in the general sense of individual, subjective, and cultural self-determination, and in its specific application to American cultures, as rendered in the concepts of heterogeneity, syncretism, and transculturation in the sense of a transformative coexistence of differences (the "racial rainbow" analogy), or of miscegenation, integration, and fusion in the sense of a more homogenized yet hybrid union of "otherness" (the "melting pot" analogy). Nevertheless, it represents the idea of transgression as a form of crossing borders and boundaries that categorize and label human beings, a theme that winds throughout this study. It will lead us to perceive and conceive forms of decategorizing and, ultimately, transcending not only what is broadly referred to as "Latin America," but also Identity in general terms, as a constitutive element of human subjectivity.

The multiplicity of Latin American identities in their condition of simultaneity (in time) and liminality (in space), and their displaced and mobile (migrant and nomadic) subjectivities, relate to the concepts of "*mestizaje*" and "hybridity." Even as the term Latin America is justifiable in reference to a cultural area, we acknowledge that the vast space to which it refers is historically determined by its apparent lack of unity: the invasions, conquests, migrations, and encounters of different cultures, superimposed in several layers, are indicative of multiple displacements and discontinuities. This also brings about the existence of contact zones as spaces of mixing of Indigenous, European, African, and Asian elements. One could speak of an encounter and, at the same time, a confrontation between the three world races and their cultural spheres, which, beginning with colonialism and continuing in neocolonial times, gave way to the formation of a hybridized culture. More notably, Latin American cultural criticism has frequently operated with terms such as "*mestizaje*" (José Vasconcelos, Leopoldo Zea, Edouard Glissant), "transculturation" (Ortiz, Rama), "heterogeneity" (Cornejo Polar), and "hybridity" (Canclini, Henríquez Ureña). These are intended to express, to a greater or lesser degree, an essence or particularity of a Latin American identity by means of a synthesizing term. Acknowledging the utility of these concepts in rendering the complexity of Latin America, it is still undeniable that they have contributed to explain only "one" or "another" version of Latin American history and culture, and to achieve only a partial definition of Latin America.

1.4 (Un-)Situating Identity: A Discursive Process of Neobaroque Transgression

From a present-day standpoint, a unifying definition of identity does not appear achievable to the extent that Identity, in its meaning of a Subject's self-determination, refers to a hierarchically imposed set of categories that are instituted by interchangeable power relations. We need not even quote Michel Foucault's take on sexuality to see identity as a discursive concept determined by the reigning *status quo* of the socio-political establishment (1980). In its traditional meaning, it implies stability. Whereas if considered in discursive terms of (symbolic) mobility, identity and its derivative idea of transitivity are not stable or uniform concepts in their very own constitution, as we will explain further throughout this book. It becomes a set of partial and mobile elements that come into dynamic contact of play or dialogue; it conforms a simultaneity of heterogeneous discourses based on local power interests and momentary relationship schemes. The identity of each subject-group-nation becomes a transitive "trans-identity": a temporary, instantaneous, and dialogical exchange of liminalities and contacts in fluctuating discursive positions of agency that are at stake; a dialogical crossing of oppositions and a decentering interference of margins in a deconstructive implosion toward fragmented centers that act on the "self"; an arrangement of mobile connections on a horizontal, non-hierarchical, and rhizomatic level (Deleuze and Parnet 1987a, 1977). Identity *becomes* alterity: plural, revolutionized, and nomadic.

Hence, our observations of select literary and performance works from Latin America lead us to argue that identity, understood as a combination of assumed but socially determined cultural traits that define an individual, is not static and is subject to (self)revision, constituting "an evolving sense of self [...] the kind of self 'in-process'" (Kristeva in Barvosa 2017: 212). As our study intends to demonstrate, identity is decentered or even dissolved in the works of Latin American Neobaroque. It is transformed into a hybrid and mobile entity of a "new mestiza consciousness," as proposed by Chicana feminist and border theorist Gloria Anzaldúa. It can be regarded as a combination of movable and shifting "alterities" or "transitivities" situated in what Anzaldúa and Keating (1987) and Cherríe Moraga (2011) associated with "*nepantla*," a transitional "space-in-between" of subjective transformation. The term "nepantlism" underlies our entire theoretical approach. As defined by Anzaldúa and Keating (2002), following pre-Columbian Native-American traditions, it refers to a spiritual "in-between" of any two or more dimensions of existence (like female and male, life and death), a state of non-exclusive transition and transformation, or shape shifting usually attributed to shamans, but attainable by any open-minded consciousness of a "borderland identity." We will develop this topic in Sect. 2.3 of Chap. 2, "Identity on the Borders."

The point of departure for our analysis is the assumption that the identity of any group or individual is the result of the superimposition or interaction of several cultural traits "assigned" by society. They tend to move and shift in certain conditions, especially in globalized transcultural societies. Identity becomes contingent on the contacts and the awareness of the subject in its immediate and past cultural contexts. In the light of postcolonial and postmodern cultural theory, the notion of identity may be defined as a mobile and exchangeable cultural construct of a dynamic and evolving self-perception. The distinctions of identity may appear as individual (solely personal) as pertains to gender and sexuality, or they may be at the group level of social, national, ethnic, racial, and (post)human-technological collectivities. Its formation takes place in the space of cultural and social interactions—at the borders, boundaries, and interstices of categories. For instance, Mary Louise Pratt speaks of the "contact zone" as a space for "the production and reproduction of those differences in the socially structured *contact* between groups bound together in their separateness" (88; emphasis in original), in a co-presence of differences, a visibility of the "other" resulting from the presence of difference, even when denied and rendered invisible. According to Joan Scott (1992), identity can be explained as the result of a culturally (also linguistically and discursively) motivated interaction—the "experience" of the subject: "Subjects are constituted discursively, experience is a linguistic event, but [it is] not confined to a fixed order of meaning" (34). Regarding the distinction between individual and collective identity, she states that "the social and the personal are imbricated in one another and both are historically variable. The meanings of the categories of identity change and with them possibilities for thinking the self" (35).

The variability of any identity becomes especially visible when referring to gender. Cross-dressed, androgynous, and transgendered characters who appear in, or are themselves the authors of the analyzed works, indicate that these subjects do not embody any single order of identity within any *one* self-contained subject claiming to be male or female, White or Black, Hispanic or (Latin/Anglo) American, but rather that, as mutants, they transgress their own selfhood, metamorphosizing into other beings and exchanging traits of other simultaneous identities (or "alterities"). The two main types of what I suggest calling "transitive identities" are *cross-dressing*, or the act of wearing the clothes and simulating the appearance and behavior of the opposite gender to the one assigned according to a supposed "biological" sex; and *androgyny*, or the psychosomatic combination of elements of the two socially sanctioned gender roles that results in ambiguity of male/female distinctions in appearance and behavior. These two transgressive sexual positions indicate forms of transitive subjectivity that relate to other categories of identity: ethnicity, race, and nationality, and even humanity (as opposed to posthumanity). Following Judith Butler's dynamic definitions of gender performativity, Ben Sifuentes-Jáuregui describes cross-dressing (or transvestism) as an acting out of gender roles, or a process of denaturalization of what historically

14   K. A. KULAWIK

has been labeled as "feminine" and "masculine" in a process that erases the dichotomy of Self and Other (2002: 3; ref. in Ch.4). In a similar way, Josefina Fernández refers to the role of transvestism in unmasking the conventionality of a categoric-binary structuring of gender (2004: 16, 63).

Combining the idea of cultural nomadism formulated by Rosi Braidotti (1994) with the concept of "nepantlism" leads to conceiving subjectivity as a collection of roles that are momentarily accepted and played out according to the need and the context of the speaking subject in any given moment, just as subject/object roles and grammatical markers of gender and number in speech are temporarily assumed and exchangeable in a discursive situation or within the structure of a sentence. Henceforth, the traditional concept of a unitary (and determined) Identity becomes an obsolete term of Modernity, giving way to a "trans-identity," or a "trans-self," in the sense of Jack Halberstam's use of "trans*" (2018). This undefined transitive entity (hence the asterisk signaling indefinability and the suspension of category) emerges in what we propose to call "trans(A) merican cultural androgyny," or the phenomenon of combining and, at times, blurring distinctive (not only gender, but all cultural) traits that coexist within postcolonial Latin American heterogeneity (Rincón 1995; Toro 1999). Our hypothesis of a movable and transitive un-identity enables us to explain how themes of fragmentation and hybridity in Latin America come to be symbolically represented in artistic discourse through multiracial, transnational, and gender-ambiguous characters in the literary and performance works of several contemporary and particularly experimental (arguably neobaroque) writers and artists. These include Cuban Severo Sarduy, Mexican-Peruvian Mario Bellatin, Chileans Eugenia Prado, Diamela Eltit, Pedro Lemebel with Francisco Casas, and Francisco Copello, Argentinians Néstor Perlongher, Washington Cucurto, Naty Menstrual and Susy Shock, Uruguayan Roberto Echavarren, Brazilians Hilda Hilst and Silviano Santiago (along João Gilberto Noll), the Bolivian ensemble La Familia Galán, and US-Latinos Gloria Anzaldúa and Guillermo Gómez-Peña. I am using a selection of literary texts (mainly narrative, with some examples of poetry and essay) and performance art topped with examples of painting that evidence transgressive non-hetero sexualities (cross-dressers, androgynes, queer characters), and racially, ethnically, and nationally plural or neutral subjects. The analysis of the experimental, polymorphous, exuberant, and, on the most part, eccentric works by these authors leads to reconceptualize the very notions sustaining any identity, this time as a movable and liminal concept situated within

1 INTRODUCTION   15

physical and figurative borderland spaces of Latin America. These works illustrate the fragmentation of Identity in terms of binary gender and any unitary form of identity (of any One subject or Self) and its dispersion into multiple, transitive, and mobile "pluridentities" or "alterities" that coexist within the plural Self-as-selves. The cross-dressed, transgendered, androgynous, or sexually ambiguous characters who appear in or are themselves the authors of the analyzed works, are discursive subjects that are indicative of cultural dispersion and decentering. They do not embody a single (sexual, ethnic, racial, or national nor "Latin American") identity within any one subject who claims to be Latin or Anglo-American, Black or White, Indigenous or *Mestizo*, male or female. In contrast, they ludically and dialogically exchange and temporarily assume several fragmented, simultaneous, and transiting identities in an exchange with "alterities," an interplay with otherness.

A consequent claim made in this book is that the transformation of identity is a subjective, but socially and culturally "interpelled" (Althusser 1970), process that takes place in the consciousness, in the discursive sphere of the symbolic dimension of the sign, as a semiotic transaction carried out in the mind of the individual. It becomes effective in the expressive speaking-writing-creative as well as the receptive-symbolic-interpretive competency of the (reading) subject. It can be explained semiotically as a meaning-making process of a decentered three-part sign that the subject is capable of recognizing. The open nature of the triadic sign was first defined in the late 1800s by American philosopher Charles S. Peirce as a three-way relationship of not only the conventional (binary) signifier and signified (as concurrently proposed by Swiss linguist Ferdinand de Saussure 1916), but also of the "interpretant," the third key and decentering semantic element of Peircean semiotics (Peirce 1991). Furthermore, the speaking subject (the individual, writer or performer), using the decentering function of the meaning-making interpretant, undergoes what José Esteban Muñoz (1999) referred to as "disidentification," or distancing from any identity "assigned" by the cultural (conventional and hegemonic) sign and reterritorializing its position. In a tertiary or triadic interpretation of categorizing signs (by extension, symbols as markers of identity), subjectivity in the meaning-making process of the sign conflates with the subject's affectivity (beyond mere reasoning) and desire (the emotional-sexual drive to connect with the "other," but also the drive toward any group identification relatable with otherness). This process resorts to external representation and interpretation which, in the case of aesthetic discourse, find recourse in the "textual surplus" of any work of art, literature, and particularly in the neobaroque text's overflowing, excessive element of erotic—by extension: formal, verbal, textual—expenditure, *la part maudite* (the cursed or damnable part), explained by French philosopher Georges Bataille in his classic essay, *L'érotisme* (1957). The decentered sign and its excessive (erotic and parodic) manipulation are the hallmarks of what Severo Sarduy (1972) branded as the "revolutionary" (because of its destabilizing, anti-normative, and transgressive nature) Latin American style of the Neobaroque.

Latin America, with its racial, ethnic, and social diversity and multicultural "contact zones" (Pratt 1993), represents a unique space of cultural coexistence and mixture, but also excess and struggle. Those fusions and conflicts have found a channel of expression since the colonial times in the American (or New World) Baroque style, as noted by José Lezama Lima (1957) and Severo Sarduy (1974) and, more recently, in the radically exuberant and experimental Neobaroque (Chiampi 2000; Zamora 2006; Figueroa 2008; Kaup 2012; Baler 2016), as we will lay out in Sect. 2.2 in Chap. 2. In the last sixty years, "[t]he critical function of the Neobaroque is not limited [...] to the pessimist vision that marks the entropy of historicist modernity. The aesthetic reappropriation of the [17th century] Baroque has also been the mechanism for recreating history in the light of new challenges in the present" (Chiampi 523). Henceforth, Latin American (Neo)Baroque art and literature have been effective in expressing this challenge of a syncretic but also conflictive coexistence of simultaneities and fusions since colonial times. As Brazilian writer Silviano Santiago stated when referring broadly to the cultural heritage of the continent, "[t]he major contribution of Latin America to Western culture is to be found in its systematic destruction of the concepts of unity and purity" (2001: 30). In this multicultural and syncretic context of the Americas, Neobaroque art can be perceived as a discursive (and disruptive) platform of a certain cultural fragmentation in the Western world. It thus becomes a staging ground for the nomadic decentering and subversion of identity within the symbolic sphere of subjectivity.

In a similar fashion, the arguably neobaroque works of Severo Sarduy, Néstor Perlongher, Pedro Lemebel, Diamela Eltit, Hilda Hilst, and other contemporary writers and performers from Río de la Plata, Brazil, Chile, Cuba, Mexico, and the United States allow us to establish trans-Latin American literary connections whose catalyst is neobaroque style and technique, notwithstanding the common themes in their works. As a resurgence and reappropriation of the Baroque cultural phenomenon in the mid-twentieth century, Neobaroque style has been effective in deconstructing the European Enlightenment-based categories of Modernity by introducing destabilizing elements in terms of sexuality and gender, and non-Western transcultured notions of ethnicity, race, and nationality by means of transgressive figuration. Its exuberant and experimental formalism operates as a postcolonial and deconstructive critique of established cultural (particularly gender) categories. The ambiguous characters populating the works that use hybrid literary and visual genres may be indicative of a "Postmodern condition," a crisis of legitimation of normative cultural classifications that Jean François Lyotard (1979) related to the hegemonically established "metadiscourse" or the "grand narratives" of History, Science, and Philosophy (1984: 37–41).

The coincidence of Neobaroque transgressions, particularly in Latin America, points to cultural and aesthetic-cultural connections that Perlongher named "the Latin American Neobaroque arch" or the "Transplatinian Caribbean" (93–100, 115, 119). The common denominator in the mentioned writers is the displacement of a subjectivity "adrift" (*a la deriva*, Perlongher 48–49) in a flow of sexual, ethnic, and racial ambiguity that is combined with a boldly experimental, mannered, and parodic style inherited from Baroque formalism. Henceforth, the Neobaroque suggests a specifically Latin American path of Postmodernity in times of an ontological crisis.

In this context, I propose to explore a set of contemporary works that are neobaroque in their exuberant forms and present a content marked by queerness, inasmuch as they display racially and ethnically mixed, but first and foremost, sexually mutant (androgynous), bisexual and transgendered, cross-dressed or ambiguously undefined characters. Examples of those include the multiracial/-cultural cross-dressers Cobra, Colibrí, Auxilio, and Socorro in the novels by Cuban Severo Sarduy, characters Dolores del Río, and María Félix in Pedro Lemebel's urban chronicles, the transcultural, bisexual, occasionally cross-dressed General José de San Martín in Washington Cucurto's novel about the independence struggle in Argentina, the cross-dressed performers and narrators Susy Shock and Naty Menstrual in the *noire* urban context of Buenos Aires, the androgynous voices in Roberto Echavarren's novels *Ave Roc* and *Diablo en el pelo*, cross-dressers La Familia Galán in Andean La Paz and Guillermo Gómez-Peña's impersonations of the transethnic and cross-gender US-Mexico border crossers Border Brujo and Naftazteca, the transnational cyborgs

Mexterminator and Mad-Mex, or the genderless posthumans Sonia and Hembros in Eugenia Prado's novels-installations. As we will explain in detail in Chap. 3, all these characters transgress normative paradigms of gender, race, ethnicity, nationality, and even carnal humanity as opposed to cyborg techno posthumanity. Their polymorphous bodily presence, ambiguous appearance, and fluid self-(dis-)identification in terms of cultural, social, and gender traits point to the conceivability of a trans-identity theory of otherness in relation to the plural self, a "subject-in-process," a "self-as-becoming" (*devenir*), a rhizomatic trans-self with multiple shifting identities that are fluid, transitive, and exchangeable. They may be perceived as voices of resistance to and subversion of the logocentric, postcolonial, and hegemonic "New World B-Order" (Gómez-Peña 1996) or "New World [Dis]Orders" (Piazza and Zimmerman 1998).

In the breaking down of categorical identities, we are opening a dimension of philosophical and political inquiry that these recent Latin American works of literature, performance, and other forms of art bring into question: that of *cultural hegemony*. If taken to broader waters of political meaning, the aesthetics of the Neobaroque, as a *discourse of resistance*, surge as a postcolonial critique of the hegemony exercised by the logocentric, patriarchal, heteronormative, and colonialist Western discourse. The Neobaroque confronts this hegemony with the transgressively disruptive power of eroticism, artifice, and parody putting into motion the decentralizing, seditious, and anti-heteronormative effect of resistance, which is also part of the broader dimension of an American "counter-conquest" signaled by Lezama Lima, and of an attitude defined by Echeverría as the "baroque ethos." Resistance also underlies the concept of Manichean struggle between binary forces of tradition and change, introduced in Angel Rama's *La ciudad letrada* (1984) [*The Lettered City*, 1996]. These multiple and frequently radical dimensions of the Neobaroque will be examined in depth in Chap. 4, Sects. 4.1 and 4.4.

1.5   Chapter Sequence and Methodology

The themes introduced here are further contextualized and explained in Chap. 2, "Neobaroque as Transgression: The Latin American Paradigm," where the topic is opened to the ensuing analysis of the literary and performance works in Chap. 3, and to their interpretation in Chap. 4 where, in the context of the Neobaroque, we combine literary analysis with queer, borderland, and nomadic theories. Firstly, Chap. 2 introduces the major concepts, setting the scene for a more meaningful reading and understanding of the examples of neobaroque literature and art (in Chap. 3), and establishes connections that link the central terminology around the book's conceptual axis of:

Latin America ⇔ Neobaroque ⇔ Discourse/Textuality ⇔ Identity ⇔ Borders ⇔ Nomadism

Chapter 2 determines the methodological and theoretical foundation for our reading of the Neobaroque as a destabilizing (textual) force that, through aesthetic and discursive means, leads to the disarticulation of normative categories of identity and the formulation of a transitive self. As a point of departure toward the analysis of transgressive subjects (that is fully undertaken in Chap. 3), Chap. 2 defines and articulates the book's leading concepts of *Latin America as a hybrid space* of coexisting and intermingling cultures, the *Neobaroque* as a characteristically exuberant Latin American style expressing such hybridity through aesthetic forms that discursively facilitate the philosophical decentering and the questioning of any essentialist cultural categories of identity, and *Discourse* as the textual-symbolic space in which the decategorizing and rearticulation of identity take place.

The first section of Chap. 2, "Latin America: Hybrid Contexts of Deterritorialization," presents Latin America as a cross-cultural space not only of migrations and crossings, encounters and contacts, but also shifts and eventual transformations of culture and identity. We refer to the by now classic Latin Americanist cultural criticism that signals heterogeneity, transculturation, cross-cultural poetics, and hybridity as part of Latin American idiosyncrasy, references that include Rama, Cornejo Polar, Benítez Rojo, García Canclini, and Glissant (1989). Newer border theory approaches to hybridity are represented by Gómez-Peña and Anzaldúa. Applying the concepts of heterogeneity and hybridity will allow us to consider the transcultural dimension of Latin America and its (post)colonial legacy of syncretism and subalternity, and delineate the cultural context for the reemergence of Colonial Baroque in its twentieth-century stylization of the Neobaroque—an aesthetic expression of this cultural heterogeneity. We propose that this particular (Latin) American cultural context of coexisting historical and cultural forces in contact is what sets the stage for perceiving cultural mobility, nomadism, and transitivity as the deconstructive forces of a plural, decentered, and nomadic (trans-)identity that characterizes the hybrid cultures of the Americas.

Section 2.2, "Neobaroque Literary and Artistic Transgressions," discusses this style as a radical cultural phenomenon reflecting hybridity, instability, and peripheral resistance to centers of Anglo-Hispanic-Western discourse and hegemony. We refer to foundational essays by José Lezama Lima (1957), Severo Sarduy (1972), and Néstor Perlongher (1997) to explain the use of this style as a form of radical literary and artistic expression carried out by means of exuberant techniques associated with artifice, parody, and eroticism. These elements liberate Neobaroque's textual-discursive potential to pursue an agenda of decentering identity, questioning categories, and producing a form of cultural resistance to the postcolonial order that Bolívar Echeverría (1994) called the "baroque ethos," a term he proposed to signal a common attitude that characterizes Latin American and Western culture.

Section 2.3, "Identity on the Borders: An Intersectional Approach to Nomadic Transits," introduces the concept of "intersectionality" as a transdisciplinary approach to the topic and a method of analysis. It focuses on defining the hybrid and fluid nature of nomadic-migrant identity situated at the interstices of categories of physical and conceptual borderlands. Insight to current Chicana feminist border theory (Anzaldúa 1987; Anzaldúa and Keating 2002) as well as the theory of nomadism (Braidotti 1994, 2002) will lead us to evince the existence of *borderland identities* in not only physical or geographical but also psychological and spiritual dimensions of consciousness, as a blurring of boundaries resulting from ethnic, racial, national, posthuman shifts (nomadism and metamorphosis). To further gage the usefulness of the concept of borderland identity, in Sect. 2.3 we link Gilles Deleuze's term of *devenir* as "becoming" of a "subject-in-process" to Chicana border theory and the notions of *nepantlism* ("spaces-in-between") and "new *mestiza* consciousness," a trans-being that straddles multiple cultures (Anzaldúa 1987; Alarcón et al. 1993). Subsequently, Part 2.3.3, "Queer becomings in trans(-itive) genders" presents the theoretic possibilities of destabilizing (as deconstructing) normative categories of gender by means of the concept of *queerness* as one of the forms of transitivity. Ideas from queer, trans, and border theories facilitate our eventual interpretation of artistic-literary works in Chaps. 3 and 4. With reference to José Esteban Muñoz (1999), Silviano Santiago (2001), Roberto Echavarren (2008), and Jack Halberstam (2018), in this section we establish the guiding theorem of this analysis: *queerness as transitivity* of gender and sexuality, an idea founded on the marked presence of cross-dressing, androgyny, and indeterminate mobile sexualities appearing in the Latin American Neobaroque. The fourth and final part of Sect. 2.3, "Eroticism as deterritorialization through excess," explains the association between the Neobaroque and *Eroticism* in its dimension of surplus, excess, and desire with reference to Georges Bataille (1957) and Severo Sarduy (1972, 1987). Making these connections among queer and borderland theory, eroticism (as surplus and desire), and the Neobaroque leads us to envision the aesthetic representation of selfhood as anti-normative transgression. We point out in the following Sect. 2.4, "Writing the Body and the Body of Writing," that identity articulation is a dynamic discursive process taking place in the textual-symbolic sphere of *writing* and *performance*.

In this last section of Chap. 2, we address the written and performative dimension of Text (the aesthetic work) as cultural embodiment of an identity destabilized in neobaroque representation. This part comprises an initial discussion of the theoretical possibilities of trans-identity, which will be detailed in Chap. 4. We establish a relationship between Identity and Discourse (Neobaroque Textuality) in the aesthetic representation of nomadism as transgressive subjectivity. The focus is on the relationship between the written/performed text and the enactment of identity in relation to both a material-empirical body and its symbolic representation. The association of body with writing/performance (the creative process) is examined considering gender as a discursive construct (Julia Kristeva, Judith Butler, Elizabeth Grosz). The Body-Writing-Performance relationship is explained in reference to performance theory (Coco Fusco, José Esteban Muñoz). In sum, Chap. 2 sets the conceptual stage for the ensuing examination of textual examples of identity transgression in Chap. 3 and their further interpretation in Chap. 4.

Chapter 3, "Subversions of Selfhood: Transgressive CharACTerS of the Neobaroque," focuses on the decentered and ambiguous characters appearing in selected textual and visual works as aesthetic representations of transgressive borderland identities. Section 3.1 presents a historical, cultural, and literary contextualization of these works. Reference to both general and specific socio-political, cultural, and literary contexts will aid in the comprehension of Neobaroque's subversive potential. Section 3.2 presents empirical examples of identity decentering and subject transitivity in select works of fiction, poetry, essay, and performance by US-Mexicans Gloria Anzaldúa and Guillermo Gómez-Peña, Cuban Severo Sarduy, Mexican Mario Bellatin, Brazilian Hilda Hilst, Argentinian Néstor Perlongher, Chileans Pedro Lemebel, Diamela Eltit and Eugenia Prado,

Uruguayan Roberto Echavarren, and the Bolivian Familia Galán, among others. Here, we identify the textual characters and narrative voices (including implicit authors in and empirical authors of the works) and examine their transformative and subversive incidence in the form of cross-dressing, androgyny, queerness, metamorphosis, cross-ethnicity, transnationality, and, ultimately, posthumanity. Examples of these are cross-dresser Cobra, Performero-Border Brujo, cross-dressed bisexual General San Martín, and cyborg Hembros.

Chapter 4, "One-T(w)o-Many: Neobaroque Articulations of Nomadic Identity," rests on the theoretical and critical premises introduced in Chap. 2, defining nomadic trans-identity and Neobaroque figurations of transitive selfhood. Here, we explain the mechanisms of identity decentering and rearticulation into trans-identity operating in Neobaroque discourse following Irlemar Chiampi (2000), Samuel Arriarán (2007), Cristo Figueroa (2008), Lois Parkinson Zamora (2006), and Monika Kaup (2012). *Neobaroque Style* is explained as a transformative aesthetic mechanism of representation that, in an analogy between form and content, configures transgressive subjects. Following the ideas of Severo Sarduy and Georges Bataille, Sect. 4.1, "Neobaroque as a Style of Instability," examines the exuberance of neobaroque elements such as artifice, metafiction, parody, and eroticism that produce a destabilizing effect on identity categories. Section 4.2, "Articulation of Trans-Identity and the Mechanisms of Nomadism," focuses on the semiotic concept of the "triadic sign" formulated by Charles Peirce as a mechanism of decentering meaning. We explain how the meaning-making process operates in a three-part/way relationship that includes the *third* (destabilizing) semiotic element, the "interpretant." The transformative and destabilizing potential of Neobaroque discourse is further validated in Sect. 4.3, "On the Borders of Identity," with modalities of gender transitivity (cross-dressing, androgyny, mutant and cyborg entities) substantiated in queer-trans theory and Chicana border studies.

We end this chapter with Sect. 4.4, "The Neobaroque Strategy: From Self to Other, from Seduction to Sedition," by addressing the political dimension of the Neobaroque in the context of postmodern relativity. The Neobaroque is considered an "alternative articulation" of philosophical and cultural thought, a "recent mode of representation [of crisis] in literature," that serves as one of the "epi-phenomena […] that have to do with the effort to forge processes of resistance […] within the frame of hegemonic forces" (Zimmerman 2001: 286). Likewise, the opulent and experimental Neobaroque style has been defined by critics like Gustavo Guerrero

(1987), Carmen Bustillo (1990), and Carlos Rincón (1996) as a radical expression of postcolonial, subaltern, and postrevolutionary resistance in Latin American literature and culture, an assessment that goes in line with José Lezama Lima's stance on the Colonial Baroque as a style of an American "counter-conquest" (1957). The decentered, refracted, and fragmented nomadic trans-self represents a subversive political stance toward patriarchal logocentrism and the market-imposed uniformizing forces of cultural globalization (García Canclini 1990, 1999). Its neobaroque representation may be considered as isomorphous with Postmodernity in an "achronic causality between the Baroque episteme and the postmodern one, […] a certain isomorphic symmetry between the rupture of logocentrism (the Baroque effect) and the mockery of capitalism (the Neobaroque effect)" (Chiampi 523). With the last claim that the Neobaroque can be perceived as an aesthetic undercurrent within the postmodern episteme of crisis, this book opens a space for further discussion.

We conclude with Chap. 5, "At the Crossroads of Nepantla," in which we assess our findings on the philosophical, cultural, and political implications of gender bending and crossing the boundaries of categorical identities and their transformations within the context of Neobaroque literature and performance from Latin America. We conclude that a plural and mobile "trans-identity" corresponds to a radical "new subject position" (Vivancos Pérez 2013: xiii) emerging from Latin America and its multiple borderlands through the exuberant and experimental forms of the Neobaroque. We highlight the discursive (and subversive) potential of this style in the process of decategorizing heteronormative impositions. The nomadic trans-self constitutes an alternative vision of identity in its fluid process of trans-ing/-iting and queer-ing with its arguably postmodern decolonializing attitude of defiance within the "baroque ethos," as proposed by Echeverría (1994). It concludes our argument about Neobaroque's subversive agency emulated by this ethos, a philosophical posture that extends beyond Latin America to any setting of multicultural encounter.

1.6   Why Experience the Neobaroque? Relevance and Scope of the Matter

Our vision of Transmerica as cultural transitivity presents "a compelling task with transformative effects, involving the encounter with two powerful multiplicities that come from completely different backgrounds," one originating in theory, the other in literary-aesthetic discourse (Soich 2021: 18).

24   K. A. KULAWIK

A theory of trans(-itivity) nested in Neobaroque discourse undoubtedly has political implications of destabilizing the heterosexual, patriarchal, and normative system of categories upon which the postcolonial order is established. It also has philosophical implications, as it proposes an opening for inclusivity of multiple, mixed, and coexisting, yet mobile and interchangeable identities transiting between oneness and otherness. The trans-self epitomizes the decentralizing strand of decolonial cultural discourse on selfhood in Latin America, the United States, and beyond.

The significance of this undertaking for Latin American literary and cultural studies, and the humanities in general, lies in the exploration of a relatively uncharted area that links identity and cultural transformations, such as queerness and inter-ethnic/-racial mixing, with Neobaroque aesthetics and its expressive possibilities. A major point of this analysis, differentiating it from the mainstream of cultural studies approaches, is that the rearticulation of identity as trans-identity (or "transentity") considers both the physical (bodily material) figuration, embodiment, and enactment of self in artistic works, as well as the discursive procedure of abstract figuration and representation by linguistic (symbolic) means. Our reasoning in this book engages two sides of the matter: Writing the Body and the Body of Writing. It establishes a connection between the material and the symbolic structures of subjectivity as they apply to the articulation of a transitive identity. This points to the underlying function of Language in the symbolic and semiotic process of any cultural experience, particularly as it applies to the formation of identity and subjectivity in the representation of the physical body.

The characters, voices, and bodies displayed in the analyzed works, many of whom are multiethnic and interracial cross-dressers, androgynes, or queer mutants, provide the empirical basis for reframing essentialist accounts of normative, conventionally and symbolically formed identities. The mobility of gender, racial, ethnic, national, and cultural traits results from cross-border and intercultural contacts. A language-based, queer and gender theory-enhanced approach conceives transitive identity as the expression of nomadic selfhood that materializes in the exuberant and radically experimental neobaroque discourse.

While it expands on classic discourses on hybridization, transculturation, and heterogeneity, this book moves beyond Latin American cultural studies to venture into the theoretical realms of Neobaroque studies supplemented with Bataille's "eroticism," Baudrillard's "simulation," Sarduy's "artifice," Perlongher's "points of passage," Anzaldúa's "nepantlism,"

Halberstam's "trans*," and Braidotti's "nomadic subjects." Reinterpreting selfhood as a symbolic-conceptual process of writing, performing, and reading the body is founded on the three-dimensionality of the "open" sign carried out by the "interpretant" in a dynamic process of subversive meaning-making. Trans-identity is formulated within the representational bounds of Peirce's decentered triadic sign that is reversible, mobile, and mutable.

Further significance of this study lies in its intersectional character, engaging multiple categories of identity (that include gender, sexuality, race, ethnicity, and nationality) from multiple perspectives (literary-cultural, gender-queer, along with border-feminist), expanding current literary-cultural, Neobaroque, and queer-gender-feminist approaches. The application of queer theory to works of the Neobaroque facilitates the figuration of trans-identity as a nomadic transit of subjectivity materialized in the trans body. The cultural potential of the Neobaroque is fleshed out with the help of queer and border theories in an analysis that displays the potential of Latin American fiction and performance to transform identity into an open, transitional, transformative entity (not category) embodied in the nomadic trans-self. This constitutes *Transmerica's* contribution to the theory of subjectivity as well as to cultural and Neobaroque studies.

Whereas our vision of trans-identity is based on queerness, it applies to transcending (mobilizing) other cultural categories of ethnicity, race, nationality, and even (post)humanity. Its significance for the advancement of general theory of identity may be measured heeding the words of the late David William Foster: "Queer studies have become a site for not only bringing race, class, and ethnicity into a discussion of homoeroticism, but for showing that it is imperative to construct a calculus of all elements of subjectivity and identity" (2006: 7–8). Hence, our intersectional and inter-disciplinary approach purports to constitute this effective calculus as it displays Latin American Neobaroque's aesthetic and political potential to disarticulate the prescriptive notions of identity on various levels, suggesting the possibility of surpassing (hetero)normatively defined, exclusive, and, in many cases, binary categories like male, female, homo or hetero-sexual, Black, White, Brown, *Mestizo/a*, Hispanic, or Latino/a. It fields a more flexible approach to assuming difference, diversity, and intercultural contact in times of enhanced (im)migration and political tension. It also hopes to achieve what Marc Zimmerman (2001) pointed out as the need for subsequent academic investigations targeting "the uncertainties and problems of an imposed order that produces a state of disorder," a need that eventually should lead to developing counter-discourses of literature and criticism, understood as "fluid representational forms [...] expressive of people's concerns and modifiable in terms of new events and possibilities" (286–87). We deem the Neobaroque to be one such counter-space and fluid representational form that provides a foundation for understanding the underlying mechanisms of not only gender and sexuality transformation, but also for the de-/rearticulation of *any* identity as defined by cultural categories of ethnicity, race, nationality, and even (cyborg post-) humanity. Our intersectional counter-discourse is an invitation for the interdisciplinary reader of Latin American literary and cultural studies to experience Transmerican nomadism in the exuberance of the Neobaroque.

The complexity of multicultural relations in times of enhanced globalization, technification, migration, and resulting cultural conflict calls for more flexible mechanisms of assuming difference, diversity, intercultural mixing, and trans-/posthuman alternatives in the nomadic transits of the Americas. It is a call to assume otherness as a value within oneness in transitive coexistence of categories. This "vision of Transmerica," as rendered in Neobaroque works, becomes relevant in times of inter-American migration, political polarization, populist demagogy, civil unrest, and deterioration of democratic values resulting from intolerant and authoritarian policies of leaders like Hugo Chávez, Nicolás Maduro, Daniel Ortega, Jairo Bolsonaro, and Donald Trump. A proposal of a trans(-itive) self hopes to create a different, more pluralistic and inclusive model of understanding identity as a decentered, mobile, and nomadic process of becoming in a multicultural America.

This book hopes to become a *de facto* reader's guide to understanding fairly recent Latin American works of Joycean difficulty and their role in cultural and epistemological transformations of the early twenty-first century. Some of the novels analyzed here have been translated to English, namely Eltit's *Lumpérica* as *E. Iluminata* (1997), *El cuarto mundo* as *The Fourth World* (1995), as well as Sarduy's *Cobra* (1975) and *De donde son los cantantes* as *From Cuba with a Song* (2000), and Bellatin's *Salón de belleza* as *Beauty Salon* (2021), among some others. The growing interest in works by Sarduy, Lemebel, Eltit, Perlongher, Echavarren, Hilst, Prado, and Cucurto extends to the themes of gender, sexuality, transgression, border crossing, cultural hybridization, and even posthuman-cyborg formations. It shows that this kind of artistic production deserves more specialized attention and explanation on the part of the critic directed in particular to an English-language reader. Neobaroque literature and performance propel us to rearticulate an idea of selfhood that enables an alternative vision of identity—as trans-identity—and opens a space for further cultural and philosophical speculation.

Transmerica's nomadic vision of *transitive identity* considers androgynous and mutant sexual identity as a neobaroque blueprint for understanding the underlying mechanisms of *any* identity (trans-)formation. It intends to be an alternative path to attaining a more flexible and tolerant approach to difference, otherness, and intercultural mixing in Latin America, the United States, and any multicultural society. The concept of a nomadic trans-self is intended to be subversive in its focus on the transgressive aesthetics of the Neobaroque. The political projections of this style disturb the hegemony of patriarchal, heteronormative, and logocentric cultural values. Representing identity as decentered and polymorphous, Neobaroque's transitive embodiments of nomadic selfhood disintegrate the notion of categorical purity. Neobaroque literary and artistic figuration of trans-selfhood materializes the coexistence of differences and interactions with otherness in a border zone of categorical transits and transitions of a normatively established Identity. Nomadic transitivity becomes an alternative path for the transformation of selfhood by using the borderlands as a conceptual space for the transgression of prescribed bounds of sameness with contact and coexistence of two sides. Nomadism becomes a way of breaking down normative categories which divide (and separate) people, an epistemological device for transiting from sameness to otherness and for opening selfhood to multiple aspects of existence in a transitory co-presence of differences within any one subjectivity. It is a nomadic impulse that leads toward new territories of cultural and philosophical thought of the future.

Our model suggests that mobile and transitive identity can be symbolically and theoretically conceived as the result of neobaroque aesthetic operations in literary and artistic works that provide the discursive foundation for understanding (cultural) queerness. A decentered interpretation of selfhood is possible considering the decentered, non-binary, and three-dimensional nature of the sign. Its destabilizing power is visible in the figuration of eccentric characters in neobaroque texts from various contexts of Latin America and the United States. In this sense, This book establishes a singular connection between discourse theory, semiotics of the Neobaroque, identity, gender and queer theory within the broader context of Postmodern and Latin American cultural studies. The three-prong relationship between Language (as Discourse), Sexuality (as the

Erotic), and Neobaroque (as Style) defines the multidimensional approach of this work. From an interdisciplinary and intersectional angle, it attempts to establish new conceptual connections linking gender and sexual identity to other categories of identity such as race, ethnicity, nationality, and even posthumanity. A critical examination of Latin American Neobaroque reveals the possibility of a fragmented oneness in its relation to a plural otherness. Ultimately, the Neobaroque relates to a postmodern aesthetic of decentering, a breakdown of any totalizing (meta)narratives that confers these literary, performative, and visual works an aesthetically radical dimension of resistance to elitist logocentric and heteronormative discourse. Queer identity of the nomadic trans-self represented in neobaroque discourse opens new perspectives for envisioning the hybrid American cultural space from the multiple angles of discourse theory, semiotics, and philosophy. With its scope reaching beyond literary analysis, this book hopes to become an inter- and transdisciplinary addendum to existing theory of identity through the lens of Latin American Neobaroque aesthetics.

Nonetheless, *Transmerica's* intention to disarticulate the idea of a stable identity (and purity) does not suppose the death of existing categories of gender, race, ethnicity, or nationality altogether. They are inexorably there but they can mobilize from the stagnant parameters of normativity with discursive mechanisms of a mobile interconnectivity and exchangeability of categorical traits within the nomadic self. Literary and performative acts of transgression become aesthetic figurations of transitivity without resorting to fixed determinations of any culturally imposed category. Any identification with or attribution of gender or sexuality, race or ethnicity, nationality or social belonging is not only limiting but equivocal for a person from different regions of the United States and Latin America. The meaning of gay/straight, White, Black, Native, Latino, or Anglo-American has different connotations for an affluent or marginalized inhabitant of Argentina, Brazil, Cuba, Mexico, or the United States. It is feasible to surpass any definite attributions of gender, race, ethnicity, or nationhood with the term "trans." Instead of focusing on the result, our attention is on the very process of transformation, transitivity, and movement *between* categories. Identity is suspended with transitivity as is Latin/Anglo-America with "Transmerica." References to Latin American hybridity are only that: temporary incarnations and points of departure for the multiple *visions* of America. Holistic identification of such hybridity has frequently been mentioned in canonical works of Latin Americanist theory and cultural criticism, whether the identification of Americanness be White–European in Sarmiento and Rodó, Indigenous or mixed-race *Mestizo/a* in Vasconcelos, Cornejo Polar, and Rama, the unified subject of *Nuestra América* in José Martí and Andrés Bello, or the Black-Afrodescendant Mulatto and Creole in Glissant's and Benítez Rojo's Caribbean. Using but stepping beyond these holistic visions, we propose the possibility of a fluid coexistence and an ongoing transfer of multiple identity variables, their contingent and momentary (even playful) assumption, a deployment of movable and shifting markers or traits within the *same* one yet fragmented and *plural* subject, regardless of attributed origin.

While using the term "Latin America" to refer to the literary and artistic works discussed in this book, it becomes clear that we are bouncing off an abstraction (which, in a way, is operationally inevitable). David Frye states in the introduction to his translation of Rama's *Transculturación narrativa*... (1982) [*Writing Across Cultures: Narrative Transculturation in Latin America*, 2012] that "Rama draws ideas and inspirations for this book from far-flung regions of Latin America and uses them to create a startling juxtaposition of ideas, revealing sudden flashes of insight into the hidden commonalities that underlie the continent's regional differences" (2012: xi). Following Néstor Perlongher's ideas about Trans-American neobaroque connections (*el Caribe transplatino* and *el arco neobarroco*, 1997: 93, 101), we also observe in these works a commonality that is the Neobaroque, despite the vast array of regional, cultural, socio-political, and geographic differences that separate the literary and artistic traditions of their respective countries of origin. Keeping in mind that any one of the cultural categories of identity referred to here has different meanings for different people in the various countries or regions, it is reasonable to put on hold the concept of (Latin) America and use it no more than as a geographical denominator that links the studied authors and their works. Also useful is Frye's nomenclature explained in his introduction to *Writing across Cultures*: "Here, I adopt Rama's habit, retained throughout this translation, of referring to all Latin America—South and Central America, Mexico, and the Caribbean—as 'the continent' or simply 'America'" (xi). Ultimately, this transcultural/continental dimension of the Americas justifies the use of *Transmerica* as a space of hybridization and heterogeneity, but more importantly, of cross-border contact and nomadic transit.

WORKS CITED

Alarcón, Norma, Ana Castillo, and Cherríe Moraga, eds. (1993). *The Sexuality of Latinas*. Berkeley: Third Woman.

Althusser, Louis. (1970). *For Marx*. New York: Vintage.

Anzaldúa, Gloria. (2007 [1987]). *Borderlands / La Frontera: The New Mestiza*. San Francisco: Spinsters / Aunt Lute.

Anzaldúa, Gloria and AnaLouise Keating, eds. (2002). *This Bridge We Call Home: Radical Visions for Transformation*. New York: Routledge.

Arriarán, Samuel. (2007). *Barroco y neobarroco en América Latina: Estudios sobre la otra modernidad*. México, D.F.: Ítaca.

Baler, Pablo. (2016). *Latin American Neo-Baroque: Senses of Distortion*. Trans. Michael McGaha. New York: Palgrave.

Barvosa, Edwina. (2017). "Feminism and Borderland Identities." *Routledge Companion to Feminist Philosophy*. Eds. Ann Garry, Serene J. Khader and Alison Stone. New York: Routledge. 207–17.

Bataille, Georges. (1957). *L'érotisme*. Paris: Éditions de Minuit.

Benítez Rojo, Antonio. (1996 [1992]). *The Repeating Island: The Caribbean and the Postmodern Perspective*. Trans. James Maraniss. Durham and London: Duke UP.

Benítez Rojo, Antonio. (1998). *La isla que se repite*. Edición definitiva. Barcelona: Editorial Casiopea.

Braidotti, Rosi. (1994). *Nomadic Subjects: Embodiment and Sexual Difference in Contemporary Feminist Theory*. New York: Columbia UP.

Braidotti, Rosi. (2002). *Metamorphoses: Towards a Materialist Theory of Becoming*. Cambridge, UK: Polity Press.

Braidotti, Rosi. (2006). *Transpositions: On Nomadic Ethics*. Cambridge, UK: Polity Press.

Bustillo, Carmen. (1990). *Barroco y América Latina: un itinerario inconcluso*. Caracas: Monte Ávila.

Certeau, Michel de. (1997 [1974]). *Culture in the Plural*. Ed. Luce Giard, trans. Tom Conley. Minneapolis and London: U of Minnesota P.

Chiampi, Irlemar. (2000). *Barroco y modernidad*. México: Fondo de Cultura Económica.

Cornejo Polar, Antonio. (2003). *Escribir en el aire: Ensayo sobre la heterogeneidad socio-cultural en las literaturas andinas*. Lima, Perú and Berkeley, CA: CELACP—Latinoamericana Editores.

Deleuze, Gilles and Claire Parnet. (1987a [1977]). *Dialogues*. Trans. Hugh Tomlinson and Barbara Habberjam. New York: Columbia UP.

Echavarren, Roberto. (2008). *Arte andrógino: estilo versus moda*. Santiago de Chile: Ripio.

Echeverría, Bolívar, ed. (1994). *Modernidad, mestizaje cultural, ethos barroco*. México: UNAM—Equilibrista.

1 INTRODUCTION 31

Fernández, Josefina. (2004). *Cuerpos desobedientes: Travestismo e identidad de género*. Buenos Aires: Edhasa.

Figueroa Sánchez, Cristo Rafael. (2008). *Barroco y neobarroco en la narrativa hispanoamericana. Cartografías literarias de la segunda mitad del siglo XX*. Bogotá-Medellín: Pontificia Universidad Javeriana y Universidad de Antioquia.

Foster, David Wiliam, ed. (2006). *El ambiente nuestro. Chicano/Latino Homoerotic Writing*. Tempe: Bilingual Press–Editorial Bilingüe.

Foucault, Michel. (1972). *The Archaeology of Knowledge*. Trans. A.M. Sheridan Smith. New York: Pantheon Books.

Foucault, Michel. (1980). *The History of Sexuality. Vols. 1–2*. Trans. Robert Hurley. New York: Vintage.

García Canclini, Néstor. (1995 [1990]). *Hybrid Cultures: Strategies for Entering and Leaving Modernity*. Trans. Christopher L. Chiappari and Silvia L. López. Minneapolis and London: U of Minnesota P.

García Canclini, Néstor. (1999). *La globalización imaginada*. México, Buenos Aires, Barcelona: Paidós.

Glissant, Edouard. (1989). *Caribbean Discourse. Selected Essays*. Trans. J. Michael Dash. Charlottesville: U of Virginia P.

Gómez-Peña, Guillermo. (1996). *The New World Border*. San Francisco: City Lights Books.

Guerrero, Gustavo. (1987). *La estrategia neobarroca. Estudio sobre el resurgimiento de la poética barroca en la obra narrativa de Severo Sarduy*. Barcelona: Edicions del Mall.

Halberstam, Jack. (2018). *Trans*: A Quick and Quirky Account of Gender Variability*. Oakland, CA: U of California P.

Kaup, Monika. (2012). *Neobaroque in the Americas. Alternative Modernities in Literature, Visual Art, and Film*. Charlottesville and London, U of Virginia P.

Laclau, Ernesto. (1996). *Emancipation(s)*. London and New York: Verso.

Lezama Lima, José. (1957). *La expresión americana*. La Habana, Cuba: Instituto Nacional de Cultura.

Lyotard, Jean-François. (1984 [1979]). *The Postmodern Condition: A Report on Knowledge*. Trans. Geoffrey Bennington and Brian Massumi. Minneapolis: U of Minnesota P.

Moraga, Cherríe L. (2011). *A Xicana Codex of Changing Consciousness*. Durham, NC: Duke UP.

Muñoz, José Esteban. (1999). *Disidentifications: Queers of Color and the Performance of Politics*. Minneapolis and London: U of Minnesota P.

Peirce, Charles S. (1991). *Peirce on Signs: Writings on Semiotics*. Ed. James Hoops. Chapel Hill: U of North Carolina P.

Perlongher, Néstor. (1997). *Prosa plebeya*. Buenos Aires: Colihue.

32   K. A. KULAWIK

Piazza, Michael and Marc Zimmerman, eds. (1998). *New World [Dis]Orders and Peripheral Strains: Specifying Cultural Dimensions in Latin American and Latino Studies*. Chicago: March–Abrazo Press.

Pratt, Mary Louise. (1993). "Criticism in the Contact Zone: Decentering Community and Nation." *Critical Theory, Cultural Politics, and Latin American Narrative*. Eds. Steven, M. Bell, Albert H. Lemay and Leonard Orr. Notre Dame and London: U of Notre Dame P. 83–102.

Rama, Angel. (1996 [1984]). *The Lettered City*. Ed. and trans. John Charles Chasteen. Durham and London: Duke UP.

Rama, Angel. (2012 [1982]). *Writing Across Cultures: Narrative Transculturation in Latin America*. Ed. and trans. David Frye. Durham and London: Duke UP.

Rincón, Carlos. (1995). *La no simultaneidad de lo simultaneo: postmodernidad, globalización y culturas en América Latina*. Bogotá: Universidad Nacional.

Rincón, Carlos. (1996). *Mapas y pliegues: Ensayos de cartografía cultural y de lectura del Neobarroco*. Bogotá: Tercer Mundo Editores.

Rivera Cusicanqui, Silvia. (2020 [2010]). *Ch'ixinakax utxiwa. On Practices and Discourses of Decolonization*. Trans. Molly Geidel. Cambridge, UK and Medford, MA: Polity Press.

Santiago, Silviano. (2001). *The Space In-Between: Essays on Latin American Culture*. Durham, NC: Duke UP.

Sarduy, Severo. (1978 [1972]). "El barroco y el neobarroco". *América Latina en su literatura*. Ed. César Fernández Moreno. México: Siglo XXI. 167–84.

Sarduy, Severo (1987 [1974]). *Barroco*. In: *Ensayos generales sobre el Barroco*. Buenos Aires: Fondo de Cultura Económica. 143–224.

Saussure, Ferdinand de. (1955 [1916]). *Cours de linguistique générale*. Paris: Payot.

Scott, Joan. (1992). "Experience." *Feminists Theorize the Political*. Eds. Judith Butler and Joan Scott. New York: Routledge. 22–40.

Soich, Matías. (2021). "Becoming Practice: Deleuze and South American Transvestite Theory." *Comparative and Continental Philosophy*. 13.1 (2021): 6–20.

Toro, Alfonso de. (1999). *El debate de la postcolonialidad en Latinoamérica*. Frankfurt-am-Main: Iberoamericana.

Vivancos Pérez, Ricardo F. (2013). *Radical Chicana Poetics*. New York: Palgrave Macmillan.

Zamora, Lois Parkinson. (2006). *The Inordinate Eye. New World Baroque and Latin American Fiction*. Chicago and London: The U of Chicago P.

Zavaleta Mercado, René. (1986). *Lo nacional-popular en Bolivia*. México: Siglo XXI.

Zimmerman, Marc. (2001). "Transnational Crossings and the Development of Latin American Cultural Studies." *Nuevo Texto Crítico*. XIII–XIV. 25/28. (2001): 267–98.

CHAPTER 2

Neobaroque as Transgression: The Latin American Paradigm

This chapter establishes connections between the central ideas that form the book's conceptual axis revolving around the notions of Latin America, the Neobaroque, Textuality and Discourse, Identity, and Nomadism as Boundary-Border transgression. These concepts relate in two-way or multiple interconnections, as illustrated in the diagram in Chap. 1—Introduction. Here, we define and articulate the concepts of *Latin America* as a hybrid space of coexisting and intermingling cultures, the *Neobaroque* style as an exuberant and transgressive technique or artistic mode that facilitates the decentering and transformation of cultural categories in the hybrid space of the Americas, *identity* as an intersectional relationship of cultural and subjective elements interacting across *boundaries*, and *discourse* as the textual-symbolic body of writing/performance representing the mobile identity of the *nomadic* trans-self.

Given that this book does not engage any particular national literature or cultural scene, but rather focuses on a few specific cultural areas ranging from the United States to Chile and Argentina, and considers the mostly Spanish and Portuguese-speaking part of the continent as a cultural whole, it will be relevant to determine the parameters of the concept of *Latin America* as a historical and geographical area and justify why the context of this vast cultural area is uniquely prone to decentering the very concept of identity and to reformulating it in terms of a nomadic transitivity of what we ultimately propose to call a "trans-self." This context encompasses both Americas, spanning from Argentina to the United States, in

© The Author(s), under exclusive license to Springer Nature Switzerland AG 2024
K. A. Kulawik, *Visions of Transmerica*, Literatures of the Americas, https://doi.org/10.1007/978-3-031-42014-6_2

which we observe the presence of the artistic and literary style recognized as the Neobaroque. Any reference to "Latin America" risks excessive generalization given the vastness and vagueness of the concept. Categories of identity such as race, ethnicity, nationality, social group, and even gender result in different meanings to a person in Mexico and Argentina, or in the United States and Brazil. But perhaps by philosophically and theoretically considering identity through the prism of border and boundary transgression, migration, transit, and nomadism, it will be possible to achieve a broader and more symbolic meaning of Latin America as a hybrid space of a cultural transition that works characterized as neobaroque exemplify in their expressions of a decentered selfhood. Focusing on the meaning of identity shifts our attention to Americanist terminology centered around the concepts of cultural hybridity and syncretism, mobility and transitivity, without obliging us to formulate any specific meaning of a Latin American identity *per se*.

Given its ubiquity, the Neobaroque, understood as an artistic style or technique, calls for adopting the notion of Latin America or even "the Americas" as a point of reference, even as problematic as this appears to be. Considering the cultural content, linguistic forms, and geographical origin of the works that we engage in our analysis, we shall refer to Latin America as the cultural regions of the vast area stretching from the border states of the US Southwest to Argentina and Chile where Spanish and Portuguese are used. In terms of cultural identity, it represents a space of plurality, a heterogeneous and hybrid area of intermingling cultures in continuous migration, contact, and transformation. In this context, the Neobaroque, as a style of conceptual and formal exuberance that decenters and questions any essentialist categories of culture, identity, and selfhood, positions itself as a subversive discourse and an attitude of cultural resistance. Before examining in Chap. 3 the specific literary and artistic works that provide examples of these cultural transformations of decentering visible in borderland nomadic identities, we will dedicate this chapter to explaining how the uniqueness of the (general) Latin American cultural context, and the occurrence of Neobaroque aesthetics as a driving discursive force of transformation, make possible the questioning of the established concept of Identity and its rearticulation in the alternative notion of a transitive selfhood. Thus, in first place, we will proceed to characterize the cultural context of Latin America as the hybrid, fragmented, transient, and transcultural space of identity deterritorialization.

2.1 Latin America: Hybrid Contexts of Deterritorialization

"History is tedious in its symmetries; the expulsion of the Moors from Granada coincides with what is, in its way, another expulsion: the discovery of America—three galleys stocked with undesirables. When they get here, from the sandy fringe of the new exile, and not by chance, Columbus calls to mind Andalusia" (Sarduy 1984b: 105). Selfhood is only defined fully when perceived from the perspective of the Other—side or self. Only after crossing the border of the sandy fringe did Columbus' transient identity acquire its full transformative meaning of nomadic transgression. It was then that he recalled Europe. America is often seen as the land of migrations and expulsions, of the exiled and outcast, and as a projection or extension of One's identity onto the Other and vice versa.

2.1.1 From Sameness to Otherness

In its way, Latin America may be perceived as a hybrid, cross-cultural space of contacts, shifts, and transformations of selfhood, often a self that is marginalized—the migrant and the exiled. This is accounted for in its history of migrations and crossings, encounters and clashes of cultures and races, of political, economic, and cultural conquests, and revolutionary upheavals. By many accounts, it is perceived as a promised land, a place of encounter for the striving and the banished, a cultural crossing of every world of race and culture. A tumultuous historical process of migrations and invasions has produced an instability that has led to a critical search for self-determination in terms of political sovereignty and economic autonomy, as well as a search for self-definition in terms of cultural identity, of conceiving the meaning of being (Latin) American. On this side of the world, this has usually occurred in contact with an "other," in opposition to and facing external dominating powers, whether they be of Europe (the colonial metropolises Spain, Portugal, France, Great Britain, and others) or the United States. Historically, this produced a certain complex of inferiority while defining a regional, national, or supranational sense of selfhood and identity, in the emancipatory sense of the word, and in regard to outside powers. As far back as the colonial times, but especially since the Independence movement in the early 1800s, establishing this selfhood has been one of the defining themes of Latin American critical thought and a major part of its literary and artistic expression (Rama 2012 [1982]: 3–5).

At the same time, it has led to the appearance of a cultural tension emerging from the dualisms of tradition versus modernization, regionalism versus universalism, and other phenomena of cultural instability, mobility, and nomadism associated with internal and external migrations. The resulting sense of movement and cultural transitivity (as flexibility and changeability) has produced an attitude of cultural conflict and resistance to the imposed external, imperial, colonial, and today's postcolonial order. As Elizabeth Ginway opportunely explains in *Cyborgs, Sexuality and the Undead* (2020), Bolívar Echeverría was the first to apply the concept of the "baroque ethos" in the sense of a cultural attitude and an agency of resistance that enables survival and prospering of a people in a context of historic injustices and economic difficulties imposed by colonialism and capitalism (10). Henceforth, we surmise that the Neobaroque artistic style stands as one of the more visible expressions of this ethos and of the complexity of America's self-definition.

In cultural terms, Latin America constitutes a "liminal" zone of borderline encounters and contacts, a space for questioning and reconceptualizing the traditional categories of cultural identity that have traditionally been founded on the unifying concepts of *mestizaje* (mixing or miscegenation), hybridity, integration, and fusion. Its "borderland" diversity of a peripheric liminal space lends itself to re-examining the formative and, at the same time, decategorizing notions of what is by some critics called "Latin American identity." One idea that stands out among the many that attempt to define Latin America is the notion of the "border," as it refers to the ambiguous space of contact and transgression.

At the beginning of the twenty-first century, Latin America appears as an ungraspable figure or, better yet, an abstract idea on the cultural world map, representative of an unusual multiformity within a shared spatial unit of the Western Hemisphere. This map is crossed by conventional discursive and conceptual dividing lines; they are lines that form geographical, political, cultural, and other divisions or borders, spaces of dialogs and crossings. This diversity is especially visible in the cultural dimension: "It cannot be claimed that there is any sense of hemispheric unity, although there is plenty of evidence of intercontinental solidarity, especially when the security of all the peoples of the New World is endangered" (Urbanski 99). In the context of this immanent heterogeneity, its constitutive (foundational) cultural traits are readily distinguishable: Indigenous (the pre-Columbian as the root of all Americanness), European, African, and, to a certain degree, Asian, which include both the Far-Eastern (Chinese,

Japanese, Korean, etc.) and Middle Eastern (Arabic, Jewish, Indian, Turkish, and Lebanese, among others). These racial and ethnic distinctions are combined with considerable social heterogeneity: a refined and wealthy oligarchy alongside a 55% of the population classified as impoverished for not being able to meet their basic needs.[1] With this added to economic disparity: the abundant natural resources in countries where more than half of the productive population is working in the informal sector; and demographic heterogeneity: the sharp contrast between the lifestyles of the inhabitants of the countryside, the province, and the economically polarized urban centers, we simply cannot speak of Latin America in terms of any viable unit. But perhaps if we take a different route, that of common languages and accompanying cultural values, we may be able to reach a common denominator.

Before we speak about the concepts of identity and Latin America, we should ask if our interpellated image of who we are referring to is considering the majoritarian presence of the feminine population combined with gender-sexual, racial, and ethnic minorities, alongside the lower social strata, the informal sector, and the migrants. And whether we are envisioning the Indigenous Latin American, the European-descended White, the Creole, the Black, the *Mestizo* and Mulatto, or the ethnically mixed person who lives in one of the urban centers or in the periphery. Or the Latin American who lives in the southern pampas of Argentina, in the Amazon rainforest, in the Caribbean basin, or in Mexico's northern deserts? Or are we talking about the Hispanics or Latinos who inhabit or arrive every day by land, air, and sea to the English-speaking neighbors of the North? On top of this, it is difficult to speak of Latin American identity without, at the same time, committing oneself to a distinction between what or who constitutes a Mexican, Argentine, Brazilian, Colombian, or any citizen within any of these nations limited by borders marked in the last two hundred years by a White elite who came to power after the Wars of Independence or during the many civil and territorial conflicts. We must ask ourselves about whose identity it is, in whose America, and *for* whom? Instead of deliberating whether there is a single or unitary Latin American identity or not, we propose first to decenter the very idea of Identity. This can be undertaken by means of gender-bending techniques

---

[1] Based on statistics in Pablo González Casanova, "The Crisis in Latin America as a Global Phenomenon" and E. V. K. FitzGerald, "Latin America in the World Economy" in *The Crisis of Development in Latin America*. Amsterdam: CEDLA Publication, 1991. 1–7, 8–22.

of cross-dressing and androgyny, as well as of homo/heterosexual (queer) mobility and indefiniteness, given the frequency of characters and voices displaying these themes in Latin American works that are identifiable as neobaroque. Their presence and transgressive characteristics, their shifting, mobile, and transiting identities that escape definability, will help us envision Latin America as a transitive plurality, or multiplicity of simultaneous, coexistent identities. This interplay of contacts, crossings, and transgressions between the multiple borders that scar the idealized and essentialized surface of Latin American culture will allow us to envision the possibility of identity as a "trans-it," a "trans-self" defined only by transitivity.

Latin America is historically defined by a lack of unity: the invasions, migrations, and displacements of different cultures, superimposed in various layers, are indicative of multiple shifts and point to the existence of cleavages, fissures, and, better yet, "contact zones" between them. One could speak of an encounter and, at the same time, a confrontation between at least three different cultural worlds, which eventually gave way to the formation of a new, mixed, and, to a certain degree, hybrid culture. Latin American cultural criticism has frequently operated with terms such as "*mestizaje*" (José Vasconcelos, Leopoldo Zea, Edouard Glissant), "transculturation" (Fernando Ortiz, Angel Rama, Mariano Picón Salas), "heterogeneity" (Cornejo Polar), "hybridity" (Néstor García Canclini, Pedro Henríquez Ureña), and "diversity" or "multiculturalism" (as the "official" discourse of the neoliberal *status quo*). All these terms attempt to express, to a greater or lesser degree, an all-encompassing characteristic of Latin American identity by means of a synthesizing and standardizing term. Certainly, all of them have contributed to fairly well explaining just *one* version of Latin American history, and to find only *one* truth in the definition of what "Latin Americanness" stands for. However, reaching any totality is not attainable to the extent that any identity, in itself as a concept, is not uniform at the base of its own constitution. As we will attempt to demonstrate, identity (as selfhood) is a set of partial elements that come into dynamic contact, interplay, and dialogue in a concert of simultaneous and heterogeneous discourses acting according to particular power interests and momentary schemes of relations. The identity of each subject, group, or nation is a temporal-instantaneous dialogue of liminalities and contacts of subjects in positions of power, an interaction of interests, competencies, and competitions; it is a crossing of oppositions, interfaces, and interferences of margins in a *simultaneous* implosion toward a defining center and a fugue toward the periphery; it is also an arrangement of mobile connections on a horizontal, rhizomatic plane of unhierarchical interconnectedness and contact (Deleuze and Parnet 1987a, 1977).

Since Hegel's "antiprophecy," or the denial of his own prophecy about "America" being the land of the future, a nostalgia of those who are tired/weary of the "historical museum of the Old Europe," and a land only echoing the Old World ways of life on the bosom of Nature, this by far Eurocentric vision of the New World as Change has indeed come to fruition: America has transited from Nature to History and Culture.[2] Hegel spoke of the future historical importance of America, possibly set in a forthcoming struggle between the North and South of America. What has resulted from this historical process is a confrontation of the North, occupied by perhaps the greatest power in the world, the United States, and a South conformed by a puzzle of fragmented nations of a vast subcontinent south of the Rio Grande: "The one of the South, with its extensive name of Latin America, it represents one of the most controversial ideas of the modern world [...]" resulting from a series of explosions that have caught the attention of the world: demographic, political, and cultural (Fernández Moreno 1982: 121–22; my translation). Still, why "Latin" and not just America? Fernández provides the linguistic explanation of colonization by three European powers that operated in the three major "Latin" languages: Spanish, Portuguese, and French. Likewise, Arturo Fox (2011: 128–29) and Edmund S. Urbanski (1978: 83) provide a similar explanation of Americanist terminology by stating the same linguistic justification, with the additional reference of Ibero America to refer to all the areas on the Western Hemisphere dominated by Europeans using Iberian languages of the Romanic (or Latin) family: Spanish and Portuguese. This could be the most general explanation of the full term that we use throughout this book. If only it accounted for the far more complex reality of an aboriginal population and its culture, there wouldn't be a need to use other terms like Indo-, Ando-, and Meso-America. In reference to the forced importation of African slaves, whose presence calls for the term Afro-America, and in addition to the presence of a variety of immigrants from Asia, forming what could be called Asian (including Sino, Nipo, and Arab) America, only then could we attain a fuller meaning of Latin

---

[2] In César Fernández Moreno, "¿Qué es América Latina?" (1982, "What Is Latin America?") in which he quotes from Hegel's *Philosophy of Universal History*, trans. José Gaos, Madrid: Ed. Revista de Occidente, 1928, p. 121.

America. The Indigenous, African, and Asian elements are the ones that give the Americas a commonality in heterogeneity that transcends linguistic, cultural, and geographical differences, as well as traditional Eurocentrism. A special case of an area problematizing all clear-cut categories is the Caribbean. Whereas a part of the "Americas," it stands as a linking cultural and geographical referent, deriving its multiplicity from its more varied colonization pattern. This intermediate region is culturally crisscrossed by not only Romanic languages, but also English and Dutch, and geographically stands in between North and South America as a kind of an island bridge, or a transitional zone of all categories. It is a particularly hybrid and syncretic area of cultural transits and the origin of many works perceived as Neobaroque, both historically and geographically.

This multiplicity in the usage of Americanist terms heightens our intention of decentering the very idea of Identity by presenting the highly complex, mobile, and transitive terms of "Latin America" and "Transmerica" that find their base in the hemispheric notion of America. The need to find a common denominator situating the cultural area that encompasses all the places of origin of the literary and artistic works in this study summons us to use "Latin America" and "Neobaroque" as common points of reference to the multiple, differing, and distant areas of the Western Hemisphere, spanning from the United States of North America to South America's Brazil, Argentina, and Chile. Their usefulness stems from their transnational dimension. The works examined in this study originate from the several nation-states but are not necessarily representative of any national literatures or cultures. They find their common denominator in the aesthetics of the Neobaroque as a transnational, inter-American technique and style. Notwithstanding Stephen Urbanski's arguments for the existence of multiple, in fact, numerous "Americas" (82), should we still look for a common denominator for all of them? We are within the hemispheric limits of the Americas, and the literature that we are dealing with is in Spanish and Portuguese, fragmentarily in English or "Spanglish"—so let our references be all- or trans-American.

A hardly definable space due to its breadth, Latin America does indeed display commonalities that should allow us to justify using the term, even if only broadly, for the purpose of discerning a common ground for the literary and artistic texts targeted in this study. One common element of special interest for us is the presence of the Neobaroque style. Its presence is due to the mobile and transitional nature of the American historical process in which nomadism stands out as a cultural commonality: a shared

2 NEOBAROQUE AS TRANSGRESSION: THE LATIN AMERICAN PARADIGM   41

past marked by being populated by migrants, from the prehistoric wanderer inhabitants arriving from Asia and Oceania to the European conquest and colonization, through the import of African slaves, and ensuing waves of European and Asian immigrants that were or have been, to this day, either economically or politically driven. This continental "(im)migrant condition" combines with a series of related factors: Latin America's common past of imperial colonialization with ensuing effects of postcolonialism, "Third World" economic dependence leading to both political and economic underdevelopment, and, in contrast with Anglo-America, the resulting social disparities of its class-divided society. At the same time, in cultural terms, (Latin) American history holds the potential of marveling and amazing with its "components of the new Western world in expansion" (Fernández Moreno 129). Thus, "Latin America" has constituted a focus of attraction and a truly global converging point of coexistence and eventual mixing for immigrants of all ethnic groups and races. In his article "¿Qué es América Latina?" ("What Is Latin America?"), Fernández Moreno follows Paul Rivet in his reasoning that:

> The New World [...] has been, from prehistoric times, a center of convergence of races and peoples. ... It is indeed curious that the historical period of American evolution is nothing but a repetition of the ethnic occurrences that conditioned its settling. Since it was discovered, America has continued to be a focus of attraction for people of the most diverse races, the same as it was during its long pre-Columbian settling. In this manner, the possible Asian and Oceanic ancestry of all American inhabitants, and the possible and immemorial geographical integration of America with Africa, are facts that give a substantial meaning to America's universality. (139; my translation)

The common element to be brought up in any cultural or historical analysis of Latin America is its historical condition of *coloniality* and dependence on foreign models. These mark its very foundations since the European conquest began in 1492 and continued through the sixteenth, seventeenth, and eighteenth centuries. Its structures permeate the republican era of post-Independence, and they linger in present-day social and economic structures, as Luis Fernando Restrepo notes:

> Despite its geographical, cultural, and social diversity, one significant unifying factor of the region we know today as Latin America has been a shared history of European colonialism. Roughly three centuries of mainly Iberian (Spanish and Portuguese) colonization have reshaped and left a marked

imprint on the cultures of the region and defined, to a great extent, its relation to the rest of the world, violently and unevenly incorporating it [Latin America] into the European modern world system. (2003: 47)

This common past of colonial dependence and European "mother country" dominance created a social, economic, and political structure that characterizes the life and culture of all the countries: namely, their status of subalternity, which in turn has incentivized the intellectual elites and artists to be constantly dedicated to the process of defining its identity at the marco-regional level (as Latin America) and the micro-regional level of nationhood.

The polarization between the urban centers and the province or regional periphery is another structuring feature of colonial hierarchy which, in turn, shaped the centralizing character of Latin American culture: "Colonial society was, in a sense, a city ruled by the men of letters, as Uruguayan critic Angel Rama suggested in his seminal work *La ciudad letrada* (1984)" (Restrepo 63). Colonial dominance brought the Latin (or Romanic) languages, religion, and a judicial and administrative system that the future countries shared, nonetheless a new post-Independence discourse of individual identities flowed out of the local conditions of each region trying to define its particularity and distinctness from the others, and this happened on two levels: internally in contrast to their neighbors, and externally in defiance of Europe and, later, the United States. The commonality of certain "American" (vs. European) traits is also signaled in sociologist Gino Germani's two polar characterizations that accord the common existence of a "Latin" America: first, the "Latin," or Greco-Roman, Christian, Hispanic, or Iberian character of the colonized subcontinent, and second, its political antagonistic and emancipatory stance in relation to an exterior power, in this case, Europe and the United States (Germani in Fernández M. 126–27). A conglomerate of nation-states that secured independence from Spain, Portugal, and France, Latin America is still in a defying position facing the imperial aspirations of the United States that are symbolically expressed in the usage of "America" as exclusively the United States of America. What became unchanged, in a large part to this day, is the underlying structure of historic determinants caused by the conquest and colonialization, as stated by René de la Pedraja:

The conquest and colonization of the Americas in the sixteenth and seventeenth centuries created the conditions for the exploitation of the vast

2 NEOBAROQUE AS TRANSGRESSION: THE LATIN AMERICAN PARADIGM   43

territories. [...] Beginning in the late fifteenth century, European imperialist expansion resulted in the defeat and subjugation of the native peoples of Latin America, the first non-European continental area to be westernized. It was not until the early nineteenth century that challenges to European domination unleashed the revolutionary forces that ended in independence. Therefore, understanding of the enduring legacies of a colonial system that lasted three centuries is fundamental to the illumination of developments and issues in contemporary Latin America. (1997: 27)

At the same time, the contact resulting from the conquest and colonization occasioned major cultural changes in the form of interracial mixing and mutual exchange, leading to transformations that later became known as "transculturation." As Restrepo further notes: "no women were included, adding other dimensions to the invasion: rape, sexual slavery, and also interracial marriages. Even though later voyages did include European women, race mixture or mestizaje occurred frequently and became from early on a defining element of the new colonial society" (49). This new colonial society in the Caribbean, with its interactions between Spaniards and the Natives, shaped the basic patterns of ensuing settlement of the continental areas. Restrepo goes on to state: "As a result, the colonial context brought together native and European cultural practices, yielding a broad range of results including syncretism, hybridism, and juxtaposition" (59), additionally noting that:

Far from the metropolis, colonial societies soon developed a regional sense of a shared history, a vernacular language, and local customs [...] [with] the consciousness developed by the white elite (criollos), expressing a proto-national identity, key in the nineteenth-century independence movements and national projects, although very problematic in terms of its selective process of appropriation and suppression of metropolitan, indigenous, and African cultural elements. (Restrepo 61)

Considering these underlying historical and cultural factors, the urge to define itself as a unity of a "Latin" America, as opposed to the US-dominated Anglo America, has always been a centripetal force for the Spanish and Portuguese "Americanized" *criollo* (White European) and, to a certain extent, *Mestizo* segments of the population of the hemispheric "south," as stated by Jorge Larrain:

44   K. A. KULAWIK

In Latin America there has always existed a consciousness of Latin American identity, articulated alongside national identities. Much of this stems without doubt from a shared history during the three centuries of Spanish domination, the independence wars in which the criollos of several countries (descended from the Spanish conquerors) fought together, the language, religion, and many other common social, economic and cultural factors. There are signs that consciousness about these common elements has been growing in Latin America in recent times. The existence of this Latin American consciousness is shown by four kinds of facts. (2000: 1)

Larrain mentions the general assumption by cultural critics that there is a Latin American identity by directly describing its four defining characteristics or by analyzing the identity of their own particular countries and then extending their affirmations to the rest of Latin America. This sense of macroregional identity has also been ascribed from the outside, specifically Europe and the United States. Larrain states: "From the sixteenth century onwards South America has been spoken of and discursively constructed in Europe as a more or less integrated whole, most of the time endowed with pejorative characteristics" (3).

The other side of the argument (that essentially there is no *one* Latin America) must be brought forth as a natural consequence of contemporary revisions of Modern cultural thought founded on a poststructuralist approach to Discourse and Identity. For instance, in the same text by Larrain we read:

I have come across only one Latin American author, Mario Sambarino, who puts forward the idea that there is no common cultural ethos between Latin American nations. For him there is no such thing as a Latin American being. The question of a 'Latin American being'—or a 'national being' for that matter—is a false problem because these are historically and culturally generated modes of living, which do not have and cannot have an ontological reality, a kind of immobile legality. Clearly Sambarino's anti-essentialist conception of identity, which is to be praised because it is so rare in Latin America, leads him mistakenly to deny the *possibility* of a Latin American, or even a national 'imagined community.' It may be inadequate to look for a Latin American or national essence, but if there is a national, or a Latin American, historically variable and relatively common way of living, then one can speak of a national identity or a Latin American identity as a *historically changing "cultural identity."* (3; emphasis added)

Although Larrain's vision does not accept a Latin American essence, he does admit the "possibility" of a national, even supranational identity that is "historically changing" in its own or more general particularities. The co-presence of these idiosyncrasies leads us to define this possibility in terms of heterogeneity, syncretism, and hybridity as the constitutive elements of the cultural process present in all areas of the Latin American subcontinent, and even to some extent the United States, as the common markers of a cultural process that is characteristically "American," but even more particularly "Latin American" without claiming to define any single (Latin) American identity.

2.1.2 Heterogeneity, Transculturation, Mestizaje, Hybridity, and Simultaneity

Heterogeneity is perhaps the most widely accepted and suitable term to characterize the complexity yet, at the same time, commonality of Latin American culture. It becomes a gateway term to other methods of approaching cultural diversity from the perspectives of transculturation, hybridity, and syncretism. "Heterogeneous culture" was coined and subsequently developed by Peruvian critic Antonio Cornejo Polar in his seminal work *Writing in the Air: Heterogeneity and the Persistence of Oral Tradition in Andean Literatures* (2013, orig. Sp.: *Escribir en el aire*, 1994). The concept is sketched out around a series of characteristics that describe the literatures of the Andean region, but with a disclaimer of its applicability to any multicultural context of other parts of Latin America. Those traits include "change," "differentiation in peculiarity of our being," "heteroclite plurality of differences that separate and counterpose the various socio-cultural universes," and the "diverse and multiply conflictive cultural configuration" of both the national (Peruvian) and international (Latin American) cultural context (1–3). Cornejo's examples are based on the specifically Andean-Peruvian colonial and postcolonial literary context, with specific reference to the heterogeneous element entering the prose of José María Arguedas, particularly the novel *Los ríos profundos* (*Deep Rivers*, 1958). Cornejo presents the optic of heterogeneity to explain "the destabilizing variety and hybridity of Latin American literature" (4), focusing on "a literature that is especially elusive because of its multi- and transcultural makeup" (3). Cornejo bases his view of heterogeneity on the contradictory, multiple, and relational aspect of the subject (as individual and social entity) that is present in Peruvian literature, and that he defines as "complex, scattered and multiple" (7), emerging from a "colonial condition" that entails "denying the conquered their identity as subjects, breaking the bonds that used to confer that identity, and imposing others that disrupt and disjoin—with intense severity" (7). He refers to this denial and intervening rupture in the sense that it "does not invalidate the powerful emergence of new, future subjects and a respect for the profoundly reshaped remains of former ones" (7), but this time, the new subjects are not uniform in their fragmented multiplicity. Cornejo's vision of heterogeneity that defines Latin America, especially when referring to the Andean region, contains his skepticism about the positive effect of any unifying force, such as *mestizaje* given its suspiciously political agenda: "I want to free myself from the shackles that impose the false imperative of defining once and forevermore what we are: a coherent and uniform identity, complacent and ingenuous (the ideology of mestizaje would be a good example)" (8). Instead, he proposes the acceptance of the differences in an oppositional, counteractive complementarity, as a driving force of not only Peruvian, but all Latin American culture.

If we allow ourselves to make any generalizations as to the possible existence of a single Latin American cultural area, it would be more viable with reference to the concept of transculturation. It best captures the dynamic and moving force of Latin American culture as a whole. It was introduced by Cuban ethnologist and anthropologist Fernando Ortiz in his most celebrated work, *The Cuban Counterpoint of Sugar and Tabaco* (1940), in which he demonstrated how Cuban (and by extension, Caribbean, and a large part of Latin American[3]) culture is structured on the binary opposition and juxtaposition of two distinct and opposing elements, but that are in contact and mutually transform by adopting certain features from each other. Ortiz defines "the word" (language) as the cultural carrier that expresses "the different phases of the process of transition from one culture to another because it does not consist merely in acquiring another culture, […] but the process also necessarily involves the loss or uprooting of a previous culture […]" (Rama 2012: 18–19). It is basically a process of reciprocal influence and cultural adaptation caused by contact, exchange, and mutual influence. Transculturation was later taken on by the Uruguayan cultural critic Angel Rama as the basis of his analysis of the fragmented cultures of the Andean region, as displayed again in the

---

[3] "[…] fundamental and indispensable for an understanding of the history of Cuba, and, for analogous reasons, of that of America in general" (Ortiz in Rama 18).

prose of José María Arguedas and extended to the entire area of the Latin American cultural sphere as its underlying structural principle. Rama (2012) identifies three phases in the process of transculturation presented by Ortiz: deculturation, acculturation, and neoculturation, which correspond roughly to the ideas of loss, gain, and creation of something new. Rama illustrates this in his detailed explanation of Latin American binaries, which he calls "American bipolarity" (e.g., city vs. province, regionalism vs. internationalism/universalism, tradition vs. modernization, national vs. foreign) (47), and in a detailed analysis of Arguedas' *Los ríos profundos* states that "the current culture of the Latin American community (which itself is a product of long-term transculturation in constant evolution) is composed of idiosyncratic values [...] creative energy that propels it forward [...] this capacity for creative originality, even under trying historical circumstances, that shows that it is the culture of a lively, creative society" (19). Ultimately, for Rama, it is also the hybrid (both autochthonous and foreign) and combinatory nature of this culture that has made possible that "the inventions of the transculturators were broadly facilitated by the existence of the continent's own particular cultural forms, which had come about through a long process of adopting foreign messages and 'creolizing' them" (34). The ultimate effect of this transcultural process is the creation of a unique and distinct culture, characterized by its lack of uniformity, plasticity, and heterogeneity, "with the least possible loss of identity to the new conditions determined by the international setting of the time" (49). This becomes especially visible in the constant influx of foreign influences that flow into the American substrate and transform it in an ongoing process of cultural transitioning.

It is only fair to complete this vision of transculturation with the concepts brought forth by Antonio Benítez Rojo (1996, [1992]) in reference to the transformative forces operating in the Caribbean region, namely the "repeating island," "organized chaos," and "polyrhythms." Again, in a bipolar setting of contrasting oppositions, Caribbean (and by extension, most of Latin American) discourse is structured on "voices that originate in differing centers of emission" and distinct moments and discourses that coexist in a dialogical form, like polyphonic music or Carnivalesque plurality of voices and that, like Mikhail Bakhtin's *The Dialogic Imagination* and Ortiz's *Counterpoint...*, its polyphony "furnishes an infinite space for coexistence" (Benítez 1996: 175). Benítez makes it clear that the counterpoint, which Ortiz models on the contrast of sugar and tobacco, is never a synthesis but a playful *co-presence* of differences in a polyphonic relation

48   K. A. KULAWIK

of polyrhythms that interact (174). Benítez states that "they relate also in the complementary and diachronic sense of mutual interdependence that recalls the complexity of power relations" (173). The "repeating island" analogy is drawn to illustrate the regular patterns governed by certain "cultural rhythms" that are visible both vertically, as governing patterns at different systematic levels, and horizontally across different spaces of the Caribbean archipelago, and across the Latin American continent. However, the binary oppositions "do not resolve themselves into the synthesis of mestizaje, but rather they resolve into insoluble differential equations, which repeat unknowns through the ages of the meta-archipelago" (26). Speaking of the multifaceted and multilingual literature of the Caribbean, Benítez states that it "can be read as a mestizo text, but also as a stream of texts in flight, in intense differentiations among themselves and within whose complex coexistence there are vague regularities, usually paradoxical. [...] Thus, Caribbean literature cannot free itself totally of the multiethnic society upon which it floats, and it tells us of its fragmentation and instability" (27). Precisely, this hybrid context of the Caribbean constitutes the birthplace of the American Neobaroque.

For the classic Venezuelan essayist Mariano Picón Salas, it was specifically the hybrid influence of the entire New World conglomerate with its "the collision of races and the violence of transplantation" that resulted in a unique Baroque art of transformation and "opposites flourishing in counterpoint" within colonial Latin America (1962: 86). Similarly, Ecuadorian-Mexican critic Bolívar Echeverría considers the very notion of *mestizaje* as an endurance strategy of the oppressed and a *sui generis* mode of resistance in the form of a "baroque ethos":

> The mestizaje of cultural forms appeared in 17th century America first as a 'survival strategy,' of life after death, in the behavior of the subjugated 'naturals,' that is, of the indigenous and Africans integrated into urban existence, which from the beginning was the predominant mode of existence. Their resistance, the persistence in their peculiar mode of symbolization of the real, in order to be effective, was forced to transcend the initial level in which the defeat had taken place and to play in the background [...]. (1994: 34; my translation)

The process of this cultural mixing occurs on the symbolic level with the underprivileged (including the economically or politically oppressed and minorities) silently resisting by means of absorption and digestion of cultural codes, a seditious assimilation of traits incorporated in baroque/

2 NEOBAROQUE AS TRANSGRESSION: THE LATIN AMERICAN PARADIGM   49

neobaroque stylistic techniques, especially that of satire, caricature, and parody (parodic appropriation). Echeverría adds that

> [i]n seventeenth-century American Spain, the dominated are the first inciters and executors of the process of codephagy through which the code of the dominators transforms itself in the assimilation of the ruins in which the destroyed code survives. It is their life that needs to have the capacity to deny in order to be fulfilled as human life [...] it nevertheless allows them to say 'no,' to affirm themselves in spite of everything, almost imperceptibly, in the line of what was their identity. (36)

This appropriation of the symbolic code is what Brazilian writers (de Andrade 1942; Santiago 2001) and critics (Madureira 2005), called "cultural anthropophagy," or a cannibalistic consumption of styles and symbolic codes of the dominant group into a hybrid combination of a new (subaltern) cultural self.

We should emphasize the link of *mestizaje* with the notion of hybrid constructs of American selfhood. Miscegenation constitutes one of the defining elements that describe the emerging New World culture. It introduces us, and most notably as early as in the decade of the 1950s, to a new view of hybridity that has dominated cultural criticism even more notably since the decade of the 1990s. Writing from the perspective of Mexico and referring to its specific socio-political and cultural context, the Argentinian-born anthropologist and cultural critic Néstor García Canclini suggests in *Hybrid Cultures: Strategies for Entering and Leaving Modernity* (1995) that Latin America, more than a peripheral and colonized scene of foreign modernization as the "dominant force replacing the traditional and what is one's own" (2–3), is a *sui generis* space of socio-cultural crossings where the traditional and the modern mix without cease or any normative prediction. Especially through mass communication, the coexistent forms of "high" art *in coexistence* with "popular" and folkloric art are massively and simultaneously diffused. This diffusion results in mixtures and fusions, in a "multicultural and multitemporal heterogeneity," (3) that appear within each country in the concurrent parameters of time and space as the new mixed with the old, the local with the foreign. García Canclini calls these fusions "hybrid circuits" that are defined by the co-presence of ethnic folk cultures with new technologies, and artisanal forms of production with their industrial counterparts (3). This process of transformation by cross-semination implies viewing intercultural mixtures from a historical perspective: the intersection of different historical temporalities in a simultaneous coexistence of the past in the present (70). As a result of this synchronic yet symbolically multitemporal hybridization, all Latin American countries demonstrate, to one degree or another, the coexistence of tradition with modernization, and the resulting conflict of these two opposing forces of sedentarism and change. García Canclini further states that:

> Latin American countries are currently the result of the sedimentation, juxtaposition, and interweaving of indigenous traditions (above all in the Mesoamerican and Andean areas), of Catholic colonial hispanism, and of modern political, educational, and communicational actions. Despite attempts to give elite culture a modern profile, isolating the indigenous and the colonial in the popular sectors, an interclass mixing has generated hybrid formations in all social strata. (46)

García Canclini makes an especially relevant point in foregrounding the inter-social, class-variable aspect of American cultural hybridization.

Traits of juxtapositions and intercultural crossings of pre-Columbian-Indigenous, Catholic-Hispanic, and modernizing North American-European-Asian elements are visible in "[t]his multitemporal heterogeneity of modern culture [...] consequence of a history in which modernization rarely operated through the substitution of the traditional and the ancient" (García Canclini 46–47). These "hybrid formations in all social strata" have produced an "interclass *mestizaje*" (or miscegenation), where it is possible to observe the coexistence of popular rural traditions of an Indigenous or Catholic nature with the simultaneous incursion of new technological mass culture (telecommunications and technology). García Canclini points to this phenomenon of intercultural and interclass transitivity between tradition and modernization to explain the simultaneous presence of multiethnic handicraft products together with cable, satellite, and digital television, or the continuity of colonial styles in interior decoration with the efficiency of the practical, fast, instantaneous, disposable, and ready-made; or even "the presence of financial magazines of monetary investments next to family rituals and religious anniversaries" (46). With these examples, García explains the process of cultural identity formation as an interrelation of discursive-symbolic elements that possess multiple forms, genres, and roots, and which are in constant transformation in the moment and space of contact, in a "transnationalization of symbolic markets and migrations" (229). It should be noted that García gives special meaning to the migratory (mobile) nature of these processes and to the aesthetic value of changes generated by "strategies of impure arts" (229).

This directs our attention to the unique symbolization achieved in the oncoming of twentieth-century Neobaroque in the context of a space that the critic defines as "cultural deterritorialization" taking place in a movement of "entering and leaving modernity" (228).

It remains to be pointed out that García Canclini's view of the unstable interrelation of tradition and modernity in the strategies of "entering and leaving" does not necessarily imply fusions into new elements, but rather relates to a fragmentary, momentary, and mobile occurrence in the so-called hybrid spaces of the limits, in which multiple and interchangeable forms coexist in the fissures created by crossings and hybridizations, without necessarily merging but rather establishing separate, interconnected spaces of constant slippage between patterns of the cultured, the popular, and the massive elements. As he states, "[w]e need rituals because we cannot bear excessive hybridization" (1990, 364; my translation).

A final notion to consider concerns Latin America as a space of *simultaneity/-ies*. In disarticulating the idea of a stable identity, we have opted for non-synthesizing, non-defining, and non-essentializing terms. Our understanding of Latin American identity, in both linguistic and philosophical terms, often points to a simultaneity of heterogeneous and marginal discourses in contact. From a historical point of view, Latin America constitutes a zone of contacts of discourses, of coexistence of cultural dialogues in search of a status shaped by a "non-simultaneity of simultaneous elements." Using this antithetical expression, Colombian cultural critic Carlos Rincón in *La no simultaneidad de lo simultaneo: postmodernidad, globalización y culturas en América Latina* (1995, "The Non-Simultaneity of the Simultaneous") explains the interaction of heterogeneous elements in Latin America as a series of constant (and playful) transitions between categories of class, nation, race, and sex. Rincón focuses on the spaces (and specific places) of these intersections-transitions and on the mechanisms that allow possible interactions-transitions between elements as diverse as the Indigenous community and the Westernized Latin American metropolis. According to this critic, the plurality of voices is perceived, above all, in Latin American literary discourse, particularly visible since the narrative renovation begun by Jorge Luis Borges, brought to its apogee during the literary "Boom" of the 1960s. In a way similar to García Canclini, Rincón focuses his analysis on the urban space of the Latin American metropolis as a space of simultaneities of juxtaposed elements, globalized by foreign influences, interactions of the ancient with the modern, the local with the international-global, due to the increased ease of communication, transportation, and world trade. It is a space of simultaneous exchanges between regional cultures and a deterritorialized global culture. The multiplicity of voices—Benítez's polyphony—present in Rincón's urban space—results in a volatile interchangeability of simultaneous, but often incompatible, discourses. In his use of the phrase "non-simultaneity of the simultaneous," Rincón interprets the element of non-simultaneity as the inability of these coexisting (simultaneous) discourses to enter dialogue, their difficult transition, and their conflictive participation in a plethora of adjoining, overlapping, and contradictory voices. Therefore, it is not a dialogue but an untuned chorus of liminalities, of points of contact, and of voices that may be incompatible but, in their simultaneity, still legitimate. According to this interpretation, in Latin America non-simultaneous (as non-compatible) elements coexist simultaneously in a shared space of the encounter of Europe, Africa, and Asia, of the countryside with the city, of tradition and modernity in which the present contains the colonial past and reaches out to the future of mercantilistic globalization, technology, telecommunications, and digital networks.

In conclusion, we reflect along with Norbert Lechner whether it would not be better to leave altogether the idea of a supposed Latin American unity with a tolerable plurality and assume social and cultural heterogeneity using the revised concepts of "collective order" and "social consensus" in the context of Postmodernity's (or unfinished Modernity's) fragmentation (1993: 129, 136). If there is any answer to the questions arising from this discussion, it will certainly not be "one" answer but an exchange of several possibilities in a dialog of simultaneities. Neither will it be a single definition of a supposed Latin American identity nor that of any part of America. It should rather be the appraisal of the unstable transitions between its multiple liminalities, its contact zones between the gray, undefined areas of hybridity and miscegenation, their intersectionality in transitivity between multiple categories that include race, ethnicity, nationality, social status, and gender. It would be more appropriate to define, through these transitions and the mechanisms that govern them, the possibilities for coexistence and dialogue of (and within) these normatively established differences. Rincón's "non-simultaneity of the simultaneous" constitutes, especially in the (Latin) American context, an exemplary cultural phenomenon of crossings of multiple liminalities. Referring to the multipositionality of the subject and following cultural theorists Brah and Gilroy, Rosi Braidotti mentions "hybrid multi-locations" that allow to de-essentialize categories of race, such as blackness, and gender (femininity), and connect the lines of subjectivity to other social variables while re-grounding the politics of identity "on the more effective principle of hybrid multi-locations" (2006: 67).

If there is one common feature among the assessments of Latin American plurality depicted by Cornejo, Ortiz, Rama, Benítez, García Canclini, and Rincón, it is most of all a critical distancing from the traditional term of *mestizaje* (miscegenation or blending) as a unifying concept of indistinguishable fusion and multicultural homogenization. To replace it, they propose heterogeneity, transculturation, polyrhythmic polyphony, hybridity, and simultaneity as a coexistence of differences. However, analogically both Latin America and Identity are abstractions that, through the discursive (arbitrary and conventional) process that forms them, are dispersed in their multiple refractions and contradictions, in voices superimposed in a pseudo-dialogical operation of cultural transitivity taking place in a "contact zone," a liminal space of the borderland. Latin America, more than or just like the idea of Identity, is an "otherness" of the multiple Americas that come into play in the same space of the incompatible (non-simultaneously) simultaneous past, present, future, or ahistorical time; just as any identity-as-oneness is conformed of a multiplicity of other-nesses. With this awareness, we ask whether, in an era of postmodern (non-unifying) globalization, Latin America stands a chance of constituting itself on the global scale as an alternative polyphonous voice that legitimates its unique contribution of syncretism and hybridity, or better yet, transculturation in a new concept of posthuman identity. Perhaps the lavish, eccentric, and experimental works of the Neobaroque and their transgressive characters can provide an answer.

2.2   Neobaroque Literary and Artistic Transgressions

The selection of literary and visual works engaged in this study is justifiable by their association with the Neobaroque. As a cultural representation of Latin American hybridity, syncretism, heterogeneity, instability, and cultural resistance, the Neobaroque is a style and a discourse that decenters and questions categories of identity and selfhood by means of exuberant aesthetics that resort to artifice, parody, and eroticism. Considered a neoavant-gardist (experimental) aesthetic mode surging in the second half of the twentieth century (Bustillo 1990, Burgos 1992), the Neobaroque represents a formal expression of Latin American heterogeneity and hybridity. Above all, it constitutes an aesthetic device that facilitates writers and artists to represent Latin America's historically and economically caused inequalities and disparities, but also the great cultural heterogeneity that resulted from the historical encounter of multiple world populations. As a subversive reaction to America's divisive differentiations, the Neobaroque has established itself as an artistic channel for expressing this fragmentation and subsequent decentering of traditional sexual, racial, ethnic, national, social, and even (post)human identities. It stands as a technique of identity rearticulation in a centerless, fluid "pluridentity" that can be referred to, following Jack Halberstam's concept of "trans*," as an open un-identity (hence the asterisk; 2018, 20). What we ultimately propose to call "trans-identity" or "transentity"—a multi-self or transitive I—embodies multi-gender, -racial, -ethnic, posthuman-cyborg traits assumed simultaneously or performed temporarily, as the characters and the narrative, performative, and visual forms in the analyzed works evidence.

The Neobaroque represents a twentieth-century aesthetic category, a literary and artistic style, mode, or discursive strategy that finds its inspiration in the historical Baroque, which itself was a cultural tendency or period, a philosophical school of thought, as well as an artistic and literary style or aesthetic modality prevalent in seventeenth- to mid-eighteenth-century Europe. From there, the Baroque was exported to Europe's overseas possessions, particularly the Ibero-American colonies by the Spanish and Portuguese, and became the preferred cultural modality of the colonizers. It was an imperial statement of an opulent lifestyle resulting from the establishment of the colonial system of land and mineral exploitation and urban accumulation of wealth, as well as of Catholic religious zeal in its evangelizing mission. However, in the Ibero-American colonies, a unique process of hybridization occurred, whereas artistic works were carried out by Indigenous or mixed-race Mestizos/Mulattoes who imbued their craft with Native American and later African stylistic elements. Thus, a new, hybrid American Baroque style emerged from this fusion, with syncretism becoming its defining feature.

To understand the functioning of contemporary Neobaroque as a transhistorical and transcultural style, it is essential to establish its connections with European Baroque. Adapting aesthetic and historical definitions from Helmut Hatzfeld (1964), Germain Bazin (1968), and Emilio Carilla (1969), we arrive at a four-point characterization of seventeenth- and eighteenth-century Baroque, encompassing its overarching presence in

2 NEOBAROQUE AS TRANSGRESSION: THE LATIN AMERICAN PARADIGM

European culture and its specific appearance in Spanish Golden Age (seventeenth century) literature. Thus, the Baroque can be considered as:

1. a pessimistic philosophical-existential attitude of crisis, which in art privileges themes related to insignificance, helplessness, or illusiveness of human efforts and their "critical reevaluation" (*Uberwertung*), that characterized seventeenth-century European philosophical thought.
2. a general aesthetic affinity for the disproportionate, the spectacular, and the monstrous, characterizing seventeenth-century European visual arts and architecture.
3. an artistic and literary tendency characterized by the profusion of ornamental elements that conform the literary (or any artistic) work.
4. a Spanish literary tendency defined by both formal and conceptual sophistication expressed in poetry (*el culteranismo*) as well as in prose (*el conceptismo*) by means of highly elaborate and figurative forms of verbal expression.

To this list, we could add another catalogue of terms that Cristo Figueroa conveniently provides from his reading of Jean Rousset (1972), defining four basic criteria of a baroque work: instability (of balance), mobility (of representation and meaning that imply displacement), metamorphosis (of multiform combinations), and dominance of decoration (replacing structure with fleeting appearances and illusionism) (2008: 46). As we will observe in Chap. 3, these characteristics prevail in the literary, performance, and visual works that we present as examples of Latin American Neobaroque.

Hence, the Neobaroque appears in the twentieth century as a stylized, yet philosophically critical and politically disruptive, transposition of these elements to the works of Latin American, but also Western (European and US-American) literature and arts, as argued and exemplified by Omar Calabrese (1992), Monika Kaup (2012),[4] and Lois

---

[4] Kaup considers the Baroque as an aesthetic and philosophical form of an "alternative Modernity." In *Neobaroque in the Americas*—her comprehensive study of "interartistic," both "word and image-based varieties" of the Neobaroque in the United States, European, and Latin American literature, and visual arts—she discusses "the transnational and transcultural as well as transhistorical dimensions of the baroque's trajectory" (1, 4). Her analysis of works by T.S. Eliot, Djuna Barnes, Diamela Eltit, María Luisa Bemberg, and US-Latino/a visual art prove her argument about Neobaroque's presence in the Anglo and Hispanic cultural spheres on both sides of the Atlantic (23–27).

56   K. A. KULAWIK

Parkinson Zamora (2006).[5] This contemporary stylization of seventeenth-century baroque elements combined with more recent contents and experimental forms of the historic Avant-garde of the 1920s–1940s, as well as the more recent developments of the Neoavant-garde of the 1960–1990s. Both avant-gardes conferred the Neobaroque elements of bold experimentation and techniques that transgressed traditional styles based on mimetic realism. Pablo Baler extends Neobaroque's scope to include baroque reappropriation in more contemporary literary styles: "By linking the imaginary of twentieth-century artistic production with the production of the historical baroque, I intend to illuminate three instances of reappropriation of the baroque in Latin America: the avant-garde, the New Narrative, and postmodernism" (2018: 2). The connection between Golden Age Baroque's "dynamic of torsion and decentering" and contemporary Latin America's "aesthetics of instability and angst" results for Baler in a Neobaroque "sense of distorsion" which he explains as "a twisting/deviation of the chain connecting a signifying center with its representation" (2–3).

Thus, the exuberant and experimental use of destabilizing discursive procedures noted in the historical Spanish Baroque can be associated, as cited in the preceding footnotes, with what critics (Chiampi 2000, Zamora 2006, Arriarán 2007, Figueroa 2008, Kaup 2012) recognized as the resurgence of Baroque poetics in a period of twentieth-century ontological instability. Neobaroque's critical operation is analogous to Baroque's

---

[5] Accordingly, we read in Zamora: "Since then, the New World Baroque has become a self-conscious postcolonial ideology aimed at disrupting entrenched power structures and perceptual categories. This ideology, termed Neobaroque in the 1970s, has provided Latin American writers the means by which to contest imposed ideologies and recover relevant texts and traditions. Under the sign of the Neobaroque, they have engaged the expressive forms of the historical Baroque to create a discourse of 'counterconquest' (José Lezama Lima's term) that operates widely in contemporary Latin America. With its decentering strategies and ironic perspectives, the Neobaroque has been considered by some critics as a Latin American postmodernism, but the resemblance is misleading. Unlike the poststructuralist categories regularly imposed by, or imported from the United States and Europe, the Neobaroque is deeply rooted in Latin America's histories and cultures" (xvi). Furthermore, Zamora explains: "For Carpentier, the kinetic energy of Baroque space accommodates the interactions of American histories and cultures, as does its dynamic impulse to expand and displace. So he recodifies the function of the Baroque, making it an instrument by which Latin American writers may subvert colonizing institutions and modern constructions of race and rationalism. For Carpentier, the Baroque has flourished in the New World precisely because cultures have collided and converged here" (xvii–xviii).

role in representing the politically and philosophically unstable period of seventeenth-century Europe marked by global-scale economic, political, and social transformations. On the American continent, the Baroque blends with transculturating elements of New World hybridization that combined with a spirit of multiethnic collectivity, dynamic socio-political structures, and polycentric spiritual-cultural perspectives capable of recognizing and including "difference" as a value.[6] In the same vein, Figueroa refers to the "constant resemantizations of the baroque that redefine it not as an essence, but rather as an 'operative function' or 'trait' capable of making more graspable the polymorphous character of Modernity (Deleuze); Baroque leads and flows into Neobaroque [...] incarnating 'a new instability' (Sarduy)" (45; my translation). Likewise, Kaup argues that "the baroque refuses to regard culture as a fixed, 'self-contained system,' the property of discrete, segregated social groups. Rather, the baroque is an 'antipropietary' expression that brings together seemingly disparate writers and artists" (3). She extends the concept to "both a historical period and a transhistorical, transcultural artistic sensibility and style" that, in its chameleon-like aspect, refuses to coalesce into an integrated totality. The Baroque situates itself as a "rebellious postscript to classicism that deforms classical norms, setting them into variation" (18). This character of belatedness suggests exhaustion of classical normativity accompanied by elements of parody, irony, cerebral linguistic tricks, and self-conscious stylization (18). Kaup projects that complex vision of the Baroque to the transhistorical and transcultural genealogy of the Neobaroque that, from its original European nucleus and in a dynamic, complex, and transnational process, has spread in a non-linear and interdisciplinary fashion in modern and postmodern literature, film, visual arts, and theory within the hemispheric framework of the Americas (2–3). Illustrating the transtemporal nature of baroque connections, Irlemar Chiampi assigns the twentieth-century reappropriation of the Baroque by a representative sector of Latin American literary production the quality of inscribing a past cultural modality in a dynamic of present crisis of Western Modernity with

---

[6] For instance, Zamora states that her objective is to relate these transcultural energies with the aesthetics and ideology of a New World Baroque, adding that: "The New World Baroque is hybrid and inclusive, and any accurate definition must include indigenous and African modes of conceiving and expressing the universe. Its transcultural energies move in many directions, of course, and as Spain and Portugal imposed their Counter-Reformation structures on America, America in turn fueled the imaginative energies of Europe [...]" (xv).

58   K. A. KULAWIK

the purpose of "confronting the enigma of its future" (2000: 17).[7] Whereas for Figueroa, it is the hybridly mixed character of Latin America that makes it a favorable ground for the settling of baroque forms in the American Neobaroque: "Indeed, the racial and cultural mixing of our peoples, with its dynamism of oppositions and its paradoxical feelings, favors the reception of the baroque which, in turn, enhances the coincidence of opposites, the variegation or the multiplicity of meanings" (2008: 87; my translation).[8] Finally, Carlos Rincón considers the Neobaroque as a "cultural universe" that does not coincide with the limits of its own system or its forms, such as new genres of visual arts or performance. Its scope is broader than the aesthetic, and does not preclude the social, the economic, and (we would add) the political: "The contemporary expansion of the aesthetic is included rather in the explosion of the field of culture, so that the boundaries of the cultural, the economic, and the social tend to become blurred" (Rincón in Echeverría 1994: 349; my translation). These positions (Kaup, Chiampi, Figueroa, Rincón) indicate the multitemporal, transcultural, and interdisciplinary (rather than solely aesthetic) scope of the Neobaroque phenomenon.

One of Neobaroque's greatest practitioners, the Cuban fictionist, poet, and theorist Severo Sarduy, referred to the (historical) Baroque as an overabundance and overflow of words and signifiers that, in its contemporary neobaroque form, reflects inharmony and breakdown of homogeneity, a

[7] Chiampi lays out the leading characteristics of the Neobaroque as indicative of the connection between the historical Baroque and the crisis of Western Modernity: "The function of the baroque, with its historical and geographical eccentricity, as well as its aesthetics, as opposed to the canon of historicism (the new 'classicism') built in the hegemonic centers of the Western world, allows us to rethink the terms in which Latin America entered the orbit of (Euro-American) modernity. The baroque, crossroads of signs and temporalities, the aesthetic reason of mourning and melancholy, of luxury and pleasure, of erotic convulsion and allegorical pathos, reappears to witness the crisis/end of modernity and the very condition of a continent that could not incorporate the project of the Enlightenment" (17; my translation).

[8] Figueroa expands on the theme of American multiculturalism and miscegenation in both racial-cultural and linguistic terms, and their effect on the propagation of the Neobaroque: "For their part, Lezama Lima and Severo Sarduy include the question of *mestizaje* at the base of their conceptions on the baroque of the subcontinent. The former emphasizes 'the two great syntheses that are at the root of the American Baroque, the Hispano-Inca and the Hispano-Negroid' (Lezama Lima 1969: 80), to explain the works of the Peruvian Indian Kondorí and the art of Aleijadinho. The second values, in a special way, the linguistic miscegenation of Latin American peoples, which enriches Baroque's proliferation 'by incorporating other linguistic materials [...] by making use of the often variegated elements provided by acculturation, from other cultural strata' (Sarduy 1978 [1972]: 170)" (88; my translation).

"structural reflection of a desire that does not reach its object" (Sarduy 1978: 176). It is possible to draw an analogy here with the same desire for linguistic and conceptual experimentation in the name of attaining transcendence that characterizes the works of Hilda Hilst, Diamela Eltit, and Eugenia Prado Bassi, as we will observe in Chap. 3. Their complex narrative presents an extraordinary relationship between the form of an exuberant poetic prose and a philosophical content marked by an eroticism (as surge of desire and affectivity) that abounds in the characters' and narrative voices' equivocal, mutant, and transgressive self-identification in terms of heterosexual, normative, binary categories.

In his seminal essay "El barroco y el neobarroco" (1972), Severo Sarduy defines the historical baroque style, in both its European and Colonial Latin American versions of the seventeenth and eighteenth centuries, in the following terms: "The baroque, superabundance, overflowing cornucopia, extravagance, and waste [...] derision of all sobriety, is also the solution to that verbal saturation [...] to the overflowing of words over things. [...] Language that speaks of language, the baroque superabundance is generated by the synonymic risks of the 'hyper' [...] by the overflow of signifiers [...]" (1978: 176; my translation). Sarduy presents the three fundamental elements that define the neobaroque style: artifice, parody, and eroticism. In combination with the aforementioned critical terms of hybridity and heterogeneity that characterize the Caribbean and Latin American cultural area, these elements constitute the formal backbone of the Neobaroque.

In *The Fold: Leibniz and the Baroque* (1993), Gilles Deleuze focuses on the Baroque experience as analogous to the shape of a fold: "Leibniz is the first great philosopher and mathematician of the pleat, of curves and twisting surfaces. He rethinks the phenomenon of 'point of view,' of perspective, of conic sections, and of city planning" (xi). Deleuze's idea that is of most relevance in our analysis of the Neobaroque in the works of (Latin) American writers and visual artists is that the Baroque refers not to an essence or a historical period, but rather to an operative function, to an existential trait. And that trait is its endless production of folds: "the Baroque trait twists and turns its folds, pushing them to infinity [...] composed of two stages or floors: the pleats of matter, and the folds of the soul" (3). The inside and the outside situate such folds of matter and soul, just as in Baroque architecture it is "the severing of the façade from the inside," where the interior, being severed yet autonomous from the exterior, still enters an interdependent relationship with it, analogously to a fold that has two interdependent surfaces of the same matter that project each other (28, 30). It is a reflection of baroque thought that directly remits us to the neobaroque concept of duality and multi-perspectivism. It also relates to central concept of the border as a folded bi-directional crossing space of two-sidedness and dual perspective. Finally, it evokes the (also baroque) motif of the mirror.

Various religious and apocalyptical evocations of the Spanish Baroque tradition along with a strong metadiscursive consciousness (e.g., instances of different narrators contradicting each other, as in Cervantes' *Don Quijote*), and other experiments with narrative form and linguistic norm, link Sarduy's novels to neoavant-garde and neobaroque currents. His style is full of displacements and instabilities of meaning that reflect a state of crisis and philosophical questioning of Western cultural values. The element of exuberance in the work of Sarduy can be considered as an attempt to fill in an existential void in the collective conscience of Western humanism, a void caused by a crisis of fixed values as offered by Modernity's discourses of Science, History, Philosophy, and Religion, with their unfulfilled promises of modernization, industrialization, and democratization, a crisis that was outlined by Jean Francois Lyotard in *The Postmodern Condition* (1984 [1979]). In Sect. 4.1, we will address in greater detail Neobaroque's key elements of exuberance, parody, and eroticism in relation to postmodern decentering.

Severo Sarduy extensively theorized the relationship between the neobaroque text and homoerotic (and ambiguously non-binary) sexuality in the essays *Escrito sobre un cuerpo* (1969), *Barroco* (1974) and *La simulación* (1982), and applied his propositions in the novels *De donde son los cantantes* (*From Cuba with a Song*, 1967), *Cobra* (1972), *Maitreya* (1978), and *Colibrí* (1984), as we will observe in the next chapter. He demonstrated the potential of metanarrative discourse which, in its form of text on paper or digital screen, becomes a symbolic construction in which the body-character-narrator and even the hand of the implied author are inscribed or "embodied." Text and writing operate as a metonymic projection of body art—the tattoo, the makeup, the clothing—(re)creating linguistically the changing identity of the characters through textual inscription or the intra or extratextual acting out of roles on the stage, as textual performance. This metadiscursive procedure of symmetry between the textualization of sexuality and the eroticization of writing, in which the text behaves as an engravable writing surface with ambiguous marks of identity, is characteristic of several other Latin American authors, whose origins span from the Río Grande to the Río de la Plata, passing through Brazil, Bolivia, and Chile. It evidences the potential of the neobaroque style to question fixed, steady identities, a potential that is made effective by its use of discursive procedures of artifice, parody, metafiction, and simulation in combination with the element of eroticism. As an example of a work portraying an ambiguous subject with transgressive and mutant sexuality, Sarduy's novel *Cobra* stands out as paradigmatic of the Neobaroque's resurgence of techniques evolved from the historical Baroque, combined with new contents of homoerotic sexuality and corporal transformation, and of the destabilizing and subversive strategy of identity deconstruction in a globally transcultural context.

Referring to a specifically baroque impulse to "capture the vastness of the language that circumscribes it, the organization of the universe [...] [and] to function as a signifying reflection of a certain diachrony [...] as images of a mobile and decentered universe [...] but one that is still harmonious" (1978: 183; my translation), Sarduy establishes a link between the historical Baroque and its modern stylization, the Neobaroque. This connection can be observed in his own prose and in that of several of the writers that we examine in detail in Chap. 3. He further states: "On the contrary, the current Baroque, the Neobaroque, structurally reflects inharmony, the rupture of homogeneity, of logos as the absolute, the lack that constitutes our epistemic foundation. Neobaroque of imbalance, structural reflection of a desire that cannot reach its object" (1978: 183; my translation). Severo Sarduy's own narrative can be defined as "Cuban Neobaroque," part of a surge of narrative authors who, starting in the decade of the 1960s, followed the steps of the style's first theorizer, José Lezama Lima, and of Alejo Carpentier, the initiator of what he himself called *lo real maravilloso* ("marvelous realism"). Other practitioners of this style in narrative and poetry were Guillermo Cabrera Infante, Virgilio Piñera, Reynaldo Arenas, and José Kozer. They used literary forms that combined the contemporary avant-garde with older Spanish baroque and American colonial techniques, and found an alternative—both conservative and radical—expression of political dissidence in the context of the Cuban Revolution. Most of them eventually opted for political exile, settling in different parts of Europe and the United States. But, foremost, it was the two initiators of this style in the 1940s, Alejo Carpentier and José Lezama Lima, who left the biggest imprint on future literary

62   K. A. KULAWIK

developments.[9] Carpentier began a critical discussion about the presence of a baroque style in American literature with reference to an inherent element of all "Americanness" that he called "marvelous reality" (*lo real maravilloso*) and that had an influence on the later emergence of "magical realism." His rather essentialist position was based on the assumption that an atemporal (essential) Baroque forms an inherent part of the "exuberant nature" of American culture and literature. In *Tientos y diferencias* (1967), Carpentier considered it an essentially proper and natural feature of American artistic expression.[10]

On the other hand, Lezama Lima's critical work pointed at a historically grounded Baroque as an expression of a typical creole Americanness of the *Señor Barroco* ("the Baroque Lord") as a manner of the American

---

[9] We refer here to the discussion on the subject of the presence of the Neobaroque in the "new Latin American literature" in the 1960s and 1970s, unleashed first by Alejo Carpentier around such concepts as "magical realism" and "baroque," as defined especially by D'Ors and Wölfflin. His position, set forth in *Tientos y diferencias* (1967), which we could call "essentialist," is based on the assertion that the baroque style is an inherent part of the "nature" of American literature. Thus, Carpentier considers it as proper to American artistic expression. The other position on this matter is that of Severo Sarduy, expressed and outlined in his essay "El barroco y el neobarroco" (1972). This position, which we would call "evolutionary," affirms that the neobaroque style is a conscious and rational resurgence of some evolved elements of an already historical style: the Spanish Baroque of the seventeenth century. Sarduy affirms that it is a process of stylization and modification of historical elements, recovered from the literary tradition. For a broader explanation of the distinction between "essentialist" and "evolutionary" Neobaroque, see the introduction to Gustavo Guerrero's *La estrategia neobarroca* (11–26). The rest of the discussion on the subject revolves around these two basic positions developed by the two Cuban authors between 1960 and 1975. There is, however, a third position on the matter, and that is that of José Lezama Lima. It could be said that it is an intermediate position between the two mentioned above, since it proposes the existence of baroque in America as the result of a fusion between the Spanish style of the seventeenth century, brought to America by the colonizer and installed in Creole (White) aesthetics—the "Señor Barroco"—and the vast Indigenous cultural substratum existing in America since before the Conquest, with the addition of the Black adstratum after the forced arrival of African slaves. These ideas are set out in detail in Lezama Lima's essay "La curiosidad barroca" in *La expresión americana* (1957).

[10] The contrast between Carpentier's and Lezama's positions on the role of the baroque in contemporary literature is summed up by Chiampi: "Carpentier, in short, elevates the marvelous real to the category of 'being,' while Lezama insists on the idea of the American as a becoming (a being and a non-being), in permanent mutation. This helps to explain, perhaps, why Carpentier speaks of taking up the baroque as a 'style' on the part of the Latin American writer, as a conscious task to represent 'our essences,' while Lezama turns the baroque into a 'form in becoming,' a continuous paradigm, from 'the origins' in the 17th century to the present day" (26; my translation).

Creole aristocrat possessing a style of his own, but an American Colonial style of "counter-conquest" of the American space from the Spanish metropolis. As Lezama explains in *La expression americana*, this self-conscious American stylization of the historical Baroque contains the constitutive elements of tension, plutonism ("the original fire that breaks the fragments and unifies them"), and plenitude of a style that, with the acquisitions of the Spanish language ("perhaps unique in the world"), expresses the opulence of the (White) Creole's mansion and the erotic delight of a "language that braids and multiplies" (1957: 32–33). Referring to Lezama, Chiampi points out that the Baroque was adopted by colonial Iberian America as its own style of oppositional (to Europe) expression.[11] She adds that "What is decisive in this Americanization of the Baroque is the orientation to modernize it with the concept of a revolutionary art, in the midst of pre-modernity" (24) (Fig. 2.1).

Lezama's New World *barroco americano* is the foundation for the emergence of a revolutionary Neobaroque in the twentieth century, exemplified in the narrative opulence of his own two novels *Paradiso* (1966) and *Oppiano Licario* (1977). In a way, these works inspired Sarduy (an admirer of Lezama) to write criticism and fiction in a similar vein, first in the Cuban literary reviews *Orígenes* and *Marcha*, and later, during his French exile, in the prominent poststructuralist journal *Tel Quel*, and to eventually specify a style that he called "evolutionary neobaroque." He defined it as such in "El barroco y el neobarroco" (1972) as a conscious, rationalized resurgence and stylization of traditional aesthetic elements *evolving* from a historical style, the Spanish Golden Age Baroque, now recovered and transposed to a new American ground. Monika Kaup (2012) presents this idea quoting Angel Rama's view on the transposition of the European Baroque to the Americas: "'The American continent became the experimental field for the formulation of a new Baroque culture'" (5). But more importantly, she highlights baroque's subjection "to never-ending flows of appropriation, resignification, and subversion that link it to new ideologies

---

[11] Chiampi explains: "Lezama's claim is clear: the baroque is 'our thing,' it is Iberian and American (it is Iberian because of the effects of the discovery and colonization, Portuguese or Spanish) and it is not possible to expand its concept as an 'artistic constant' or 'will of form.' [...] *La expresión americana* (1957) is the essay that takes up these hypotheses to develop the concept of the American becoming as an imaginary era, in which the baroque appears as a moderating paradigm and authentic beginning of the American fact. It is the aesthetics of 'curiosity,' of igneous, Luciferian or Faustian knowledge—a demonic *poiesis*, we would say [...]" (22; my translation).

Fig. 2.1 Colonial baroque façade of San Lorenzo Church in Potosí, Bolivia. (Photo by author)

and political subjects" (6). The historical Baroque becomes the raw material for new articulations of alternative, critically baroque modernities in Europe and the Americas that take on the form of the Neobaroque. It acquires a decolonizing force of the American (colonial and postcolonial) baroque. In its return in the twentieth century, the Neobaroque is seen by Kaup as one of the decolonizing, anti-institutional voices of "alternative modernities that deviate from the notion of a single, universal modernity modeled on European history in general, and Enlightenment ideology in particular" (6, 8), as well as a "central strategy of the postcolonial revision of modernity" (Chiampi in Kaup 7).

Meanwhile, other Latin American neobaroque connections have been broader and far more reaching (than the solely Circum-Caribbean) since the mid-twentieth century. It is even possible to trace a cartography that connects the neobaroque nuclei from the place of their first theorizations in the 1940s and 1950s in Cuba (with Lezama and Carpentier) and Argentina (with Angel Guido), to the narrative boom in the 1960s to 1980s, encompassing both the Caribbean and South America (Kulawik 2009: 40–43). Similar to a "creative leprosy" (Lezama 1957: 53–54), the Neobaroque spread in an exquisite outbreak and resurfaced in echoes, but also of rumblings, bounces, propagations, and displays in an exuberant trans-Latin American literature of a markedly formalist cut. From the 1970s onward, in what Néstor Perlongher calls the "neobaroque arch," the style extends from the Caribbean through Mexico to the Southern Cone, where it marks its three main nuclei: the Brazilian, the *rioplatense* (of the Río de la Plata region comprising the capital cities of Argentina and Uruguay), and the Chilean. He also gives it the name of *Caribe Transplatino* (1997: 99–101). The connections are ample, and there are parallels and links with other literatures, notably Eastern European. In an unpublished 2002 interview with Kulawik, Diamela Eltit stated that she knowingly rec-reated the themes and style of both Severo Sarduy and Polish Postmodernist Bruno Schulz (1892–1942). The theme of the old merchant shop invaded by the mob and mass culture of cheap supermarket junk was a propitious metaphor for the changing social structure of post-dictatorial Chilean society. Following Sarduy's and Schulz's footsteps, to depict this phenom-enon, Eltit used an exuberant and experimental prose style, which in both the Chilean author's and the broader Latin American context has been referred to as "neobaroque" (Ortega 1984, Christ 1997).

Therefore, the Neobaroque can be defined as a parodic and critical, but fully conscious utilization of the ornamental and conceptual seventeenth-century Baroque style in twentieth-century literature. Chiampi acknowl-edges that:

> Neobaroque is a continuity of that tradition; without rupture, but with the renovation of previous experiences (hence the neo), without cuts, but with the intensification and expansion of the experimental potentialities of the

66   K. A. KULAWIK

'classic' Baroque recycled by Lezama and Carpentier, but now with a strongly revisionist inflection of the ideological values of modernity. Modern and counter-modern at the same time, the neobaroque informs its postmodernist aesthetics, [...] as an archeological work that does not inscribe the archaic of the Baroque if only to allegorize the dissonance of modernity and the culture of Latin America. (29; my translation)

It can be considered a reaction to certain contemporary cultural phenomena, and an expression of a conflictive and non-homogeneous perception of reality, as Carmen Bustillo observed after Sarduy.[12] The use of baroque elements by the Neoavant-garde confers this narrative an aesthetically postmodern dimension and, ideologically, a postcolonial stance. Here, once again, we understand "postmodern" in Lyotard's terms as decentered and critical of the totalizing narratives of Modernity, and "postcolonial" along with Frederic Jameson (1991) and Homi Bhabha (1992) as assuming a subaltern voice of the periphery. Neobaroque narrative, especially in the case of Diamela Eltit in Chile, Osvaldo Lamborghini in Argentina, and even Bruno Schultz in far-away interwar Poland, portrays the downfall of the individual in a globalized and massified marketplace that is invaded by centralizing neocolonial economic interests. The highly opulent, poetic, and figurative use of language and of metafictional devices becomes a tool of political resistance against the encroaching mediocrity, uniformity, and consumerism, but also unemployment resulting from economic changes in both peripheral societies of Chile and Poland. Once again, Kaup points to the particular peripheral context of Latin America in its pre and postmodern contextualization of baroque forms:

Modernity should be conceived as having multiple, alternative forms resulting from the complex interplay of colonial and indigenous elements. The

---

[12] Carmen Bustillo points to Sarduy's stance on the link between the historical Baroque and contemporary Neobaroque: "Perhaps it is not necessary to insist on the relationship of the Baroque with that conflictive perception of reality. However, it is worth bringing up a very important difference that Sarduy points out between the 'founding' Baroque and the present one: the mobile and decentered universe of the Spanish and colonial Baroque still preserves, according to him, a certain harmony, a certain logos with the two epistemic axes of the century: God, and his terrestrial metaphor, the king. But for Sarduy, the Baroque is not only a transposition of that rupture, but it goes beyond it, transgresses, and its 'colorful, sometimes strident, motley and chaotic' language tries precisely to challenge the falsity of a 'given' logocentric entity: it becomes the spokesman of a revolutionary zeal that 'metaphorizes the disputed order, the judged god, the transgressed law'" (111–12; my translation).

New World baroque and the Latin American neobaroque constitute such a site-specific, hybrid modernity from the global periphery, where imported European and native, modern and premodern forms are joined to generate an eccentric New World modernity that deviates from the metropolitan prototype. (9)

Based on the studies by Ortega (1984), Guerrero (1987), Chiampi (2000), Zamora (2006), and Figueroa (2008) on the critical and vindicating function of the neobaroque in Latin American art and literature, this discussion may be extended to the possibilities and capacity of the Neobaroque to destabilize and deterritorialize, but also to reformulate the concept of identity in light of what we presented earlier as the presence of hybridity, heterogeneity, *mestizaje* (mixing), and transculturation that characterize Latin American culture in the context of a more general crisis of unitary values of Western Modernity and cultural fragmentation. Is it feasible to harbor a neobaroque epistemology that makes possible the formulation of a transitive cultural subject, a Trans-(Latin) American "Self"? Along the lines of Lezama's idea of an American Baroque "counterconquest," Chiampi (26, 31) and Zamora (2006: 286, 295) associate neobaroque aesthetics with revisionism and rupture of homogeneous discourses and categories of Modernity (as a "countermodernity"). Zamora even referred to this as a "neobaroque provocation" (285). Accordingly, Sarduy (1987) and Perlongher (1997) suggest that a "neobaroque creative leprosy" has managed to spread as a style, technique, and subversive intention in several latitudes of Iberian America, as Perlongher's previously mentioned "neobaroque arch" and "Trans-Rioplatinian Caribbean," spanning the Latin American continent from the Antilles and Mexico to Brazil and the Río de la Plata (1997: 101). This trans-American resurgence of neobaroque poetics points to its philosophical character of a deconstructive technique that disarticulates the heteronormative subject in terms of its subjectivity and identity signs. Its dynamic corresponds to a postmodern and postcolonial anti-establishment intentionality. As a style of seduction (in its opulence and eroticism), it becomes a style of sedition (in its radical and revolutionary dimension), as we will further explain in Sect. 4.4.

The textual presence of sexually (as well as racially, ethnically, nationally, and socially) unstable and transgressive subjects leads the critical reader to assert that the Latin American Neobaroque, as a system of meaning-making, is indicative of a broader cultural, philosophical, and political phenomenon of (arguably postmodern) decentering. Perhaps it is the multiculturally hybrid space of Latin America that enhances the potential to re-envision and reformulate the very concept of identity. The works of Latin American literature and performance that utilize neobaroque artistic forms become an aesthetic and discursive space for conceiving a plural idea of the self—both individual and collective—founded on ambiguity, hybridity, coexistence, and, most of all, transitivity of cultural traits. Ultimately, the concept of a trans-self projected by neobaroque aesthetics evinces the fragmented and shifting identities as a form of socio-political resistance referred to as a "baroque ethos" (Echeverría 1994), a creative attitude that defines hybrid cultural spaces in Latin America, the United States, and potentially any other areas where human (thus cultural) migration occurs, and cultures intermingle. This formative space of cross-cultural nomadic identity corresponds to the borderlands, where the nomad transits the contact zones of the "in-between," a space evincing the Native American concept of *nepantla*.

2.3 Identity on the Borders: An Intersectional Approach to Nomadic Transits

The transformative processes displayed by Neobaroque poetics involve the concept of *borderlands* and "borderland identity," as formulated by Chicana border theory. Movement and change are the key components in the non-linear processes of these multi-level transformations taking place across intersectional categories of gender, race, ethnicity, class, and nation (and even posthumanity) that form web-like connections. As Rosi Braidotti opportunely stated: "The only constant in today's world is change, but that is neither a simple nor a unilinear process. It rather operates with web-like sets of simultaneous shifts and contradictory trends" (2002: 264). The concepts of Identity and Border are linked in nomadic transits across cultural boundaries. Zones of contact constitute the formative space for the creation of transitive subjects—the ambiguous characters appearing in neobaroque works analyzed in Chap. 3. These spaces of "in-betweenness" and "points of passage," constitutive of Borderland Identity, will lead us in Chap. 4 to articulate "transentity"—a nomadic identity of a transitive selfhood situated in the cross-cultural space of the border.

2.3.1 Intersectional Theorizations of Borders and Boundaries

Identity articulates differentially in situations of contact along lines or spaces of separation, the physical and cultural borders and boundaries that distinguish One from the Other. Feminist Chicana border theory (Alarcón 1993, Sandoval 2000, Anzaldúa 2002, Moraga 2011) emphasizes the physical aspect of the word "border" as a transitory space of crossing of multiple political, cultural, and symbolic dimensions. An example of a physical, geographical, political, and cultural border appears in some of the analyzed works is the US Southwestern border with Mexico. Since the determination of its current position, largely as a result of the Mexican American War (1846–1848), the US-Mexican border has constituted a contact zone between two nations and heritages, a passage point for migrants, and a transitory space of intermingling of Mexican Hispanic, US Anglo, the Native American, and multiple other Latin American cultures in transit to the North. Considering aspects that go beyond its geopolitical determination, it has acquired the symbolic dimension of a cultural icon in the collective imagination of both the United States of America and Mexico, especially in more recent times of the massive migration of undocumented immigrants of the late twentieth and early twenty-first centuries. Their estimated number in the United States in 2010 was over 11.5 million (Fox 365, USAFacts.org), and has remained close to that number before 2020.[13] Beyond the Border Wall controversies that are presented in the news and the press, this boundary constitutes a theme of both aesthetic and ontological significance, depicted as a hybrid contact zone of transit. Many neobaroque works represent border crossing by way of incorporating "borderline" decategorizing concepts of non-heterosexual ambiguity—cross-dressing, androgyny, trans*, and queerness—and racial/ethnic mixing, or *mestizaje*.

The artistic rendition of liminal spaces and identities occupying the border between the United States and Mexico proliferates in US-Latine

---

[13] This number has remained stable since the all-time high of 11.8 million in 2007. "In 2018, there were an estimated 11.4 million unauthorized immigrants in the US" in USAFacts, "Unauthorized Immigrants." *US Immigration & Border Security Statistics and Data | USAFacts* and Bryan Baker, *Population Estimates, January 2021* (2021). U.S. Department of Homeland Security. *Estimates of the Unauthorized Immigrant Population Residing in the United States: January 2015–January 2018 (dhs.gov)* (2). Both sites accessed on February 13, 2023.

literature. Examples abound in testimonial essays, poetry, and novels by authors such as Rodolfo "Corky" Gonzales, Gloria Anzaldúa, Cherríe Moraga, Ana Castillo, Emma Pérez, and Sandra Cisneros, among others. In visual arts, the US Anglo-Latino cultural borders have been enacted in the transform-ist/-ative gender-bodily transgressions in the performance of Nao Bustamante, Carmelita Tropicana, Coco Fusco, Guillermo Gómez-Peña, and the Pocha Nostra troupe. An example of the cinematic depiction of the border as a posthuman space of the cyborg migrant laborer is Alex Rivera's sci-fi thriller *Sleep Dealer* (2009). From both sides of this cultural frontier, artistic and literary works critically point to the border themes of migration, crossing, and transgression layered with gender-bending themes of cross-dressing. These artistic and philosophical expressions have an intersectional character, as they highlight simultaneous contacts between the ethnic, racial, national, and sexual "other" within the border zone. Interest in the border between Mexico and the United States—analogous to the US-Latino cultural border—in the artistic activity of Chicane artists and feminist border theorists like Anzaldúa and Moraga represents and symbolically reconceptualizes the basic tenet of the border in times of increased controversy around deportations and border walls. This literary and artistic activity highlights the borderline interstices/in-between spaces and crevices that mediate between sameness and otherness, both in the physical-political and symbolic spheres that form the ethnic, racial, national, and sexual identity complex of the Americas. The analysis in Chap. 4 will refer to the theory of the border—a Native American, Chicane, Mexican, Anglo-Latin American transit zone, viewed intersectionally as a conglomerate of racial, ethnic, national, sexual, and posthuman formations.

A dynamic perception of the border emerges from the works of four contemporary Mexican and Chicano artists. Visual artist Guillermo Gómez-Peña affirms in *The New World Border*, a book of essays that he calls "a disnarrative ode to hybrid America" (1996: i), that his conception of America encompasses the entire continent and not only a single country (the U.S.) traceable on geopolitical maps. His performances and essays propose "opening the matrix of reality and introducing unsuspected possibilities" (6), one of which is gender-bending cross-dressing that is symbolically related to border crossing. In a figurative dimension of her testimonial-poetic book *Borderlands/La Frontera: The New Mestiza*, Gloria Anzaldúa proposes an equally symbolic, if not always physical, transgression of the border between the United States and Mexico by

2 NEOBAROQUE AS TRANSGRESSION: THE LATIN AMERICAN PARADIGM   71

means of the figure of the "new *mestiza*," a bisexual and gender-fluid, cross-border and cross-cultural being (2007: 99–105). On the other side of the border, the equally "borderland" prose of Mexican-Peruvian fictionist Mario Bellatin opens new narrative spaces in his experimental novels that cross the borders between multiple simulated spheres of subjectivity with transvestite and mutant characters in works that transit literary genres. By the visual medium of the feature film *Sleep Dealer* (2009), the US-Latino filmmaker of Peruvian descent, Alex Rivera, achieves a spatial-temporal manipulation of the southern US border, this time at the cybernetic level, virtualizing the national boundaries of Mexico and revealing the neocolonial economic domination of transnational corporations. At the same time, he reveals technological and aesthetic possibilities of transgressing, in the sense of disguising or visually cross-dressing, the historically and politically established political boundaries by means of remote labor technology and the ambiguous posthuman figure of the cyborg. The works of these four artists reveal transgressive identities that disclose new conceptual possibilities of subjectivity with the figures of the techno-ethnic cross-dresser, the new *mestiza*, the mutant, and the cyborg. They open aesthetic possibilities of representation with their hybrid artistic and literary genres of drama with the cross-border performance of Gómez-Peña, testimony with Anzaldúa's poetic essay, narrative with Bellatin's novels, and cinematic with Rivera's science fiction thriller. We will engage these works in Chap. 3 to behold Neobaroque's representative potential in depicting nomadism as borderland identity.

From a theoretical and intersectional angle, Elena Ruiz-Aho situates feminist border thought as "a socio-political theory that articulates the barriers towards inclusiveness and recognition of cultural differences in multiethnic societies" and considers it "an emerging paradigm for understanding and revising disciplinary discussions that center on identity-based issues such as class, race, gender, and ethnicity, as well as for formulation of new methods of cultural analysis that can respond to the complex needs of cultural and ethnic minorities in multicultural democracies" (2011: 357). One of the tenets of feminist border thought, one that guides our neobaroque vision of Transmerica, is the concept of intersectionality as it pertains to categories of ethnicity, race, and sexuality. The focus on interstitial boundary zones corresponds to fluid and fragmented subjects who simultaneously transgress (live out) multiple categories of identity. An intersectional approach allows to perceive the transitory and intertwined (intersectional) nature of the border in a simultaneous crossing of multiple categories/entities. Tina Fernandes Botts presents the multidimensional aspect of intersectionality: "By turns a research program, a description of personal identity, a theory of oppression, a counter-hegemonic political agenda, a symbolic antidote to mainstream (liberal) legal theory, and a critique of the methods and practices of mainstream philosophy, the concept of intersectionality (or simply 'intersectionality') wears many hats" (343). She points to the concept's broad scope and its centrality for contemporary research in the social sciences and humanities, its relevance for feminist theory and practice, as well as its still systematic dismissal by mainstream philosophy. According to Botts' definition, intersectionality is a research program that "stands for the proposition that no phenomenon is adequately researched or understood without factoring in the ways in which socialized identity markers like race, gender, sexuality, ability status, and class interact and affect the phenomenon being researched (McCall 2005)" (343). In reference to the individual, Botts presents intersectionality as a disruption of the concept of personal identity as definable in neat, linear, and timeless categories. In terms of a theory of oppression, intersectionality refers to the existence of forms, modes, or 'axes' of oppression (such as race, gender, class, sexuality, and ability status) that overlap and fuse in the subjectivity of the oppressed subject to present "an account of oppression that highlights its complexity" (343).

Basing her explanation of border feminism on Gloria Anzaldúa's "multiplicitous subjectivity" and "multiethnic cultural identity," Ruiz-Aho proposes interpretive alternatives to the conceptions of selfhood and cultural identity in a context of neoliberal economic policies, increased migration of Latin Americans into the United States, and shifting paradigms of globalization (350). She speaks of the new turn in Latin American social theory toward *pensamiento fronterizo* [border thought] "as a sociopolitical perspective or organizing concept around which complex narratives of displacement associated with multiethnic identity, migratory life, and multicultural citizenship can be theorized" (351). She emphasizes that the "decolonizing agenda" of this discourse engages "complex intersections of race, gender, and ethnicity that are so central to contemporary discourses of citizenship and rhetorical constructions of national identity" (351) in the wake of the historical legacy of Latin America, marked by colonization, exploitation, and resulting migration.

Feminist border thought offers an alternative to traditional essentialist discourse of Modernity as it "takes into account articulating the complex workings of intersectional oppressions such as race, class, gender, and ethnicity on women of color" (352), as well as the additional layers of differences that marginalized the Chicanas within traditionally White Anglo-American feminist movements. Thus, this particular brand of feminism is complemented by "positionality in multiple cultural and social realities" that enabled the voice of "the Chicanas' multiple perspectives" and "double consciousness" situated outside the dominant cultural constructions of selfhood or normative identity (352). Border theory's strong link to the real-life setting and practical dimension of its applicability sheds a light on borderland life as "a unique set of contradictory cultural experiences that result from inhabiting multiple yet conflicting frames of reference" (352). This experience has a particularly adverse effect on women given colonization's double protocol of racial inferiorization and gender subordination (354). Ruiz-Aho's assessment emphasizes key notions of feminist border thought in relation to the multicultural subject "whose lived-experience is structured by *flux*, *change*, and *cultural discontinuity*," whose state of mind straddles multiple and asymmetrical cultural contexts. The resulting borderland subject is a "new hybrid, multicultural self [that] has the added burden of *reconciling different strands* of one's identity" (354; emphasis added).

The intersectional character of queer theory is reflective of border theory's emphasis on multiple and simultaneous contacts across categories of cultural normativity. The interdisciplinary way in which queer theory approaches personal identity, sexuality, knowledge, politics, and generally the human experience (referenced by Botts in the work of Michel Foucault, Judith Butler, and Eve Sedgwick), allows it to focus its inquiry into the ways the discourse of difference is formulated ("created") as a result of what is determined as "natural" and "unnatural," especially in the realms of (gender-sexual) identities and acts. Queer theory highlights the fluidity and instability of categorizations and its potential for bringing on changes in perception as a result of its power to decategorize:

> Motivating queer theory is the debunking of stable (sexual) identities in favor of understanding identity as a conglomeration of unstable identities. Queer theory, like intersectionality theory, is 'world-making' (Duong 2012: 371), that is, it has the power 'to wrench frames' (Duong 2012: 371). It is capable of producing schemas of reality that are beyond preconceived (metaphysical and epistemological) sense-making mechanisms. Queer worlds, thus defined, transcend conventional notions of personal identity and politics to create room for countercultural (sexual) practices, ways of

being in the world, and alternative accounts of phenomenological experience (Halperin 1990; Ahmed 2006). Such a vision of personal identity is central to the concept of intersectionality. (Botts 2017: 346)

Intersectionality as a theoretical approach offers our study of neobaroque forms of expression of subjectivity a method for the simultaneous inclusion of multiple categories of race, ethnicity, nationality, gender, sexuality, and any other socialized identity markers while considering the *interaction* of these categories in the lived-represented experience of a single subject. The same applies to the varying modes of oppression that act upon subjects simultaneously and operate in tandem, revealing their intersection in multiple categorical distinctions. "If the concept of intersectionality has any lasting lesson, in other words, it may be that the key to combatting oppression is a radical openness to the other" providing a way to "get beyond intersectionality as an abstract ideal and back into the specific particularities of the individual lives of the oppressed" (Botts 2017: 353). The essence of intersectionality's approach seems to be a radical openness to the "other" outside the dominant cultural constructions of selfhood" (352), an approach that eschews mainstream philosophy's focus on abstraction, creation of categories, distinctions, and universal principles. It directs attention to its amorphous, fluid, and subjectively grounded nature of shunning the imposed structures of order and points toward a multivariate personal identity, but also to the multiple forms of its oppression. This means to propose a complexity and instability that the boundaries of traditional disciplines (including philosophy, sociology, and psychology) hold within their limits.

> For intersectionality is not a theory, nor an epistemological paradigm, nor a fantastical metaphysical fantasy designed to reinforce its own privileged status in the Western intellectual hierarchy. Instead, it is a sober acknowledgment of the epistemological, metaphysical, ethical, and political value of the lived experience of the vast majority of human beings on the planet (who are not white, male, heterosexual, 'able-bodied,' or wealthy). (Botts 2017: 353)

This is not to acknowledge the risk of this quantitative multiplicity that may lead to a pluralistic fragmentation without any apparent coherence in the consciousness of the subject. Following an intersectional approach, Braidotti proposes a stance on adopting qualitative (or substantial) changes of consciousness amid the quantitative accumulation of temporary and transitive identity markers (2002: 258). In our approach to decentered selfhood, based on the fluid transitivity and fragmentation of the literary-artistic subjects, voices and characters, we certainly want to avoid excessive relativization by multiple labeling of "transgressions," which could represent the neoliberal consumer-oriented and official market-driven cultural tendency of "anything (that pays) goes," a hegemonic stance of tolerance intended to attain the system's fuller control of a normative *status quo*. Intersectional tools of border theory allow us to perceive these qualitative changes of self-perception, behavior, and appearance taking place in the fragmentary (yet still coherent), mobile, and transitive nomadic subject. These tools are associated with the overarching concept of "borderland identity" that leads to a flexible "borderland state of mind" attained in nomadic transgression, transitivity, and metamorphosis. The critical and artistic works engaged here are exemplifications of nomadic borderland processes. Before looking more closely at them, we shall further explain the conceptual tools of borderland thought.

2.3.2 Borderland Identities and Nomadic Transits: Perspectives on Crossing Borders

The *borderlands* as border, boundary, or the contact space of "in-between" represents both the physical-empirical and the subjective-conceptual space in which identity is reformulated in relation to the ongoing effects of such phenomena as ethnic, racial, national, posthuman mixing, nomadism, and transformation (metamorphosis). It can be considered a space of crossing (also transgressing) and blurring of borders as divisive lines: walls, fences, or any normative categorizations. Referred to by Gloria Anzaldúa as an intermediate zone (or dimension) of *nepantla*, it represents a state of mind and body, an existential state of being, that relates to what the Chicana author calls a "new mestiza consciousness." This borderland condition is associated with the concept of "becoming," which in both Spanish and French translates as *devenir* and appears as a tenet of poststructuralist philosophy, as developed by Gilles Deleuze and Guattari (1987b [1980]). It is related to Rosi Braidotti's concept of nomadism, furthered in Chicana border feminist theory by Gloria Anzaldúa, Cherríe Moraga, Norma Alarcón, and Ricardo Vivancos Pérez.

Borderland identity is related to the previously explained phenomenon of interracial mixing, or *mestizaje*. A significant contribution to complement *mestizaje* was made by Bolívar Echeverría, whose "baroque ethos"

76   K. A. KULAWIK

concept appears as one of the key elements of Latin American cultural resistance enclosed in any syncretic form of culture. The framework of Echeverría's theory of *mestizaje* in conjunction with the baroque ethos provides an adequate context and explanation for borderland and nomadic identity transformation and rearticulation. It also relates to Neobaroque's subversive dimension encoded in its parodic hybridity. More importantly, Echeverría compares miscegenation and cultural hybridization to a "baroque strategy," a kind of technique and an operation taking place on the same wavelength as the neobaroque works that we proceed to analyze in Chap. 3. What is more, the baroque aesthetic/philosophical mode constitutes a discourse of opposition to the governing cultural system and questioning its value order. Thus, Echeverría perceives the baroque as a style of quiet "affirmative" resistance, elaborately inverting the established order:

> It is possible to say [...] that the strategy of cultural miscegenation proper to the Ibero-American tradition is a *baroque* strategy, which coincides perfectly with the characteristic behavior of the baroque ethos of European modernity and with the post-Renaissance Baroque attitude vis-à-vis the classical canons of Western art. The expression of the 'no,' of the negation or opposition to the will of the other, must follow an elaborate path; it has to be construed indirectly and by exaggeration. It must be carried out by means of a subtle game, with a plot of 'yeses' so complicated that it is capable of overdetermining the affirmative meaning to the point of inverting its sense, of turning it into a negation. To say 'no' in a world that excludes this signification, it is necessary to work on its value order: shake it, question it, awaken its foundations, demand that it give more of itself, that it move to a higher level so that it can *integrate* even that which for it are counter-values. (1994: 36; my translation, emphasis added)

It is a strategy illustrative of the operational mechanism of irony, satire, and parody. It directly relates to Sarduy's observations about neobaroque's techniques of emphasis: artifice, overabundance through proliferation, substitution, and hyperbole (as exaggeration)—a style that will do anything to convince. Moreover, it reminds us of the technique of cross-dressing—a hyperrealistic exaggeration of what is masked as absent yet is still desired. The coveted "no," as the mark of the void, is supplemented with a chain of "yeses" that is nothing more than the simulation of an inexistent presence, of a negation of any presence. As the subject transits, the border is voided. There are no limitations, no borders that cannot be crossed. A borderland analogy can be drawn between the cross-dresser's transgression of normative gender (and sometimes sexual orientation) and the opulent linguistic subversion of neobaroque representation as surpassing the word (as sign). Both the cross-dresser and its form of representation situate on both sides of a fictional boundary.

Indigenous Perspectives on Crossing Borders. Notwithstanding Western poststructuralist feminism, there are at least two Indigenous, Native American-based avatars of feminist discourse that, in their dealing with borderland identity, become the *de facto* conceptual "borderland" or a contact zone of theories all in itself. The critical discourse of two bicultural theorists becomes a space in which identity is perceived as delimited, then decolonized, disarticulated, and ultimately reconstituted in relation to the ongoing effects of ethnic, racial, national, posthuman contact, mixing, hybridization, nomadism (as transit and mobility), and transformation (metamorphosis or integral change). Amerindian-rooted feminist voices of Gloria Anzaldúa and Silvia Rivera Cusicanqui collude with Rosi Braidotti's Western, feminist-based concept of nomadism, and eventually join with queer theory, borderland Chicana, and Indigenous decolonial perspectives representing feminine discursive forces. Their purpose is to propose feminine futurities that emerge from the damaged spaces of colonization, capitalistic extractivism, and patriarchy. Besides presenting a Transatlantic connection of compatibility, their discourse offers critical revisions that enable the study, reconceptualization, and recreation of new textual spaces. They envision conceptual worlds that represent a reconstitution of the notion of identity as a movable, shifting, transitive, and open space of desire, affectivity, and cross-fertilization of traditionally exclusive gender, sexual, ethnic, racial, social, and national categories. The common denominator of their discourse is that of the *borderlands*: the border, boundary, or space of "in-between," a space of transit, flow, movement, crossing (also transgressing), and blurring of limits. Referred to by Gloria Anzaldúa in her poetic testimony *Borderlands/La Frontera* (1987) as an interstitial space of *nepantla*, the border conjures a state of mind and being that the Chicana author identifies as *nepantlism*, or a state of transitioning of an in-between space of becoming a "subject-in-process" of a "new *mestiza* consciousness" (2007: 99).

Somewhat later and farther south, in the Andean context of Bolivia, Silvia Rivera Cusicanqui publishes *Ch'ixinakax utxiwa: Una reflexión sobre prácticas y discursos descolonizadores* (2020), a study of the migration routes of women who create communal territory in the midst of colonial oppression and capitalist exploitation. This work generates a *sui generis* border epistemology, unsettling all categories instituted by colonial patriarchy, mixing temporalities in border spaces of transits and spiraled, non-linear, and multilayered time dimensions in which border spaces and migrant routes coexist. These routes reflect the migrations taking place in Latin America and across the US border, migrations that are both internal and external. By way of migration and transformations, Rivera decolonizes Western epistemology in its categorical determinations of cultural belonging. She introduces the native talisman concept of *ch'ixi* to designate an undefined, and formless "motley mix," adding on to cultural *mestizaje* and hybridization the idea of a double existence or coexistence of "one" and "other" with a third element resulting from the interaction of both. The concept reflects the Aymara idea of something that is and is not at the same time, situating it in a logic of including a third element into the binary. The example Rivera gives of *ch'ixi* is the color gray as an incorporation of both white and its opposite, black (2020: xxi).

Ch'ixi represents an Indigenous way of non-binary thinking that has its multiple references to the "third sex" in several other cultures, like the North American Zuni whose figure of the *berdache* combines man and woman. In a broader cultural frame, it refers to a mixed society with a coexistence of multiple cultural elements that do not blend but instead negotiate their belonging and mutual influence (Rivera 66). Applied to the cross-border subject, it deftly represents the multiple identities that conform a transitive borderland identity.

The borderland states evoked by the Indigenous concepts of *nepantla* and *ch'ixi* are compatible with the Western concept of "becoming" that in both Spanish and French translates as *devenir* and appears in the post-structuralist philosophy of Gilles Deleuze. It is also relatable to the concept of nomadism in the theory of Rosi Braidotti who developed the concept of "nomadic subjects" used in feminist and Chicana border theory. The epistemological contribution of US Latinas to the concept of borderland identity expands significantly the philosophical inquiry of subjectivity. It was introduced by way of feminist and Chicana border theory writers Anzaldúa, Moraga, Sandoval, and Alarcón starting in the 1980s. After 2010, their feminist discourse of the border was recapitulated by Ricardo Vivancos Pérez with reference to nomadic theory introduced in the 1990s and early 2000s by Australian critic Rosi Braidotti.

Rosi Braidotti's Nomadic Subjects in the Borderlands. As a major contribution to feminist and decolonial identity studies, Braidotti's nomadic subject theory of corporeal materiality provides meaningful insights to the analysis of Neobaroque literary and artistic works that represent decentered identities. In *Nomadic Subjects* (1994), Braidotti presents nomadism as a theoretical option and a philosophical tenet, a figurative style of thinking that evokes a "vision of female feminist subjectivity in a nomadic mode" (1). In *Metamorphoses* (2002), she further develops the idea of transformative nomadism into a "materialist theory of becoming" which ultimately evolves into "nomadic ethics" in *Transpositions* (2006). She relates transformative nomadism to conceptual figuration in "a style of thought that evokes or expresses ways out of the phallocentric vision of the subject," defining her work as a thinker in terms of "a succession of translations, of displacements, of adaptations to changing conditions" (1994: 1). The idea of figuration constitutes "a politically informed account of an alternative subjectivity" (1). She redefines a materialist theory of feminist subjectivity in a trans-mobile mode, committing to utilizing parameters of the fragmented postmodern cultural condition in order to present new possibilities of inquiry that pivot on the notion of *positionality*. Within this historical condition, concepts, definitions, and any determinations of subjectivity "can be alternatively perceived as positive or negative depending on one's position" (1994: 2).

It is also meaningful to observe a close link between Braidotti's idea of positionality and Susan Brison's take on the concept of "relational selves" as identities forming only in relation to other selves in linguistic terms, that is, verbally through words. According to this perspective, they are positioned or determined only temporarily and in a perceptual (and symbolically verbal) relation to another self, always in a position that is changing or replaceable. That is to say, identities determining the self (or selfhood) are fundamentally relational entities with other selves (218). Brison defines relational selfhood as:

> a self [that] is an embodied, socially constructed narrative. [...] I argue for the less obvious view that other persons also *constitute* me as who I am; that is, they participate in the ongoing process of my self-constitution. By "self-constitution," I mean, not the constitution of a self all by itself, but rather the process by which a self is constituted, however that happens. In my view, other selves are essential to this process. More specifically what others do with words plays a crucial role in my self-constitution. (2017: 226; emphasis in original)

The ideas of positional, nomadic-as-transiting, and relational selves represent the most adequate theoretical formulation of a transitive subjectivity perceptible in the Neobaroque work, which carries linguistic-aesthetic potential of representing the nomadism of relational selves. Following the analysis of select Latin American writers of fiction and performers of Neobaroque Neoavant-garde from the last five decades will allow in Chap. 3 to fully comprehend the relational and nomadic dimension of transitive identity.

Braidotti's "nomadic subject theory of corporeal materiality" emerged from a twofold lineage: on the one hand, from previous poststructuralist Deleuzian thought on nomadism and rhizomes (horizontal and non-hierarchical relations) and, on the other, from classical feminist materialism in the line of Luce Irigaray. This double line of thought proposes a "transmobile materialist theory of feminist subjectivity [...] [as] opening up of new possibilities" that are centered, again, on the notion of *positionality* that relates to *intersectionality* (1994: 2).

Works of the Neobaroque style, whether written as text or enacted in visual forms or performative acts, are the symbolic and material incarnation of a transmobile materialist theory of feminist (and queer) subjectivity that Braidotti expands in her first three major theoretical works. For the redefinition of subjectivity in her project of nomadism, *Nomadic Subjects* (1994), Braidotti lays the foundation for her nomadic theory, describing it as "a new form of materialism, one that develops the notion of corporeal materiality by emphasizing the embodied and therefore sexually differentiated structure of the speaking subject," consequently rethinking the bodily (material) roots of subjectivity as "the starting point for the epistemological project of nomadism" (1994: 3–4). The body or embodiment of the subject is to be understood as neither a biological nor sociological category, but rather as "a point of overlapping between the physical, the symbolic, and the sociological," all within the frame of "a radically anti-essentialist position" (1994: 4). Braidotti continues to expound the feminist underpinnings of her nomadic framework: "The nomad is my own figuration of a situated, postmodern, culturally differentiated understanding of the subject in general and of the feminist subject in particular" (1994: 4). This bodily (materialist) dimension of nomadism and identity in relation to textual representation is a point to which we shall return in greater depth in the next section.

The role that literary and artistic creation plays in the realization of this nomadic subject is apparent when subsuming "the potency and relevance of the *imagination*, of myth-making, as a way to step out of the political and intellectual stasis of these postmodern times. Political *fictions* may be more effective, here and now, than theoretical systems" (1994: 4; emphasis added). The exemplary role conferred to imagination, and consequently to artistic and literary discourse, in this process and its function in the Latin American Neobaroque, becomes relevant as they may be projected to the extratextual realm. This occurs when the nomadic subject is enacted and embodied on the epistemological (textual) and empirical (performative) levels in the concrete socio-cultural context of the characters, narrators, performers, through representation in the literary-artistic works. By resorting to the neobaroque style as a transgressive technique of visualizing and representing the nomadic self, the subjects in the works enact (carry out or display) a decentered vision of subjectivity.

The intersectional structure of nomadic theory provides the framework for Braidotti's feminist reformulation of Western philosophy of subjectivity: "In so far as axes of differentiation such as class, race, ethnicity, gender, age, and others intersect and interact with each other in the constitution of subjectivity, the notion of nomad refers to the simultaneous occurrence of many of these at once." (1994: 4) The concept of nomadic subject becomes a creation of simultaneity and transitions, an "intellectual myth" of sorts, that is to say, a political fiction that allows the author "to think through and move across established categories and levels of experience: blurring boundaries without burning bridges" (1994: 4). The intersectional approach stands out in nomadic theory, similarly to Rincón's previously mentioned concept of simultaneity. Our examples of transitive and nomadic subjects intersectionally involve cross-gender, racial, ethnic, national, social, and posthuman characters/figures. Intersectionality is further developed in *Transpositions*, Braidotti's third work on nomadic theory in which she quotes bell hooks' [lower case intentional] stance on intersectionality: "Radical postmodernism calls attention to those shared sensibilities which cross boundaries of class, gender, race, etc. that could be fertile ground for the construction of empathy—ties that would promote recognition of common commitments, and serve as a base for solidarity and coalition (hooks 1990: 27)" (Braidotti 2006: 78). In terms of other categories of identity, such as nationality and ethnicity, it is the aspect of multiplicity present in webs of interconnections and alliances that forms the basis for a refiguration of subjectivity, one that is founded on multiple belongings and flexible forms of citizenship. Braidotti affirms that nomadism "allows for complex allegiances and multiple forms of cultural belongings" (2006: 79), dismantling the us/them binary and replacing a fixed notion of citizenship, nationality, and national identity with a flexible and movable concept of transitory identifications.

Braidotti adds the concept of "nomadic shifts" in taking on performative roles as creative ways of becoming, as metaphors that allow for unique encounters and unanticipated bases of interaction in terms of experience and knowledge. "In a feminist perspective, I prefer to approach 'the philosophy of <<as if,>>' however, not as a disavowal, but rather as the affirmation of fluid boundaries, a practice of the intervals, of the interfaces, and of the interstices" (1994: 6). She subsequently provides an example of this transformative power of artistic expression in Laurie Anderson's performance art as "another great example of effective parodic nomadic style, in the 'as-if' mode […] the art of reversibility," Braidotti goes on to affirm: "What I find empowering in the practice of 'as if' is precisely its potential for opening up, through successive repetitions and mimetic strategies, spaces where alternative forms of agency can be engendered. […] In other words, parody can be politically empowering on the condition of being sustained by a critical consciousness that aims at engendering transformations and changes" (1994: 7). Here, a link can be established with Sarduy's vision of parody as one of the tenets of Neobaroque technique, forming part of the general element of "artifice" (comprising "substitution," "condensation," and "proliferation"), and one of the three general pillars of neobaroque poetics, alongside "eroticism" and "revolution" (1978: 174–76).

"The nomadic subject as a performative image" allows Braidotti to express her own conceptual preference for a "postmetaphysical vision of subjectivity" conjugated with feminist politics in a "figurative approach to nomadism" (1994: 7–8). The relevance of the imaginary and creative element in the aesthetic realm of the artistic, literary, and textual work of the Latin American Neobaroque is the realization of this figuration of subjectivity in a nomadic mode. The key concepts of mobility and transitivity of the nomadic subject are ever-present in Braidotti: "But there is no triumphant *cogito* supervising the contingency of the self; the nomad stands for movable diversity; the nomad's identity is an inventory of traces" (1994: 14; emphasis in original). The idea of decolonizing and deconstructing identity as such and its dispersal into movable parts-molecules is of fundamental relevance in this approach: "Nomadism: vertiginous progression toward deconstructing identity; molecularization of the self" (1994: 16). Braidotti expresses an "affection for the places of transit […] in between zones where all ties are suspended and time stretched to a sort of continuous present. Oases of non-belonging, spaces of detachment. No-(wo)man's lands" (1994: 18–19).

As a key precept for our further inquiry into transitive identity, we propose to adopt Braidotti's definition of the nomad as "a figuration for the kind of subject who has relinquished all idea, desire, or nostalgia for fixity. This figuration expresses the desire for an identity made of transitions, successive shifts, and coordinated changes, without and against an essential unity" (1994: 22). This rejection of deterministic fixity becomes the guiding principle for the configuration of a fluid, mobile, and transitive notion of identity that is formulated in Neobaroque aesthetics; it is founded on openness and fluidity that lead to relativization of categories making up the trans-identified self. In a more philosophical sense, identity is conceived as a nomadic consciousness that assumes perspectives that do not remain fixed or attached to any one position and are movable: "Nomadic consciousness is also an epistemological position. [...] This transdisciplinary propagation of concepts has positive effects in that it allows for multiple interconnections and transmigrations of notions" (1994: 23). Identity is "a form of resisting assimilation or homologation into dominant ways of representing the self. [...] The nomadic style is about transitions and passages without predetermined destinations or lost homelands" (1994: 25), which leads to "a passionate form of post-humanism, based on feminist nomadic ethics" (1994: 29). It is best summed up in Braidotti's idea of nomadism as an "invitation" (30). We will examine it as we progress through ornate textual spaces drawn out by the exuberant works of the Latin American Neobaroque.

Further Perspectives on Borderland Identities. From a feminist perspective, Edwina Barvosa (2017) describes the imposed divisive and exclusive aspect of identity categorizations, stressing the socially determined nature of its structures: "borderlands identities are configurations of multiple identities that include elements socially constructed as mutually exclusive at a given time. Such divided identities are usually cast as an impassable social division such as woman/man [...] however, these constructed divisions are encompassed in the life of a single person" (215). Before more fully approaching transgressive forms of queerness in its condition of transitivity, liminality, and simultaneity, and in its adoption by shifting and mobile identities, it is necessary to return for a moment to the concepts of "*mestizaje*" and "hybridity" as the underlying components of borderland identity. Particularly useful is the idea of the "new mestiza consciousness," developed by Gloria Anzaldúa in *Borderlands/La Frontera*

84   K. A. KULAWIK

(2007 [1987]), which in her approach means "a tolerance for ambiguity," "the juggling of cultures," and "a plural personality" (2007 [1987]: 99–101), not synthesized under any defining term. In a similar way as Mary Louise Pratt defined the "contact zone" (1993), this Chicana author displaces the concepts of center and margin in what is a supreme example of transitivity. Anzaldúa refers to a playful linguistic, cultural, and sexual transgression of the "border," understood in her work literally as the wall that crosses the desert from California to New Mexico, and then on to the Rio Grande, but also understood figuratively as the cultural divisions resulting from the imposition of categories that discriminate between being Mexican, Mexican American, American, gringo, Chicano/a, Latino/a, man, woman, gay, lesbian, etc. Anzaldúa defines the borderland as a "space" and, in opposition to the dominant phallocentric cultural paradigm, as "a consciousness of woman," "a consciousness of the border/Borderlands," or "bilingual consciousness," always transgressive and transitive (77). It is situated in a place of contact and crossing (as the physical border in the Rio Grande Valley) where, as a child, Anzaldúa experienced borderland transits and figurative passing, which she practiced throughout her life); it is the result of cultural confrontation and perpetual transition. In this borderland space the "mestiza woman" is created as a composite being with a "tolerance for ambiguity" that relates to Braidotti's nomadic subject. She combines cultures in a pluralistic mode by adopting multiple perspectives of the Indigenous, the Mexican, and the Anglo-American. Her plural personality learns to juggle multiple cultures, while sustaining contradictions and using ambivalence as the cohesive element for transiting between categories (Anzaldúa 2007: 101).

Anzaldúa adds that mestiza consciousness results in a breaking and transcendence of duality, characteristic of Western thought, in terms of hierarchy (subject/object), gender (male/female), and race (black/white). The idea she suggests is reflective of the long-heard call to accept the other in oneself, which goes in line with Homi Bhabha's question of "How can the human world live its difference; how can a human being live Other-wise?" (1992: 207). The Chicana author displays an acute perception of a torn subject that functions through transgressive interaction between the two sides of the border. The *Mestizo* being combines the two sides and is situated in the contact zone, mediating differences in a projection of presences and a mutual recognition of differences. Finally, it is important to note that in the line of thought denoted by Anzaldúa, it is not a matter of overcoming duality in search of unity that again would represent an essentializing and totalizing entity, but of learning to play with duality and multiplicity in one's own space of contact, of the border, of the systemically imposed limit by means of movement, transit, transgression, and ultimate transcendence of categories. Anzaldúa proposes a "cultural juggling" (of the "Chicano-gringa," as the Mexican American author defined herself) that best describes the consciousness of the "mestiza woman" extending to other forms of nomadic selfhood.

Current border studies establish a conceptual bridge with previous subaltern and postcolonial studies on more than one occasion. This is perceived, for example, when rescuing the notion of the "contact zone" proposed by Mary Louise Pratt (1993) as a theorem to "de-center the communal and fraternal modes of understanding that have organized the discussion on the nationalisms and sub-nationalisms" (87). She defines the "contact zone" as a virtually existing or latent boundary space (or "zone") *within* a self-determined group (national, racial, sexual, etc.), but also as a space of co-presence, coexistence that allows for a visibility of the "other" that is typically defined by mutual invisibility or segregation. Contrary to the accepted idea of identity, and departing from a contact perspective, differences and separations (internal borders) between individuals are created by critically interacting and sharing the same (contact) space in which an inevitable co-presence, in the least, or eventual miscegenation, hybridization, and transculturation may occur (Pratt 88). In this regard, it is useful to recall *Hybrid Cultures* (1990) by Néstor García Canclini and Fernando Ortiz's *The Cuban Counterpoint of Tobacco and Sugar* (1995 [1940]) to realize how these processes of hybridization and transculturation take place within the same "contact zone" defined by the co-presence of non-binary subjects, politically divided by the discourse of oligarchic colonization.

Migratory movement across the border results in contacts that produce exchanges and mixtures. These can be applied to various signs of identity (ethnic, national, racial, sexual, and even posthuman) and, at the same time, to artistic genres that represent this phenomenon, such as the new experimental artistic forms of cyber-tech, cyber-punk, Internet Art, installation and performance, cybergothic cinema and borderland science fiction (Donohue 2018); not to omit Anzaldúa's critical work and poetic testimony in Spanglish prose and verse, or the open narrative forms of Bellatin's "novel-in/as-process" (Kulawik 2012). In Chap. 3, we will examine examples of such artistic incursions to illustrate just how the process of representing these concepts of border, boundary, and borderland identity unfolds in the broader field of borderland art and literature. This conception of the border no longer associates it with a fence, a wall or dividing line between human groups, or even with the national, political, or geographic borders marked on a map, but rather conceives it as a conceptual point of intersection, contact and opening of subjectivity; that is, as a contact zone, that leads to the decentering of identity. In Chap. 4 we will return to the concept of border/boundary, represented in these works in its symbolic dimension, using the notions of queerness as a crossing and transitivity of sexual categories, borderland consciousness as a situational-positional identity in the transitive space of the porous boundary, and eroticism as the desire-driven mechanism that propels the transgression of boundaries through surplus and excess. All along, these concepts converge as the defining features of the Neobaroque as a discourse of self-transcendence.

Following Braidotti's commitment to ethical accountability in the conception of a nomadic identity, we have attempted to present a borderland, non-unitary vision of the subject. Although the perspective adopted in Braidotti's *Metamorphoses* places emphasis on the need for "a new ethics for non-unitary cyborg-subjects that undergo met(r)amorphoses/meta(l) morphoses," for the purposes of our study and its proposal for configuring the nomadic subjectivity of the trans-self "without altogether losing sight of the norms and values of the human condition" (2002: 267–68), we propose the applicability of nomadism to a broader, cross, and intersectional array of identity categories like gender, race, ethnicity, nationhood, and humanity that all form "borderland identities." We adhere to Braidotti's emphasis on the continued need for the existence of "a subject," as well as for "a dispersed form of affectivity, a flowing type of coherence and for the necessity of reconfiguring the subject" (2002: 268). This approach should lead us to a "feminine" (as flexible and open) morphology of the subject in the form of cartographic accounts of many, often-contradictory, intersecting positions. Neobaroque aesthetics should allow us to perceive a high-tech, mobile, and accountable figuration of border-crossings that connects such transitions, transits, and transformations of the sexual body to the body of writing, to textuality and performance. We intend the "borderland identities" perceived in neobaroque works to exemplify "a nomadic vision of the subject that, however much in process and in becoming, is still there" (Braidotti 2002: 268).

2.3.3   Queer Becomings in Trans(-itive) Genders

As a component of borderland subjectivity, queerness (or queer identity) plays a critical and theoretical role in the deconstruction and rearticulation of gender identity. Analogically, the exuberant and experimental nature of the Neobaroque constitutes a way of "queering" normative communication and undoing the definitions previously established by realist-mimetic literary discourse, as well as by social and scientific discourses. We understand "queering" as a subjective or creative activity of realizing sexual ambiguity by diverging from heteronormative gender/sexual categories and by departing from a binary version/representation of gender identity. Similarly to the cross-dresser's performative act envisioned as queering, the neobaroque text queers communicative (denotative) language through its extravagant style. By means of verbal opulence and the frequent use of rhetorical figures such as syllogisms, irony, parody, metaphors, and similes (all examples of artifice), neobaroque texts reveal the discursive and artistic modes that erase established categorizations, relativize and transgress the norms, parodically "stripping" discourse—frequently in a metadiscursive way—down to the same mechanisms that official discourse (mimetic, realistic, communicative) employs to categorize and institutionalize identities. The texts that we are presenting adopt a position of political dissidence through "queering means" of the cross-dressed, androgynous characters, on the one hand, and through a symbolic cross-dressing of language in the exuberant textual representation, on the other. This creates resistance and opposition to the cultural system of administration of officialized fixed meaning, meaning understood as a control mechanism created by the centers of dominant power.

The term "queer" has been defined by Annemarie Jagose, following Teresa de Lauretis (1987), as a concept and a practice representing the idea of reinvention of sexualities by means of a different ("another") discursive horizon, a different way of thinking the sexual (2015: 26). In traditional terms, it has been described as a way of recommitting to a non-heteronormative yet still foundational identity object, described plainly as "homosexuality" or more elaborately as "male and female homosexualities" (2015: 29). Inasmuch as the primacy of queer's antinormative character stands out in political terms of resistance, Jagose proposes to reevaluate "queer's" antinormative presumption so as to add as equally relevant to its critical dimension the destabilizing, uncategorical, and intersectional character it possesses in conceptual and theoretical terms.

88 K. A. KULAWIK

Founded initially on solely gay and lesbian discourse, the concept of queerness has evolved to encompass any destabilizing, antinormative, and non-binary, or better yet, indeterminate staging of traditionally hetero-normative categories of sexuality by means of theoretical or aesthetic discourse (2015: 26–27). Similarly, Eve Kosofsky Sedgwick admits its traditional use "to denote, almost simply, same-sex sexual object choice, lesbian or gay, whether or not it is organized around multiple criss-crossings of definitional lines" (2013: 8). However, she adds that queer can refer in an intersectional manner to many other options as

> an open mesh of possibilities, gaps, overlaps, dissonances and resonances, lapses and excesses of meaning when the constituent elements of anyone's gender, of anyone's sexuality aren't made (or *can't be* made) to signify monolithically. [...] At the same time, a lot of the most exciting recent work around "queer" spins the term outward along dimensions that can't be sub-sumed under gender and sexuality at all: the ways that race, ethnicity, post-colonial nationality criss-cross with these *and other* identity-constituting, identity-fracturing discourses [...]. (8; emphasis in original)

Following Jagose and Sedgwick, we propose to adopt an open and inter-sectional understanding of "queerness." Moreover, the intersectional character of queer theory provides the perspective from which "queer" stands as a foundational idea for our interpretation of "trans-identity" in Chap. 4.

Within the hegemonically imposed categorical bounds of gender, the two main types of what I suggest calling "transitive identities" are *cross-dressing*—the act of wearing the clothes and simulating the appearance of the "opposite" gender assigned according to a supposed "biological" sex; and *androgyny*—the psychosomatic combination of elements of the two hetero-socially determined gender roles resulting in ambiguity of male/female distinctions in appearance and behavior. These two transgressive and performative gender behaviors are particularly indicative of an emerg-ing form of a transitive, indeterminate, and unstable "borderland" subjec-tivity that also applies to other categories that include ethnicity, race, nationality, social class, and, ultimately, humanity (as opposed to cyborg posthumanity). Reference to queer and gender theory (Echavarren, Santiago, Foster, Muñoz, Jagose, and Halberstam) will help us determine how queerness is relatable to Neobaroque representation through linguis-tic ambiguity, artifice, and parody, and how this theoretical possibility of "queering" identity through language, a language that itself is "queered," is achieved in the neobaroque literary and artistic representation by Latin American writers and artists. The overflowing, erotic, experimental, and boundary-breaking character of neobaroque textuality allows the reader/spectator to notice and conceive how the categories of heteronormative sexuality are surpassed and more effectively queered in neobaroque discourse. The textual and performative attempt to find transcendence through aesthetic-discursive means has often been noted by critics and stated by the authors of these works in interviews. The fluid and transgressive nature of gender and sexuality is best explained with the concept of gender/sexual transitivity, developed with Jack Halberstam's concept of trans* (2018), the figure of "*travesti*" in Don Kulick's (1998) study of Brazilian cross-dressers/drag queens and in the testimonial texts of Argentine transvestite activist, Marlene Wayar (2019). These concepts are complemented with the idea of "disidentification" introduced by José Esteban Muñoz (1999).

The process of identity "invention" or "negotiation" takes place at the "collision points" of determined discursive perspectives that cultural critics call essentialist and constructivist. An example of this antinormative negotiation of categorical discourses is when identities "deviate" from (hetero)normativity within artistic representation, as in the cases of literary creation and performance. In *Disidentifications* (1999) Muñoz states: "The version of identity politics that this book participates in imagines a reconstructed narrative of identity formation that locates the enacting of self at precisely the point where the discourses of essentialism and constructivism short-circuit. Such identities *use* and are the fruits of a practice of disidentificatory reception and performance" (6; emphasis in original). As an example, when applied to the figures of Qadós, Cobra, or the anonymous cross-dresser of Bellatin's *Beauty Salon*, all of whom we will examine in more detail in the next chapter, the idea of disidentification as a negotiation (rejection and adoption) of binary identity fragments allows us to understand the figuration of a trans-identity with these characters' textual-symbolic-representation. It is aimed at achieving transcendence in terms of surpassing any categorization and un-determining any identity-defining terms.

The point we wish to make further on in our analysis, especially in Chap. 3, is that the exuberant language and fragmented narrative structure are the textual reflection of a liminal existence, of a borderline and transitive identity facilitated by neobaroque discourse. It represents the transition of beings between bodies (and sexes, races, ethnicities, and human/cyborg states) and ultimately between life and death. As we shall also see later, neobaroque eroticism opens possibilities for conceiving a transitive subject, exemplified in Halberstam's concept of "trans*" as an open, unfinished, undefined, and unteleological (without a set outcome) bodily transition in open sexual relations, an "embodiment as a more fluid architectural design" (2018: 24).

Sexuality transitions and becomes all-ambiguous in the search for transcendence embodied in a divinely undivine "one-in-many" that coincides with the search for wordS (not *the* Word, but rather its fragments) that could express its plurality, in a metonymic extension of being-existing-writing. As we shall see later, the characters' transformation from man to woman and vice versa, and their subsequent metamorphosis into animal states, result in a shifting, mutable, and unstable self-identification of the characters and narrative voices. Their fragmented, and sometimes split or shattered identities and inverted sexualities, unbridled in an all-libidinous eroticism, lead to conceiving subjectivity in terms of transitivity. The cross-dresser's passing identity can be situated in a space of transition of a trans-identity by applying Halberstam's concept of "trans*": a fragmented and fluid "category" of self-identification without the determination of any finished identity.

The title of Halberstam's book containing the prefix "trans*" reflects the intended opening up of the term to category variations organized around but not confined to forms of gender variance. As we will see in our examples of neobaroque works, this un-naming device of an open-ended word or prefix allows us to interpret the ambiguous subject as a fluid trans-identity that does not conform to being labeled to any category, preferring to be unnamed as a transitive and fluctuating subject. Halberstam's concept of trans* offers an explanation of the ambiguous characters and narrative voices, and a theorem for conceiving the "trans-self." Trans* leads to conceiving the body as a fluid and flexible set of dynamics defined by motion, transition, and transformative precariousness of the in-betweenness of nepantlism. Its placement in front of any normatively defined category provides an optic that recognizes openness and fluidity of subjective experiences rather than their diagnosis in categorical terms.

The relationship between the categories of sex and their symbolic representation is also addressed by Chilean critic Nelly Richard (1996). She maintains a radical position similar to North American and French feminists, affirming that "sexual difference" is inscribed in the prevailing discourses of patriarchal-logocentric power and, therefore, has a discursive and symbolic character. However, Richard distinguishes herself from them by highlighting the enunciative site from which her theoretical and critical discourse originates: the "postcolonial periphery" of Latin America. She focuses on the local particularities that must be glimpsed in the discourse on sexuality in order not to exclude from the "central" theoretical discourse the reality of the "peripheral experience" of the multiple ethnic, racial, and social groups, as well as address the concrete experience of these groups in the marginal context of Third World countries (733–36). As an example of a peripheral and transgressive sexual experience, Richard mentions the figure of the Chilean transvestite—a being with ambivalent sexual marks—and his/her=*hir* parodic discursive representation in aesthetic discourse. Examples may be found in the narrative of Diamela Eltit, the chronicles of Pedro Lemebel, paintings by Juan Dávila and Carlos Leppe, and theatrical plays by Sergio Vodanovic and Eugenia Prado. From a Latin American perspective, such representations place symbolic and discursive marks of Western culture into a deconstructive (because parodic) mode (Richard 1993: 72–73). Transvestism, as a decentering cultural technique, reveals the indeterminate, ambiguous, flexible, and open element associated with "feminine writing," as an alternative to a normative masculine (thus closed) cultural framework. Richard explains in *Masculino/Femenino* (1993) that the discourse of postmodern feminist criticism considers identity as a mobile and dynamic construction, a "multipositionality of the subject" that presents itself by means of cultural symbolizations that are shifting and mobile (86–89). It questions the integrity of the classical male subject and the stability of gender (79). Like Bellatin in fiction, Richard suggests in her theoretical criticism that "the 'woman' position articulates reading as an active mechanism that stimulates the reader to critique the forced meaning and formulate new contracts of interpretation now favorable to the emergence of alternative and dissident subjectivities" (1996: 744).

In sum, sexuality is a key component of the complex technologies of the self. It appears so in the networks of power that determine the definition and interplay of categories. Nomadic selves are subjectivities beyond gender, "in the sense of being dispersed, not binary, multiple, not dualistic, interconnected, not dialectical and in a constant flux, not fixed" (Braidotti 2002: 80). Once again, emphasis is on the importance of sexual difference, and its reformulation through antinormative queerness, as determining, more than a boundary, a threshold for the elaboration and the expression of other differences within a subject, extending beyond gender and sexuality, beyond humanity. Following Irigaray's theory of the "virtual feminine" and to Deleuze's theory of the becoming-woman/animal/machine/imperceptible, Braidotti argues that "this is a new kind of political subjectivity which no longer assumes the unitary, self-evident subject of modernity or even of 'standpoint' feminism [of multiple but determined positions or perspectives]. This is rather a non-unitary, multiple, complex subject that inhabits several locations and [most importantly] moves between them, though not always with ease" (2002: 261–62). New cartographies are needed to map out different embodied and embedded positions of the nomadic subject of the borderlands. A cartographic account of the trans-subjects of the Neobaroque kaleidoscope of characters and works that we will engage in Chap. 3 creates a critical dialog set up around exchanges of queer, feminist, Chicana borderland and (Latin) Americanist cultural theories, theories that form such cartographies "in a new alliance with nomadic readers" (2002: 262).

Our cartography of borderland and nomadic subjects is based on the frequent sexually ambiguous characters and the themes of androgyny, transvestism, homo and bisexuality, indeterminacy and ambiguity, and physical metamorphosis that appear in the narratives of Hilst, Sarduy, Bellatin, Eltit, Prado, and Echavarren in a prose described by Jo A-mi as "degenerate literature that hybridizes genres […] in a relentless narrative flow" (2016: 291). It is tenable to argue that this combination of the exuberant (neobaroque) form and the presence of characters who are ambiguous and transformative in terms of their sexual identity produces in the text a categorical transgression and transcends hetero and logocentric exclusiveness, largely founded on dualism and binarism in terms of categories of gender, sexuality, and, by extension, literary genre. The fiction that we are dealing with does not adhere to generic limitations of narrative prose and uses forms of other genres in the frequent incursions of dramatic and poetic forms. In the trans-generic discourse and the characters that are represented or speak in the works, the text attempts at transcendence through aesthetic means, something that has been stated by the authors themselves in interviews.[14] Their prose presents itself as a discur-

---

[14] For example, Hilda Hilst states: "I think writing is more for endurance, for existing outside ourselves, in others. […] That is why I think that what drives me to write is a will to surpass myself, to go beyond the petty condition of finitude" (Cristiano Diniz, 2013 *Fico besta* 29–30; my translation). Also, see Hilst's statements in Eliane Robert Moraes (1999: 117) and Sarah Gerard ("The Hilda", 2013: 1).

sive and aesthetic space for surpassing the limiting categorizations of sexuality, a space that lends itself to conceiving it in terms of a transitive multiplicity of binary and non-binary attributes, in the mode of a transitive identity of the trans-self.

Our claims enter a dialogue with gender and queer theory as they explain the role of representation and reception in the process of articulating sexuality and gender. Similarly, language and discourse are key players in the process of decentering and queering normative identities (Butler 1990: 13). This is demonstrated in the (central and decentering) assumption of queerness as "trans*" (Halberstam) and "transvestite" subjectivity (Kulick, Wayar), and as a form of "disidentification" (Muñoz). The role of language in destabilizing sexuality relates to Judith Butler's proposition about the mobilization of gender categories through "disidentification" from the regulatory norms of heterosexual discourse, in the same symbolic space in which identity is both constructed and deconstructed (1993: 4). We argue that the literary and performative discourse of Neobaroque fiction and performance offers effective means for this mobilization and destabilization of sexuality. Queer borderland identities of the Neobaroque work open an aesthetic-discursive space for the emergence of a culturally androgynous America, a "Transmerica" in which a transitive identity—a trans-identity or transentity—of the nomadic self appears.

2.3.4   *Eroticism as Deterritorialization Through Excess*

A connection can be established between desire, body, and textuality by the destabilizing presence of eroticism, which is another subversive element of the neobaroque work (Sarduy 1978 [1972]: 181–82). In the chapter titled "Transits," in *Transpositions* (2006) Braidotti introduces the term "transports" to argue for a sustainable "subject of difference" that she defines in terms of identity production complemented and sustained by the notion of desire, a longing of otherness as a force of positivity in a process of complementarity and interconnectivity with elements that are immanent to all "others" and hence more powerful (in the sense of creative potential). She calls it "the becoming-imperceptible" in otherness. As an example, she provides Virginia Woolf's stream of consciousness technique as a channel for the literary expression of "the radical immanence and structural contingency, of the patterns of repetitions by which differences occur" (189). This radical immanence and contingency (as complementarity with difference) are structural elements of the process of becoming imperceptible with the erasure of the fixed identity of a subject that becomes camouflaged, undetectable, that is, unstable, blurred, and fluid as a result of mixture with otherness. Desire and eroticism, as the mechanics of attraction between "one" and "other", constitute one of the key components for the realization of the transformative process of identity exchangeability, leading to its eventual blurring and dilution.

Similarly, in her conclusions to "Transits," the nomadic theorist goes on to explain that transformation of the self (in relation to an "other") triggers processes of metamorphosis in nomadic transits of subjectivity. As a playful, wasteful, and excessive figuration of desire and affectivity, eroticism exerts a central role in the process of dis- and rearticulating selfhood. "This theory of radical immanence is very simple at heart and intuitively accessible (pace Benhabib). What happens is really a relocation of the function of the subject through the joining of memory and the imagination into propelling a vital force that aims at transformation" (2006: 200). This erotic force is propelled by desire. It can be affirmative and positive in its drive for encountering the Other, or negative in its destructive impulse of excess and (self) annihilation, as observed in the acts of sadomasochism. Artistic and literary representation allow these mainly positive forces to flow into self-realization and creativity: "Locating the potential of affirmation in the realm of not only reason but also of imagination— artistic and literary creation is the site of its recreation and realization, producing a new theory of desire" (200). Into this conceptual space enters the "ethical moment" that Braidotti proposes as an act of transcending ego-oriented negativity itself, transforming it into something positive. This transformation becomes real only if the subject does not assume a judgmental stance regarding oneself or others and recognizes (within oneself) the challenges of not giving into the paranoid-narcissistic self-nexus of exclusive One-ness. Braidotti goes as far as mentioning the point of utter destitution of one's "self" as the ultimate site of undertaking the transformation of exclusive negativity into affirmative inclusiveness (2006: 201). Overcoming the negative forces of desire (domination) is affirmation, the result of a process of transformation of negative into affirmative passions, as an intrinsic expression of (erotic) joy and positivity. As a process, it is constitutive of the subject's potential and capability of enduring or sustaining the actualized form of "finite wholes" for a certain amount of time. As complements with otherness and difference, these wholes can be understood as thresholds for ethical sustainability of nomadism: forces that manage to assemble and combine multiples in one, at least for a while. "They are collective becomings, which involve a selective sort of plurality. They assemble by relations of positivity or affinity with other forces, and they insist or persist in becoming" (2006: 201). In this sense, subjective transformation as "becoming" is a mobile process set in time and space. As painstaking and non-self-evident as it may be, the very process by which the transformation takes place is just as important as its result. Bolstered by eroticism, the driving force behind this process is Desire for change and transformation. It is a question of playing on, winning, playing, losing, but playing on (2006: 202).

What becomes notable in this line of thought is the importance of literature, the arts, theater, music, and film as forms of representation of the transformative process of nomadic subjectivity and of the erotic desire that drives it. It constitutes the expression of a transitional subjectivity emanating from this force of affirmation, the result of the potency of "a joy that goes beyond the metaphysical divide of sexual or other forms of differentiation." The desire for *potentia* (the potential force) as transformative change allows the subject to stretch toward "the outer boundaries of his or her capacity to endure, pushing them open so that they turn into thresholds of becoming" (2006: 202). The name Braidotti gives for this process of in-depth transformation driven by desire (and, in our terms, expressed in the erotic surplus of the transgressive characters and their exuberantly neobaroque aesthetic representation) is "metamorphoses."

In the context of the Neobaroque, eroticism appears as surplus, excess and transgression, the result of desire and a driving force for change, a drive for transgressing limits, breaking the bounds of categories that limit Identity as a normative concept. It constitutes the force that leads to transcending the stable and unitary Self with sexual desire and force, expressed in the body through love, art, and textuality. Eroticism conforms the third underlying component of Borderland Identity along with the previously mentioned intersectional transitivity and queerness. As a desire-driven force, eroticism has been theorized by Georges Bataille in the empirical context of sexuality, ritual, and economy as an element of surplus and overspending; it was also described by Severo Sarduy as linguistic/discursive excess and exuberance in the space of the neobaroque text. Both authors reach similar conclusions about eroticism's destabilizing effect of transcending one's subjectivity toward otherness through excess, a transcendence that projects to the transgression of social and cultural norms.

96   K. A. KULAWIK

In their formal exuberance (marked by artifice, playfulness, and meta-fiction) and thematic opulence (sexual transgression and eroticism), the works of a number of writers and performers in our study create what we propose to call an "eroticism of the word." This coexistence of the erotic element within the aesthetic domain of the literary-artistic work points to Georges Bataille's ideas about eroticism as a surplus (excessive) element of culture, and to Severo Sarduy's reflections regarding the Neobaroque as a type of symbolic textual and cultural overflow figuratively exemplified in transvestism, in which erotic and vestmental trespassing are analogous, in a figurative-metonymical dimension, to transgression in the Act of Writing. The Neobaroque text, semantically considered in a "speech act" (Austin 1962, Searle 1980), assumes a subversive function: it acts upon and against (transgresses) literary and social conventions while seeking a metaphysical and transcendental meaning (Sarduy 1978 [1972]: 181–84). Referring to the writing of Brazilian Hilda Hilst, Eliane Robert Moraes notes that "the writer exceeds her own measure, which results in a remarkable expansion of the concept of transcendence" (117). Similarly, Susanna Busato observes that eroticism in Hilda Hilst's work occupies language, transcends it in its linguistic play with the word that experiences *itself*, self-referentializing, "undressing" discourse (Reguera 11, ref. in Ch.4). The neobaroque literary operation of erotically overflowing/exceeding the word in ambiguous (or queer) sexuality and of surpassing heteronormative forms of sexuality in the exuberant (and erotic) word is precisely one of the transcendental aspects of the works of these writers and performers. It becomes the thematic-structural axis of the fiction, poetry, essay, performance, and painting that we proceed to examine in Chap. 3. Eroticism is also one of the key constitutive mechanisms operating in the articulation of border-land identity. It can also be seen in terms of the erotic of "becoming woman" as a vitalist sensuality, one that remains deeply attached to the embodied subject. This follows the previously mentioned tradition of "enchanted materialism" that Braidotti brings forth in the line of both Deleuze and Irigaray (or French and Continental philosophy). The fact that this tradition, so close to libertine literature or to the *ars erotica* that to Foucault's regret had left mainstream culture, only makes it historically all the more stimulating (Braidotti 2002: 60).

It is meaningful to stress the role that the material body plays in the conformation of the subject and identity, which in our case refers to the double dimension of the empirical (textually or performatively repre-sented) body and the textual body represented through writing and performance in the literary and artistic works. In the last chapter of *Transpositions*, "Transcendence: Transposing Death," Braidotti further develops "the concept of sustainable ethics with reference to my [her] project of nomadic subjectivity as eco-philosophy of the subject" (204), using the materialist, body-oriented approach of philosophical immanence of the "embodied foundations of the subject" as the basis for an ultimate extension of the bodily element through the affective and the erotic, with the erotic understood here as affectivity and desire: "That implies that the crucial mechanism by which the subject operates is the expression of his or her innermost core that is affectivity and the capacity for interrelations" (205). The nomadic ethical-political project is conceptually founded on becomings and transformations as a sensible (and sensuous) approach of pragmatism that stresses the need to act at the empirical level of experimenting with alternate modes of figuring subjectivity and relating to alterity. This, in a philosophy of radical immanence that Braidotti proposes after Deleuze and Irigaray, points to alternative modes of dealing with or relating to the material body ("inhabiting our corporeality" in Braidotti's terms). The critic emphasizes adopting a rigorous stance that does not romanticize philosophical nomadism as an "anarcho-revolutionary philosophy," while maintaining its ascetic style of material-physical bluntness and pragmatism: "Accordingly, nomadic politics is not about a master strategy, but rather about multiple micro-political modes of daily activism or interventions on the world" (205).

The materiality of the body as the carrier and determining force of the self's subjectivity remains vital in the configuration of a nomadic borderland identity. The presence of borders, whether physical or conceptual, remains a point of reference for the subject's situation as a physical entity, a body that is experienced and lived in its transit, transition, and transformation. The body and the border are there, and they remain real and have to be, as markers of human diversity, providing possibilities of transiting spaces between differences of the situated body in the space of the border. "Boundaries must be set and reset; boundaries become thresholds: 'it is less a question of abandoning the politics of specific identity than of supplementing and complicating it' (Massumi 1992: 210)" (Braidotti 2002: 167). This amounts to the recognition that the processes of borderland identity continually go on in an internally differentiating manner. Crossing, trespassing, and transgressing borders and boundaries is a constant rhizomatic and nomadic movement of body/ies on the borders, bodies as carriers of multiple transiting identities.

2.4 Writing the Body and the Body of Writing: Neobaroque Enactment of Identity

The enactment of identity in the Neobaroque work possesses a distinctively material dimension stemming from the reference to the physical body of the represented (intratextual) or empirical (extratextual) subject, on the one hand, and its (also physical) textual and performative representation in the literary and artistic work, on the other hand. The nomadic subject's transgression occurs analogically on two levels. A parallelism may be established between the material embodiment of transgressive identity by the characters (subjects) represented in the aesthetic works and the equally transgressive (because linguistically experimental and genre-breaking) act of writing/performing/visualizing. The aesthetic act represents the symbolization and representation of embodied trans-identities in the literary-artistic works that we proceed to analyze in Chap. 3. Establishing this analogy between the material enactment-embodiment of trans-characters and its transgressively neobaroque written-performative-visual representation renders possible our articulation and theorization of trans-identity (or *transentity*) in an open model of the mobile trans-self. Similarly, focusing on Latin American speculative fiction in *Cyborgs, Sexuality, and the Undead* (2020), Elizabeth Ginway perceives the pragmatic dimension of the body-text relationship in the literary work that conveys a deeper meaning of crisis and transformation in Latin American society. She argues that:

> by focusing on the body—changes in sexual identity, the presence of prosthetics or artificial bodies, and the traits of the living dead and the undead—the authors of these stories were able to convey in an effective and powerful way prevailing anxieties about society, politics, and technology. Thus, in Mexico and Brazil, the transformed, artificial, or distorted body is not simply a rewriting of colonial chronicles or a product of magical realism, but rather a symptom of crisis and change in these two large, industrialized, and ethnically diverse countries. (19)

The material-bodily dimension of the characters sustained in the physical body, or its technological extensions, corresponds to the physical nature of the text as a cultural artifact materialized in writing and performance. The aesthetic act represents a projection of identity transgression (and crisis) through the imaginary-recreated physical embodiment and the representation of this embodiment in writing, performance, and artistic creation by means of "material" bodies marked by signs of sexuality, gender, race, ethnicity, national, and social belonging.

2.4.1 Body, Text, and Performance as Spaces of Transgression and Embodiment of Selfhood

Nomadic displacement and transgression of fictional characters (and empirical subjects) is represented in Neobaroque poetics with the unstable, mobile, and shifting nature of the text, the carrier of dislocated and shifting meaning. The discursive forms symbolizing the body of the nomadic subject are materializations of the decentered and self-conscious nature of the neobaroque work. Its textualization reflects nomadic fluidity and instability through its metadiscursive awareness of being a (discursive) simulation of the nomadic body. With its exuberant forms, Neobaroque representation multiplies the signifying power of the sign and language's plurality of meaning proliferated in the literary/performative work. The text, especially in its aesthetic dimension, shows that it is *per se* transitive and multiple, as is what it represents—the transitive self. In its formal framework, the work, with the signs that conform it, recreates the meaning of nomadism by textually incorporating the values of transitivity, multiplicity, difference, and dialog. The neobaroque text builds on multiplicity in dialog, transitivity, and mobility. It constitutes a transformative aesthetic tool conjoined with the potential to re-configure processes of change of subjectivity with a positive perception of difference that will allow to experience identity "against the centuries-old habit that consists in pathologizing and de-valuing all that is 'different'" (Braidotti 2002: 267). The Neobaroque work would appear in this context as textual "sets of radical mutations acting on the g-local' stage [...] actually *signifying* nothing [fixed]. Beyond signification, these transformations could be taken as the positive [material] expression of nomadic, non-unitary subjectivity" (2002: 267).

Nomadic subjects, however displaced, dispersed, and technologically or naturally structured, are discursively and physically performative in the text/on stage, thus embedded and embodied in the material dimension of writing and performing. By the textual sign's power of signification, they correspond to actual extratextual bodies that are sexualized, ethically and racially marked, socially and nationally situated, and accountable for their own spatial-temporal locations. Therefore, Neobaroque discourse-as-representation allows the nomadic subject's mobility and shifting of categories in textual/staged performativity to articulate a materialized transitive identity, as well as an open and fluid subjectivity, as "the first step towards a new ethics of accountability" (2002: 267), as actual effects of

Neobaroque's meaning-making potential that materializes in an actual (extra)textual trans-self. Ultimately, the reader/viewer of the work articulates the meaning of nomadism as a form of transitive selfhood.

The transgressive character of identity, perceived in the characters of the analyzed works, is the result of transgressive symbolization of open meaning-making that the neobaroque text induces in its exuberance and fragmented, multi-level, metadiscursive character. What matters in the process of nomadic transformation is that it does not occur through a sign based on binary, zero-one, deterministic relationship of signifier and signified, as an object/image representing a conventionally determined and fixed idea or meaning. The representation of the nomadic position of transitive selfhood does not engage the unilinear and dualistic, binary model of the sign as a fixed relation of the signifier and the signified, developed by Ferdinand de Saussure (1955 [1916]). It calls for the application of a triadic (three-part) model of signification, borrowed from Charles S. Peirce (1991). It is a semiotic model of meaning-making that operates with a fragmented and open-ended mode of signification. Identity transformation in the transgressive characters and the resulting/emerging concept of a Trans-Self are hermeneutically conceivable when comparing the identity process to the functioning of the dynamic (three-part or tertiary) sign, as presented in Peirce's semiotic model. It is based on the opening of meaning of the sign carried out by the meaning-carrying element of the "interpretant."

Thus, identity is determined semiotically in a dynamic, movable process of symbolization of a mobile three-part sign. The self refers to a textually materialized (represented) imagined body that shifts between categories; it is ambiguous as it moves, transforms, and combines with multiple other identities. This plural, combinatory, and mobile "trans-identity" is the result of the process of meaning displacement in a plurality or multiplicity of simultaneous identities. They are the result of an historical context of contacts, crossings, and transgressions between the multiple borders-boundaries that have historically formed in the Americas. Gender and sexuality and other categories of race, ethnicity, nationality, socio-economic status, and posthuman condition cross intersectionally in the transitive identity of the nomadic trans-self.

Textual and visual-performative works constitute linguistic, discursive, thus material venues for the destabilization of identity by means of the represented body. Nomadic transgression of borders and boundaries is executed through a semiotic process of creative (artistic) and receptive (reader-viewer) meaning-making activity. Aesthetics achieve meaning as

2 NEOBAROQUE AS TRANSGRESSION: THE LATIN AMERICAN PARADIGM   101

the sum of their creators' writing/performance and the reader/viewer interpretation. Textual and performative representation of transgressive characters (as bodies and voices in the works) ultimately leads the reader/spectator to a transformative mode of experiencing subjectivity and conceptualizing a decentered, fragmented, shifting and fluid image of nomadic trans-identity, situated as on the border of categories.

The act of writing becomes the embodiment, the physical-material projection of the empirical body (as flesh) by the physical representation of the text: the readable script, the visual work, the staged performance. The neobaroque text operates with representational techniques that enable the reader to articulate transformative states of subjectivity and identity transitivity by the inscriptive effect of the "written/visualized body," a body that is enacted. The metadiscursive (self-conscious) character of the neobaroque work facilitates such semanticized somatization of the text as a surface of inscription of identity markers carried out in writing. It is a transformative process of creation, a feminine operation of cultural transgression of the categorical-masculine norm.

The textual representation of the subject—body, voice, persona, or character—through the act of writing is the metonymical equivalent of marking, staining, tattooing, piercing, lacerating, incising, burning, or scarring the body, "the body as inscriptive surface" (Grosz 1994). Writing and, by extension, the body are entities in which uncertainties fluctuate in the blank spaces left between letters, lines, paragraphs, on the non-tattooed parts of skin and extremities. The novelistic and performative characters constitute examples of this bodily inscription—as bodily alteration—taking place on the ornamented surface of the exuberant text (plot) by means of linguistic representation of dress and makeup.

Referring to the process of writing on the bodily surface as a feminine operation of opening meaning by not-naming, in *Gynesis* (1985) Alice Jardine uses Jacques Derrida's deconstructive precepts (especially, his notion of "the logic of the between"[15]), to demonstrate that (literary-

---

[15] Jardine presents an extensive explanation of this concept in Chap. 7 of *Gynesis*, "Thinking the Unrepresentable." The essence of the concept of "in-between" that Derrida uses to deconstruct the presence of the Subject in written representation is summarized in the following excerpt: "For what Derrida *is* working on has no name or place—at least not yet. Lacan's Real? Not exactly. The trace of *différance* is even more thoroughly unnamable, unrepresentable, than Lacan's Real: 'There is no *name* for it at all' (Derrida, *Margins of Philosophy* 26). Neither inner nor outer, it is in-between (*entre*), it enters (*entre*), it inter-venes between all metaphysical oppositions. And, as we shall see later, 'When the middle of an opposition is not the passageway of a mediation, there is every chance that the opposition is not pertinent. The consequences are boundless' (*Margins* 255–56)" (132; emphasis in original).

artistic-fictional) writing is a feminine operation of un-fixing the presence of a stable Subject, thus, of forming a space of ambiguity: "Rather, it is woman that must be released from her metaphysical bonding and it is writing, as 'feminine operation,' that can and does subvert the history of that metaphysics. The attributes of writing are the attributes of 'woman'— that which disturbs the Subject, Dialectic, and Truth is feminine in its essence" (183). The formation of the subject in its material-bodily dimension is the result of both fictional and documentary/critical "feminine writing process" of fluidity and opening, a radical immanence of bodily materialization, a process of symbolic inscription on the body's physical, material surface.

When Cherríe Moraga (2011) speaks of the transformative experience of the shaman's teachings of the Old Way, she situates her selfhood in "that blessed moment between breaths in meditation where time is of no consequence and the 'I' disappears. Such acts bring one back to a profound place of origin and shared identity, where me is subsumed by we, and violence against any part of that we becomes unthinkable" (81). Connecting this experience to the writing-creative process, Moraga adds that "[w]riting too is one of these acts. The best of creative writing [...] is able to traverse great borders of mind and matter. The distinctions disappear. Our present moment becomes history. History is enacted myth" (81). Likewise, Derrida's logic of in-between leads to several epistemological consequences: imbalance and erasure lead to violent operations of text-/sex-ual disarticulation in the discursive act of naming and un-naming. It is a textual operation carried out in writing that does not preclude an inherent violence in the attribution of a "named" category: "[...] if naming is always violence, is the process of being un-named through a re-naming-in-parts any less violent?" (Jardine 183). According to Jardine (who refers to Sarah Kofman), the mutual approach of the text to the corporeal-sexual "form" is expressed as a "sexualization of the text" and a "textualization of sex": "[...] swinging between the sexes, no longer opposed but heterogeneous, the object of speculation becomes strange as it moves toward that space [of in-between] of general equivalence, so constantly devalued by our history. It opens onto a new dimension of heterosexual erotics" (182).

2 NEOBAROQUE AS TRANSGRESSION: THE LATIN AMERICAN PARADIGM 103

This two-directional operation of sex-/text-ualization is precisely what occurs in the decategorizing operation taking place in the exuberant discourse of the neobaroque text. The disintegration of sexual categories is the semantic effect of the destabilizing discursive procedures of artifice, parody, and formal exuberance, accompanied by metadiscursive awareness. Illustrating this operation, René Prieto points to how the body, in its materiality, relates to the act of writing by "getting rid of words" in the avant-gardist work of Argentinian Tununa Mercado:

> Tearing away the classic unities and modifying the typically passive posture of readers are not the only features Mercado alters in her iconoclastic revision of the novel. Even the wall that traditionally stands between the sexes topples in the act of love as she portrays it: 'penis and vagina simultaneously one and the same' (110 -Mercado). Erasing differences and bringing about a fusion by means of erotic love is the key to an innovation whose highly poetic imagery introduces a fresh way to envision the relationship between reader and writer. Mercado feels the time has come to get rid of words in order to focus on the tasks of the body. The bodies she portrays are focused on physical pleasure, on jouissance; their genders and the roles they play are not explicitly defined. Given the high degree of ambiguity concerning genders and situations, the reader, like the characters in the fiction, ends up actively relying on his or her imagination and freely engaging with a text that has forsaken coercive strictures of traditional prose fiction designed to plant a single image in our minds. (2000: 252)

This symbolic/semiotic process of bodily sexualization (or any other category marking) within the written/performed text is attained in Mercado through the open, blank, indetermined spaces that correspond to the sexually indeterminate bodies of the characters. It takes place through reception, in the reader's imagination. The process of writing as textualization of sexuality, gender, or any identity category is represented in the neobaroque text metadiscursively as discursive ambiguation or generation of open meaning. This semantic effect is attained by the works that we will discuss in Chap. 3. The resulting ambiguity of body-sex-gender-(literary) genre is not the only consequence of the discursive operation noted by Prieto in Mercado's narrative. The violence of appropriation through naming, which is implicit in language's denominative action, is destabilized in the secondary displacing operation of connotation, especially if it is charged with eroticism. The violence of representation and un-representation (discursive deconstruction) is denoted by the text in the erotic pleasure of the sexual act; other times, it is in the explicit contents and images of sexualized bodies in violent acts involving the infliction of pain and mutilation. Erotic violence is represented in the morpho-syntactic disintegration of the text itself, in the visual aspect of the work at the connotative level of blank spaces/silences, in the bold metaphors and ruptured words, voice intonation and pitch, in the cleavages between the broken lines of the disintegrat-ing/-ed text, in which coherent meaning disperses and dissolves, and with it, the categories of identity undergoing fragmentation and ultimate erasure.

In "Violence of Rhetoric" in *Technologies of Gender*, Teresa de Lauretis draws on Peirce's three-part sign as a relationship of the iconic meaning carrier (*representamen*) to its represented *object* by means of an *interpretant* (the processor element). She refers to the sign's meaning-making process as a type of violence implicit in all writing and representation that inevitably has to go through a semiotic process of "somatization" (or embodiment): "Thus, as we use signs or produce interpretants, their significant effects must pass through each of us, each body and each consciousness, before they may produce an effect or an action upon the world. Finally, then, the individual's habit as a semiotic production is both the result and the condition of the social production of meaning" (41). Both the institutionalized (categorized) and transformed (transgressive and subversive) representation of the body become carriers and producers of meaning in categories that are linguistically determined through symbolizations of power and its opposing transgressive subjectivity.

Body and text—the textualization of the body and the somatization of the text—are complementarily interrelated. The structuring of identity is determined in a two-way transit between semiotic-discursive textualization of a psychoanalytically inscribed set of affections or codes and the corporal flows of a materially biological body. The role of the material dimension of the body and its un-natural and simulated (social, symbolic, and representational), but also unessential (not codified nor discursively enforced) open condition in the neobaroque text enhances the structuring of a nomadic and metamorphous subject that moves between the material and symbolic. Neither is the bodily material nature of this subject biologically determined but rather socially and symbolically (self-) constructed by an interplay of affective forces taking place in the process of representation:

The embodiedness of the subject is a form of bodily materiality, not of the natural, biological kind. I take the body as the complex interplay of highly constructed social and symbolic forces: It is not an essence, let alone a biological substance, but a play of forces, a surface of intensities, pure simulacra without originals. This 'intensive' redefinition of the body situates it within a complex interplay of social and affective forces. This is also a clear move away from the psychoanalytic idea of the body as a map of semiotic inscriptions and culturally enforced codes. I see it instead as a transformer and relay point for the flow of energies: a surface of intensities. (Braidotti 2002: 20–21)

The image of the body as a transformer represents a bundle of contradictions, a zoological entity, a genetic databank, transferer of energies and intensities (both material and symbolic), also a bio-social entity in the sense of codified, personalized memories. This makes it part animal, part machine, notwithstanding the dualistic opposition (and separation) of these two dimensions maintained by our culture. The body of the borderland involves the multiple variables that form nomadic identity with its representation in its material referent—the body. These variables cross intersectionally as Braidotti observes:

> The embodied subject is thus a process of intersecting forces (affects) and spacio-temporal variables (connections). I take the concept of the body as referring to the multifunctional and complex structure of subjectivity. This is the specifically human capacity for simultaneously incorporating and transcending the very variables—class, race, sex, nationality, culture, etc.—which structure it. This in turn affects the notion of the social imaginary. The process of becoming-subject requires sets of cultural mediation; the subject has to deal with material and semiotic conditions, that is to say institutional sets of rules and regulations as well as the forms of cultural representation and sustain them. (2002: 21)

The semiotic, representational, culturally mediated aspect of subjectivity as "becoming subject" is part of the social imaginary that is textually materialized in the aesthetic expression of the neobaroque work in the written, painted, and performed text.

2.4.2 Writing-Performing the Nomadic Body: A Material and Symbolic Relationship

Writing (extended to Performance) and Reading can consequently be perceived as discursive experiences in the symbolic process of "becoming," in its extended meaning of nomadic becoming minoritarian. This includes the material experience of perceiving and living the represented body in the sense of embodying identity in multiple transitory forms. Texts, as forms of the subject's bodily representation, are not closed, unitary entities, but can rather be assimilated, consummated, taken up, used—or not—in the dynamic interpretation process. Transgression and identity transition occur in the act of writing/performing and, on the other end of the communicative spectrum, in the act of reception which corresponds to the fulfillment of a text by the reader/spectator. Accordingly, "texts are accounted for like territories, regions, or embodied areas of enframed and formatted intensity" (Braidotti 2002: 96). The dynamic nature of this writer-reader relationship becomes particularly evident with then neobaroque text because of its symbolizing potential of transgression and subversion.

Following the Deleuzian reading that Braidotti carries out, we can assume the act of writing as a symbolic and material vehicle of deterritorialization, of a nomadic dis- and rearticulation and reconfiguration of identity. Consequently, the Neobaroque as "style" acquires a special role, speed and intensity, engaging *certain textual effects* that engender processes of becoming. The body-text relationship is a contribution of Gilles Deleuze in "a sort of pragmatics of the affective forces that shape certain texts" (2002: 96). Deleuzian-based French feminism follows a strategy of positionality in terms of situating the body strategically and intersectionally in its textual representation and performance:

> Irigaray 'brings the body back into play, not as the rock of feminism, but as a mobile set of differences' (Chanter 1995: 46). The body is then an interface, a threshold, a field of intersecting material and symbolic forces; it is a surface where multiple codes (race, sex, class, age, etc.) are inscribed intersectionally; it is a cultural construction that capitalizes on energies of a heterogeneous, discontinuous, and unconscious nature. The body, which, for Beauvoir, was one's primary 'situation,' in reality is now seen as a situated self, as an embodied positioning of the self. This renewed sense of complexity aims to stimulate anew a revision and redefinition of contemporary

2 NEOBAROQUE AS TRANSGRESSION: THE LATIN AMERICAN PARADIGM   107

subjectivity. This vision of the body contains sexuality as a process and as a constitutive element. (Braidotti 2002: 25)

The body, in the sense conferred to it by Irigaray, is a situated entity in its material and empirical existence, also in its textual/semiotic representation. The aesthetic (literary and artistic) expression of the body materializes in "style" of which the Neobaroque is an example. This discursive/ textual relation of the nomadic subjectivity with its embodiment in a material-physical self—a sexually, racially, ethnically, socially, technologically marked physical body that lives out plurally its incarnations—applies to the very crux of the decentering of identity as a twofold process of body relating to writing/textuality, which then relates back to the body.

The metatextual character of neobaroque discourse, conscious of its arbitrariness, facilitates the explanation of the relationship between the mutant corporality of the sexually transgressive characters and the genre-breaking experimentation of the ornate metafictional character of the neo-baroque text/visual work. For Alice Jardine, writing is an eroticized (bodily material) operation of metadiscursivity (or the consciousness of the writing process), marked by the sign of the ambiguous sex. It is also equivalent to the mobility and openness of feminine signification. In *Gynesis*, she puts forward Derrida's thought on the feminine function in the dissimulation, ornamentation, deception, and artifice that constitute the artistic work (1985: 195).[16] The space of writing acquires identity-formative and erotic (claimed as feminine) dimensions through which ambiguous sexuality is created through the act of writing in the space of the "gendered" text/performance. The narrative, in its literary written from, is textually allegorized in the representation of the body-as-writing, materialized as writing of the subject's body. In its textual form, it is metaphorically transposed into the "body" of and in writing—the site of identity creation. The text, as well as the performative act, creates a figurative-but-materialized body, a staged or textually represented subject whose identity is in fugue. The desired—open, transgressive, and

[16] "The 'feminine operation' is designated by the spacings in and by Nietzsche of 'woman'—as *affirmative*: 'she [woman] is twice model, at once lauded and condemned. Here, in a manner like to that of writing, surely and safely [...] she plays at dissimulation, at ornamentation, deceit, artifice, at an artist's philosophy. Hers is an affirmative power' ([Derrida cit. by Jardine] *Spurs*: p. 67). [...] Woman is not to be found through the Truths and Lies of concept and knowledge, 'yet it is impossible to resist looking for her' (*Spurs*: p. 71)" (Jardine 195; emphasis in original).

108 K. A. KULAWIK

transitive—identity becomes textualized, and acts out its materiality in the textual or visual (and staged) work of art.

In Neobaroque works, writing corresponds to the eroticized body in the haptic, usually sexual act of physical contact of intercourse, caress, but also slashing, incision, razor cutting on the skin, or the pen and ink on paper. Writing is presented as an erotic act, at once intersubjective, intimately affective, occasionally violent, but also artistic, literary, communicative and, by extension, political. An affective or violent erotic relationship becomes a metaphor for the political situation of a marginalized racial or ethnic group, a country enduring dictatorship or revolution. The act of writing as a narrative theme (in a metanarrative dimension), visible especially in the works of Sarduy, Bellatin, Eltit, Prado, and Hilst, is explicitly related to the transformative sexual and erotic, sometimes violent and sadistic act. Within the narrative texts of these authors, the process of writing is figuratively (metonymically) associated with erotic, desire-driven sexual activity. The dimensions of textual-creative and erotic activity are confused and, indeed, indistinguishable. The body-writing relationship in these works is achievable in the form of a strong metadiscursive consciousness of the creative process of writing and performing.

The body is a symbolically inscribed material surface to the extent that meanings are inscribed on it from birth. It is sexed, gendered, racialized, and de-humanized by technology with categorical inscriptions that, as conventional signs, can be "opened" and interpreted in multiple ways through the "interpretant" function/capacity of Peirce's triadic sign. In this line of thought Elizabeth Grosz proceeds with her body-sex-writing relationship, taking into account male and female distinctions in the constitution of the physical body as the main point of reference for its interpretation:

> I am suggesting that, in feminist terms, at least, it is problematic to see the body as a blank, passive page, a neutral 'medium' of signifier for the inscription of a text. If the writing of inscription metaphor is to be of any use for feminism—and I believe that it can be extremely useful—the specific modes of materiality of the page/body must be taken into account: one and the same message, inscribed on a male or a female body, does not always or even usually mean the same thing or result in the same text. (1994: 156)

These conventional symbolizations and meanings of the body are discursively constituted and articulate a subject's identity in an assigned manner. They are marks placed externally by others (as social stigmas) or internally (subjective choice of clothing, adornment, tattooing and piercing) in the communication of emotional states and distinctions of identity. Alice Jardine (1985) denominates the process of identity formation with the term *gynesis*, which she defines as the "becoming of feminine identity" with the mediation of the woman's body in the discursive-cultural process of interpretation. The body is like a linguistic sign that involves the presence of the interpretant: a formative symbolic space, dynamic, unfinished due to its insertion in a specific and ever-changing social context. She agrees in this respect with Elizabeth Grosz: "Not being self-identical, the body must be seen as a series of processes of becoming, rather than as a fixed state of being" (1994: 12). An important part of Grosz's feminist theoretical proposal is the reevaluation of the body in her analysis of culture, considering it a formative element of identity, a dynamic element in the process of "becoming." Here, she coincides with Deleuze and Perlongher in their take on the concepts of *rhizome* and *devenir* as horizontal relationships of culturally ascribed traits of identity. Grosz stresses the importance of the different physical marks made on the dynamic and transforming body, considered as the surface of "social incisions" as meaning-making signatures, following previous philosophical and methodological blueprints of Lingis, Nietzsche, and Freud.[17]

The articulation of a nomadic trans-self benefits from Jack Halberstam's proposition of constructing the trans* body on the basis of Lucas Crawford's idea of understanding the body through an architectural logic: "If we shift our focus, as Crawford proposes, away from the housing of the body and toward the notion of 'transition'—perpetual transition—we can commit to a horizon of possibility where the future is not male or female but transgender" (131).[18] This transition would apply to multiple categorical lines of identity, situated on the axes of the material and the textual body of Writing/Performance. Trans* bodies point to fragmented, unfinished, broken-beyond-repair forms to illustrate the body as a physical entity *always under construction*. Whatever the social, cultural, and legal

---

[17] As Grosz explains that: "Alphonso Lingis sketches an account of the body as a surface of erotogenic intensity which combines elements of the Nietzschean notion of the body as a surface of social incision, the Freudian and phenomenological conceptions of the libidinal investments in narcissistically privileged bodily zones and organs" (1994: 138).

[18] Halberstam quotes Crawford's association of sexuality with a body architecture: "I am taken with the idea that, as Crawford puts it, 'transgender and transsexuality may even be exemplary architectural practices' [...] Crawford goes one step further and looks at the way an architectural logic informs our understanding of the body" (131).

implications of perceiving trans* bodies are, they are "also a site for invention, imagination, fabulous projection. Trans* bodies represent the art of becoming, the necessity of imagining, and the fleshly insistence of transitivity" (135–36). This space of invention and imagination brought up by Halberstam takes us to the textual-verbal-discursive dimension of refiguring the body through symbolic and semiotic means, in the space of the Sign and its Interpretant, in the realm of literature and visual art, in the sphere of textuality and performance, in the open-ended forms of neobaroque exuberance. The Neobaroque, as a destabilizing style of artifice, parody, and eroticism, enhances the relationship between textuality, sexuality, and actual physical embodiment of nomadic subjects. As Braidotti states, "[t]he notion of the embodied or fleshed subject is central to my understanding of the kind of philosophical materialism which I support. […] [in] the extent to which it highlights the bodily structure of subjectivity and consequently also the issues of sexuality and sexual difference" (2002: 20).

The following "transformative flow" chart in Fig. 2.2 illustrates the process of embodiment through writing, considering the Act of Writing as a form of embodiment of subjectivity in the process of nomadic identity trans-formation. It explains the relationship between the sexual Body and the performed/written Text in the process of symbolization of sexuality and the formation of a transitive Identity that takes place in the Neobaroque text, a literary representation of the social fabric of culture. Additionally, it illustrates the semiotic process on the two levels of the relationship between text (semantics or meaning-making form—in the lower line) and context (pragmatics or meaning-generating content—in the upper line):

Fig. 2.2 Stages of the literary-semiotic process of identity formation

The two levels of content and form (upper and lower row, respectively) show the relationship in the meaning-making process between transgressive identity formation (in the upper row)—from body-sexuality to identity to socio-cultural convention—and its textualization (in the lower row) in Writing and Neobaroque style and Literature as literary-cultural representation of nomadism.

2.4.3 Performative Transits of Selfhood: Unwriting Genders and Genres

In the nomadic process of borderland subjectivity, identity becomes a performative act, a material (textual or staged) embodiment of discursive roles assigned by society, embedded in convention and governed by power structures. It constitutes the assuming, living, and playing out of roles in a combinatory adjustment to two spheres: one is the socio-political and cultural context, the second relates to affectivity and desire at the individual level. The performative character of selfhood articulation underlies the process of formulating nomadic selfhood within the neobaroque text. As a transgressive act, it also leads to modelling a trans-self as a conceptual possibility for a theory of transitivity.

In "El barroco y el neobarroco" (1972), Severo Sarduy considers the playful and performative aspect of eroticism as one of the constitutive characteristics of the baroque aesthetic space marked by un(re)productive (erotic) squandering, and establishes a relationship between artistic creation, writing, eroticism, and the performativity of identity constituted in the playing out of sexual roles:

> [...] this obsessive repetition of a useless thing [...] is what determines the baroque as *play*, in opposition to the determination of the classical work as work [...] How much *wasted* work, how much play and waste, how much effort without functionality! [...] Play, loss, waste and pleasure, that is, eroticism as an activity that is always purely ludic, which is nothing more than a parody of the function of reproduction, a transgression of the useful, of the "natural" dialogue of bodies. (182; my translation, emphasis in original)

The performative character of the identity-forming process is perceived as an "embodied" enactment of otherness from its discursive/textual perspective of rhetorical (and aesthetic) distancing—through parody and satire—necessary for acquiring cultural and categorical neutrality. One of

112   K. A. KULAWIK

performance art's leading practitioners and theorizers, Coco Fusco states that "[o]ur [performative] project concentrated on the 'zero degree' of intercultural relations in an attempt to define a point of origin for the debates that link 'discovery' and 'Otherness'" (1995: 39–40). The key component of Performance Art as an artistic genre, with the leading example of Fusco's and Gómez-Peña's work, is the blurring of all kinds of distinctions (boundaries) between the disciplines (intersectionality) and between the art object and the body (as acted or embodied performance), between fantasy and reality (as live spectacle), and between historical documentation and its dramatic reenactment (use of dioramas as props). The scene (or staging) of the performative act with living subjects—the artists and the spectators, even the guards—provides an interactive and "parodically didactic" setting for performance that goes beyond the reach of textuality and the literary text (Fusco 62). This appears to be, in Fusco's terms, performance's biggest potential in the identity dis- and rearticulation process. However, the issue with such dramatization lies in the interpretative mechanism of a direct, live, and preconditioned (prejudiced) spectator who is figuratively "put on the spot." In performance, "[h]ow does one prove that our fiction, which only could exist in the live interactions with others, was a scripted event and that editing could have only reconstituted it? How does one impress upon documentarians that a performance artist's likeness is not raw material but self-consciously constructed art?" (62). This constructive dimension is the result of a cultural text composed in the writing-creative process. With its simulating, fictional-imaginary, and linguistic dimension, performance appears as a self-conscious symbolic textualization of history and the cultural document in the ambiguous borderland space of the aesthetic-theatrical imaginary.

The transformative process of identity nomadism takes place in the act of performance with the technique of creative or strategic mimesis as a "positive simulation" of cultural categories that does not essentialize an "original," but rather parodically plays on its copy/-ies. Performative simulation resembles the fugue-like neobaroque text: the transformative pulse of evolving, a copy of a copy, a parodic simulation of a prescribed model rather than a confirmation of an original, as we will explain in Chap. 4 with Jean Baudrillard's theory of simulacra and the neobaroque text's use of simulatory techniques of masking. From this perspective, Writing becomes a metaphor for transvestism, a simulating "textual mask" that functions in the same way as the "false" and displaced exterior appearance of the transvestite. Cuban Severo Sarduy, whose novels share in this sense similarities

2 NEOBAROQUE AS TRANSGRESSION: THE LATIN AMERICAN PARADIGM   113

with Bellatin's, explains in *Escrito sobre un cuerpo* [Written on a Body, 1969] that:

> The apparent exteriority of the text, the surface, that *mask* deceives us, "since, if there is a mask, there is nothing behind it; surface that hides nothing but itself. [...] The mask makes us believe that there is a depth, but what it masks is itself: the mask simulates dissimulation to dissimulate that it is nothing but simulation." [quoted from Jean-Louis Baudry] (1987: 262; my translation, emphasis in original)

Sarduy determines an analogy between writing and transvestism. The figurative dimension of language, especially in poetic literature that emphasizes "signifiers" as linguistic signs that create an "effect of meaning," resembles the simulation and masking (of meaning and gender) that the cross-dresser performs in *hir* symbolic use of clothing and makeup (Sarduy 1990: 224). The transvestite breaks the social law by exceeding and overstepping ("hypertelically"[19] according to Sarduy) the categories of gender, and even of life and death. Even so, for Sarduy language constructs meaning in the symbolic analogy of dressing and putting on makeup, and in other activities of the cross-dresser. The Cuban author draws an analogy between the act of writing as simulation (by way of "cross-dressing" literal meaning) and the disguise that a transvestite makes of *hir* sexuality, transgressing the distinctions of the two sexes, prescriptively established according to binary patterns: "Transvestism [...] would be the best metaphor for what writing is: [...] *the very fact of transvestism* [...] the coexistence, in a single body, of masculine and feminine signifiers: the tension, the repulsion, the antagonism that it grows between them" (Sarduy 1987: 262–63; my translation, emphasis in original). The use of the mask, disguise, and makeup are classic forms of performative simulation based on artifice, a key component of the neobaroque text. Analogously, in *Trans*: A Quick and Quirky Account of Gender Variability*, Jack Halberstam points out that young people of today who cross-identify have the capability to imagine themselves into other bodies, making them feel truer to who they are (2). On the other hand, the author warns about the insufficiency of the process of naming (as labeling) these bodies and all the new emerging identities. Bodies and identities in their performative

---

[19] The word "hypertelic" appears in the *Novo Dicionário Aurélio* (2005) and is associated with "hipertelia": "1. Zool. Extreme degree of coloration or ornamentation that cannot be explained in terms of utility" (n.p., digital CD version; my translation).

character are just that: bodies in transit, in movement of meaning. Trans-identity as un-identity, as the un-named, or unnamable, is a performative act carried out by simulation of the unnamable:

> [...] countless transgender men and women fell between the cracks of the classifications systems designed to explain their plight and found themselves stranded in unnamable realms of embodiment. Today we have an abundance of names for who we are, and some people actively desire that space of the unnamable again. This book explains how we came to be trans* and why having a name for oneself can be as damaging as lacking one. (4)

Performance's "theory-making power" in the identity deconstruction process of "unnaming" the self is exalted by José Esteban Muñoz in *Disidentifications* (1999). He presents an array of queer performers of color as cultural transformers and creators of cultural theory by means of the art of performance, stating that "[... presenting] artists who are considered here as not only culture makers but also theory producers is not to take an anti-theory position. My chapter on Davis' terrorist drag employs Antonio Gramsci's theory of organic intellectuals in an effort to emphasize the theory-making power of performance" (33–34). Muñoz uses the term "queer of color" to describe most of the Latino and Afro-American cultural performers/makers who appear in his book, while expounding performance art's possibilities to represent "these subjects' different identity components that occupy adjacent spaces and are not comfortably situated in any one discourse of minority subjectivity." He calls these performers' presence and location "hybridized identificatory positions" that are "always in transit, shuttling between different identity vectors" (32). Speaking of performance as a live, interactive form of art, Muñoz also points to the role of the viewers who, many times minoritarian, are not merely passive subjects marked by traditional paradigms of identity, but "they are active participant spectators who can mutate and restructure stale patterns within dominant media" (29). This indicates that performance's capacity to transgress stable patterns of both gender and genre lies in the potential of active, live, and critical representation based on the use of parody and humor. According to Muñoz, performance has the ability "to unpack meanings in an effort to dismantle dominant codes of culture" and achieve, through what he calls "disidentificatory methods," a paradigm of oppositional (critical) reception (26).

One must be cautious not to reinvest in "newly" categorical or normative, readopted notions of femininity or queerness in the process of exposing gender hierarchies. It should be a precaution to not re-essentialize trans-identity in terms of a mere spectacle, a theatrical playing out of roles, when approaching figurative representations of the body. Performance's role as an act or technique is that of articulating the fragments of identity that are left once the subject transits the borderlands of *nepantla* and transgresses the normative, prescriptive notion of a determined (assigned) identity (the remaining pieces of Man, Woman, White, of Color, American or Latino). Performance as representation is not foundational of a new fixed or determined identity. This art is a representation of the transitivity of identity, summed up in the term "trans*" as trans-identity.

We are aware that some versions of feminisms are critical of viewing femininity as pure artifice, as theater and performance. Some trans* theorists (Halberstam cites Julia Serano) resist this notion of femininity, or gender in general, as pure performance. Their concern is that "adopting performativity as a theoretical rubric implies, in a transphobic way, that trans* gender is not real, material, authentic" (120). However, we argue that even the close relationship between queerness and gender performativity (as could take place in transsexuality) can adopt a non-essential, non-performative relation to materiality. Halberstam points to the fact that indeed "[t]here are transsexuals who seek very pointedly to be non-performative, to be constative, quite simply, to be" (121). We understand this caveat as an opening to the complexity of the relationship between the "real-life" empirical experience of identity and its figurative representation in artistic contexts of the fictional text, of performance and the visual work. The semiotic approach that we propose in this analysis may still be, according to Halberstam, a theoretically or philosophically based avenue to "articulate in a gloriously complex way many of the misgivings that transgender theorists felt about queer conjuring of gender flexibility, gender plasticity, and gender performance. This emphasis on the real for trans* people was a valuable intervention in the late 1990s" (121), and continues to be in this study of Neobaroque aesthetics.

Crafting selfhood in real-world activities still involves an element of performance—as use of visual methodologies of embodiment of identity. It entails disturbing normative clichés by representing without fetishizing bodies that simply display an inversion of categories or are lodged between binary gender/racial labels to an audience expectant of orderly arrangements of categories. To achieve this, Halberstam points to the possibilities of performative ambiguation offered by "haptic" experiences (perceived directly by visual or physical con-tact) of performance in the real-life material experience of the body, as "a path around the conundrum of binary visual plane (what is not male appears to be female, what is not female appears to be male). Indeed, the haptic offers a great aesthetic frame for trans*representation in general" (89–90). This implies resorting to an interactive, sensorially perceived art, such as the Neobaroque works that we engage in our analysis. As we will observe in Chap. 3, the haptic effect of nomadic identity embodiment is a crucial element in the performance of Susy Shock, Naty Menstrual, the Familia Galán, Francisco Copello, Eugenia Prado, and even in the narrative and critical prose of Severo Sarduy, Diamela Eltit, and Roberto Echavarren.

Haptics reveal associations between the body and its symbolic recreation through performance. The different ways that identity's meaning can be read by way of experiencing the physically contained body is expressed in performance as:

> "a visual erotics that offers its object to the viewer but only on condition that its unknowability remain intact, and that the viewer, in coming closer, give up his or her own mastery" [a quote from Laura Marks, *Touch*: 20]. As this quote indicates, hapticality organizes meaning, knowing, and seeing in ways that exceed rational, sense-making enterprises and instead force the viewer to examine their own relations to truth and authenticity. This is a perfect frame for the trans* body, which, in the end, does not seek to be seen and known but rather wishes to throw the organization of all bodies into doubt. (90)

Haptics in art constitute a will to know and a remapping of the gendered body, foregoing the symbolic Phallus-Logos, and seeking knowledge via the hand, the finger, the arm, the body in bits and pieces. The haptic body and self are not assumed in advance. They are acted out, improvised, and performed repeatedly by a willful subject capable of freeing a sense of liberation through bewilderment (91–92). Halberstam takes the haptic along with a sense of queer temporality in the nameable and unknowable experience of embodiment as the foundation for examining how trans bodies have been represented in the last decades in film and literature to demonstrate the indefiniteness, non-specificity, and open-endedness of trans* representation (92). In the context of transgressive characters in Latin American performance, this affects the identity-forming process of transformation into nomadic borderland selves, as exemplified in the next chapter.

The haptic element of neobaroque narrative and performativity constitutes a catalytic and political force of excess of representation of the hereto-now unrepresentable, eccentric, and non-static multiplicity that has been culturally coded as the hybrid and displaced "feminine":

> By dialectical opposition, Woman as the Other of this [masculine, universal] subject is deprived of all these attributes. She is thus reduced to unrepresentability within the male symbolic system, be it by lack, by excess or by perennial displacement of her subject-positions. Even feminine sexuality is defined by Irigaray (1997) as not-one, that is to say multiple and complex and ex-centric to phallic genitality. (Braidotti 2002: 24; emphasis in original)

As such, Neobaroque textuality and performance represent an eccentric, exuberant, and boundary-breaking mode of expressing the unrepresentable "feminine," the nomadic trans-self.

These political implications lead Braidotti to the conclusion that, through the strategy of textualizing the feminine by both feminist and aesthetic discourse, the "other of the Other" is represented as a trans- or meta-identity, a *transentity* embodied in the nomadic trans-self. The representation of otherness as gender queerness is materialized in performance, as in the neobaroque text. The relativization of the masculine and feminine leads to perceive sexuality as a textual and performative representation. It can be written and acted out as a fragmented entity with undefinable attributes, in a fluid process of dynamic and unstable combinations of selfhood. According to Deleuze, it is a "becoming," a passage between multiple states of self-realization of the "I." This "dialogical" state of the subject's self-constitution presents itself through the (erotic) "waste" of signifiers in performance. It appears on the textual page or performative stage, and, by extension, in the conceptual realm of subjectivity, as a subversive squandering (*dépense*) of a surplus—Bataille's "eroticism." Sexuality is transitive, fluctuating, and dialogical. The subject, as a unit, is "de-subjectified" through figurative-performative procedures of masking-simulating a self-in-otherness, in different forms of cross-dressing and androgenizing, in queerness. Writing and performance achieve this through the exuberance of attributes, the overflow of signifiers, of words, the linguistic-narrative procedures of aesthetic representation.

The "de-subjectification" or dispersion of the unitary-homogeneous subject, transformed into a plural-nonhomogeneous "one," may be represented schematically in Fig. 2.3.

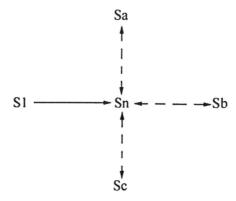

Fig. 2.3 Dispersion of unitary Subject/Identity (S1) into plural-transitive subjects/identities (Sn > a–c)

Following Judith Butler, Julia Kushigian considers the dispersion and (re)articulation of identity a discursive (symbolic) process of a desire-driven, emotionally conditioned "erotic struggle" of creation of the body in "a kind of action that goes beyond the binary oppositions of masculine and feminine gender. It produces an erotic struggle to create new categories born on top of the rubble of the old ones, to find a new way of creating a body within the cultural field" (1999: 1614; my translation). This performative process of identity creation taking place in neobaroque discourse presents the possibility of formulating a model of the nomadic trans-self. It refers to the concept of "becoming," explained by Néstor Perlongher (who himself relies on Deleuze[20]), that defines the performative constitution of subjects without center, the de-subjectified, dynamic individuations that form "transentity" as "collective *agenciamientos*" ["agencings"], "instantaneous individuations," "minorizations and marginalizations" in centrifugal movements from the periphery, from the margins (1997: 66–68). Perlongher's view of "becoming," which we will

---

[20] We refer here to Perlongher's and Deleuze's ideas of "nomadism" and "displacement" applied to the process of identity formation. This process is allegorically compared to the movement of a caravan and camels in constant displacement and transition. Perlongher's reflection on nomadic identity in *Prosa plebeya* (1997) is founded on *Dialogues* by Gilles Deleuze and Claire Parnet (1987a: 34–42).

examine in greater detail in Sect. 4.3, relates to the state of in-betweenness of the nomadic subject in its process of identity formation:

> These processes of marginalization, of escape, to varying degrees, release *devenires* (molecular particles) that throw the subject adrift along the edges of the conventional pattern of behavior. [...] To become is not to transform oneself into another, but to enter into an (aberrant) alliance, into contagion [contact], into *inmistión* [immersion] with (the) different. Becoming does not go from one point to another, but enters into the "between" of the medium, it is that "between." (68; my translation, emphasis in original)

This new conception of transitive sexuality and gender expressed in hybrid multi-genre literary and artistic forms no longer represents a unity but a dispersion, dialog, and "becoming" in a process of nomadic transition. It is the result of figuration carried out by Neobaroque discourse in the conceptual space of identity categories. It is a gateway for modeling a new discourse on the transformative dispersion of identity, a decategorization or disidentification of the subject, whether sexual or cultural, in the space of postmodern fragmentation. The nomadic trans-self that applies to undefining the (Latin) American self, and (post)human identity as such, is exemplified in the transgressions of the ambiguous characters, voices, and subjects in the works of several Latin American writers and performative-visual artists whose works we proceed to examine in the next chapter. There, we invite the patient reader to undertake a textual and semiotic journey across the American continents with stops to delve into literary and artistic pieces at sites where writers and artists transgressed the categories of identity and destabilized the notion of selfhood.

Works Cited

Alarcón, Norma, Ana Castillo, and Cherríe Moraga, eds. (1993). *The Sexuality of Latinas*. Berkeley: Third Woman.

A-mi, Jo. (2016). "Do sublime e do grotesco: a obscenidade em Hilda Hilst." *Acta Scientiarum. Language and Culture* 38.3 (2016): 291–99.

de Andrade, Mário. (1942). *O movimento modernista; conferência lida no Salão de Conferências da Biblioteca do Ministério das Relações Exteriores do Brazil no dia 20 de abril de 1942*. Casa do Estudante do Brasil. Departamento Cultural, Rio de Janeiro.

Anzaldúa, Gloria. (2007 [1987]). *Borderlands / La Frontera: The New Mestiza*. San Francisco: Spinsters / Aunt Lute.

120 K. A. KULAWIK

Anzaldúa, Gloria and AnaLouise Keating, eds. (2002). *This Bridge We Call Home: Radical Visions for Transformation.* New York: Routledge.

Arriarán, Samuel. (2007). *Barroco y neobarroco en América Latina: Estudios sobre la otra modernidad.* México, DF: Ítaca.

Austin, J. L. (1962). *How to do Things with Words.* London: Oxford UP.

Baker, Bryan. (2021). *Population Estimates, January 2021.* U.S. Department of Homeland Security. *Estimates of the Unauthorized Immigrant Population Residing in the United States: January 2015–January 2018 (dhs.gov),* p. 2. Accessed: February 13, 2023.

Baler, Pablo. (2016). *Latin American Neo-Baroque: Senses of Distortion.* Trans. Michael McGaha. New York: Palgrave.

Barvosa, Edwina. (2017). "Feminism and Borderland Identities." *Routledge Companion to Feminist Philosophy.* Eds. Ann Garry, Serene J. Khader, and Alison Stone. New York: Routledge. 207–17.

Bazin, Germain. (1968). *The Baroque: Principles, Styles, Styles, Modes, Themes.* New York: W. Norton.

Benítez Rojo, Antonio. (1996 [1992]). *The Repeating Island: The Caribbean and the Postmodern Perspective.* Trans. James Maraniss. Durham and London: Duke UP.

Bhabha, Homi. (1992). "Interrogating Identity: the Postcolonial Prerogative." *Anatomy of Racism.* U of Minnesota P. 183–209.

Botts, Tina Fernandes. (2017). "The Genealogy and Viability of the Concept of Intersectionality." *Routledge Companion to Feminist Philosophy.* Eds. Ann Garry, Serene J. Khader, and Alison Stone. New York: Routledge. 343–57.

Braidotti, Rosi. (1994). *Nomadic Subjects: Embodiment and Sexual Difference in Contemporary Feminist Theory.* New York: Columbia UP.

Braidotti, Rosi. (2002). *Metamorphoses: Towards a Materialist Theory of Becoming.* Cambridge, UK: Polity Press.

Braidotti, Rosi. (2006). *Transpositions: On Nomadic Ethics.* Cambridge, UK: Polity Press.

Brison, Susan J. (2017). "Personal Identity and Relational Selves." *Routledge Companion to Feminist Philosophy.* Eds. Ann Garry, Serene J. Khader, and Alison Stone. New York: Routledge. 218–29.

Burgos, Fernando. (1992). *Vertientes de la modernidad hispanoamericana.* Caracas: Monte Ávila.

Bustillo, Carmen. (1990). *Barroco y América Latina: un itinerario inconcluso.* Caracas: Monte Ávila.

Butler, Judith (1990). *Gender Trouble.* New York: Routledge.

Butler, Judith. (1993). *Bodies That Matter: On the Discursive Limits of Sex.* New York: Routledge.

Calabrese, Omar. (1992). *Neo-Baroque: A Sign of the Times.* Trans. Charles Lambert. Princeton, NJ: Princeton UP.

2 NEOBAROQUE AS TRANSGRESSION: THE LATIN AMERICAN PARADIGM 121

Carilla, Emilio. (1969). *El barroco literario hispánico*. Buenos Aires: Nova.

Carpentier, Alejo. (1967). *Tientos y diferencias*. Montevideo: Arca.

Chiampi, Irlemar. (2000). *Barroco y modernidad*. México: Fondo de Cultura Económica.

Christ, Ronald. (1997). "Extravag(r)ant and Un/erring Spirit." In: Diamela Eltit. *E. Luminata*. Trans. Ronald Christ. Santa Fe, NM: Lumen. 205–34.

Cornejo Polar, Antonio. (2013 [1994]). *Writing in the Air: Heterogeneity and the Persistence of Oral Tradition in Andean Literatures*. Trans. Lynda J. Jentsch. Durham and London: Duke UP.

Deleuze, Gilles and Claire Parnet. (1987a [1977]). *Dialogues*. Trans. Hugh Tomlinson and Barbara Habberjam. New York: Columbia UP.

Deleuze, Gilles and Félix Guattari (1987b [1980]). *A Thousand Plateaus. Capitalism and Schizophrenia*. Trans. Brian Massumi. Minneapolis: U of Minnesota P.

Deleuze, Gilles. (1993 [1988]). *The Fold: Leibniz and the Baroque*. Trans. Tom Conley. Minneapolis and London: U of Minnesota P.

Diniz, Cristiano, ed. (2013). *Fico besta quando me entendem. Entrevistas com Hilda Hilst*. São Paulo: Editora Globo.

Donohue, Micah K. (2018). "Borderlands Gothic Science Fiction: Alienation as Intersection in Rivera's *Sleep Dealer* and Lavin's 'Llegar a la orilla'." *Science Fiction Studies*. 45 (2018): 48–68.

Echeverría, Bolívar, ed. (1994). *Modernidad, mestizaje cultural, ethos barroco*. México: UNAM-Equilibrista.

Fernández Moreno, César. (1982). "¿Qué es América Latina?" *Cuadernos Americanos*. 41. 240 (1982): 121–39.

Figueroa Sánchez, Cristo Rafael. (2008). *Barroco y neobarroco en la narrativa hispanoamericana. Cartografías literarias de la segunda mitad del siglo XX*. Bogotá-Medellín: Pontificia Universidad Javeriana - Universidad de Antioquia.

Fox, Arturo. (2011). *Latinoamérica: presente y pasado*. 4th ed. Boston: Prentice Hall.

Fusco, Coco. (1995). *English is Broken Here. Notes on Cultural Fusion in the Americas*. New York City: The New Press.

García Canclini, Néstor. (1990). *Culturas híbridas: Estrategias para entrar y salir de la modernidad*. México: Ed. Grijalbo.

García Canclini, Néstor. (1995 [1990]). *Hybrid Cultures: Strategies for Entering and Leaving Modernity*. Trans. Christopher L. Chiappari and Silvia L. López. Minneapolis and London: U of Minnesota P.

Gerard, Sarah. (2013). "Body of the Text: Hilda Hilst's 'The Obscene Madame D'". *Los Angeles Review of Books*. 21 abr. 2013. https://lareviewofbooks. org/article/body-of-the-text-hilda-hilsts-the-obscene-madame-d/. Accessed August 29, 2021.

Ginway, M. Elizabeth. (2020). *Cyborgs, Sexuality, and the Undead: Body in Mexican and Brazilian Speculative Fiction.* Nashville: Vanderbilt UP.

Gómez-Peña, Guillermo. (1996). *The New World Border.* San Francisco: City Lights Books.

Grosz, Elizabeth (1994). *Volatile Bodies: Toward a Corporeal Feminism.* Bloomington & Indianapolis: Indiana UP.

Guerrero, Gustavo. (1987). *La estrategia neobarroca. Estudio sobre el resurgimiento de la poética barroca en la obra narrativa de Severo Sarduy.* Barcelona: Edicions del Mall.

Halberstam, Jack. (2018). *Trans*: A Quick and Quirky Account of Gender Variability.* Oakland, CA: U of California P.

Hatzfeld, Helmut. (1964). *Estudios sobre el barroco.* Madrid: Gredos.

Jagose, Annemarie. (2015). "The Trouble with Antinormativity." *Differences: A Journal of Feminist Cultural Studies.* Brown University. 26.1 (2015): 26–47.

Jameson, Frederic. (1991). *Postmodernism or the Cultural Logic of Late Capitalism.* Durham and London: Duke UP.

Jardine, Alice. (1985). *Gynesis. Configurations of Woman and Modernity.* Ithaca, London: Cornell UP, 1985.

Kaup, Monika. (2012). *Neobaroque in the Americas. Alternative Modernities in Literature, Visual Art, and Film.* Charlottesville and London, U of Virginia P.

Kosofsky Sedgwick, Eve. (2013). "Queer and Now". *The Routledge Queer Studies Reader.* Eds. Donald E. Hall and Annamarie Jagose. London and New York: Routledge.

Kulawik, Krzysztof. (2009). *Travestismo lingüístico: el enmascaramiento de la identidad sexual en la narrativa latinoamericana neobarroca.* Madrid and Frankfurt am Main: Iberoamericana-Vervuert.

Kulawik, Krzysztof. (2012). "Des-escribir el hombre y la mujer: *performance* de la sexualidad enmascarada en algunas novelas de Mario Bellatin." Eds. Claudia Gronemann and Cornelia Sieber. *Fiestas infinitas de máscara: actos performativos de feminidad y masculinidad en México.* Hildesheim, Germany: Georg Olms Verlag, 2012. 169–83.

Kulick, Don. (1998). *Travesti: Sex, Gender and Culture among Brazilian Transgendered Prostitutes.* Chicago: U of Chicago P.

Kushigian, Julia A. (1999). "Severo Sarduy, orientalista posmodernista en camino hacia la autorrealización. *Une ménagerie a trois: Cobra, Colibrí y Cocuyo.*" *Sarduy. Obra completa.* Eds. Gustavo Guerrero y Francois Wahl. Madrid: Galaxia Gutenberg –Archivos. 1605–18.

Larrain, Jorge. (2000). *Identity and Modernity in Latin America.* Cambridge, UK: Polity Press.

de Lauretis, Teresa. (1987). *Technologies of Gender: Essays on Theory, Film, and Fiction.* Bloomington and Indianapolis: Indiana UP.

Lechner, Roberto. (1993). "A Disenchantment Called Postmodernism." *Boundary.* 220. 3 (1993): 122–39.

2 NEOBAROQUE AS TRANSGRESSION: THE LATIN AMERICAN PARADIGM 123

Lezama Lima, José. (1957). *La expresión americana*. La Habana: Instituto Nacional de Cultura.

Lyotard, Jean-François. (1984 [1979]). *The Postmodern Condition: A Report on Knowledge*. Trans. Geoff Bennington and Brian Massumi. Minneapolis: U of Minnesota P.

Madureira, Carlos. (2005). *Cannibal Modernities: Postcoloniality and the Avant-garde in Caribbean and Brazilian Literature*. Charlottesville and London: U of Virginia P.

Moraes, Eliane Robert. (1999). "Da medida estilhaçada". *Cadernos de Literatura Brasileira*. 8 (1999): 114–26.

Moraga, Cherríe L. (2011). *A Xicana Codex of Changing Consciousness*. Durham, NC: Duke UP.

Muñoz, José Esteban. (1999). *Disidentifications: Queers of Color and the Performance of Politics*. Minneapolis and London: U of Minnesota P.

Ortega, José. (1984). *La estética neobarroca en la narrativa hispanoamericana*. Madrid: José Porrúa Turanzas.

Ortiz, Fernando. (1995 [1940]). *Cuban Counterpoint: Tobacco and Sugar*, Durham, NC: Duke UP.

de la Pedraja, René. (1997). "The Historical Context." Ed. Richard S. Hillman. *Understanding Contemporary Latin America*. Boulder, London: Lynne Rienner Publishers. 27–50.

Peirce, Charles S. (1991). *Peirce on Signs: Writings on Semiotic by Charles Sanders Peirce*. Ed. James Hoopes. Chapel Hill: U of North Carolina P.

Perlongher, Néstor. (1997). *Prosa plebeya*. Buenos Aires: Colihue.

Picón Salas, Mariano. (1962). *A Cultural History of Spanish America: From Conquest to Independence*. Trans. Irving A. Leonard. Berkeley-Los Angeles: U of California P.

Pratt, Mary Louise. (1993). "Criticism in the Contact Zone: Decentering Community and Nation." *Critical Theory, Cultural Politics, and Latin American Narrative*. Eds. Steven, M. Bell, Albert H. Lemay y Leonard Orr. Notre Dame: U of Notre Dame P, 83–102.

Prieto, René. (2000). *Body of Writing: Figuring Desire in Spanish American Literature*. Durham and London: Duke UP.

Rama, Angel. (1996 [1984]). *The Lettered City*. Ed. and trans. John Charles Chasteen. Durham and London: Duke UP.

Rama, Angel. (2012 [1982]). *Writing Across Cultures: Narrative Transculturation in Latin America*. Ed. and transl. David Frye. Durham and London, Duke UP, 2012.

Restrepo, Luis Fernando. (2003). "The Cultures of Colonialism." Ed. Philip Swanson. *The Companion to Latin American Studies*. London: Hodder Education. 47–64.

Richard, Nelly (1993). *Masculino/Femenino. Prácticas de la diferencia y cultura democrática*. Santiago, Chile: Francisco Zegers.

Richard, Nelly. (1996). "Feminismo, experiencia y representación". *Revista Iberoamericana*. LXII. 176–77. (1996). 733–44.

Rincón, Carlos. (1995). *La no simultaneidad de lo simultaneo: postmodernidad, globalización y culturas en América Latina*. Bogotá: Universidad Nacional.

Rivera, Alex, dir. (2008). *Sleep Dealer*. US-Mexico: Maya Entertainment Film. DVD.

Rivera Cusicanqui, Silvia. (2020 [2010]). *Ch'ixinakax utxiwa. On Practices and Discourses of Decolonization*. Trans. Molly Geidel. Cambridge, UK and Medford, MA: Polity Press.

Rousset, Jean. (1972). *Circe y el pavo real*. Barcelona: Seix Barral.

Ruiz-Aho, Elena. (2011). "Feminist Border Thought." Eds. G. Delanty and S.P. Turner. *Routledge International Handbook of Contemporary Social and Political Theory*. London: Taylor and Francis.

Sandoval, Chela. (2000). *Methodology of the Oppressed*. Minneapolis: U of Minnesota P.

Santiago, Silviano. (2001). *The Space In-Between: Essays on Latin American Culture*. Ed. Ana Lúcia Gazzola. Trans. Tom Burns, Ana Lúcia Gazzola, and Gareth Williams. Durham and London: Duke UP.

Sarduy, Severo. (1978 [1972]). "El barroco y el neobarroco." *América Latina en su literatura*. 5th ed. Coord. César Fernández Moreno. México: Fondo de Cultura Económica. 167–84.

Sarduy, Severo. (1984b). "Deterritorialization." Trans. Naomi Lindstrom. *Review of Contemporary Fiction*. 4 (1984): 104–09.

Sarduy, Severo. (1987 [1969]). *Escrito sobre un cuerpo*. In *Ensayos generales sobre el Barroco*. Buenos Aires: Fondo de Cultura Económica. 229–317.

Sarduy, Severo. (1990). "Writing/Transvestism." *Modern Latin American Fiction*. Ed. Harold Bloom. New York: Chelsea House. 221–24.

de Saussure, Ferdinand. (1955). *Cours de linguistique générale*. Paris: Payot.

Searle, John. (1980). *Speech Act Theory and Pragmatics*. Boston: D. Reidel Kluwer.

Urbanski, Edmund Stephen. (1978). *Hispanic America and Its Civilizations: Spanish Americans and Anglo-Americans*. Norman: U of Oklahoma P.

Wayar, Marlene. (2019). *Travesti / Una teoría lo suficientemente buena*. Buenos Aires: Muchas Nueces.

Zamora, Lois Parkinson. (2006). *The Inordinate Eye: New World Baroque and Latin American Fiction*. Chicago and London: U of Chicago P.

CHAPTER 3

Subversions of Selfhood: Transgressive CharACTerS of the Neobaroque

> *But I, like other queer people,*
> *am two in one body, both male and female.*
> *I am the embodiment of the* hieros gamos:
> *the coming together of opposite qualities within.*

—Gloria Anzaldúa, *Borderlands / La Frontera (2007: 41)*

This chapter begins by contextualizing the literary works and their authors with an overview of their historical and literary backgrounds. A history of hybridization in the Americas has led to the emergence of (neo)baroque literary and artistic genres that adapt their forms to cultural heterogeneity and nomadism. This brief introduction (Sect. 3.1) is followed by Sect. 3.2 with a detailed description of ambiguous, category-bending characters that appear in the fictional, critical, performative, and artistic works of the Neobaroque. They exemplify different modes of transgression and borderland identities that we contemplate in the light of neobaroque stylistic and narrative techniques used in their representation. A common feature of the works selected in this study is the presence of subversively eccentric characters, voices, and performers. Their recurrence indicates unstable and hybrid contexts that are fertile grounds for articulating a model of transselfhood. The common stylistic features and techniques of these works are pointed out as transformative devices in the decentering of identity. Nomadic subjects are presented according to the modes of their transgression: cross-dressing, androgyny, queer ambiguity, metamorphosis,

© The Author(s), under exclusive license to Springer Nature Switzerland AG 2024

K. A. Kulawik, *Visions of Transmerica*, Literatures of the Americas, https://doi.org/10.1007/978-3-031-42014-6_3

125

posthumanity, and borderland transit. The objective of this chapter is to explain how these works exemplify cultural transitivity and lead to conceiving a nomadic trans-self by means of neobaroque discursive devices.

3.1 Historical Determinants and Literary Environments

Latin American Neobaroque literature and art are the result of a migratory historical, socio-economic, and cultural development of the Americas fraught by historical conflict, but also by encounters and mixings, fusions and cross-seminations. The multilayered hybridization of the Americas is the result of the multiple upheavals that especially Latin America endured throughout its turbulent history: conquest, colonization, independence, and revolution. European conquest and colonization resulted in the transformation, if not extinction, of native cultures during the three centuries of colonial domination. As Edwin Williamson (2009) states, "the heterogeneity of the Indian world has not been taken into account [...] to interpret historical change in the new world as a tragic loss of cohesion and authenticity in native cultures" (84). In areas dominated by the Spanish Crown, a high degree of miscegenation, or *mestizaje*, occurred giving way for the birth of a new blend of mixed, hybrid, and syncretic cultural forms. The imposed colonial system induced a transposition of European cultural values held in place by European privilege. The demographic contact of the Amerindian, White Caucasian, and later Black-African racial groups resulted in the mixing and transformation of world populations on an unprecedented scale. Dynamic shifts were held in check by conservative forces of the Crown and later by the Republican state elites of the 1800s in an attempt to define a new feeling of national belonging.

During the colonial period, the Indigenous subaltern underwent a much more radical transformation due to its status of dependency and marginalization in the European-mandated colonial setting. Carlos Malamud (2010) states in his *Historia de América* that "[t]he main factor of social mobility of the Indians was outside and not within the Indian society, and it was simply the possibility of joining the Spanish society" (147; my translation). Through such mobility and contact, both the Native and European cultures experienced modifications by way of mutually induced transformations (Williamson 85). The European invaders also underwent a process of transculturation, as we mentioned in Chap. 2 with reference to Fernando Ortiz (1947), the result of which was the creolization (Americanization), or even Indigenization of European models of lifestyles, cultural practices, arts, letters, architecture, and attitudes toward selfhood. One example of this is the adoption of the European Baroque style in cultural life, education, and thought and its transformation into an American Colonial Baroque, proper of the "*Señor Barroco*," defined by José Lezama Lima as the impersonation of the already Americanized creole but seated on his *own* possessions, dominating his own scenery (1957).[1] His (still masculine and patriarchal) cultural attitude evolved into the syncretic forms adopted by the American Baroque. The physical labor of creating this style was carried out by the mixed-race/bicultural *Mestizo* or the Native-American artist and builder who silently added their own autochthonous elements to the imported and prescribed European themes. Lezama Lima provides examples of artist Indio Kondori, whose work on the façades of the churches of Potosí (in today's Bolivia, see Fig. 2.1) as the first great synthesis of styles and the preparation for the rupture from Europe in the forthcoming rebellions (52).

This cultural scene would not be complete without the addition of the third great racial and cultural component. The Black-African element was introduced to the Americas forcefully in the slave trade and contributed to the further transformation of American culture as the third element and final catalyzer to the White, Native, and newly formed *Mestizo* components. Lezama explains the influential presence of the *mulato* artist Aleijadinho in Brazilian Baroque as the synthesis of the Luso-Hispanic and Black-African elements in the affluent mining town of Ouro Preto (53). As a result of the centenarian exploitation through forced labor in the fields and mines, the rebellious presence of the Afro-descendant became especially visible since the first emancipatory movements of the mid- to late eighteenth century in Brazilian *quilombos,* Caribbean *palenques,* Haitian sugar-cane plantations, but especially in the momentous and successful revolt of 1791 which resulted in the Haitian Revolution and the Republic of Haiti that in 1804 brought a bitter end to the French colony of Saint Domingue. The African population attained socio-political but nor economic emancipation during the course of the nineteenth century,

---

[1] Lezama explains: "Thus we see that the American Baroque master, whom we have called the authentic first installed in what is ours, participates in, watches over, and cares for the two great syntheses that are at the root of the American Baroque, the Hispano-Inca and the Hispano-Negroid" (53). Similarly, in terms of scenery, he affirms that "[w]hile the European baroque became an inert game of forms, among us the baroque master dominates his landscape giving new solutions to Western scenography by now sweating in plastered cast" (119; my translations).

when slavery was gradually abolished in the newly independent Latin American republics after 1820, and much later in the 1880s in Brazil and the last Spanish colonies of the Caribbean.

The Independence Wars and the founding of the Republics were another defining moment for Latin America in political and cultural terms but conserving social-racial disparities remained unresolved throughout the republican era, and well into the twentieth century. Although nominally politically liberated, the new nation-states were still economically dependent on European and North American powers, and national societies remained divided along racial, ethnic, social, and gender lines. The patriarchal, white, male-dominated, economically privileged postcolonial order of European and North American economic and cultural hegemony prevailed in Latin America, even when cultural and racial miscegenation was taking place at the lower to middle echelons of a continuously classist society. Colonial legacy did not hinder the creative potential of a hybrid America. Williamson observes that:

> far from being paralyzed by its colonial past, Latin America has changed profoundly after opening up [...] in the nineteenth century. [...] The explosion of creativity which has fascinated a worldwide public since the middle of the twentieth century shows that the colonial legacy was by no means a disabling influence [...]; rather it was a rich inheritance that writers and artists have drawn upon in order to make sense of the continent's place in the modern world. (615)

Neobaroque's twentieth-century awakening entailed a stylization of the Colonial Baroque with a subversive explosion of creativity as the expression of a Postmodern crisis of Modernity's hegemonic values.

The Republican era of the nineteenth century, while offering economic consolidation for the privileged elites of the White minority, did not resolve the fundamental issues of foreign economic dependency, determined in a postcolonial *status quo*, and of the deep social division into a class system of economic (racially determined) inequality. The inheritance of European colonialism, unresolved by eighteenth-century European Enlightenment-based philosophical and economic liberalism, resulted in the ensuing revolutionary turmoil that plagued Latin America throughout the twentieth century. As Williamson explains: "The white creoles operated within their countries much as their forebears had done since the Conquest: [...] the hacienda [...] dominated the economy more fully than ever and continued to be the prime source of status. Society, as a result, remained rigidly patriarchal, stratified along racial and economic lines" (313). The twentieth century saw an inherent struggle between tradition and change. The first relied on the élite's power to monopolize agrarian and mineral export markets through political deals and to concentrate wealth in aristocratic consumption and lavish lifestyle. Change came in the 1900s in a series of social (and in some cases revolutionary) disruptions to the century-long established order of the postcolonial oligarchy enhanced by the expansion of urban centers and the growth of the middle class as a result of the influx of immigration from Europe and the Far East. Revolutions brought about some transformations in Mexico and Bolivia (and considerable changes in Cuba) but matters cyclically returned to an undemocratic and economically polarized establishment. The control was often in the hands of the military, who, as a defensive reaction to maintain "order and progress" and with some success, took control of government and finances, as in the case of the regimes in Brazil (1964–1985), Argentina (1976–1983), and Chile (1973–1989). Latin America's situation in the twentieth century can be characterized in the least as highly unstable. In Carlos Malamud's words,

> The second half of the 20th century was very difficult for Latin America, since almost every door that opened towards development and democratic consolidation was closed by the action or omission of Latin Americans themselves. Neither autarchy, nor import substitution industrialization, nor developmentalism, nor openness, nor the Washington Consensus and neo-liberalism were able to put the region on the path of economic development. The same can be said of democracy, since neither the Cuban Revolution, nor the populisms, nor the military authoritarianism of the 1970s were able to stabilize the political systems, which were subject to the tensions that interrupted the institutional progress of their countries. (455; my translation)

However, referring to the first decades of the twenty-first century, Malamud uses the phrase "*época de cambios*" or "era of changes" defined by the rebirth of (social) democracy with a marked shift toward the Left (497).

Assessing the historical development of nineteenth- and twentieth-century Latin America, Roberto Echavarren explains the contrast between the utopian visions of the republican era and the delegitimized revolutionary drives of the twentieth century that led to more dictatorships and suppression of democratic freedoms: "The imperative of historical change

became, for some, more important than individual freedom, which justified the terror practiced by the 'dictatorship of the proletariat.' The dictatorship has meant a crisis of the model of the state and the state of legality"
(2010: 21). The socio-political and cultural developments in the second
half of the twentieth century in the United States have additionally influenced the formative context of the neobaroque works that we propose to
analyze, as Echavarren points out:

> After the Second World War, but above all through the sixties, a new view of
> politics became manifest. Indians, blacks, US minorities together with newly
> formed groups of gay and queer militants, the women's movement, student
> revolt, new youth styles attached to music, drugs such as marijuana and
> LSD, outsider varieties of life outside the 'system,' protests against the war,
> articulated visible operating demands. People from these groups […]
> brought a new sensibility, a new behavior, a new attitude, and the new
> image. […] A micropolitics of civil disobedience developed. (2010: 21)

The Americas' historical and cultural development can be summed up as a
convergence of the forces of these peripheral groups mentioned by
Echavarren in addition to the races, ethnicities, interest groups, minorities
and exiles, internal and external migrants who converge in a space of contact, and whose hybridization has been enhanced by the accelerating process of communication and globalization that has transformed traditional
cultural patterns in late twentieth and early twenty-first centuries.
Williamson sums up this phenomenon:

> Globalization accelerated the modernization of Latin American cultures and
> societies, as technology and mass media exposed the population to influ-
> ences from abroad, and as migrants from disintegrating rural communities
> and, say, the Andean highlands found themselves earning a living alongside
> people of myriad nationalities and the permissive ambience of the great
> Western cities. This direct experience of the pluralism of modern society
> fostered an ideology of individual and civil rights which contributed to the
> undermining of patriarchal values that had shaped Latin America over cen-
> turies. (573)

The historical pendulum of forces and changing values at work in Latin
America is projected in the literature and arts. The opposing historical
forces of political and cultural multiplicity and migration-induced contact
are determinants in Neobaroque's revolutionizing of literary and artistic forms.

Establishing these historical contexts also allows us to detect the forces that have triggered the northbound migration of Latin American population and the expanding presence of its culture across the United States. The continuous flow of economically and politically driven migration has produced additional identity frictions, hybridizations, and transculturations in the transit border and urban zones of the United States. As new capital-intensive agribusiness entered the rural economy of most Latin American countries, causing further migration to the cities, the overflow of jobless seeking employment shot up, also the result of public spending cuts and trade liberalization. This, in turn, produced a lack of jobs in the cities and pushed a large number of Latin American workers to enter the United States, legally and illegally, throughout the 1990s and the new millennium (Williamson 572). Additionally, factors such as violence induced by trafficking drugs and arms, natural disasters, and political repression have turned migrants into exiles. The US-Mexico border has become a contentious boundary, both politically and culturally, a wall that intended to block the flow of population and cultural values, affecting interactions of Anglo-America with the feared Hispanic "other." Notwithstanding, major US cities, especially in the West and South, received the overflow of displaced Latin American populations, which added to the reach of Hispanic culture in the United States. These factors have contributed to identity transformations in the Latino/Hispanic and US-American subconscious. Juan Flores (2004) states that "This nomadic, migratory dimension of the Latino imaginary is anchored in historical reasons for coming here, and in the placement assigned most Latinos in US society. Unlike earlier waves of European immigrants, Latinos typically move to this country as a direct result of the economic and political relationship of their homelands, and home region, to the United States" (613–14). The postcolonial relations of hemispheric inequality explain the causes and patterns of migration, as much as they explain the not-always-so-desirable position of Latinos in US society.

By the mid-2000s, Hispanics had become the largest minority, with projections indicating they would constitute 25% of the total US population by 2050 (Williamson 572–73). Both the Texas Rio Grande Valley and California are the setting for Chicane struggles represented in the hybrid critical works of Gloria Anzaldúa, Cherríe Moraga, and Guillermo Gómez-Peña. As we will see later, they textually and performatively represent Latine and Chicane identities as a selfhood in process, a nomadic borderland identity forming in the transnational/cultural context of the

US-Mexico border. The political undertones of these authors, critical of *both* sides of the border, cannot be underestimated, as Cherríe Moraga declares:

> Beneath the shadow of a giant wave of U.S. and Mexican flags I stand among the sea of protesters on the May Day March for Immigrant Rights. I wonder what we are really protesting amid this bold display of bicultural loyalty to the countries that betray the immigrant from both sides of the border. *Immigrant*, a bitter and ironic misnomer when the increasing majority of undocumented workers are migrant Indigenous *Americans* displaced from their lands of origin. (89; emphasis in original)

The US Census of 2020 provides meaningful figures, which can help us consider the cultural transits between Latin America and the United States, part of the great inter-American phenomenon of hybridized co-existing cultures and shifting identities on the move. According to this data, "[t]he Hispanic or Latino population, which *includes people of any race*, was 62.1 million in 2020. The Hispanic or Latino population grew 23%, while the population that was not of Hispanic or Latino origin grew 4.3% since 2010" (Jones et al. 2020, 1; emphasis added).[2] The words "people of any race" imply that being Latino/Hispanic is not a racial distinction anymore, but the result of a complex interracial and interethnic mixture of Latin America. These figures point to a population in movement, whose identity is shifting, just as it displaces the perceptions of the cultural "other." It is a population that is illustrative of modern-day trans-American nomadism as it engages the formation of a hybrid (Latin) American culture and a mobile transitive identity.

The **literary environments** of the analyzed works have been shaped by the above-mentioned historical contexts of a multicultural hybrid America. The selection of the works making up this study is founded in the recurrence of neobaroque techniques that constitute their common feature. The Neobaroque appears in mid-twentieth century as an artistic stylization of the historical seventeenth-century European and American Colonial Baroque. Attaining its heyday in the 1960s and 1970s as a stylistic modality in narrative, poetic, essayistic, and visual works in several Latin American countries, the Neobaroque has continued to mark its presence

---

[2] These figures and statement are from the article by Nicholas Jones, et al. "2020 Census Illuminates Racial and Ethnic Composition of the Country," https://www.census.gov/library/stories/2021/08

in the first decades of the twenty-first century. Originally perceived as a style consecrated to the service of political and religious domination, in the New World the Baroque evolved to acquire a sense of contestation and, in the words of José Lezama Lima, of a "counter-conquest," an attitude of resistance and rebellion (1957: 32, 52). It represents a postcolonial and hybrid, distinctly American idiosyncrasy in an historical moment of transformation, sometimes described as the postmodern crisis of Western civilization.

In order to further contextualize works that resort to this opulent style marked by the use of artifice, parody, and eroticism, we propose to establish five "neobaroque nuclei" within the Latin American regional literary and artistic scenes. They include Cuba (part of the broader Antillean region), Mexico, Chile, Argentina (part of the Rio de la Plata region including Uruguay), and Brazil. The existence of an initial Caribbean Neobaroque nucleus has been demonstrated in the critical studies by Gustavo Guerrero (1987), Carmen Bustillo (1990), and Roberto González Echevarría (1987). First and foremost, we point to Cuba, given the major role that Severo Sarduy (1937–1993) played in the inception and theorization of the Neobaroque. His direct predecessor and model was José Lezama Lima (1910–1976), Cuban poet, novelist, and essayist who situated first Neobaroque's origins in the American Colonial Baroque and theorized about its viability in twentieth-century Latin American art and literature. He also put his theories into practice in two grand novels: *Paradiso* (1966) and *Oppiano Licario* (1977). Other contemporaries of Lezama and Sarduy associated with the opulence and experimentation in the neobaroque vein are Guillermo Cabrera Infante (1929–2005) with his playful novel *Tres tristes tigres* (1967; *Three Trapped Tigers*), and Reinaldo Arenas (1943–1990) with the fantastical novel *El mundo alucinante* (1966; *Hallucinations*). The list would not be complete without Alejo Carpentier (1904–1980), who famously advocated the baroque nature of American art and the poetics of the *real maravilloso* ["marvelous reality"], influencing Gabriel García Marquez's and Isabel Allende's newer forms of "magical realism." His internationally recognized novels in this vein are *El reino de este mundo* (1949; *The Kingdom of this World*) and *Los pasos perdidos* (1953; *The Lost Steps*).

In the context of Mexican narrative, Mario Bellatin stands out as a solitary figure in his own right with his "novel-as-process" and "dynamic writing." His work has been described by Julio Ortega as "exploratory writing" along with that of Chilean Diamela Eltit, Argentine Néstor Perlongher, and Peruvian Enrique Versátegui (Ortega and Dávila 2012: 8). The predecessors of narrative innovation in Mexico are Juan Rulfo (1917–1986), whose book of harshly (sur)realistic short stories *El llano en llamas* (1953, *The Plain in Flames*) and short novel *Pedro Páramo* (1955) take on the specters of the Mexican Revolution while adopting Modernist and Avant-gardist techniques akin to William Faulkner; Carlos Fuentes (1928–2012) with the darkly Baroque-like complexity of the novel *Cristóbal Nonato* (1987; *Christopher Unborn*) and the early experimentations of *La muerte de Artemio Cruz* (1962; *The Death of Artemio Cruz*) and *Cambio de piel* (1967; *A Change of Skin*); Fernando del Paso (1935–2018) with a more neobaroque tint in his "total novel," *Palinuro de México* (1976) and the historiographic novel *Noticias del imperio* (1986; *News from the Empire*); and Jorge Volpi (b. 1968) with the more recent experimental "crack novel" (crack as a "breakthrough") *En busca de Klingsor* (1999, *In Search of Klingsor*), a work protesting "light-type literature" while introducing darker, more critical, and apocalyptic themes.

Chile's narrative predecessor to Diamela Eltit's formal experimentation and dark-tinted contents of queer sexuality was José Donoso (1924–1996). Baroque elements abound in his acclaimed novel *El obsceno pájaro de la noche* (1970; *The Obscene Bird of Night*), and in *El lugar sin límites* (1966; 1972, *Hell Has No Limits*) topics of homosexuality and cross-dressing are central. Another notable name representing narrative innovation in Chile is Jorge Edwards (b. 1931) with the novels *Persona non grata* (1971) and *La Casa de Dostoievsky* (2008).

The Río de la Plata (Argentinian and Uruguayan) nucleus is marked by a long tradition of literary, particularly narrative, innovation that influenced New Narrative in Latin America. In terms of conceptual innovations that marked a "postmodern" turn in future Latin American narrative, we could not omit Felisberto Hernández (1902–1964)—the Uruguayan precursor of magical realism—and Macedonio Fernández (1874–1952)—the Argentine pioneer and mentor of experimental avant-garde narrative. His followers were Jorge Luis Borges (1899–1986) with his conceptual narrative inventions of *Ficciones* (1944) and *El Aleph* (1949), and Julio Cortázar (1914–1984) with the radically experimental novel *Rayuela* (1963; *Hopscotch*), the stories *Bestiario* (1951) and *Todos los fuegos el fuego* (1966; *All Fires the Fire*). This narrative modernization paved the way for more recent writers in the Río de la Plata (including Uruguay with Juan Carlos Onetti, Cristina Peri Rossi, and Roberto Echavarren) who were at the forefront of the so-called post-Boom narrative from the mid-1970s

3 SUBVERSIONS OF SELFHOOD: TRANSGRESSIVE CHARACTERS... 135

onward. To this group we add Luisa Valenzuela (b. 1938), given the formal ingenuity (as well as feminine and political content) of her expressionistic, metafictional, and transcultural novel about the destructive effects of power and discourse, *Cola de lagartija* (1983; *The Lizard's Tail*), and Manuel Puig (1932–1990), whose novel *El beso de la mujer araña* (1983; *Kiss of the Spider Woman*) also focuses on the relationship of politics, power, and homoerotic sexuality.

Finally, in Brazil, the literary influences that set the stage for Hilda Hilst are found in the Modernist prose of Mário de Andrade (1893–1945) with *Macunaíma* (1928), in the linguistic and narrative experimentation of Oswald de Andrade (1890–1954) in the poems of *Pau-Brasil* (1925) and his novel *Serafim Ponte Grande* (1933). In the same line emerges the linguistically, formally, and conceptually modernizing, hybrid narrative of João Guimarães Rosa (1908–1967), with in his masterpiece (and only) novel *Grande Sertão: Veredas* (1956; *The Devil to Pay in the Backlands*). In a meaningful way, the novel closes with the sentence: "Travessia. O homem humano" ("Crossing. The hu-man human-being") followed by the symbol of infinity, as a nod to one of the main themes of *Transmerica*—transcendence and boundless infinity. Perhaps a somewhat lesser-known figure outside of Brazil, nonetheless of equal importance, is Osman Lins (1924–1978), whose novel *Avalovara* (1973) earned him the reputation of one of the leading innovators of twentieth-century Brazilian literature. Also, the solitary figure of João Gilberto Noll (1946–2017) is analogous to Hilst's isolation and focus on erotic themes through narrative experimentation. Finally, the Brazilian writer most closely resembling Hilst in terms of linguistic and conceptual experimentation is internationally acclaimed Clarice Lispector (1920–1977), whose novels *A Paixão Segundo G.H.* (1964; *The Passion According to G.H.*), *Água viva* (1973; *The Stream of Life*) and *A hora da Estrela* (1977; *The Hour of the Star*) indicate most advanced solutions in terms of linguistic-conceptual experimentation and philosophical speculation. Our focus also rests on the novelistic and essayistic production of Silviano Santiago, an innovative voice in terms of both open narrative form and content laden with themes of transgressive sexuality and queer characters in his novels *Stella Manhattan* (1985) and *Em Liberdade* (1982), as well as in his volume of essays on transculturation, *The Space In-Between* (2001).

This overview of the literary predecessors from the five main cultural areas is not meant to be exhaustive. Its purpose is only to signal familiar names and outline a context for the authors whose works eventually lead

136   K. A. KULAWIK

to perceive a Latin American "neobaroque scene" and to articulate a transitive selfhood. The works of the mentioned authors from the five areas as well as others from Bolivia and the US-Mexico border provide us a wealth of characters that transgress and destabilize the concept of identity.

3.2   Nomadic Transgressions of Identity in Latin American Fiction, Performance, and Painting

The works of Latin American writers, performance, and visual artists presented in this chapter illustrate characters that are ambiguous and unstable in terms of their uncategorizable and fluid identities. They transgress normative categorizations of gender, ethnic, racial, national, and human identity, exemplifying mutant, transitive, and nomadic selves that transform within the plots of the stories or in the performances they partake. At the same time, the experimental literary and performative devices that these works adopt, as well as the exuberant linguistic and visual effects they utilize, are indicative of the Neobaroque. The presence of this style produces a destabilizing effect and a conceptual transformation of the represented characters, voices, and their identities. It leads the reader/spectator to envision a nomadic trans-self embodied in the mutant characters that we proceed to distinguish in their particular forms of transgression.

3.2.1   Cross-dressing

A common feature of the neobaroque works of the mentioned authors is the notable presence of cross-dressing, or transvestism. It is a gender-bending activity of wearing clothes of the "opposite" (to assigned) sex (from Latin *trans* as "across" and *vestis* as "clothes"). Its objectives range from gender and sexual self-realization to the adoption of a dissident stance on sanctioned norms of gender exteriorization. Its techniques are manifold: theatrical, humorous, and parodic, as in *drag*; or simply *gender-bending* as in dressing markedly feminine and masculine attire while inverting assigned gender categories (Ellis y Abarbaniel 1961, 1012).

Spanish-language literature displays a tradition of gender bending, which dates back to colonial times with the adventures of Catalina de Erauso in the play *La Monja Alférez* [*The Nun Ensign*] by Spaniard Juan Pérez de Montalbán (1635). The protagonist, a runaway girl from a well-to-do family turned nun, cut her hair, dressed as a man, and set out to

3 SUBVERSIONS OF SELFHOOD: TRANSGRESSIVE CHARACTERS... 137

experience her new male identity enlisting in the Spanish army in the New World. The case of Catalina represents the necessity to cross-dress in order to attain personal (sexually motivated) and political goals in a prohibitive, male-dominated environment. It is also visible in the inverted gender role play between Sor Juana Inés de la Cruz and the Bishop of Puebla contained in the nun's epistle-riposte, "Respuesta a Sor Filotea de la Cruz" (1691); it is present in the sentencing of Juana Aguilar, a suspected hermaphrodite tried for sodomy in early nineteenth-century Guatemala.[3] It will be much later, in the extravagances of modernist poets, such as Uruguayan Julio Herrera y Reissig or Colombian Porfirio Barba Jacob, that transvestism would emerge with an additional aesthetic value as a sexual desire of otherness. In the twentieth century, more sublimated gender-bending figures appeared in the works of Cubans José Lezama Lima, Severo Sarduy, and Reynaldo Arenas, along with the explicitly cross-dressed protagonist in Donoso's novel *El lugar sin límites*.

Severo Sarduy

The cross-dresser's chameleonic, transient, and thus ambiguous character set in a highly mobile transcultural framework is represented in Sarduy's exuberant and experimental neobaroque narrative forms. In his novels *De donde son los cantantes* (1967), *Cobra* (1972), and *Colibrí* (1984), the protagonists are transvestites, bisexuals, mutants, and androgynous individuals displaced between multiple geographical and cultural spaces. In an elaborately contrived and artfully stilted narrative style, their changing sexual and cultural identities mutate in a framework of (not only) Latin American geographical and cultural elements, juxtaposed with the "otherness" of European and Asian settings in combinations that produce a transcultural mixture of Western and Oriental themes. This is reminiscent of more contemporary Chilean novelist Roberto Bolaño, whose characters and fragmented plot lines also move in a transitory, transnational, and transcultural space.

Cobra embodies a metamorphosing and name-changing cross-dressed dancer at the Teatro Lírico de las Muñecas in Havana. He is oppressed by his patroness, the despotic Señora. Initially called the White Dwarf, the transvestite flees to France with a desire to transform his body and sex. He is compelled to travel on to Morocco to seek the services of the

---

[3] This case was studied broadly by Maria Elena Martínez in her article "Archives, Bodies, and Imagination: The Case of Juana Aguilar and Queer Approaches to History, Sexuality, and Politics" in *Radical History Review*. 120 (2014): 159–82.

surgeon-alchemist, Dr. Ktazob. Cobra shrinks and reincarnates as Pup—a doll-sized baby, again coopted by the despotic Señora in his/her double incarnation. Cobra/Pup escapes again to Paris, now identifying as a gay supermacho, involved with a gang of S-M motor bikers who, in their drive toward transformation, decide to travel to a Buddhist monastery in Tibet where they futilely seek spiritual enlightenment. There, Cobra is brutally murdered by the police (as a representation of the homophobic state and its authorities) after being recognized as a drag queen dancer. In this convoluted story, the protagonist succumbs to a series of plastic and cosmetic transfigurations, in the course of which, by way of metamorphosis, *hir* sexual and gender attributes are repeatedly inverted or combined in mutant configurations: "Up to her neck she was a woman; above, her body became a kind of heraldic animal with a baroque snout" (94).[4]

The bodily and sexual mutations of both Cobra and her dancer companion Cadillac begins in the Lyrical Doll Theater under La Señora's (the Master Lady's) absolute control. Both remain in their state of dwarf dolls, still with masculine attributes, as noted in the use of the object pronouns and noun endings in masculine form in the opening sentences of the novel:

> She'd set *them* in molds at daybreak, apply salt compresses, chastise *them* with successive baths of hot and cold water. She forced *them* with gags; she submitted *them* to crude mechanics. She manufactured wire armors to put them in, shortening and twisting the threads again and again with pliers; after smearing *them* with gum arabic she bound *them* with strips of cloth: they were mummies, [male] *children* of Florentine medallions. (3; emphasis added—italicized pronouns are masculine *los* or *-os* in the Spanish original)

The process of sexual transformation of Cobra and Cadillac by surgical (and textual) means of mechanical artifice (opulent and overflowing language) is observed in the subsequent change to feminine pronominal forms and adjective endings:

> *She* began to transform at six for the midnight show; in that crying ritual *one* had to deserve each ornament: the false eyelashes and the crown, the pigments, which the profane could not touch, the yellow contact lenses—tiger eyes—[…] So the *Go Between* came and went […] all day *the mutants* slept,

---

[4]For quotes in English, we use the translation by Suzanne Jill Levine of Severo Sarduy. *Cobra*. New York: E.P. Dutton, 1975.

3 SUBVERSIONS OF SELFHOOD: TRANSGRESSIVE CHARACTERS... 139

imprisoned in machines and gauze, immobilized by threads, lascivious, smeared with white facial creams. The network of *her* route was concentric, *her passage* was spiral through the *baroque setting* of mosquito nets. (3–4; emphasis added for feminine pronouns/grammatical and lexical forms and general baroque artifice)

The intricate plot, with the continuous bodily transformations and mutating identities of the characters, takes place in a shifting transcultural context set between the West and East in a nomadic narrative that interweaves the body-sexuality theme with metatextual procedures. This baroque technique of the fugue is evidenced in the convoluted narration and ornamental language. Figuratively, it evokes a verbal weaving of language—a codification analogous to the mutant body of the protagonist marked by makeup, tattooing, and alteration of the size of his/her limbs and body, e.g., in the change of Cobra into his double, the Pup doll: "Cobra = Pup^2/or else/Pup = $\sqrt{Cobra}$—" (27), or in the alteration of Cobra's reproductive organs during his transsexual transformation in Morocco: "The Alterer A will be able to practice his modeling force on the Subject to convert him into Subject prime [S^1], a force whose stabbing vector will be suffered by, in this case, the altered girlie out there (a), she of course being transformed, by the coaching therapy, into optimal receiver (a^1) prime. The whole thing can be represented by the graph of the mutation: Diamond." What follows in the text is a diamond-shaped geometrical graph of the mutation showing vectors for the mutation of $S>S^1$ and $a> a^1$ (59–60), and dramatized discourse in dialogic form (64–65).

In a metonymic dimension, the text (the act of writing) assumes the sense of a surgical operation and, later, an erotic performance in which the narrator symbolically marks the gender/sex of the characters with symbols, consequently changing the grammatical forms in the ensuing description to depict their metamorphosis. In an equally bizarre footnote, the mutation of the combined bodies of La Señora, Cobra, and the hybrid offshoot Pup is transcribed as an equation: "[Mme. + Cobra (+/=) Pup =(3/2)]" (46). It recreates the mutating sexuality and identity of multiple combined characters into one threefold entity resulting from the sum of two mutated characters. The subjects—the characters, narrators, even the implied authors and readers—overlap in multiple metatextual layers of the narrative, muddying the reader with transposed distinctions of the protagonists' gender that fluctuates and inverts between masculine and feminine, and between the multiple cultural spaces that serve as the setting for the story. Cobra's continually

140   K. A. KULAWIK

shifting spatial-cultural references to Paris, the South of France, Morocco, India, Tibet, and Ceylon potentiate the effect of ambiguity.

Just as in the erotic relationships of the protagonist, so too in the meta-narratively presented act of writing there is a (con-)fusion of all subjects (including the implied author and reader), whose identities as well as voices and roles in the story are intertwined with the equivocal use of subject pronouns: I, you, he/she. The narrator's bursts of reflection addressing the transformed protagonist are highly ironic, if not sarcastic, indicating the artifice and simulation involved in the presentation of the character: "[...] on Judgement Day, under what guise and nature will the ill-fated appear before the Creator and how will he recognize her without the attributes that he knowingly gave her, remodeled, redone, and handmade, like the circumcised?" (47–48). The exuberant language and centrifugal syntactic/narrative structure of the novel are analogous to Cobra's mutating identities in *hir* continuous flight across shifting transcultural spaces. The character's displacements and mutations are described in opulently baroque detail (Fig. 3.1):

> Her makeup was violent, her mouth painted with branches. Her orbs were black and aluminum-plated, narrow beneath the eyebrows and then elongated by other whorls, powdered paint and metal, to her temples, to the eyes, but in richer kaleidoscope colors; instead of eyebrows, fringes of tiny precious stones hung from the rims of her eyelids. Up to her neck she was a woman; above, her body became a kind of heraldic animal with a baroque snout. (80–81)

Cobra's character constitutes a supreme example of how the exuberant neobaroque linguistic and stylistic procedures disarticulate and transform the identity of the cross-dresser into a transgressive mutant being that chameleonically lives out *hir* plurality to the fullest as a way of chameleonically adapting to adverse circumstances, a way of surviving in a world of oppressive categories of selfhood.

In the novel *Colibrí* (1984), the characters' changing identity becomes the engine of the novel's centrifugal plot. It is about a robust and agile blond youth named Colibrí (Hummingbird) whose (nick)name in itself symbolizes the ease with which he had jumped from the boat that was taking him as prisoner on a river in the middle of a sumptuous American (by all textual accounts) jungle to a sadomasochist brothel, called La Casona. However, imprisoned again, he ends up working there as a hired

Fig. 3.1 Cover of Severo Sarduy's *Cobra and Maitreya*. Dalkey Archive Press, 1995. (Courtesy of Deep Vellum Eds.)

wrestler-pugilist. His most memorable fights are with the overweight Japonesón [Big Japanese], with whom he eventually engages in a romantic relationship. However, the tyrannical owner of the brothel, the Lady-Regent, falls in love with Colibrí, producing an amorous conflict. Pushed by the immanent violence that threatens him at the Casona, Colibrí escapes

142 K. A. KULAWIK

again, this time with his opponent-turned-lover, the Japonesón, to the jungle where they take refuge. After several hunts carried out by the tyrannical Regent's henchmen, and after more spectacular escapes, Colibrí remains in the jungle where he indulges in his sexual relation with the Japonesón and with the multiple incarnations of the Regent's assistant, the Dwarf, and even with her metamorphosed double, the Gigantito. Finally, Colibrí decides to return to the Casona with the same hunters who were commissioned to capture him but who finally rebel, betraying the Lady (Regent). Together, they defeat her and Colibrí ironically, in a political role reversal, turns into the new despot of the Casona.

In the panoply of characters that appear in this novel, most stand out for their ambiguous ever-changing sexual orientations and mutating incarnations. Their relations portray an exuberant yet unstable eroticism that combines mutual pleasure with sadomasochistic violence. The sexual identity of the characters Colibrí, Japonesón, and La Señora-the Lady is repeatedly inverted between homo and heterosexual roles in an array of fluctuating masculine and feminine appearances. Along with effusive attributes of beauty mentioned by the narrator: tall, stout, blond, golden-haired, black-browed, wavy-bodied (13–14),[5] which make him sexually attractive to the other characters, Colibrí is a victim of the Regent's sexual abuse and tyranny. During his escape from the Casona, he reveals his tender homoerotic side in contrast with the (also inverted) despotic masculine impersonation of La Señora: "Colibrí's hand, still dulled by sleep, approaches the other body, naked and fresh. [...] Without speaking, they caress each other. [...] *one in the other* they slept together again" (149; emphasis added). The two contrasting characters fuse their bodies into one in a homoerotic relationship that is the central motor of the plot.

The play of sexual roles reaches its apogee of ambiguity when Colibrí returns to the Casona for the last time to defeat La Señora and take full control of the brothel. But he turns out to be as despotic as she was. His sexual orientation fluctuates, as he rejects homosexuality and adopts macho masculinity as the dominant order: "They're finished forever, did you hear that? [...] forever in this house, alcohol and weed. No more anything that corrupts and weakens [...] And besides, stop being faggots.

---

[5] All examples and quotes are from the 1st Spanish edition of Severo Sarduy's *Colibrí*, Barcelona: Argos Vergara, 1984. All quotes are my translations, as there is no published English translation.

Power is a male thing" (177). In this sexual reversal, the meek and sympathetic "bird" becomes the new Regent of the Casona, demonstrating sadistic traits of hypermasculine domination. This metamorphosis, taking place in the arbitrary transition from effeminate homosexuality to authoritarian, masculine-driven machismo, points to the combinatory effect of roles within the space of one subject, a duality or multiplicity of facets that constitute the character's metamorphic sexuality, and similarly as in *Cobra*, helps him to navigate adversity and homophobic oppression.

In *Colibrí*, transvestism is signaled with artifice—makeup, cosmetic alterations, and attire—as the most outstanding feature of a distinctively American tropical environment that abounds in the sumptuous descriptions, as seen in the caricaturized description of the male cross-dressed Regent-La Señora: "how was she dressed?—Horrid, as always [...] As if she wanted to lose her identity, she had smeared her face with white stucco: only her lips emerged, straight and purplish [...] with violent make-up" (117–18). In *Colibrí*, as in *Cobra*, caricature plays a key part of the neobaroque element of parody. The narrator's sexual orientation is questioned in a parodically metanarrative comment made to him at the end of the novel by a voice that identifies itself as the narrator's father, suggesting that he is the implied writer of the novel (with the last name of Sarduy). The meta-narrator, as the writer, appears in the story as another destabilizing metafictional figure that questions the narrator son's homosexuality, scolding him: "You are already a man and of the Sarduy family, so far, there has been no bird. And I don't want anyone to point me out in the street. So right now, you're going to burn those four pieces of shit too. Who has ever seen a man playing with glittering fruits?" (129). The inverting-mutating identities and homo/heterosexual orientations of the characters evolve analogously to the ambiguous relationship established by the narrator with the text and its implied author. Amidst the lush setting of the American rainforest, identities are put in a free flow (and fall) of inversions and mutations.

Cobra and *Colibrí* constitute examples of how the ornamentation and artifice of Sarduy's neobaroque narrative create cross-dressed mutant characters, whose identity subverts binary sexual attributes of masculinity and femininity as a survival strategy within a power system that exploits them. Gender and sex binaries are combined within the (textual) body of the same character. Transvestism, bodily metamorphosis, and transition of sexual orientations represent in these two novels the fluctuation of the neobaroque sign that articulates a nomadic trans-self in the figure of the bisexual cross-dresser.

Mario Bellatin

Transvestism appears in the novels *Salón de belleza* (1994; *Beauty Salon*) and *Lecciones para una liebre muerta* (2005; "Lessons for a Dead Hare"— no published English translation) in a schematic, albeit natural and direct way, without introductions or explanations, more as part of a textual construct of an illusory character than a plausible representation of a character's identity. It is a form of an arbitrary, textually encoded transformism that recreates conventional attributes of masculinity and femininity. Diana Palaversich considered this illusive, superficial, and mutable nature of Bellatin's characters as a reflection of the narrative and teleological disarticulation of the postmodern text, asserting that these characters "are a mere creation of the text and not a plausible representation of extraliterary identities" (2003: 33).

Salón de belleza is a novel about a hairdressing salon turned into a morgue for the terminally ill after a strange contagious disease spread through a large city (possibly Mexico City, considering narrative hints). At the age of sixteen, the protagonist escapes from his mother's house. Having accumulated some savings while working in "the north of the country," he returns to his place of origin and decides to open a beauty salon that soon attracts a profuse female clientele. In the evenings, when the salon closes, the clerk and his two employees dress up as women and go out in search of men on the main avenues of the city. In the meantime, an unknown disease begins to claim victims rapidly, which is why the protagonist feels the need to house a few dying people in his salon. Little by little, the salon is turned into a *moridero* [morgue], whose function is not to rehabilitate the sick but to offer a place for them to spend their last days. Parallel to this, the protagonist cultivates a particular taste for breeding aquarium fish that share the care given to the terminally ill. Two plot lines alternate, the first around the salon's and its acquariums' role during the epidemic and the second focusing on the origins and the future decline of the narrator's business, providing the story with a certain symbolism around beauty and the fleetingness of life in illness and death.

Ambiguity conditions several narratological elements of this work such as time, space, and characters, since no date, place, or name of any character is ever mentioned. Likewise, the illness suffered by the guests of the beauty parlor is never named, although certain hints indicate AIDS. There are random mentions of the narrator being a cross-dresser who would regularly change clothes with his male friends:

3 SUBVERSIONS OF SELFHOOD: TRANSGRESSIVE CHARACTERS... 145

The women didn't seem to mind being attended by male stylists dressed in women's clothes. [...] There were three of us working in the salon. A couple of times each week we would all get dressed up after closing time, pack up a small suitcase and head off to the center of the city. We couldn't travel dressed as women for we had already gotten into dangerous situations more than once. Which is why we packed up our dresses and our makeup and carried them with us. (13–14)[6]

By way of a metadiscursive intertextual game, in Bellatin's later novel *Lecciones para una liebre muerta*, we observe the inclusion of the same transvestite character from *Beauty Salon*: "Some years ago, while the author of 'Lessons for a Dead Hare' was trying to write his book *Beauty Salon*, a friend began to frequent his house who, while studying philosophy, used to cross-dress in the evenings. This discovery of a transformist philosopher seemed interesting enough for him to dedicate entire afternoons to listen to him talk, not only about his nocturnal adventures" (*Lecciones*... 107; my translation). The change of clothes is presented as a playful, almost natural phenomenon of symbolic-external (re)presentation of the opposite sex to the "biological" or conventionally assigned one, with social-communicative implications, done as a way of personification, performance, pretending, or simulation of certain roles played out as split or parallel personalities. Thus, in *Lecciones* ... we read:

> The writer recalls that the transvestite philosopher would arrive home, make himself a cup of tea and begin to refer to the myth of the eternal return or criticize the Kantian categories. He always carried with him a briefcase with some books and the necessary items for his nocturnal incursions. As he spoke he would take out the earrings, lipstick, and wigs that he would wear later. Without any modesty s/he would take off his trousers and put on a pair of black stockings with diamond-shaped designs. (107; my translation)

Alicia Vaggione (2009) explains in terms of a "specular game" this double nature of the protagonist "and the philosopher as one who not only relates to an aesthetic, that of his own performance, but also to thought and truth. On the plane of this re-writing, the cross-dressed hairdresser-*travesti* in *Salon*... has become a philosopher, a character connected to the search for knowledge" (484; my translation). The narrator himself,

---

[6] All quotes are from the English translation by Kurt Hollander of Mario Bellatin's *Beauty Salon*, San Francisco: City Lights Books, 2000.

transitioning between external-heterodiegetic (third-person) and internal-homodiegetic (first-person) voice, like the cross-dresser himself, refers to the transformations of the transvestite philosopher as "incursions into the game of changing sexual identity" shared with an "early passion for reading" (*Lecciones...* 115). The dual nature of this deceptive and displacing identity is noted. The author enters the narrative and erotic game metadiscursively. We read that "mario bellatin [*sic*] saw [...] how this shy student was transforming into the aggressive woman who, night after night, took different risks in her searches around the city" (*Lecciones...* 107). The text clearly illustrates the mobile and performative character of cross-dressing.

In Bellatin's case, it is important to observe the parallel development of the transformation of the transvestite character in his externalization of sexual roles and the transformative evolution of the "cross-dressed" narrative with its unexpected plot twists. Parallel stories such as those of the aquariums appear as do intertextual mentions of other "real"-existing novels by the author, simulating double presences of a novel within a novel. This is also the case of the Mexican writer Margo Glantz transformed and cross-dressed into "a young trainee lawyer" in *Lecciones* (73), or the peasant transvestite poet in the novel *El libro uruguayo de los muertos* (2012). All are accompanied by metadiscursive explanations of the narrator that transform the novels into a laboratory of narrative metafiction. Vaggione observes that "[i]n the framework of the drifts through which the text passes, the flashes of the golden genres, used for the exercise of a nomadic, clandestine and open sexuality in the framework of the city, are replaced in the space of the *moridero* by the clothes [of the transvestite]" (481; my translation).

Bellatin's use of the narrative fugue, a genuinely baroque technique of composition, becomes more visible in the destabilizing function of the transvestite characters. Likewise, we note that this textual and character transformism itself constitutes one of the bases and, at the same time, keys to Bellatin's writing. Following our previous observations about writing as a type of masking, we notice that, in his narrative, an unstable representation of characters fluctuating between the masculine and the feminine is achieved, as observed by Palaversich: "bodies that mutate from male to female constitute the norm. These bodies [...] unsettle [...] by their tremendous power to destabilize any concept of character unity and transparent narrative meaning" (2005: 11–12). The fragmentation of the narrative structure and of the sexual attributes of the characters entails other mutations: of time, space, bodily state, and identity. According to Palaversich, it is a textual transformism with "signifiers that float freely in Bellatin's narrative, in an infinite free play" (2003: 34). As previously observed in *Salón de belleza*, there is an ironical naturalness to the cross-dresser's routine: A couple of times each week we would all get dressed up [...] pack up a small suitcase and head off to the center of the city. [...] Before standing on a busy street corner dressed as transvestites we would hide the suitcases in a hole at the base of statues of national heroes (13–14).

The change of clothes is presented as a playful—almost natural—activity, in tune with the casual representation of the characters, with the random unfolding of their personalities in fortuitous combinations of the plot. In Bellatin's text, multiple boundaries are crossed, as narrative and identity transitivity complement each other in their transgressive flows.

Silviano Santiago's novel *Stella Manhattan* (1985) transits queer sexuality, politics, and intercultural connections. The action is set in New York City in the period of cultural and political ferment of the late sixties. Echoes of Brazil's military regime (1964–1985) resound with political intrigue in New York City's psychedelic cultural scene of 1969. The novel presents an array of sexually diverse characters of the Brazilian and Hispanic community living in Manhattan. Homosexuality and transvestism intertwine with radical movements of an anti-government conspiracy organized by clandestine Brazilian and Cuban left-wing rebel groups. They plan a series of hijackings of consular officials in Brazil and the United States. The structure of the novel displays a characteristically neobaroque decentered, fugue-like form of three parts with intertwined actions interrupted by shifting metanarrative discourses. The dimensions of time and space in the narration interweave confusing webs that disrupt the binaries of United States/Brazil, New York/Rio, rightist/leftist politics, sexuality/gender, submission/domination. The performative inversions of characters' identities are reflected in the multilayered, fragmented narrative which includes the overt appearance of the book's writer disputing with the narrator.

The main character, Eduardo, was forced from his native Brazil by an unforgiving father, embarrassed by his son's homosexuality and transvestism. "Badly dressed, afraid of his own shadow, and depressed; that's how Stella Manhattan, alias Eduardo da Costa e Silva, arrived in New York" (7).[7] He lands a job in the Brazilian consulate in New York, prearranged

---

[7] For quotes from this novel, we use the English translation by George Yúdice of Silviano Santiago's *Stella Manhattan*, Durham & London: Duke UP, 1994.

by his father's old military friend, Coronel Valdevinos Vianna, "working" in the United States for the military government. Eduardo establishes a relationship with Vianna, who is also a cross-dresser. Eduardo aids Vianna (as a possible payback) to "come out of the closet" with his alter-ego, the leather-clad super macho, sadomasochist Black Widow.

The storyline is filled with double dimensions of lived reality and fantasy lives created (acted out) by the characters. The protagonist Eduardo's consular office position interweaves with his *alter ego* personal life as cross-dresser Stella:

> *She* exhales and stretches out her arms like a vedette in final apotheosis in a burlesque show at Tiradentes Theater. If *she* stood before a staircase, *she* might sashay up the steps regaled in plumes, rhinestones, and sequins, luxuriously making *her* way to the top where in a long and tuneful trill she would bless her delirious admirers with a star-shower of kisses as they screamed: 'She's the greatest! She's the greatest!' Amid frenetic clapping *her* voice would reverberate against the vaults of Manhattan's skyline. Stella Manhattan, the star of Manhattan. (4; emphasis added)

Eduardo adopts the feminine identity of Stella (with last name Manhattan) when in his "off" time he cross-dresses and goes out to village clubs to meet his boyfriends. Throughout the novel, personal pronouns transition from masculine to the feminine "she-hers" when the action focuses on Eduardo's personal life with his partners. This usage is interchangeable with the masculine "he-his" in official settings, e.g., in the consulate.

Eduardo/Stella establishes relationships with other Latinos, like the neighbor Paco-La Cucaracha, a Cuban anti-Castro exile, and his American boyfriend Ricky—the stereotypical 1960s happy-go-lucky youth and model lover. In this gay milieu, s/he impersonates a double identity that undergoes transformative trances, with the added biracial element reflected in *hir* Afro-Brazilian features: "Actually, Maria da Graça went easy on him, she didn't tell him that people were gossiping about his Afro. That mountain of ringlets brought out his negroid features more clearly. 'He looks like a Black Panther,' they'd say" (17). Transiting between the two opposing factions of the military and the revolutionaries, Eduardo is apparently apolitical, dreaming of an idealized Brazil s/he left behind, set in a cloud of nostalgia for *hir* native country brimming with more sexually liberal and erotically effervescent, multiracial values. Yet, in *hir* apparent exile in

New York, he (still as Eduardo) is thrown into a political intrigue in his relationship with Coronel Vianna—the cross-dressed Black Widow—surrounded by a group of Brazilian guerillas who attempt to press Eduardo into their service to entrap the coronel. Drawn into the conflict between the Brazilian government (by whose "generosity" he is employed in the consulate) and its communist opposition (most of his gay friends), Eduardo/Stella is caught between his desire originating from his double sexual identity and his political commitments split between rightist-military Brazil (with its US ally) and the oppositional inter-Latin American leftist revolutionary movement (tied to his intimate life). Eduardo-Stella's divided persona transits the double sexual and political planes of homo/heterosexuality and the conservative versus liberal-radical visions of Latin America. As external political forces dispute for power, Stella and his friends lead a secret life of passions in multiple apartments, nightclubs, and streets.

Neighbors Eduardo and Paco-La Cucaracha negotiate their foreign identities as they attempt to reconcile their differences within the US context of the unifying concept of "Latino." They fluctuate between Portuguese and Spanish, between "masculine" and "feminine" forms of homosexuality, between Paco's Cuban rightist political values and Eduardo's more liberal stance. However, as Susan Quinlan (2002) remarks, "ironically, it is New York society that casts them as one, collapsing Brazilian and Cuban identities into 'Latino.' They are beset with the construct of Latino because Eduardo and Paco both possess African features, speak with accents, have trouble communicating in English" (219). Racial and national identifications come into play in the US-American context of stereotyping Latinos. English becomes the "third" neutral code (after Portuguese and Spanish) in their communication. The linguistic triangle analogously reflects the triple possibility of gender combinations stemming from the sexual relations among the characters fluctuating between masculinity, femininity, and ambiguous transitivity as cross-dressing. Transgressive sexuality may also be regarded as a political stance of these exiled Brazilian and Cuban citizens in a contentious relation to the repressive dictatorial governments in their respective countries. They are caught in the middle of a power struggle between the dictatorial-masculine—represented by the oppressive patriarchal values of their homelands' political regimes—and the progressive liberal-feminine stance represented by their transgressive/-itive sexualities.

150   K. A. KULAWIK

As an illustrative example of this cultural-political split in negotiating identity in the dual space of in-betweenness, the two main characters, Stella and Paco, undertake a heated discussion:

> Paco can't stand maricones who analyze themselves or others. He feels they have three defects. The first is that they are too loose, too uninhibited, as if you could be a faggot twenty-four hours a day. You lose your sense of convenience. Eduardo says that it's a way of taking on an identity and that it's good. Paco retorts that it's like being possessed by the devil. [...] Of course it never occurred to Paco that Eduardo held him up as an exemplary faggot, a maricón with a true sense of self. Paco's life was *no longer that of a man or a woman*. He had style. Not an individual style, his and his alone, but a style that recuperates and sums up and synthesizes *all the inventive gestures* and behaviors of an entire class of people. In a conversation with Eduardo, Marcelo said the main characteristic of today's bicha [Port. "gay"] is a *constant search* for his own faggot *style*. (158; emphasis added)

This reference to identity in the transitive space of in-betweenness (Paco being neither man nor woman and his constant search of a "style") is reminiscent of Roberto Echavarren's emphasis on style (and not fashion) as the distinctive feature of the androgyne and the mutant: the creation of one's selfhood, based on negotiating identity in a dialectical, self-appropriating manner of combining elements from both sides of the binary spectrum of opposites (2008: 7, 11–13).

After finding out that he is persecuted by the police and after his friend, mentor, and lover—Coronel Vianna—refuses to help him escape back to Brazil, Eduardo suffers a breakdown. His self disintegrates and his body willfully transforms in an effort to articulate his identity, a metamorphosis achieved through figurative language:

> Eduardo loses all sense of direction; he knows no shortcuts. [...] He wants to exist. He rolls on the floor, running into the furniture, feeling in his skin the marks of the hits and misses. Eduardo wants all things to be reborn out of nothing right where they are and he invents magic tricks with the movements of his body rolling on the ground. [...] His body is now a circumference around one of the bed's legs. [...] Eduardo recreates from nothing the possibility of the existence of the world, and within it, the possibility of the existence of the movement of life. (176)

3 SUBVERSIONS OF SELFHOOD: TRANSGRESSIVE CHARACTERS...   151

The final transformation of Stella into an animal-like fugitive remains only a conjecture: "by now the puto's [Port. vulgar for gay man] probably already had a plastic surgery, changed his identity and who the fuck is going to recognize him, lying on the beach on some tropical island in the Pacific. That's where American intelligence sends their stoolies" (202). Stella vanishes, just as his ephemeral identities had.

The cross-dressed characters Stella and Leila (the erotically rebellious, cross-dressing wife of a right-wing Columbia University professor) both disappear at the end of the novel, without any disclosure of the ending. This is reminiscent of the vanishing cross-dressers Cobra and Colibrí in Sarduy's novels. After the attempt at Coronel Vianna, the guerrilla plot is revealed to the authorities and Eduardo/Stella falls victim to CIA and police persecution. We are not sure if he wanders off anonymously amidst the streets or night clubs of New York City, or if he returns to his yearned Brazil to blend incognito in the gay milieu of Rio. The character vanishes, and *hir* return is awaited by *hir* NYC companions like that of a Billy the Kid, who will eventually tell the unknown "truth." It is an open ending of a story of an open, double faced, and indeterminate protagonist caught in between multiple binary forces. "Santiago manages to describe the space in between but leaves us no literal meaning" (Quinlan 223).

Santiago's *Stella Manhattan* plays with the ambiguous and performative nature of the concepts of masculinity and femininity in Latin American cultural discourse. At the same time, the novel proposes a transitional in-between space of the "third" sex (the cross-dresser) set between aesthetic representation and political reality of exile and homophobia. Displaying the multiplicity of categories of "otherness," genders and sexual orientations transit in *Stella Manhattan*. They are "invented" as disguises for desired self-identifications in which "[t]he stages may move, yet the performers continue, inventing and reinventing disguise after disguise, gender after gender (gender after genre)" (Quinlan 228). As the metatextual epigraph at the end of the book states, the narrator and characters are intended to be flexible.

Diamela Eltit

In the works of this neoavant-garde Chilean writer, cross-dressing becomes more than a theme of alternative sexual identity. With her use of experimental narrative and language, it acquires the dimension of political agency of resistance and transgression of Chile's dictatorial, neoliberal, heteronormative order. In defiance to masculine heteronormativity, Eltit disguises the

152   K. A. KULAWIK

clear meaning of sexuality using the technique of textual, visual, and performative simulation. In Eltit's novels, the opposition to official cultural discourse is carried out symbolically by means of violent confrontations of sexually ambiguous characters who operate in contrasting linguistic registers. These elements are characteristic of and have been described by critics as "neoavant-garde," "post-boom," or "neobaroque" (Burgos 1992, 252–60; Maíz-Peña 1997, 293–94). The novel *El cuarto mundo* (1988; *The Fourth World*) represents a rupture of sexual and cultural identity in a story about twins that begins in the womb of the mother and moves on through the birth and the stages of life of the two siblings. When they reach puberty, a family crisis caused by conflict between the parents occurs. This induces the male twin (the first narrator) to cross-dress and approach his sister in an incestuous and sexually ambiguous relationship. As a result of this incest, the two conceive a "bastard" child whose birth is awaited in tension until the end of the novel. In a metafictional twist, the second narrator—the female twin—unveils as Diamela Eltit, the implicit author of the text, becoming one of the characters of the novel. She turns out to be the mother of the illegitimate "*sudaca*" [a disrespectful word for South American] child/text "born" at the end of the story. This metafictional procedure increases the level of ambiguity of voices and cross-dressed appearances in the text and confers the story an allegorical dimension of an ironically named "fourth world"—a South American socio-cultural borderland.

The newborn's uncertain sexual identity perplexes amidst the contrasting affections and authority of the parents, as in the symbolic act of naming the children. The sexual identity of the cross-dressed son is ambiguously dual from the beginning of the novel, as seen in the act of receiving a name: "They gave me the name of my father. They also gave my sister a name. My mother, looking at me deviously, said I was the same as María Chipia, that I was she. Running her slender hand over me, she said: 'You are María Chipia' [...] Then my rebellious infirmity became the epicenter of chaos" (14).[8] The problematic sexual identification of the child narrator can be observed when he was lying in bed with his twin sister María: "we were each just half of one another, unnaturally complementary, all of which forced me to consider my hybrid nature" (16). The two bodies fuse and their gender distinctions are blurred in what the narrator calls a "habit of transfusions" (42). In a characteristically avant-gardist procedure of

---

[8] For all quotes, we use the English translation by Dick Gerdes of Diamela Eltit's *The Fourth World*, Lincoln: U of Nebraska P, 1995.

3 SUBVERSIONS OF SELFHOOD: TRANSGRESSIVE CHARACTERS...   153

spatial-temporal dislocation, the narrative resorts to flashbacks and fast-forwards, as in the scene when still in the womb of the mother, the male narrator feels the influence of his twin sister: "The feminine counterparts, which were dominant in this situation, carried persistent messages. Trying to escape her desperation was impossible; so, instead, I opted for openly imposing my masculinity [...] despite our attempts to *change positions*, the space would not contain us [...] my sister maneuvered herself to a position underneath me" (11; emphasis added).

The trespassing of boundaries between the two bodies occurs in their attempts to "change positions," as their bodies eventually blend into one hybrid being: "I would become frightened as we rubbed up against each other in the dark, but I also began to think that there was neither one precise place for anyone nor were we each one individual person but, instead, we were each just half of one another, unnaturally complementary, all of which forced me to consider *my hybrid nature*" (16; emphasis added). Sexual distinctions are blurred when the male, cross-dressed narrator admits to his fluctuating selfhood when lying in bed with his twin sister: "It was impossible for me to conceive of life without my sister. A part of me ended in her, perhaps the most stable and permanent part" (38). The transitive connection with the sister's "other" is symbolized by "transfusion": "Without really knowing whether this act was an attempt to fuse myself with her or, to the contrary, I was making her responsible for unleashing my blood, we intuitively pulled away from each other—fearful of establishing the habit of transfusions" (42).

Eltit's narrative displays a playful, if not experimental, use of language that parallels the theme of cross-dressing. Using the Spanish original, as the translation does not render this experimental play, we quote: "Intenté bloquearme y leer para partera, emití la imagen de un peligroso bisturí, aluciné palqui" (*El cuarto mundo* 115) ["I tried to keep things going, maybe learn how to be a midwife, but I hallucinated images: a dangerous scalpel and palqui bushes would appear in my mind"] (75). Unexpected changes occur in the narrative voice which fluctuates between homo (first person) and heterodiegesis (third person). The voice passes from the male narrator protagonist to that of the female—the twin sister—who cedes her feminine name to the brother, who is now cross-dressed: "My twin brother adopted the name María Chipia and, like a transvestite, became a virgin, for a virgin could predict the birth" (69). Eltit's *The Fourth World* is a notable example of how trans-identity is conceived with the fluid passing of subjectivity from male to female positions on the body of the

154   K. A. KULAWIK

transvestite character. This happens in a double dimension of the literal cross-dressed body and its allegorical projection of a marginalized "fourth-world" peripheral identity of the Latin American "other."

Pedro Lemebel (with Francisco Casas)
The works of contemporary Chilean writers-visual artists Pedro Lemebel and Francisco Casas utilize cross-dressing as a parodic weapon to undermine normative identity formulations of an order imposed by heterosexual, patriarchal, and dictatorial power structures. Partaking in the exuberant and ornamental language of the neobaroque, these authors and performers highlight in their urban chronicles and novels the transgressive figure of the cross-dresser as a political statement of resistance in the context of Chile's military dictatorship in the 1980s and the ensuing transition to a neoliberal, postcolonial, yet still hegemonic heteronormative system.[9] The use of artifice, as neobaroque linguistic expenditure, is related to the cross-dresser's simulation, an artistic and discursive technique of masking that reveals the conventionality of the categories instituted by the patriarchal masculine-heterosexual system.

Since the 1990s, Pedro Lemebel became known for his fictionalized chronicles in which he explored the social margins of neoliberal urban Chile of the democratic transition. The chronicle *La esquina es mi corazón* (1995; "The Street Corner Is My Heart", n.t.) presents a politicized view of sexuality in Santiago, a city of neoliberal paradoxes. Lemebel's partner in the Yeguas del Apocalipsis [Mares of the Apocalypse] project, Francisco Casas, published his memories of their performances in a collection of fictionalized testimonials titled *Yo, yegua* (2004; "I, the Mare," n.t.). In both chronicles, the cross-dressed first-person narrators Dolores del Río and María Félix who, using the names of classical 1930s–1950s female Mexican film stars, apparently refer to the *alter egos* of the empirical authors as they embark on a textual/sexual journey through a city still besieged by dictatorial control and the imposed neoliberal economic and social order. As they transit the nameless, faceless, anonymous city of the consumer masses, they reveal spaces of social and political dissent. These spaces include artistic

---

[9] It is to be noted that Pedro Lemebel was also an accomplished novelist and Francisco Casas a poet. However, for a lack of space, we will not comment on these works, even if the presence of cross-dressing is notable in them. Such is the case of Lemebel's *Tengo miedo torero* (2001), in which the love affair between the cross-dressed protagonist Loca del Frente and young political activist Carlos is romantically set in the historical context of Chile's military dictatorship to depict the failed assassination attempt of General Augusto Pinochet in 1986.

happenings, performances, movie theaters, bookstores, political rallies, parks, and shantytowns—the *callampas santiaguinas*—all part of the sprawling, hybrid, and unequally "modern" Latin American metropolis.

Using a playful and parodic narrative, Casas' and Lemebel's texts present transvestism as a radical artistic and political stance to decenter notions of identity, not only sexual, but national, ethnic, and social. The figure of the transvestite represents a rupture with the heterosexual traditionally White Chilean male subject, representative of the official culture, privileged by political and economic control. The city of contrasts serves as a backdrop for the narrative in which the instability and mobility of the urban space turn the text into a symbolic "accomplice space" in the transformation of the characters' gender, ethnic, and social identities. Lemebel's and Casas' performances highlight the figure of the cross-dresser, whose images illustrate several book covers. On the Seix Barral edition of *La esquina es mi corazón* (EC after forthcoming quotes), Lemebel appears in a photo-installation using partial drag and an alligator on his lap' (Fig. 3.2).

Fig. 3.2 *Sin título* [*No title*], Pedro Lemebel, 1990. (Photo by Pedro Marinello. Courtesy of Archivo Pedro Lemebel)

Fig. 3.3 *Las dos Fridas* [*The Two Fridas*], performance by Pedro Lemebel and Francisco Casas, 1990. (Photo by Pedro Marinello. Courtesy of photographer)

Among several others, the covers of Lemebel's *Loco afán* and Casas' *Yo, yegua* also feature the authors' performances or photo-installations (Fig. 3.3). The chronicles of *Yo, yegua* by Casas (YY after forthcoming quotes) tell the story behind the performance work of the Yeguas del Apocalipsis. Like *La esquina…*, it features transvestite (cross-dressed) protagonists, whose voices, gazes, and actions are narrated in a storyline of urban adventures. The narrator voice fluctuates between the homodiegetic "I" and the heterodiegetic and omniscient third-person collective voice of the "habitat of poverty," the "neo-liberal inheritance of this demos-gracia […] cannon fodder in the traffic of big politics," "South American wasteland" (EC 35–36; my translation). The action situates in documented

3 SUBVERSIONS OF SELFHOOD: TRANSGRESSIVE CHARACTERS... 157

urban spaces such as Parque Forestal, Plaza Italia, Nagasaki cinema, Alameda, neighborhoods such as Florida, Brasil, San Miguel. These sites contain a symbolic meaning associated with transgressive actions of the two *locas* [drag queens]. The image of the city in the chronicles is blurred, fractured, and ambiguous. In an interview Lemebel called it "a shifting territoriality [...] a movable, transfugal territory" (Jeftanovic 2000, 74), describing it in his chronicle as an "obscene x-ray of the family album, or complicity of passions [...] as flows that permeate the metropolitan free flow" (EC 49). They are passions that look, according to Casas, "between the cracks of the city destroyed by the bombing [during Pinochet's military coup]" (YY 21; my translation).

In *La esquina...*, cross-dressers appear concealed among a series of textual contrasts that are characteristically neobaroque in the ornamented yet abject images of the city, a fancy yet vulgar vocabulary, slang intertwined with elaborate syntax, street talk with poetic figures and experimental techniques. Their voices fuse with what they sarcastically call a "habitat of poverty" (35–36). The testimonial text becomes a mocking performance of social condemnation of the postmodern city, carried out from a queer perspective of a drag queen. It is a "*loca*-crazy" cartography of a drag queen's "*ciudad-anal*" gaze (a pun roughly meaning "citizen's anal gaze of the city") of Santiago's "*ver-ano*" ("sum-mer" or "gaze of the anus"). It constitutes a subversive and radical rewriting of the city's "behind" as it unveils the furtive activities of the marginal street characters: vagabonds, drug addicts, artists, street performers, and cross-dressers, banned in public spaces. The benefits of the "official" city of the neoliberal free-market economy inundate it with their limitless offer of trinkets and paid sexual pleasures, ironically reflected in the exuberant language of the chronicle.

The figure of the transvestite is linked to contrasting images of disguised love, prostitution, and homophobic violence. These images are constructed with a highly figurative, ornamental language reminiscent of the Baroque, as seen in the violent scene of the stabbing of the drag queen:

> Holding back the vomit of *copihues*[10] she flirts him [...] the night on the wasteland is the arena of a fight, a handkerchief in a coliseum which in a flamenco flight taints it in scarlet. Red foam of the faggot which *andalusiates* him in flames while cutting through. Toreador of topaz is the moving boy who slices him, orange-blossoms him in boiling corduroy, shattered Macarena. (167; my translation and italics with foreign terms)

[10] A characteristically Chilean lily-like red flower.

The overload of poetic figures recalls the seventeenth-century Baroque techniques of masking and veiling literal meaning behind exuberant imagery, a textual *maquillaje* (cosmetic makeup). The neoliberal façade of economic prosperity masks the city's inner self of poverty and abjection, represented in the exuberant ornamentation of Lemebel's neobaroque style: "Thus, at the flash of December, the city dresses up as a Christmas Eskimo. […] Lots of glitter and strings of lights to decorate the filthy face of the buildings" (EC: 147). The imagery of the sumptuously masked abject is yet another element of neobaroque simulation.

The figurative and sonorous baroque discourse of Lemebel's and Casas's chronicles portrays street corners populated by exuberant, outlandish transvestite figures that glide through the cityscapes censored by the vigilante apparatus. In *La esquina…* we read: "That is why every night she crosses the bower of her feathers and does not mind coagulating with other men, who meander the paths like lost anacondas, like red-headed snakes that are recognized by the traffic lights urged by their rubies" (EC 24–25). In Casas *Yo, yegua*, we see them represented with baroque splendor that makes references to Rome's famous fountain: "[…] scenes of copulating birds, slender toucans trilling the glittering gazebo of that sunken Trevi Fountain" (YY 24). The crude space of the city is transformed, together with the transvestite characters and by means of an opulent language, into a sumptuous mythical space of erotic desire. The encounter of the two protagonists takes place on the banks of the polluted and fetid Chilean stream flowing through the heart of Santiago, now transformed into the Egyptian Nile:

> Dolores del Río and María Félix spend their afternoons reclining on one of the benches that rest next to the Frenchified southern bank of the Mapocho River. Seen from a distance, they resemble perverse Cleopatras next to an obsessive Nile, through whose torrent pink flamingos blaspheme the dream of Anubis. In drunkenness they see Caesar's matchless galley sailing downstream. The two prissy ones see the legs of the young emperor decorated with an erectile mound that shudders them. (YY 18; my translation)

The nomadic presence of the cross-dressers transforms the destitute urban spaces with their performance of "miserable opulence" (YY 18) among "the cardboard shacks proliferating like mushrooms" (150). In their neobaroque simulation, they confer it a tone of a carnivalesque masquerade.

3 SUBVERSIONS OF SELFHOOD: TRANSGRESSIVE CHARACTERS... 159

Throughout the chronicles, the narrative voice fluctuates between the first person of the characters and the third of the external and neutral guide-observer (voyeur) who assumes a plurality of foci and a polyphony of voices that originate in the multifaceted and fragmented city.

Lemebel and Casas take their parodic simulation to the political level with their cross-dressed/nude performances of the Yeguas del Apocalipsis. They crash into poetic, cultural, and political events: a book fair in the Parque Forestal (on the edge of the Mapocho River), the homage to poet Raúl Zurita in the residence of poet Pablo Neruda—La Chascona; the elitist celebration of Bastille Day at the Alliance Française in the new and remodeled Cultural Center of the Mapocho Station. During the inauguration of the first post-dictatorial democratic president, Patricio Aylwin, the two half (un)dressed and posed as the Mexican artist Frida Kahlo to simulate a blood transfusion between each other in a photo-performance at the Chilean Human Rights Commission titled *The Two Fridas*. It represents a pastiche of Frida Kahlo's famous double self-portrait of the same title, depicting the duality of the split, as much as transitive, self that embodies a double subjectivity of "one" and/in "other," symbolically interconnected by blood vessels (Fig. 3.3).

In *Yo, yegua*, Casas mentions another notable intervention of the Mares in 1987, this time in a direct demonstration protesting to the dictatorship's repressive policies. The two naked performers mounted a horse that was led through the streets of Santiago to the Art Faculty of the University of Chile. Their bodies sharply contrasted with the ongoing student demonstrations, repressed by the military police. Referring to the event in his intricate chronicle, Casas resorts to figurative embellishments of an otherwise stark narration of the dramatic events of that day (Fig. 3.4):

> Paper rain, followed by dry applause, falls on the naked bodies of María Félix and Dolores del Río. The Lady Godivas are mounted on the mare Parecía. Dolores governs the bridle [...] María [Lemebel], holding Dolores [Casas] by the waist, places her buttocks on the wide rump of the draft beast, which advances gracefully, trotting as if it were carrying a fresh bundle of costine lettuce. The violent protests of the students demanding the resignation of the military rector have been going on for several days. They are shouting throughout Chilean territory for the country's return to democracy. The demonstrations leave hundreds of students injured, the riot police confront them with tear gas bombs and water cannons. (YY 167)

Fig. 3.4 *Refundación de la Universidad de Chile* [*Refounding of the University of Chile*], Las Yeguas del Apocalipsis, 1988. (Photo by Ulises Nilo. Courtesy of Archivo Yeguas del Apocalipsis)

Casas' text establishes a connection with Spanish Golden Age baroque literature as it plays intertextually with Miguel de Cervantes' (2004) *Don Quijote de la Mancha*. In a parodic twist, Casas presents the theme of the lustful "mares" (María Félix and Dolores del Río) inversely echoing the scene of Don Quijote's horse, Rocinante, overcome with desire to rub elbows with "the lady mares" (*Don Quijote*, Part III, Ch. 15: 130–31). Noteworthy is the parodic parallelism between the immodest encounter of Don Quijote's horse with the "Galician mares" and the wanderings of the apocalyptic "Mares" around the streets of Santiago in search of amorous adventures.

In the chronicles by Lemebel and Casas, the subversive presence of the cross-dresser in the context of the city encumbered by hegemonic political and economic structures claims a space of resistance. It does so by transgressing the public domain of the street with cross-dressed or naked bodies. The sexualized body constitutes the medium of expression of a nomadic subject, whose transgressive sexuality stands in opposition to the oppressive political system. The ostentatious and parodic performance of the drag queens in their simulation between the masculine and the feminine are expressed in the verbal and figurative lavishness of the exuberant neobaroque text (Fig. 3.5).

Fig. 3.5 Pedro Lemebel (in red feathers). (Photo by Joanna Reposi Garibaldi. Courtesy of photographer)

Naty Menstrual
This Argentine performer, writer, and graphic artist published *Continuadísimo* in 2008 to much critical acclaim, as reflected in positive reviews and ensuing interviews (Peralta 2010, 116).[11] The collection of twenty-four short stories, or vignettes—brief scenes reminiscent of the urban chronicle—portrays the passionate, sometimes romantic yet usually violent scenes, occurrences, and anecdotes involving relationships of a first-person narrator who focuses on the experiences of cross-dressers. The setting are the streets, love motels, X cinemas, and apartments of Buenos Aires. The inversions of identity, or the subversions of sexual, gender, ethnic, and social categories, are the distinctive features of a narrative that is transgressive in its crudeness and graphically eschatological expression, but one that also contains a good measure of ornamental-poetic exuberance and popular flair.

[11] Cf. Jorge Luis Peralta, "La narrativa travesti de Naty Menstrual." *Lectora*, 17 (2010): 105–22.

162   K. A. KULAWIK

The collection adopts a traditional story format with everyday life scenes of the urban underworld, yet the dynamism of the language and its abundance of slang and jargon, with the addition of poetic, romantic, and fantastical vocabulary, and the agile twists of spatial and temporal dimensions, give Menstrual's prose a neobaroque feel of grotesque profusion and verbal excess. The upside-down world of usually violent relationships of the depicted characters is construed and reflected in a "rebellious linguistic object" (Peralta 108)—the crude, graphic, yet overabundant language of Buenos Aires' trans underworld. In typical neobaroque fashion, the profusion of otherwise harsh slang combines and contrasts with the more poetic tone of sophisticated vocabulary and figurative imagery: "She was walking among the trees like a leopard on the hunt, looking at the glare of the lights of the machines that formed a twisting chain edging the forest. A lot of brand-new cars and brand-new kids, although there were also regulars who had already lost their unbeaten streak" (22; my translation).[12] The characters, most of whom are transvestites, show signs of a desired femininity attained in a process of continuous transformation of the body in multiple, colorful, artificial forms, achieved with craft:

> Her name was Sissy Lobato. She had given herself that name when she decided to cross-dress for the first time. She swore she had the palatial glamour of Sissy the Empress and the overwhelming eroticism of a prima vedette like Nélida Lobato. She had done everything possible in those twenty years to look like one of them, she injected as much liquid silicone as there was [...] First a little bit of BREAST, then a little bit of HIP, later the mirror pointed to the NOSE [...]. (15; capitals in original)

This femininity is concealed under a shell of "masculine" determination to survive in a harsh world of sadistic aggression. Sissy was the victim of a brutal attack by a well-to-do and apparently kind man. In self-defense, she killed the aggressor with a frying pan and cannibalistically castrated the corpse at the end of a brutal scene. This story, like most, portrays the cross-dresser's victimization in an intolerant, homophobic, and classist society.

Minita [Lil' Gal], a transvestite from the story "Fantasía final," felt a strong identification with femininity. She desired to be pregnant and have

---

[12] Quotes from Menstrual are my translations from the edition: Naty Menstrual. *Continuadísimo*. Buenos Aires: Eterna Cadencia, 2008.

a baby of her own. She could not stand her masculine body, she desired the feminine. Again, artifice was her method toward mutation: "How could she allow herself to undress and discover the truth that was wounding her to death without remedy? Alone was better and she could. Everyone wanted her and she knew she was beautiful. Feminine. Delicate. Balanced, with long, slender hands, beautiful breasts full of hormones recommended to her by a good friend" (28). She simulated her pregnancy and carried it out by means of artifice, stuffing her belly. Her transformation reaches fulfillment when, during a bank robbery when Mina happened to be standing in line, the thief fired at her swollen womb. She was carried out by a guard with whom moments earlier she had established a romantic bond, and who in accepting her "double" lie did not reject her after seeing that no blood ran out of her belly. It is one of the unusual romantic scenes of acceptance of a character's inverted identity. Genuine transformation occurred when "[h]e let her know that it was all right, [...] and sealed her mouth with a kiss of desperate love. She understood that something had died ... but something much more real ... had just begun" (32). Thanks to that loving touch, the transformation of identity in Mina was now complete as she attained the acceptance of her femininity in spite of her despised male body.

In the story "Sabrina Duncan y su linda cabellera" ["Sabrina Duncan and Her Beautiful Hairpiece"], the feminine identification of the transvestite is clear, but the male-female roles invert during the sexual encounter:

> She didn't work as a transvestite, she just let herself be driven by her feminine need when she was horny. [...] A nice pair of small tits, they imagined those were.—"I'm straight," said one of them after calling Sabrina and sticking his head out of the window. [...] She adjusted her dirty, burnt, cheap *canecalon* wig and ran her tongue over her swollen lips, half twisted by the home-made botox injections.—I'm a little girl ... or didn't you notice? Each one agreeing with his lie sustained in a world of absurd fantasy, they went together to a dark corner to pamper themselves unrestrainedly. (21–22)

Menstrual's narrative depicts the inversion of the concept of self in closed homo/heterosexual terms and defined roles in sexual practices. This inversion is noted in the fluctuating attitudes toward defining selfhood by the cross-dressed characters. Transvestite identity shifts are performed textually by linguistic means and in intricate narrative form that "constructs the margin" (Peralta 105). These inversions reject the affirmation of any defined sexuality, shunning both hetero and homonormativity. There is an absence of typically heterosexual and homosexual characters who would present standard and normative perspectives of sexuality. Menstrual carries out a narrative focused on the dubious and inverted male-female relationship from within the transvestite perspective, using the first person and omniscient narrator who shares first-hand the experience of the characters, understands and empathizes with them, or directly takes part in the action. This perspective of the "authentic" experience is affirmed in the narrator's references to Menstrual being a cross-dresser, as well as an artist and writer herself, as autobiographic themes abound in her stories, giving them a testimonial flair. In "Continuadísimoooo," after a pleasant relation with the unusually "perfect" partner, the narrator reveals: "He asked me what I was doing [in life], so I told him that, among other things, I was writing and he told me oh, you're an artist" (134).

The expression of sexuality is notably modeled on the feminine role. But in frequent inversions, this portrayal rejects any essentializing categorization of sexuality, shunning from adopting the patterns of male/female (not even mentioning them), preferring inversions of active/passive roles in relationships. The cross-dressed (male) characters express a "feminine feeling" that cross-identifies them. In his analysis of Menstrual's narrative, Jorge Luis Peralta observes:

> Thus, we could think that in this narrative universe, transvestites have built their bodies and their identity signs on the basis of female models, but that, at the same time, women have adopted certain features of the transvestite idiosyncrasy, which causes an interesting fracture in the conventional gender binomial. In the end, what does it mean to be a woman or to be a transvestite? Menstrual questions the generic imperatives while showing the artificiality and contingency of its presuppositions. (Peralta 108; my translation)

The characters' roles as active or passive agents are inverted in multiple ways: in the narrator's questioning of the true "macho" identity of her male partners and in the active rather than the expected passive the role of the cross-dresser in the sexual act.

Exemplifying a crossing of multiple identities on different levels of gender, sexuality, race, and ethnicity, the character La Mr. Ed "[...] was unique. Ugly as she was. A Tucumana of pure stock, brunette, almost Black, of Aboriginal ancestors. Nothing had prevented her, in spite of her enormous ugliness, from becoming a faggot first and then a travesti. [...]

But she loved being queer. That's why she quit. She never returned to her province" (73–74). Homophobia and racism are what the *mestiza* transvestite experiences, a rejection of all the negative traits of her minoritarian standing in a society of White masculine hegemony: "Those same fascists who filled their mouths in coffee chats censuring everything were the ones who most asked for their asses to be filled when it was time to sleep with a *trava* [derogatory for 'transvestite']" (73). With La Mr. Ed we see one of several examples of an ending that is a complete metamorphosis of the character. After accidentally moistening medicinal seeds that she had received from a witch doctor to cure the symptoms of AIDS, and after ingesting them wet, her body, in a bathtub, turned into a vine that grew along with other seeds that she had accidentally watered all around the inundated apartment where she was cohabiting with friends. No one saw her body anymore, as La Mr. Ed vanished, transforming into a plant: "In the bathtub ... a drop leaking from the shower ... unintentionally watered ... a little bud that was being born" (81).

As seen in La Mr. Ed's mutation into a plant, a feature of Menstrual's prose is the use of fantasy along with the theme of metamorphosis. This is usually accompanied by a good dose of parodic humor. Her characters undergo transformations from human to ethereal, plant, or animal states in a casual, almost "natural" way, appearing as ruptures within the otherwise realist logic of the story. Besides transformations or transits between gender categories, identities evolve to new ones, as some characters undergo a complete transformation from human to non-human or animal states, or combine part-human, part-other creature-like forms, depicting symbiotic mutants. One example of such a transformation is the story "Amada [Beloved] Kombucha." It narrates the process of incorporation of an organic, edible kombucha fungus into the body of a lonely, depressed, and sickly bloated transvestite (narrating in first person) who bought it from a neighbor to cure her uncontrolled and embarrassing onsets of bloating. After ingesting the fungus in exaggerated amounts, the "woman" begins to feel that it is taking her over from the inside. When a handsome plumber arrives to fix a clog (one that she hadn't even reported!), both desiring bodies become involved in sexual intercourse during which a "Kombucha monster" emerges from her anus and devours the visitor:

> I felt the vinegary taste of the Kombucha in my throat ... but suddenly at the best moment I felt something strange inside my body ... a twisting of

the guts ... an internal hecatomb ... no ... just now I felt like shitting ... just now ... [...] something strange was happening with my organism ... the Kombucha started to move frantically inside ... to roar like a lion in heat and the plumber thought he was the one making me roar ... noooooo ... it was the angry and jealous Kombucha that wanted to get out ... it was Sigourney Weaver in *Alien* ... for Goddd's sake ... [...] the Kombucha took advantage and fiercely stuck its sticky head out and stuck its big tongue out and looked at me and winked an eye and at the horrified look of my snazzy brand-new lover the Kombucha looked at him opened its mouth wide and ate him ... when it had digested, it cracked out a terrible belch with the smell of freshly chewed male and crawled back into me. (58–59)

The woman narrator is astounded but content: "since that day I am no longer depressed. ... I am happy ... I no longer need a man around ... noooo ... what for? Close? Not a chance ... if I already have one inside me" (59). Another empowering transformation comes to fruition in this humorous example of Menstrual's handling of the crude reality of the cross-dresser's social abjection. It brings us back to Spanish seventeenth-century Baroque prose, where the presence of comical monsters plays a satirical-moral role in Francisco de Quevedo's *Sueños* and Baltasar Gracian's *El Criticón* (Fig. 3.6).

As in the Baroque, the abject and monstrous are sublimated in artistic forms including the use of contrastive language, combination of vocabulary of high- and low-popular registers, hyperboles resulting in monstruous, grotesque, and macabre scenes, characteristic of baroque and avant-garde imagery of the *esperpéntico* [exaggerated and absurd]. A good example comes from the story "Qué tren, qué tren" [What Train, What Train? n.t.]:

The tits were already a mass that was confused with the waist—which on top of that had never existed—. She could not distinguish well if what she saw in the mirror was a nipple or a navel. The hips ... one at calf level ... the other at an ankle. The mouth ... the mouth was something else. [...] It was like ... it was as if she had tried to eat two rump steaks but had not been able to swallow them, and then they were hanging from her lips, waiting to be digested. (33–34)

Ironically, in the story "Medialuna de Manteca," the only one in which Menstrual overtly includes police characters, the transvestite is not a victim of violence. Instead of being the object of homophobic aggression,

3 SUBVERSIONS OF SELFHOOD: TRANSGRESSIVE CHARACTERS... 167

Fig. 3.6 Naty Menstrual at a reading in Buenos Aires, 2020. (Photo by Augusto Starita, Ministerio de Cultura de la Nación. Source: Wikimedia Creative Commons)

her transformed body is accepted as source of pleasure and fulfillment of her trans-identity. Menstrual does not intend to portray a transphobic perspective; instead, s/he shows an array of multiple outlooks that may be out of line with both the defenders of heterosexism and a "politically correct" homonormativity (as another essentializing categorization). Her intention is to portray the displaced sites of bodies that are rejected and marginalized, that do not matter in our society. Perhaps we could consider the abject bodies of Sissy Lobato, Sabrina Duncan, La Mr. Ed, and the many others in the twenty-four vignettes, as the abject element that, according to Kristeva "disturbs an identity, a System, an order" (Peralta 118), as disorderly subversive cross-dressed bodies opposed to the binary norms imposed by society, and whose role is to reflect the image of otherness, necessary for the fulfillment of oneself in a nomadic plurality of selves.

Susy Shock has been a part of the *travesti* activist movement in Argentina since the first decade of 2000. As poet, singer, performer, and social advocate, she contributed to the *MU Magazine* of the Lavaca cooperative and has collaborated with Marlene Wayar in the Futuro Transgénero collective in Buenos Aires. Her political engagement is evident in "Oración

168   K. A. KULAWIK

a la divina trans" ("Prayer to the Divine Trans"), which reveals a poetic
subject and performative persona of a trans resistance fighter:

> Lady of the Trans/Dirty from hair to tail/And so blessed. … /Grant me the
> will to enlighten and illuminate/Give me strength to battle/With my shin-
> ing sword of ideas/With my lumpen butterfly of loving/And the humility
> of knowing I'm a diamond/Of my own creating. … Amen. (Zarranz and
> Ciancaglini 2019: 9, my translation)

With ideas (sword) and affection (butterfly), she intends to be the agent
of change creating a subject of her own conjuring, a trans-identity personified in her self-designation as a *travesti*, a *trans-trava-sudaca*.[13]

Referring to Shock's work in the article "Trans Formarse," Claudia
Acuña remarks: "How do you change the world? Not that world of the
utopian category, but this one that we trample on every day, avoiding
obstacles? […] but [in] another, different [world] that allows other possibilities, all of them, even those that we do not even imagine today?" (TF
11; my translation).[14] Susy Shock's role in that project of identity (and
political) transformation is with her poetry, performance, and activism.
Acuña sums up Shock's work with "a disturbing term: heterofugue" that
troubles us with outlining a horizon for conceiving identity with the
baroque technique of the fugue; here, of subjectivity and desire. Shock
explains this poetically: "my gender is hummingbird: the only bird that
dies if it is locked up" (TF 22).

Susy's project intends to do away with stigmatization and labeling; in
her art, binary categories melt down. The artist responds to the question
about identity: "What am I? Does it matter? I am art. […] Actually, we are
all art. […] we are talking about rethinking male and female roles" (TF
39–40).[15] Shock explains how art needs to allow to transit genders and
genres in a terrain of a great unknown, in connection with the Earth, as a

---

[13] *Trava* is an abbreviated form of the term *travesti* (Spanish for transvestite or cross-
dresser), that may also include the transgender category. *Sudaca* is short for South American,
and a European derogatory term for immigrants from that part of the world (Martínez &
Mora 23).

[14] The quotes marked as (TF) are my translations from the edited collection *Trans
Formaciones* comprising essays, interviews, and creative works, edited by Zarranz and
Ciancaglini. Buenos Aires: 2019.

[15] From the article and interview with Susy Shock by Luis Zarranz, "Teoría (y práctica) del
Shock" in *Trans Formaciones* (39–40).

return to traditional, ethnic, provincial values. Thus, Shock's performances combine poetic recital with song and percussion instruments. Many include her poems from *Poemario Trans Pirado* (2011) accompanied by traditional folk songs, such as *coplas* and *bagualas*.[16] By means of her deep, disconcerting voice, she produces a cross/multi-genre spectacle in which she performs, recites, and sings her verse in the traditional *baguala* song, addressing ways to avoid gender, racial, ethnic, and social binarism. While not denying identities, she sees the need to adopt a way of transiting them:

> And the Pachamama: I have a great connection with the Earth, even being *porteña* [inhabitant of Buenos Aires] as I am, but I allow myself to find it in certain sonorities. [...] The *baguala* allows your voice to go through certain canons or, in any case, through none of the established ones. It allows you to play with masculinities and femininities. [...] I do not deny the masculinity I have because it is part of my construction, of the being I am aiming at. Now, I don't know where that construction will go: that is my search. But I also know that politically I need—and it is needed—for a guideline to be established. (TF 40–41)

The performer adopts an "unclassifiable radical alterity" (Martínez and Mora 2020: 1, 3–5) that she describes in her writings and interviews as "monstrous." In an intersectional crossing of several cultural categories, gender identifications of the transvestite are imbued by elements of North Argentinian folkloric traditions and the real-life contexts of both the rural province and urban Buenos Aires. These lines of hybridization escape the homogeneity of any categorized identity.

Both Zarranz (*Trans Formaciones* 2019, 41) and Martínez and Mora (2020: 17–19) observe how Shock's performance goes beyond a purely linguistic-textual representation. The role that hands, even fingernails, makeup, gestures, mimicry, but above all, Susy's voice play in her performance enables a transformative experience of deconstruction and transitive rearticulation of identity. As Shock states: "Art, in itself, does not have a genre, and, in any case, if it does, the academy has given it to it. I speak of an art as a space of exploration that each and every one of us has, to bring out what we have to bring out. Therefore, it has no genre, it has no

---

[16] Martínez and Mora (2020) state: "Her poetic performances include songs that can be framed within the national folklore musical genres, both urban and rural—such as *vidalas*, *coplas* and *tangos*. Her unique stamp comes from the appropriation of a traditional cultural product in the voice of a trava" (2–3).

title" (TF 41). Her *travesti/trava-sudaca* identity is not theoretically conceived, as much as it is part of the collective undertaking of a *teoría trans trava latinoamericana* with another trans-writer and critic, Marlene Wayar. Their selves flow from the desiring and affective experience of "real-world" life, originating outside of aesthetic representation: "The bonds of affection are the basis from which we have to put into practice these ideas for the world we dream of. […] I am saying it from the street, I am not saying it because I am an artist or a café citizen: I am in the street" (TF 43).

The creation of identity as a personal endeavor of artistic and subjective formation is expressed in *Poemario Trans Pirado* of which one fragment mentions: "My right to explore myself/to reinvent myself/to make my mutation my noble exercise/to summer me, to autumn me, to winter me: /the hormones/the ideas/the hunkers/and the whole soul!!!!!! … Amen" (TF 43; my translation). The poetic subject asks and responds: "What am I? Does it matter? […]/'I am art,' I say while I flutter my hips and get lost among the people and their smoke/[…] Travesti outlet/splendor of an angel/[…] and it doesn't matter what we are, if we manage to be able/to become … the rest is machine/and I'm not" (my translation).[17] Artistic creation is perceived as a process of creation of identity. The cross-dresser is the channel (or outlet) for the representation of this polyvalent subjectivity with all its inversions and aversions toward the machine-like impositions of systemically prescribed roles. The label of identity does not matter if the quest for identity is driven by desire and affection.

In her prologue to Marlene Wayar's (2019) *Travesti: Una teoría lo suficientemente buena*, Susy Shock speaks of the constant reinventing of a non-binary gender by means of one's own artistic creation of oneself: "'the first art object to be created that we are' […in] that founding and still revolutionary act of making oneself, betraying hegemonies and their mandates. […] that is why the Latin American trans *trava* theory is ready to think about oneself and think in general, to discuss about oneself and discuss all over" (*Travesti* 14–15).[18] The mobile, temporary, and simultaneous character of a transitive identity is the main proposal of Shock's artistic work and theory: "from the Latin American trans-*trava* theories […] we try to get out of the systemic pair: 'I am not a man, I am not a

---

[17] Available on Susy Shock's webpage: http://susyshock.com.ar/poemario-trans-pirado/
[18] All quotes marked as (*Travesti*) are my translations from Marlene Wayar, *Travesti/Una teoría lo suficientemente buena*. Buenos Aires: Ed. Muchas Nueces, 2019.

woman, today I am being a transvestite.' This gerund explains my being only for today but does not close it to crisis and transformation" (*Travesti* 25).

In *Travesti...*, there is an interview and a transcription of Susy's recital of a poem illustrating the transformative character of any artistic activity as it dissolves all stable and binary identity into ether or centrifugal flows:

> in the sea of your forms/my hands vines/are deformed/they will never be binary/No, never/Sometimes they masculinize you or me/and other algae females invent your dream [...]/they are simply/ether/or centrifugal light [...] (Susy sings:) Millenary melodies I remembered/Allpa mama/ Pachamama, light of life. (56–57; my translation)

Self-transformation involves a connection with Earth, Nature, and Native-American tradition in a cross-cultural and cross-philosophical bonding of selfhood's elements into what shapes to be a trans-nomadic self.

Ariel Martínez and Ana Sabrina Mora argue how Shock's uniqueness derives from the appropriation of traditional musical forms (*copla, baguala,* and *tango*) combining her voice of a "trava" with reciting her poetry. In her performance, the materiality of a voice with a cross-gendered register becomes part of the performative deconstruction of the normative (heterosexual) image of femininity. Her voice modulates the tones and vocal registers that are part of a folkloric style, reaching a diverse, subjective positioning that disrupts the image of a coherent identity in terms of both gender and ethnicity. The use of that style of complex crossovers and overlapping transforms the performative scene into a space where the artist can claim "monstrosity" as a part of her transitive identity: "[...] the text of her poetry reclaims the *right to be a monster.* [...] However, we point out [...] the multiple elements that intricately tie together to make her performative scene shape the monstrosity [...] that bursts in that constitutive element of the scenic performances, which is impossible to capture in linguistic categories" (MM 3; emphasis in original).[19] The voice in the performative act (the scenic element) allows for an alternative negativity of difference that is unnamable in categorical (linguistic) terms, and is expressed as an intersectionality of performed existences (identities),

---

[19] Quotes marked with (MM) are from the article by Ariel Martínez and Ana Sabrina Mora, "The Scenic Performance as Subversive Negativity: Radical alterity and *trava sudaca* performance in the voice of Susie Shock." Available in http://seet.ufrgs.br/presença

because on stage everything (text, music, voice, acting, and appearance) plays out at the same time, producing an "overlaying and simultaneity of multiple identitary cores that are present in one single subjective position and its scenic presentation" (MM 7).

Reclaiming her existence as a Monster, Susy Shock does not represent its literal meaning on stage and in her poems. She uses it as a semiotic strategy, a meaning-making decategorization of otherness in the performative act, using the modulated sound of her *trava* voice. In a complex interaction with other elements from her performative *mise-en-scène*, her monstrosity is a semiotic fugue that "escapes the possibility of being precisely articulated in any full identitary meaning" (MM 13). The use of voice takes place in multiple scenarios of a singular enunciating subject. There is no single *real self* represented with one totalizing identity, "since the self is scattered in the multiple voice as well as in the interstitial spaces between the voices and between the terms that language provides us to name identities. Even when there is a single agent, the differences within reclaim multiple voices that the limitations of language cannot resolve" (MM 15).

It is that surplus element of sonic excess in the scenic act that confers performance the more encompassing reach of a dramatized representation that goes beyond language's or written text's ability to express the simultaneity and converging of multiple identities. What Martínez and Mora call (after Judith Butler 1990) "subtle corporal acts" constitutes an interaction of the multiple axes of meaning and power that intersect beyond the restrictive use of language when it attempts to "name" identity (MM 17). It is possible to claim that the performative surplus and semiotic excess of the scenic sign indicate an affinity between the modern neobaroque representations of Susy Shock and the theatricality of the historical Baroque, considering that drama was a preferred genre in the expression of the complexities of selfhood (Lope de Vega, Calderón de la Barca, Molière, with their predecessor Shakespeare, to name a few).

In an attempt to pulverize the limit, Susie does not capture any taxonomic identity for herself. Affirming herself a monster situates her symbolically and semiotically in a place of radical alterity that destroys the abusive limitations of any system of identity categories. Performance acts by Susy Shock compliment queer theory by illustrating the power that lies in the way in which scenic presentations dissolve identities. "As a good mutant, Susie Shock projects in her palms the beautiful monstrosity and the right to exist without fitting in any box. She resists being captured in binary terms and in any label that closes down the possibility of escaping to other becomings that allow her to constantly reinvent herself, following her desire" (MM 10). Following Martínez and Mora's argument about performance's ability to transcend the limitations of language in textual expression, we conclude that the scenic element of performance uncovers the different dimensions of identities intersecting in a single instant, in a single trans-self.

The radical alterity of the *travesti-trava un*-identity, represented on stage and ungraspable in otherwise textual forms, is a multiple scattered self, built on transits. The shattered, undefinable "I" produces a void in self's transitive center (the border) that is irreplaceable with linguistically definable categories. Scenic excess (of the sign) is an attempt to replace that void with performance, filling the borderland space of the disjected self with alterities. As explained with the typically baroque *horror vacui*, that fear of the empty space, performance resorts to the excess of a "neobaroque" representation. In this attempt, "[Shock] indicates the ungraspable power of interrupting the illusion of coherence of any identity. [...] the void of meaning can harbor the negativity that can threaten the solidity of any normatively sedimented discourse. The monstrosity that Susie Shock reclaims reminds us of that" (MM 22).

Susy Shock's performance style rejects any attempt to reduce identity/alterity to a single concrete representation of a stable subjective positioning. In an attempt to avoid the exoticization of the Other as an essentialized difference, Shock proposes the shifting idea of *travesti* or "trans" as the Other's counterpart (the other of the Other). Susy's *travesti*, as the cross-dressed figure of staged representation and poetic/theoretical voice of her texts, creates a multiple presence of alterities that intersect. In their impossibility of being named, they do not find a single identitary location. The result is an artistic persona without a clear or defined identity position, a fictional poetic and stage character that is decategorized, but also an empirical self whose gender, ethnic, racial, national, and social traits are multiple, unstable, and—most importantly—transitive. Susy Shock represents her self-claimed Monster as an incarnation of a nomadic identity.

La Familia Galán

From the Bolivian highlands of South America, La Familia Galán demonstrates how normative categories of identity are transgressed and ultimately deconstructed in the performance of "transformist" activists. "Our Family was initiated from transformism, as a cultural, artistic action using the body as a space of aesthetic pleasure" (Danna Galán in Araujo 2007, 132). As a performative collective of cross-dressers, the Galans took on transvestite identity to wider grounds of artistic production combined with political activism. Not only is cross-dressing a way of life, as we have seen in Naty Menstrual's narrative, but it constitutes a far more reaching artistic and political stance of forging social change toward the acceptance of otherness.

The Galans constitute a "family" in the sense of an artist commune, a group that not necessarily lives together, but shares performative, artistic, and intellectual activity in the public sphere. "We proposed ourselves as a family that questioned the exclusive belonging to a biological family, opening the doors to a political family, a large family, with the right to decide" (2018: 25).[20] Its leading spokesperson, Danna Galán (artistic name for David Aruquipa Pérez), defined this group as more than cross-dressers or drag queens. S/he refers to themselves as "transformists," adding that a transformist is a "performer who changes costume and adopts the mannerisms of the opposite sex in a show. In this way, s/he 'transforms' *hir*self into another person in a character s/he imitates, or into another character of *hir* own creation" (2016: 452).[21]

Speaking of the familiar dimension of the collective, Aruquipa explains how their proposal was based on each member's personal choice of selecting their belonging and the role in the family as "the outcome of affections, common creative interests, the fascination by and the desire for transformism as a medium of the fight to question the binarism of gender and sexuality. Our sole presence was in itself a political interpellation" (2016: 455). The Galan Family represented cross-dressed, interracial/-ethnic, nomadic figures in their performative interventions since 1997 until the late 2010s. They transcended the urban spaces of the capital La Paz to reach the provinces, and also the national confines of Bolivia to present their proposal of transformism in transnational settings of LGBTQ activism (2016: 456). After adding "La Familia" to the *Galán* last name in 2004, they took a more critical and theoretical approach with the arrival

---

[20] All quotes marked as (2018) are my translations from the article by David Aruquipa Pérez, "La Familia Galán: Una historia sobre zancos." *Diario Página Siete.* La Paz, Bolivia. May 20, 2018, 23–26. Web: https://issuu.com/revistarascacielos/docs/rascacielos_17/26

[21] All quotes marked as (2016) are my translations from the article by David Aruquipa Pérez, "Placer, deseo y política: la revolución estética de La Familia Galán." *Bulletin de l'Institut Français d'Études Andines.* 45.3 (2016): 451–61.

Fig. 3.7 La Familia Galán, "Una historia sobre zancos" ["A Story on High Heels"]. (Photo by Antonio Suárez, published in *Zona Trans*. Courtesy of Comunidad Diversidad)

of Susana Rance (pseud. K-os Galán), a sociologist and academic researcher whose affinity with feminist and gender theory introduced the group to critical thought. As Aruquipa states, "K-os was fascinated with our proposal and constantly repeated that she saw in all of us the performative theories of Judith Butler, alive, from our bodies, with the foams, the high-heels and wigs. We were the deconstruction of gender" (2018: 25) (Figs. 3.7 and 3.8).

The main characters Danna, K-os, Kris-is, and Paris, along with other twenty plus members of differing sexual and identity orientations, performed between 2001 and 2007 in numerous happenings and political interventions, at markets, festivals, and fairs. The first memorable public presentation was at the Festival of Sexual Citizens on the central Abaroa

Fig. 3.8 La Familia Galán in La Paz, Bolivia, with Mt. Illimani in the background. (Courtesy of Comunidad Diversidad)

Square of the Sopocachi business and upscale residential district of La Paz, Bolivia, on December 2, 2001 to celebrate the 53rd anniversary of the Universal Declaration of Human Rights. It was a march of a few of the first drag queens appearing publicly in the city in their exuberant, ultra-feminine, and outlandish costumes, full of feathers, wigs, and high heel platform boots. These were considered their "instruments of power" due to the height advantage they provided. The artists were transvestites of indeterminate sexuality, as they never defined themselves as anything more than cross-dressers, eschewing terms of hetero or homosexuality. Later, these shows of drag and theatrical skits that questioned the current state of affairs were repeated on the central historic Murillo Square (in front of the Presidential Palace, the Legislative Assembly, and the Cathedral), in the Paseo del Prado (the main boulevard crossing the modern part of La Paz), in addition to the cultural markets and art/book fairs, and on multiple streets, plazas, in supermarkets and discos in the vicinity, as well as in theaters while taking part in plays and skits. Danna/David refers to them as "urban transgressions," "irruptions of reflection about scandalizing and crossing borders" (2018: 4).

After attaining notoriety in the early 2000s, the Galan Family entered academic circles to present their hands-on strategy of gender bending: "The high heels, the makeup, the lashes and the costumes accompanied us in various public actions and debates about politicized bodies in Bolivian society" (2018: 25–26). Cross-dressing in public was a daring "street politics" approach in a conservative society such as the Bolivian, and it also defied the "comfortable actions of gay groups that from behind the institutionalized desk thought about changing the society [...] formalized in a politics of social enclosure of a 'gay ghetto'" (2018: 26). The Family played an important role in the founding of the TLGB movement of Bolivia (LGBTQ in the United States), especially when Danna/David became its vice-president. As a group, they participated in national congresses of this organization. More notably, La Familia Galán mounted several photo exhibits of their performance work, thus reaching the official spaces of Bolivian art and culture. The most notable ones were "Lenguajes Corporales: Transgresión Transformista" ["Bodily Languages: Transformist Transgression"] (2003), "Mi Otro Yo" ["My Other Self"] (2004), and "Metamorfosis" (2014). They performed the theatrical pieces "Las memorias de Katherine" ["The Memories of Katherine"] (2004) and "Las mal-criadas" ["The Spoiled Ones"] (2006), a parody of Jean Genet's "Las criadas" ("The Maids"), among others. In the later phase of their activity, they partook in traditional celebrations, like El Gran Poder ["The Great Force"] of La Paz, in villages outside the capital, and at the famous Carnival of Oruro, thus making incursions with gender and sexual role reversals in Indigenous festivals and dances. One example was the female personification of the traditionally male Waphuri, the central figure of virility and power, as the leader of the large female group called the Kullaguada or the "weavers of life" (*las hilanderas*). "Obviously, we gave the *waphuri* character *marica* [faggot] traits and a new high heel aesthetic" (2016: 457). This role reversal in the play and dance caused considerable commotion and criticism in various official/traditional circles, perceived as a distortion and undermining of the role of this character, but it was generally accepted by the crowd with interest and applause. It represented a new variation of the Andean Indigenous tradition with disruptive elements of syncretism, hybridity, gender role inversion, and overall transgression of ethnic and social boundaries at different levels (Fig. 3.9).

"The illustrious daughters of audacity," as Aruquipa calls the Galan Family, utilized transformism as a tool of resistance and political struggle of the LGBTQ community in Latin America, a method of questioning

Fig. 3.9 Danna Galán as Waphuri, Oruro Carnival, 2012. (Photo by Pablo Céspedes. Courtesy of Comunidad Diversidad)

fixed identities based on the belief that gender is a social construct in permanent movement. "Our work is a cultural device, actively political, allowing to interpellate the politically correct" (2018: 26). Their acts of transgression in performances contain the additional element of theoretical and critical reflection. With K-os (Susanna Rance) also being an academic, Danna and others took to formal writing about their activity.

Another feature of Galans' transformist activism is their cross-border, international outreach. Not only do they seek to transform the concept of open citizenship of the marginalized minorities in Bolivia, but they have spread their transformist activism across various countries, either as performing, presenting, or living abroad in Brazil, Chile, Argentina, Great Britain, France, and the United States. There is a certain air of transnational nomadism in their image of transitive transvestite identity that is perceived in the transgression or neutralization of categories of national identity: "If we refer to all Bolivian, we could essentialize Bolivianness. What we are *not* interested in is to look for what is Bolivian. […] The Family does not look for origins, it is not interested in identities. […] The question of Bolivian culture is optional; we are not looking for Bolivian

Fig. 3.10 *Estéticas Galán 1* (Danna in yellow). Oil on canvas by Alfredo Muller. (Courtesy of artist)

essentiality or to rescue or try to show what is Bolivian in our appearances" (Araujo 136; my translation and emphasis). When Danna dons a traditional Aymaran *saya* [skirt, or here a mini-dress] (as seen in Alfredo Muller's painting, Fig. 3.10), it is with the intention of temporarily adopting that identity as a passage point to a plural trans-self. To be noted is the placement of a mask in line with the made-up face.

Aruquipa explains his personal motivations for transformism as the result of his early searches of liberties, to live and express his sexuality, his pleasures and desires that in his life were marked by wounds on his body. "These marks of disciplining are still part of my bodily map" (2016: 452).

180 K. A. KULAWIK

The family constituted an affective, communitarian space that helped to heal those wounds on the transvestite's body (as previously seen in Menstrual's stories) with the help of performative ritual, humor, sarcasm, and the transformist aesthetics. In a presentation at the Universidad Academia de Humanismo Cristiano in Santiago, Chile, in 2007 (moderated by Diamela Eltit), impersonating Danna, he stated:

> We use the body as the stage of transgression, as the space of subversion […], as the space of questioning of gender roles. We open the debate about genders, and our provocation stems from our body. Our body, as Diamela Eltit says, is the space in which the entire oppressive load of culture is written. So *we* [femenine "nosot*ras*" in Sp.] use the body as the stage for subversion to say that the natural has not been natural. (Araujo 128; my translation and emphasis)

With its exuberant, artifice-laden neobaroque forms of spectacle and parody, Galans' performance becomes art, a path to the creation of new transformative spaces of the self. The artistic expression they adopted corresponds to the transformist aesthetics of the drag queen, which in its exaggerated forms correlates to neobaroque techniques of artifice and parody. "We take our appearance to the extreme, giving it a playful and transgressive connotation, colorful wigs, gaudy outfits" (2016: 454). However, the Galans moved beyond the early drag queen persona to adopt more ambiguous characteristics. "As the Galan Family, we left behind the image of the 'Barbie figure transformism' to opt for more androgynous, zoomorphic drag queens, with more colorful wigs and galactic space suits. We were very ludic and showy figures" (2016: 456). During the same presentation with Diamela Eltit in Chile, K-os Galán observed that "we are imitating a model [of femininity] that in reality never existed. We conceived our play of genders as a continuous theatrical piece, without understating its superficiality and plainness. We are not seeking depth, we like superficiality, appearance, and the flat, the bodily" (Araujo 130; my translation). Adopting femininity takes them to the open space of a transitive nomadic identity that does not imply taking on only the transvestic inversion of genders. It also opens the space of subjectivity to other forms, such as androgyny, animalization, and monstrosity. According to K-os, "in the Galán Family not everything is based on the imitation of the feminine, because there is the androgynous, the zoomorphic, there is every type of performance that does not fit in the male/female binary" (Araujo 139).

The Familia Galán represents an artistic attempt to find new strategies of destabilizing the system with mutant appearance and provocative behavior. The emblematic figure of the China Morena, a female dancer in Bolivian folk celebrations, now exemplified by homosexual men and transvestites, caught on in Bolivian mentality and, according to Aruquipa (2016: 459–60), has modified the political perception of popular culture in Bolivia. These interventions, paired with artistic creation, entered social and academic discourse to produce several articles and a testimony to Galans' work in the book *Memorias colectivas* (2012). It is a testimony of how La Familia Galán was able to use transformism as a tool of political resistance. David/Danna wittily sums up the work of the Familia: "We keep up the provocation that says: we are daring, awesome, and arrogant. Heels, wigs and can-can [Parisian music hall dance], that's what we are, the Galán" (2018: 26).

Alfredo Muller Suárez

In his hyperrealistic neobaroque portraits of religious, Indigenous, and cross-dressed figures, Bolivian painter Alfredo Muller expresses the ambiguous and transitive identity of diverse subjects, particularly in terms of sexuality. This rendition of what we perceive in his paintings as nomadic (mobile) identity is construed by means of the sexualized human body, specifically in its expression of nude and cross-dressed figures.

Alfredo Muller (b. 1958) is from Santa Cruz de la Sierra where he currently lives and teaches drawing along with graphic design at the Universidad Privada de Santa Cruz de la Sierra, and where his most recent exhibit "Señor de los señores" ["Lord of the Lords"] was inaugurated in April of 2022.[22] Muller's paintings focus on the study of the human body in the nude and in costume. Since he portrays nudes using religious figures of saints, the Holy Virgin, and Christ, his work has been the object of much controversy from the conservative circles, and the victim of hate through its vandalization. Considered as "one of the most irreverent artists" in an interview published on the website of *Sociales.Ed* in 2017,[23] he admits that his life and his work have been shaped by the homophobic persecution that he has experienced from his childhood at home and school, and later as an artist in Santa Cruz. His works have been slashed, spray-painted, and burned on numerous occasions, "and when they wanted to burn me, they were there with scissors,

---

[22] https://www.upsa.edu.bo/es/noticias-upsa/1830-exposicion-de-docente-upsa
[23] https://eldeber.com.bo/sociales/alfredo-Müller-suarez-arana-hubo-figuretis-que-intentaron-anularme_20043

ropes and spray when I exhibited, and they had to close the Casa de la Cultura for three days" (Sociales.Ed interview, n.p.; my translation). He admits that there have been "figurettes" of prominence who have tried to bring him down, but he remains firm in his initial purpose of recreating the multigendered and sexual body and its mobile subjectivity. "My delirium for the human body is what led me to paint" (Sociales.Ed interview). As a deeply religious man, he states: "I think that God, in creating man and woman, contemplated them as I contemplate a painting when it comes out well and I want to show it. Man and woman are the most beautiful work of creation" (Sociales.Ed interview). Hence, his focus is on the combinations and crossings of gender lines, as well as on the relationship between hetero and homosexuality.

Muller crosses the terrain of double/multiple identity with depictions of Native Andean figures, orienting his art toward the common folk: "I have painted hundreds of virgins and for a while I dedicated myself to the indigenous Virgin and the people wanted to massacre her. The humble people did see the Virgin. When I lack strength, I paint for the humble" (Sociales.Ed interview). As he approaches native Bolivian ethnicity, Muller takes the hybrid, transcultural paths of the Neobaroque. He admits that the historical Baroque was his school of choice for his technique: "In art nothing is new; now I take the Baroque, I give it shades of modernity" (Sociales.Ed interview). When asked why his latest virgins were dressed, **he answered:** "For the challenge of the Neobaroque and it is not that the last virgins were dressed; I already come with a history of dressed virgins" (Sociales.Ed interview). Indeed, most of his works show affinity to Spanish Baroque portraiture with echoes of Francisco de Zurbarán, José de Ribera, and particularly Bartolomé Esteban Murillo. The influence of the baroque technique is visible in the profound realism, deep contrast between light and dark (*chiaroscuro*), and in dramatic facial-bodily expression, besides the recurrent religious theme, reminiscent of the Spanish Golden Age masters. Yet, his modern take on the Baroque is what makes him Neobaroque, especially in terms of the subjects and identities he depicts, such as stylized religious figures from the Catholic book of saints (many nude), Bolivian Indigenous women, and cross-dressers. His use of baroque techniques on the human body, particularly the nude, stands out as the most prominent feature of his paintings.

Muller's studies of cross-dressed figures go deeper into the terrain of fluctuation in gender and sexuality, as they portray transvestites in performative poses. States of nomadic identity transits are observed in his

Fig. 3.11 *Andrómeda 1* (Miki). Oil on canvas by Alfredo Muller. (Courtesy of artist)

extreme care given to detail, where the subject's outside femininity disguises tints of masculinity in bodily posture, gesture, and mimicry. His inspiration and model for cross-dressed figures has been a local transformist of Santa Cruz, whose artistic name is Miki. His cross-dressed performances in both drag and conventional feminine attire are studies of the fluid series of assumed identities, often "masked" or "simulated," as the performer himself calls them.[24] They are visible in the two *Andrómeda* paintings in Figs. 3.11 and 3.12.

Another cross-dressed model for Muller is Danna Galán, the transformist performer from La Paz, whose portraits in elegant feminine and traditional Aymara attire show a crossing of multiple identities on the body of one subject, as depicted in paintings from the "Estéticas Galán" series

---

[24] This information comes from my personal, unregistered interview with Miki during my visit to Santa Cruz de la Sierra in April 2022.

Fig. 3.12 *Andrómeda 2* (Miki). Oil on canvas by Alfredo Muller. (Courtesy of artist)

(Figs. 3.10 and 3.13). In both Miki and Danna, the markedly female clothing with outlandishly tall platform boots indicates a surpassing of femininity (the ultrafeminine, as in the cross-dresser analyzed by Echavarren 2008). This excess of detail and colorful effervescence point to the neobaroque elements of hyperrealism and light-shadow contrasting. Bodily traits suggest masculine composure; a subtly ironic facial expression of performance behind a mask of makeup indicates flows of a double identity that fluctuates between femininity and masculinity.

The presence of diverse outfits, one being Andean Indigenous (Fig. 3.10 in previous section on La Familia Galán), indicates a cross-ethnic identification of Danna, whose descent could be Hispanic (White) Bolivian or *Mestizo*.

Fig. 3.13 *Estéticas Galán 2* (Danna in blue). Oil on canvas by Alfredo Muller. (Courtesy of artist)

Finally, the presence of masks, eyeglasses, and heavy makeup symbolizes the intent to simulate feminine appearance. All the paintings depict features associated with the Neobaroque: use of vivid color, contrast of light-darkness; hyperrealist (almost excessive) rendition of detail, the subject's body as the topic, the human figure in solemn or official portraiture, and the religious theme of the Virgin, angels, and saints' martyrdom, frequently observed in Muller's portraiture. These historically Baroque themes are undertaken, reappropriated, and stylized in Muller's postmodern painting, which further leads us to consider it as "neobaroque" (Fig. 3.14).

Muller's study of transvestism exemplifies an artistic attempt to visualize and articulate an identity that is fragmented and mobile, plural and transitive, a case of nomadic "trans-identity." When asked in an interview

Fig. 3.14 Muller (right) and Miki (left) in the artist's studio in Santa Cruz, Bolivia in 2022, with Muller's portraiture in the background. (Photo by author)

about social intolerance of diversity ("How much does it cost to recognize oneself as different?"), he replied: "Those are values [categories] that frighten, like many things [words] that are made to feel fear, but you let go ... and that's it. There have always been faggots and wh...s in this world. [...] When I talk about diversity, yes, but the asshole out there has created a genocide, he has burned people, he has tortured them and that is not diversity" (Sociales.Ed interview).

Juan Dávila
Another (by now classic) example of a cross-dressed figure in painting comes from Chile. Dávila is associated with the same political and cultural context as the Chilean writers and artists previously mentioned, that is, the neoavant-garde scene of the 1970s–1980s called La Avanzada, and the literary-artistic collective CADA. The portrait is a mixed technique of oil

Fig. 3.15 *El Libertador Simón Bolívar* [*The Liberator Simón Bolívar*] by Juan Dávila, 1994. Oil on canvas on metal. (Photo by Mark Ashkanasy, © Juan Davila. Courtesy of Kalli Rolfe Contemporary Art, Melbourne)

with graphics on metal, painted by Juan Dávila in 1994. It represents the Liberator Simón Bolívar on horseback with a female body, cross-dressed as a woman with heavy makeup, showing an obscene gesture (Fig. 3.15).

The painting was exhibited in 1994 at the Hayward Gallery in London, however the circulation of postcards with its reproduction caused a scandal in the political and artistic media of post-dictatorship Chile, a case analyzed by Nelly Richard (2001: 187–94) and Francine Masiello (2001: 53–56). In a true "carnival of identities," the image of the venerated male hero is anamorphically distorted by feminine elements. To that we should

188   K. A. KULAWIK

add the *Mestizo*-Indigenous dark-skinned Afro-descendant facet to produce a juxtaposition of multiple "sub-identities," all in motion, in nomadic
transit within the same subject. Additionally, the combination of mimetic
and abstract styles results in a parodic hybridization that puts in tension,
according to Richard, the "official Latin Americanism, of how the inversion of sexual gender violates the virile protocol of a history that repro-
duces the ideologemes of patriarchal discourse through an iconographic
gallery [...] of civilizing discourse" (2001: 189; my translation). The
image of a cross-dressed Simón Bolívar produced in official cultural registers of normative decency what Richard calls "a semantic disorder that
made the border between One and Other rock and reel" (190). She goes
on to state:

> The twisting of signs that committed the barbarism of which the work was
> accused can be summed up in the figure of transvestism: a figure that parodi-
> cally conjugates the masculine and the feminine in a zone of sexual ambigui-
> ties [...]. Transvestism breaks the binarism of sexual opposition by
> superimposing and disqualifying gender representations; [...]. Moreover,
> transvestism detaches sexual identity from the realism of the original body to
> reconjugate the marks of the masculine and the feminine through a rhetoric
> of artifice, masking, and simulation. (189–90)

Massiello adds that "the cross-dressed Bolívar suggests to viewers that
even marginal citizens have the right to interpret their national hero,
thereby reversing the common symbolic legacies that have excluded considerations of gender" (2001: 54; my translation). We observe an analogy
of this image in Washington Cucurto's novel *1810: La Revolución de Mayo
vivida por los negros* (2008), in which the protagonist, South American
Independence War hero General José de San Martín, is presented as a
transculturally Africanized homo/bisexual. It suggests a reinterpretation
of normative symbols of White heterosexual order set in official historical
discourse. The accumulation and combination of artistic styles and genders (sexual and artistic) with the erotic content of the transvestite figure,
all in the single space of Dávila's painting, refers us to the notion of a
(characteristically neobaroque) total work, with its contradictions and
ambiguous transitions representing crisis and the revision of a fragmented
and mobile identity.

3.2.2 Androgyny, Queerness, and Ambiguity

Roberto Echavarren

Works by this contemporary Uruguayan poet, novelist, and essayist display sexually and culturally ambiguous subjects whose identities are marked by androgynous mutability. The key points to consider when approaching the novels *Ave Roc* (1994) and *El diablo en el pelo* (2005) are the shifts of binary categorizations of gender and sexuality, and the mobility of ethnic, racial, and national categories. Echavarren's narrative creates a cross-cultural dialogue of displacements, mixtures, and hybridizations that occur in the multicultural American context.

The gender-sexual indeterminacy of the androgyne, combining both male and female traits, makes it an illustrative example of a nomadic identity in its fullest ambiguity. In his essays *Androgynous Art* (2008) and *Performance* (2000), Echavarren describes the mutant as close to the cyborg, "a creature beyond man and woman" (2008: 12), "as a third way to generic classifications" (2000: 16), "a possibility of escape from stable identities, which allows the production of monsters" (2000: 358). Mutants evade a fixed identity because they are in the process of constant becoming, transiting "points of passage" mentioned by Néstor Perlongher. In Echavarren, they are depicted as feedback between Western pop culture and Amerindian traditions, reminding the transculturation defined decades earlier by Fernando de Ortiz.

An illustrative example of an androgynous subject is Julián in the novel *El diablo en el pelo*, in which a first-person narrative voice depicts a non-conformist, socially marginal, *Mestizo* Uruguayan youth. He places outside the typically Uruguayan frameworks of ethno-racial and sexual identity. The narrator, in the course of a romantic relationship with the protagonist, reflects on Julián and construes *hir* androgynous *mestize* persona within a minoritarian social stratum of the River Plate region that typically had not been given a voice. The fluctuating narrative abounds in its diverse approaches and focuses, in its lexical and figurative abundance toward an eroticism impregnated with humor that invades the subculture of Uruguay's underprivileged youth. The desire that overflows in the androgynous volubility of this ephebus becomes a survival strategy stuck between the economic scarcity of a marginal group and the upward ascension of a consumerist society. The figure of the androgynous Julián, indeterminate and fluctuating between feminine and masculine, White-Hispanic (*criollo*) and Charrúa-*Mestizo*, opens with intensity and violence, liberating spaces in the constitution of a plural identity of a Uruguayan mutant transgressing the confines of national and ethnic belonging.

The rebelliously eccentric and androgynous figure of Jim in the novel *Ave roc* invokes the historical Jim Morrison, the controversial singer of the Californian band The Doors. Both masculine and feminine attributes in his looks and stage performance make him an icon of sexual liberation of the sixties, on par with Elvis Presley and Mick Jagger. His defiant behavior on and off the stage propels him to become the political voice of a rebellious and non-conformist youth in the era of the Civil Rights movement, the Cold War, and feminist and homosexual liberation.

The novelistic Jim presents a complex personality and an ambiguous identity across intersecting lines of several categories. Not avoiding bisexual contacts, he has relationships with women, like Nitro (a.k.a. Nico, the singer of the band Velvet Underground), and with men like the transvestite Peter and the masculine narrator who reveals himself as Jim's childhood friend and faithful companion. The narrator directs his discourse to Jim in the second-person singular "you." He is omnipresent in all of Jim's actions, so the reader can assume his "real" existence as a close friend. But he is seldom approached physically or even addressed by Jim in dialog. His presence is almost ghost-like. He perceives Jim in all interactions and addresses him often, but Jim doesn't ever seem to perceive his presence. Therefore, as much as physically present or not—ephemeral and reflexive—as the first-person narrator appears, he is more likely some form of an inner voice or omnipresent consciousness, perhaps of Jim's alter ego speaking to himself. He represents an analytical, reflexive, and omniscient voice more than a true character participating in the plot's events. More likely, he is a narrator metafictionally projected in Jim's (or the implicit author's) own imagination or dreams. Using this unusual narrative device, Echavarren creates a dream-like metafictional account of historical occurrences and characters involving Jim Morrison, the band Doors, and the broader musical, cultural, and political scene of the late sixties in California, the United States, and Europe.

By projecting this narrative voice of a "shadow conscience," the author opens ample room for reflection about Jim's chameleonic personality, complex sexuality, and his quest of a nomadic identity that trespasses all normative categorizations. The narrator's admiration for Jim is founded on one particularly unique element of his ambiguous sexuality (visible in his behavior and appearance) that is his *androgyny*. Jim combines masculine and feminine attributes as the main feature of his nomadic transiting

3 SUBVERSIONS OF SELFHOOD: TRANSGRESSIVE CHARACTERS... 191

that attracts the narrator "friend" to him and triggers his homosexual desire for him. The narrator's admiration focuses on the ambiguity and bipolarity of Jim's androgynous sexuality:

> What others call identity and even the essence of the person, always seemed to me material of contradiction. I later found that many men who sleep with men prefer to reinforce the masculine vertex. [...] These individuals remained prisoners of an imaginary identity, of poles that they subverted but confirmed: they were attracted to the same sex, but it was *that* sex. Your appearance, on the contrary, from what you perfected later, had to do neither with one nor with the other. The equivocation was liberating for me as something that I always suspected, and that you and some others, even after having slept with women, or because of that, managed to maintain. (26–27; emphasis in original)[25]

The narrator is critical of closed, defined identifications, especially with binary "essences" that he calls "material of contradiction." Throughout the novel, he continues to reflect on the simulative and fictional character of any determined identity imposed from the outside by fashion. He criticizes Jim for giving in to the influences of the commercialized management of his artist-persona, especially in his looks: "The only thing that justifies one or the other appearance is the joy of disproving, or confirming, the fiction that a man is a man and a woman a woman. You, with the new [hair]cut, had become one of the boring boys. You were too well adjusted to what was imposed on you" (28). Many of these reflections are a narrative projection of Echavarren's ample theorizations on art, fashion, style, and gender transgression contained in his essays *Arte andrógino*, *Fuera de género*, and *Performance* (Fig. 3.16).

Jim undergoes a process of transformation of identity in the broad (intersectional) sense of many categories that include sexuality, race, and ethnicity. It began in his youth and continued during his vibrant, albeit short, musical career. He understands from his readings and relationships with older and experienced friends (like the well-read doctor who handed him a copy of Shakespeare's *Tempest*) that he can become a borderline subject transiting between the two poles of a liberating sexual world: a monster (Caliban) who eats raw men and a reconciliating angel (Ariel) without a sexual definition. While still living in Florida, with his friend

---

[25] All quotes from the novel that follow are my translations from the edition of Roberto Echavarren, *Ave roc*. Buenos Aires: Mansalva, 2007.

Fig. 3.16 The Doors. Promotional photo of Jim Morrison about 1970. (Photographer: Pictorial Press. Reproduced under license from Alamy, Inc.)

doctor, he visits pubs with drag queen shows that expand his perception of gender transitivity and ambiguity, and perhaps bisexuality. A meaningful example of transformation is when, on the wayside of a Texas road, he witnesses an accident involving several Native Americans on the verge of death. As a witness, he experiences a transformation that results in absorbing the spirit of and identifying with the dying Amerindians who, in Jim's critically rebellious conscience, were marked by binary Anglo-White culture as the "Caliban monsters": "The disgrace of the Calibans wrenched a vow from you. You resolved that you were their brother, that the feathered ones did not die because their breath passed to you, and later, by means of makeup, jewelry, and clothing, you recreated that forbidden luxury" (31). Jim would later use androgynous elements of Native-American gender-bending makeup and outfits in his emulated eclectic persona on stage and off. Besides his appearance, Jim's identification with the Indigenous took the form of frequent outings to the Californian and Mexican deserts to experience the transformative hallucinogenic effects of the nopal cactus—the peyote plant. "Later, the innate calfskin pants, the silver plastrons that you hung from your hips, the dark gelatin that you distributed over your skin, marked a complete victory of the Indian over the soldier" (31). Here, the narrator is referring to the Western movies that they both liked to watch as teenagers, and Jim's empathy for the "Indians," and not the White soldiers and cowboys. The protagonist's identification is with the cultural (and sexual) "other." He displays an affinity for passing as Native American and as female with the techniques of androgynous gender bending.

As Jim's intimate friend who witnessed his early transformations, the first-person narrator comments on the artist's androgynous inclinations: "From then on, the seducers of cinema were no longer women. Nor, by the way, were they men, but the new mutants on motorcycles, dressed in leather and with guitars: Marlon Brando, James Dean, Elvis Presley, who spoke in a whisper, shook their nipples, and shouted high-pitched screams" (46). Jim's love life is revealed by the narrator as sumptuously erotic and adventurous, distinctly bisexual. During his steadier heterosexual relationships with girlfriends like Nitro, he did not stray from random adventurous sexual encounters with androgynous or cross-dressed, or even distinctly mannish, homosexual partners. His attraction to transvestites and other mutants is visible with Peter, Jim's groupie and lover, of "a more advanced appearance than yours, more abandoned. He wore black metal-tipped boots and strings of bird-shaped medallions after the style of the Hopi, violet fingernails"; "[…] the boy who […] had been taken for a girl. Peter had lips like trays, eyes of greenish water, heavy eyelids like those painted by Ingres, an immense hoop in each ear" (71).

Jim's sexuality became a constant search evolving from both hetero and homosexual relationships toward more ambiguous ones, as he was experiencing a transition into androgyny. This process is represented in the novel through language that is opulent and contrived in its syntax and vocabulary, like in the display of felts, velvets, brocades, washers, leathers, and spandex in the decadently lavish interior of the modernist mansion invaded by Jim's group of rockers in the highlight years of the band. The erotic scenes are narrated in such ornamental detail, sumptuous language, eccentric imagery, and figurative devices (notable use of the hyperbole) that, besides the masculine pronouns, distinctions of gender and sexuality become obfuscated. The now androgenized narrative voice of the fluctuating external-internal observer and the language s/he uses are again fully reminiscent of the neobaroque style:

[from his underpants] emerged a toy, the thin, hard scruff of a stuffed swan topped by a crown of diamonds. The swan's feathers enveloped the parts. [...] You separated the swan molding the genitals. They were, you then noticed, covered with gold dust. The penis was the size of a canvas sewing needle. [...] He demanded that you first make him enjoy. You collapsed in each other's arms, you more than him. You asked him to insert his fingers through your sphincter. He didn't want to because he was afraid of breaking his very long fingernails. [...] Inside your guts a thorny dome opened like a peyote button. (50)

The narration undergoes experimental alterations in syntactic structure and cohesion in scenes involving the narrator's engagements with Jim and in moments of hallucinations induced by alcohol or narcotics. An example is the fragment in which the narrator reasons about fashion and style (again, reflective of Echavarren's critical essays on the topic), using a notably lavish, poetic style and complex imagery. Noteworthy are the artful vocabulary, convoluted syntax (especially the last sentence), and elaborate metaphors that display a high level of artifice:

Your gasping is the outline of a vortex. It enters from below and bathes and programs me. Fashion is invented from the top down, it is hierarchical, aristocratic. The state [referring to "style"], the other way around (you wheeze), comes from the bottom up, rises from the perineum, is invented by an electrician and a truck driver. [...] It was not what could be expected of a boy: to break the mirror of roles and the 'natural' law for the style, ambidextrous Indian, creature of another space, you inhabited this one. (73)

The narrator's perception of Jim is that he is someone from another dimension, breaking and liberating conventional roles, but ultimately not being able to sustain his determination of otherness by falling victim to outside pressures, or simply losing himself to alcohol and drugs, and crossing a limit into a point of no return.

In his many outings to the borderland (US-Mexican) desert in search of more transcendental forms of transformation, he encounters enlightenment among the natives, first the Hopi, later the Tarahumara. His androgynous sexual transformation occurs participating in the tribes' rituals: "The following night it was the turn of the *amujerados* to dance. The term had been applied to them by the Spanish missionaries, but in their language, they were called by a word that meant 'neither man nor woman,' or beyond man and woman" (81). A series of narcotically induced metamorphoses occurs. These are narrated in a surrealistic language but as

3 SUBVERSIONS OF SELFHOOD: TRANSGRESSIVE CHARACTERS... 195

real-life occurrences, with a narrative naturalness of mimetic-like verisimilitude: "That night you and I, transformed into lepidoptera with spiritromps and four wings covered with scales, walked along a stone with erect antennae, free from the similarities in the quicksilver of others" (97). The final trip to the Sonoran Desert is full of encounters with androgynous and hermaphroditic beings, both the Indigenous who perform the rituals of peyote cleansing, and the White visitors in search of transformation into more complete, complex, and nomadic selves: "The blond, I thought, is an androgyne, he has neither one sex nor the other. The hermaphrodites, on the contrary, with silicones and appendix" (117); "I am a man and a woman. I play the violin" (123).

The narrator admits that his (real or imaginary) relationship with Jim was a "liberating" experience. In the third part of the novel, he relates the mutant artist's final demise and departure in his early death, the memory of which was marked only by his distant grave in Paris, sumptuously described in the fans' pilgrimage to the Père Lachaise Cemetery. The meaning of his eccentric experimentation with identity roles and his nomadic passings between categories of gender and ethnicity may be viewed as his ultimate legacy: "It was not attractiveness as we know it. It was the Turkish love, the love of androgynous people. Not the love of another man, but the call of a planet where they had spent another life. You insisted that the other life was this one. You dedicated to breaking the mirror of the roles of 'natural' law in love" (105) (Fig. 3.17).

The demise of Jim is narrated using a method of reminding the "qualms of conscience" of the protagonist, as a reproving voice of possibly Jim's own conscience explaining his ultimate trespassing to the other side without return. The narrator/Jim's reflections admit that he created something that he surpassed and was not able to retain. The final appearance of Jim with an overweight body and overgrown facial hair represents a figure that transgressed the boundaries of his own selfhood but forsook the image that he had created in his effort of transforming into an icon of style. That image surpassed him but touched others, his imitators:

> On the side sat a Dutchman who looked to me like a replica of your rock figure. Black fishnet T-shirt, high boots, hair sculpted strand by strand with aerosol spray: a dressed-up dude. The lazy, brutal lips, designed and augmented by brown eyeliner: the doll you had given soul to. The spirit of the world was now peeking out of the Dutchman's mask, while your eyes were shipwrecked in your beards. You had transposed the pose, which the Dutchman assimilated, from the dolls of the Sunset Strip. (146–47)

Fig. 3.17 Jim Morrison 1969, author: Elektra Records. (Source: Wikimedia Creative Commons)

Jim's self-annihilating impulses brought him to his downfall, as he gave in to the destructive forces of inner fragmentation and instability as "the rebel and the inverted king who would fall at the end of the festival" (150). In his final alcoholic and narcotic daze, he cedes to the materiality of his body's cravings: "'Longing to annihilate myself is the only thing I feel, seafaring is dead, my *fix*, fixity,' you thought. […] Now you became not a drug of life, but a still perfection, a transparent glass, a spine of a frozen cat. The happiness in the belly lasted until after the loss of consciousness, which is not the last word of anything, or anyone" (153; emphasis in original). The narrator implies that happiness and life, or the meaning that it produced in the persona that Jim created, do not end with death; the meaning of one's work of creating an androgynous multicultural self-image continues transcendentally in others. "'The death,' said Peter over the phone, […] 'was early Friday morning, from an overdose'" (152).

3 SUBVERSIONS OF SELFHOOD: TRANSGRESSIVE CHARACTERS... 197

Hilda Hilst

In the novellas *Qadós* (1973) and *A obscena senhora D* (2012 [1982]; *The Obscene Madame D*) by this contemporary Brazilian novelist, poet, and playwright, we observe how language and narrative technique represent a sexuality that becomes ambiguously changeable; it is simulated, mobile, and plural, like a transvestite. The multiple voices of the characters fluctuate between male and female positions. In their frequent metamorphoses, they transform and transit between gender categories, body and spirit, life and death, seeking a transcendental dimension of "transidentity."

An example of the fragmentation and transcendence of a sexually ambiguous subject appears in *Qadós*. The eponymous protagonist-narrator presents himself as an extravagant and opulent, but lonely man. His sexual inclinations, in combination with his philosophical concerns, alienate him from society. The narrative voice loses coherence, shifting from the first to the second, and subsequently to the third grammatical person. The word endings indicate both masculinity and femininity of the same subject-protagonist whose attributes oscillate between the two genders. In his journey in search of himself, Qadós changes (transcends, reincarnates) from one body to another and converses with an "other" who appears to be his wife, lover, or, simply, his alter ego. Interpersonal dialog shifts to internal dialog and monolog that takes the form of a stream of consciousness. The hermaphrodite magician Karaxim helps the protagonist to reconcile his dual nature, embodying him in a multiple transitory subject, androgynous and bisexual, even animal: "Qadós, man-question" (96), "Qadós woman-raped" (97–98), "Qadós man-woman," "Qadós man-woman-female dog" (100), "Qadós The Whole Desired [...] a [feminine] one or two" (104–05).[26] The fluctuation of narrative voices, grammatical markers, and the inconstancy in the character's personality are produced by linguistic artifice, lexical and syntactic exuberance, and prolific ornamentation.

Playfully combining narrative voices and transitioning between identities, Qadós perturbs the one-dimensional narrative-mimetic and heterosexual-masculine order when he ventures into bisexual relationships: "I was intimate for she-one or two, I don't even remember [...] gluttony to possess me whole, if it was a woman she told me the same

---

[26] Given that no published English translation is available, for quotes from the novel *Qadós* I am providing my translation from Portuguese from Hilda Hilst, *Rútilo nada. A obscena Senhora D. Qadós*. Campinas: Pontes, 1993.

gluttony to possess you whole, Qadós, if it was a man too, there I hid myself" (104); "I won't be happy, I CHANGE-ALWAYS, NO-NAME […] longing for continuous softness" (122, capitals in original). Qadós's mutation resembles the transformation of the transvestite or mutant, who positions *hir*self in a fluid and mobile space between genders, between homo and heterosexuality.

Qadós abandons society joining up to travel with an "other" who is sometimes male, sometimes female. The two androgynous mutants achieve a state of bisexual wholeness in the presence of a third party—an "absolute being"—who may be the consciousness of Qadós himself or the sought-after deity. The quest ends when the subject "I" merges with the deity in an attempt of transcendence, either as wholeness in oneself—the "Nameless One" (143)—or in union with the other: "Qadós looked at the beautiful. Time of ten thousand years, lustful Qadós smiled, and *no longer knew his own identity*, […] and one day the two would never be […] and in whose body would they join?" (143; emphasis added). He admits, however, that the union of beings is only temporary. Qadós is able to transit the duality of genders, life and death, to at least momentarily reach a third dimension.

The transitivity of the sexually ambiguous body in Qadós goes through stages of transformation to reach, transiently, a higher state of reconciliation (and fusion) of the opposites of masculinity and femininity that coexist in a state of queerness. The fluctuation in the identity process, which we distinguish with Jack Halberstam's concept of "trans*" (2018), allows us to see Qadós's different avatars (cross-dressed, androgynous, queer) and his desired encounter with divinity. The novel's exuberant language and fragmented narrative structure are a textual reflection of a liminal existence, a borderline and transitive identity achieved in the opulence of Hilst's neobaroque discourse.

The Obscene Madame D is built around a long, erotically charged conversation between a defunct man, Ehud, and his widowed wife Hillé on the mezzanine of a staircase and in the space below. Madame D-Hillé also assumes different names-avatars: "I, Hillé, also called by Ehud Madame D, I Nothing, I Nobody's Name, I searching for the light in a silent blindness, sixty years searching for the meaning of things. Dereliction, Ehud would tell me, Dereliction—for the last time Hillé" (35).[27] Also here we

---

[27] For quotes from *A obscena Senhora D*, I use the English translation by Nathanaël of Hilda Hilst. *The Obscene Madame D*. Callicoon, New York: Nightboat Books, 2012.

3 SUBVERSIONS OF SELFHOOD: TRANSGRESSIVE CHARACTERS... 199

observe the fluctuation of the character's multiple names with the multiple narrative voices, which leads to the fragmentation of the plot and the integrity of the characters. A large part of Hillé's conversation and monologs revolve around the sexual relations she had during her life with Ehud before he died, but also with an ambiguous being named Pig-Boy [*Porco-Menino*]. The narrative voice leaves the suspicion that Hillé is an incarnation of Ehud or his consciousness, or the superego of an implied author who is writing a book within the narrated story (note the similarity of the names Hillé and Hilda). Metafiction, as a neobaroque narrative device, is employed frequently by Hilst. It produces the effect of decentering and queering of the characters. The female identity of the sometimes-male narrator is expressed at the end of the story with "a being-woman" (78). Although the text grammatically indicates a female protagonist, Hillé questions her own gender, combining her voice with other, sometimes male, individuals: "there are some living ones [Port. masc.] inside beyond the word, they [masc.] express themselves but I don't understand, they pulsate, they breathe, there is a code at the center" (38).

In transitivity of identities and narrative voices, Hillé and Ehud's discourses join to blend in an erotic bodily fusion: "you and me, a single spiral ball, never separate, [...] I lick you slick, I suck hairs, smells, I find thigh and sex, I wanted to swallow you, Ehud, you went down in UMM through my larynx, UMM through my guts, [...] your mixing with me, within me undone, you are no longer Ehud, you are Hillé [...]" (64). The characters' discourse confounds the grammatical "I," "you," and the third-person narrative voice: "I am not I-Ehud experienced in you, you see me as I could never see myself, I Ehud am not the one you experience in you, you are Hillé who can be happy only being thus touched, isn't it good?" (65–66). The voices of Hillé (I) and Ehud (you) alternate in their approach to an Other ("this," a divinity?). Finally, the narrative assumes Ehud's voice (masculine), but identifies itself as a feminine being, "a being-woman" (79). The end of the plot presents a dissolution of characters with no clarification of whether Hillé-Madame D was talking to Ehud, her deceased husband, to another lover, or to herself. Perhaps it was God (the Other) whom she evoked so much. The narrative resorts to the characteristically neobaroque artifice: fragmentation, proliferation (as dispersion), condensation (as fusion), and metanarrative in the representation of mobile and transitive identities with several alternating voices. Meaning is left open in the fragmented discourse of the novel, saturated with voices and words in fugue, erudite linguistic trappings, and baroque syllogisms.

The boundary between characters' bodies is obscured in the opulent representation of the erotic relationship that becomes figuratively abstract, overflowing with words, many of them neologisms.

Diamela Eltit

Queerness appears as another theme in the novels of this Chilean author. In her first novel *Lumpérica* (1983, 1997; *E. Luminata*), Eltit experimented with textuality, taking linguistic and narrative forms to the extremes of figurative simulation of a queered protagonist. The fragmented plot presents a destitute, homeless woman of the same name as the title of the novel (E. Luminata in the English translation),[28] who wanders about the streets and the central square of the Chilean capital, Santiago. Only the glow of a few neon lights illuminates her during her nighttime vagrancies and multiple activities: combing and cutting her hair, putting on and taking off her clothes, confronting passersby and the police. An external narrative voice makes descriptions of her from different perspectives like the focus of a movie camera. The narration changes to a metanarrative level as it addresses the very techniques of narrating and creating images. The action ends when the neon lights are turned off and a new day awakens the streets of Santiago. The narrator makes nighttime incursions into Lumpérica's inner world and produces several displacements of time and place to present E. Luminata in a hospital, in parks, in different neighborhoods. A pedestrian is arrested and taken by the police for interrogation to account for the suspicious (politically subversive) acts of the indigent woman. It is not certain whether the woman lives on to see another day or dies in the park as a result of a beating in an allegorical depiction of dictatorial repression by the military regime.

The piecemeal articulation of the multifaceted figure of the wandering female protagonist is visible in the narration on various occasions: "All her possible identities have sprouted wildly—pinning down her anatomical points—overshooting her beyond her areas" (16).[29] It is also visible in name changes: "[Her] identities are being celebrated. They are their own godparents who are being received and she, she's the one who is

---

[28] The main character's name in Spanish is a play on two words that are joined in the compound that is "Lumpérica": "lumpen" as Marx's term for the underclass or working class, and "*América*" referring to the feminine allegory of the American continent.

[29] We use the translation by Ronald Christ of Diamela Eltit, *E. Luminata*. Santa Fe, NM: Lumen, 1997.

rechristened in each one of them. It's a feast" (19). The distorting effects of light and sound suggest the simulating effect of technology in deconstructing the image of the character: "Synthesizing in their singular name all the others cast down by the illuminated sign to the point of gathering unto themselves the identity based on their diverse appearances" (27). Other fragments suggest the character's ambiguous sexuality: "That way turning back the canons of identity across the lump sum of bodies which neutralize individual features to the utmost" (21). The character's identity appears as a simulation, a creative effect of the narrative voice's fluctuating perception and fluid figuration of the character: "she compounded falsification upon falsification. In the midst of that artifice maybe she was not real either […] even she herself was an excess" (197).

Body alterations further deconstruct the identity of the fragmented character. Violent bodily inscriptions indicate a metonymic relationship between the body as text and the character's identity: "slits the skin and the blade delays the cut. Embellished she warns that the softness is even more alarming. Skin and leather delicately opened prevent each other + feast on its new condition" (167). The eight incisions on the skin of the right forearm, each one of them representing a fragment of Chap. 8, "Dress rehearsal," provide visual metatextual support of the narrative (149). They appear on a photograph of the implicit (and empirical) author, referred to in the text as "Diamela" (Fig. 3.18). The image represents Eltit's performative intervention in 1982 in a protest of the Pinochet regime. The cutting and shaving of the hair and the incisions on the skin of the artist's-writer's arms are metonymical "real-life" extensions of transformative bodily alterations that in the text ambiguate the identity of E. Luminata in her erotic excesses paralleling on discursive exuberance of the narrative. The erotic-bodily act increases the ambiguity and defiance of appearance: "cracks it does her skin and the blade delays the cut/[…] + she celebrates herself in her new condition and her legs resist too but their solidity is only a matter of appearances" (173). Identity becomes a matter of appearances that are simulated-performed and fleeting. These acts of erotic bodily-textual transgression and subversion of identity through corporal-syntactic-narrative alteration correspond to an act of antihegemonic protest (Fig. 3.18).

Parallelly to the bodily transformations, linguistic forms undergo a process of explicit, metatextual deconstruction by means of morphological and syntactical forms, and in the inscription of the text in different registers: "she broaches the opposite meaning of her phrase. She deconstructs

Fig. 3.18 *Zona de dolor: Diamela Eltit* [*Area of Pain*]. (Photograph by Lotty Rosenfeld, 1980. Courtesy of Diamela Eltit)

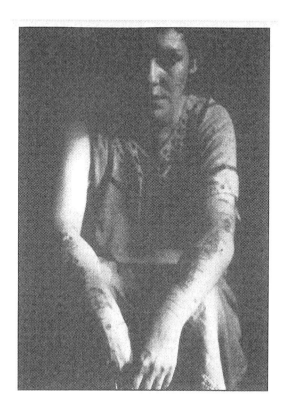

the phrase word by word, syllable by syllable, letter by letter, by sounds. Twisting its phonetics [...] she converts it into a foreign tongue. [...] She has disorganized language" (43). In her/narrator's monologs, she deconstructs language, phrases, words: "She does not cross and she is not crossed with pack of mutts yapping/mutt pack [...] thimpossible a cinch [...] thinflammation of the bitch/thinfection of those mutts" (94; punctuation and spacing in original). The transgression of sexual gender, literary genre, and grammatical forms defies the authority of the "dominators" and is carried out as the narrator's "graffiti inscriptions" of the woman's acts, as narrative marks left in the urban space: "[...] all for the reader who reads her, in writing she would even get so far as foreign language: English, French, Provençal alphabet or of the disdained Aymará, Mapuche, to please the dominators, [...] Over thresholds would pass genres chivalric/

pastoral/picaresque/serial/troubadour/bourgeois   drama/pamphlet/
tragedy and comedy/[…] speeches, proclamations/graffiti" (110; spacing
in original).

The ambiguous identity of the protagonist and the dismemberment of
the text are induced by the exuberant imagery, the experimental language,
and narrative techniques. Feminine subjects such as E. Iluminata, María
Chipia (in *The Fourth World*), and Coya (in *Fatherland*, 1986) never
appear determined in their gender, nor is their sexuality defined as homo
or hetero. They are assigned momentary, shifting, and ambiguous qualities. This lack of ontological integrity of the subjects takes us to perceive
queerness as the most characteristic element of these mutant characters'
nomadic identities.

3.2.3   *Metamorphosis and the Posthuman*

Severo Sarduy

The presence of transgressive and transforming characters is a constant
feature of Sarduy's works. In his novel *De donde son los cantantes*
(1967; *From Cuba with a Song*, 1994), two particularly equivocal, ambiguous, and metamorphic characters appear. Auxilio and Socorro, as their
names indicate, are parodies of characters with partially human features;
they resemble ephemeral, fairy-like creatures: "slender and symmetrical"
(1994: 15), "Bald Divinities," "Living-Dead," "they are piranhas, leprous
angels who sing 'Metamorphosis, metamorphosis'" (35).[30] They play a
double role: they are bearers of the narrative voice (contesting the narrator, like the chorus in classic Greek theater); they are also wild cards in the
plot because of their omnipresence, omniscience, and their ability to easily
transform their look (and sex) into multiple auxiliary characters. Their
gender fluctuation is reflected in their appearance that constantly mutates,
as do their equivocal roles in the story. The intricate plot is composed of
three parts in a multicultural triptych that corresponds, according to the
author's "Note" at the end of the book, to the "Three cultures, at least,
[that] have been superimposed to constitute the Cuban—Spanish, African,
and Chinese—three fictions alluding to them constitute this book" (1994:
154). In the first part, which represents the "Chinese" (Oriental)

---

[30] For quotes from this novel, I use the English translation by Suzanne Jill Levine of Severo
Sarduy, *From Cuba with a Song*, Los Angeles: Sun & Moon Press, 1994.

component, a general of Spanish origin falls madly in love with Flor de Loto, a transvestite vedette of the brothel El Shanghai in Havana's Chinatown. It is a story of evasions and persecutions that ends with an assassination attempt on Flor by the General. The two assistant chorus girls-narrators, Auxilio and Socorro, serve as intermediaries in this love affair. The second part of the novel, corresponding to the African (Black) component, tells the story of Dolores Rondón (possibly a metamorphosed Flor de Loto), a Mulatta who achieves fame and wealth as the wife of the Creole Havana senator and politician, Mortal Pérez. After a life dissipated among the high spheres of military dictators (presumably Gerardo Machado and Fulgencio Batista) and the fall of Mortal from his high rank, Dolores returns to provincial Camagüey (n.b., the birthplace of Sarduy), where she dies impoverished. The third part refers to the Hispanic (White) component of the Cuban cultural mosaic. It begins with the search for Mortal throughout Spain by his two secret lovers, Auxilio and Socorro. It continues with a pilgrimage of the two from Santiago de Compostela— fantastically transformed to Santiago de Cuba—to Havana with a wooden statue of Christ, as incarnation of the disappeared and ill-fated Mortal— now metamorphosed as Fidel Castro—to end with the sumptuous "Entrance of Christ to Havana," as an allegorical representation and a parody of Castro's triumphal entry to the capital after the victory of the Cuban Revolution in January of 1959.

The multiple facets of Auxilio and Socorro combine with their diverse roles in the plot of the novel. In a parodic game of words, their names, besides being two fairly common feminine first names in Spanish, have the same meaning—they both translate as "assistance" or "Help!" Their equivocal and ambiguous sexual features are noted from the beginning of the novel: "Feathers, yes, lovely brimstone [...] feathers on her head, a feather, hummingbirds and raspberry hat [...] Help's [Auxilio's] smooth orange nylon hair stretches to the ground [...] And Help, in stripes, an Indian bird behind falling rain [...] She peeps out, Baroque: [...] Look at yourself. Your tears have made a furrow in the first five layers of your makeup" (11–12). The feminine marks of Socorro and Auxilio become predominantly masculine (but still effeminate) in the next chapter, "Dolores Rondón," when the two assist the two narrators disputing the narration in a heated dialogue (inscribed in dramatic form, n.b. the shift in literary genre from narrative to drama) trying to find a way to keep the narration coherent. The parenthetical annotations of the implied author— now as playwright appearing on a metadiscursive level—characterize them as revolting gay and cross-dressed males "coming out of the closet," instead of aiding the protagonist:

HELP [Auxilio] (*red-haired and waxen youth with a high and hysterical voice*): With toad tack!

NARRATOR ONE (*protesting*): Oh no, out of the question! I will not stand for those three queens, horrible creatures.

NARRATOR TWO: Come on, for God's sake (a figure of speech), more simplicity, more modesty [...] listen quietly. These are Dolores's witnesses, her attendants. Let them express themselves.

HELP (*leading a protest by the trio, real leader of the masses style, very confident*): We strive to come out!

MERCY [Socorro] (*sprecht-gesang*): Like the tortoise from his shell, like the chicken from his egg, like the corpse from his hole, yes! (59)

The use of parody is again evident. The two are transformed into two tireless adventurers who travel throughout Spain in search of their ephemeral lover (Dolores' ex-husband), Mortal. In a figurative-symbolic plan, they adopt or metamorphose into different beings such as nun, martyr, and masochist, in their journey to bring Mortal back to Cuba. The result of these two cross-dressed characters' constant metamorphoses and parody—two characteristically (neo)baroque devices—is the novel's articulation of a transitive multicultural nomadic identity.

Mario Bellatin

Metamorphosis in Bellatin's novels takes place in two parallel dimensions: first, of content, by means of transformative characters that fluctuate between human and animal, masculinity and femininity; and secondly, of form in the metamorphic and intertextual narrative structure of the novels, with the apparently random relationships among its characters. These texts surpass traditional, mimetic realist narrative, opening up the novels to avant-garde solutions of an experimental nature. Metatextual procedures question the boundaries of both sexual gender and literary genre. In

206   K. A. KULAWIK

a fragmented and combinatory narrative that resorts to associations of facts and characters, Bellatin's narratives present mutants who are highly unstable in their appearance and acts, and who undergo processes of reincarnation and metamorphosis. On the other hand, Bellatin transgresses the boundaries of narrative genre by injecting the novel with a self-conscious extratextual metadiscourse that situates the text between fiction and nonfiction. Its fragmentary structure is made up of threads of diverse narratives that take on different story lines, interwoven as free associations, but organized by the superior voice of a narrator situated at a meta-discursive level. This voice additionally interlaces the text with historical (or apocryphal) documentary references.

Thus, we observe multiple discursive levels in the novel *Jacobo reloaded* (2014), in which the narrator appears as an implicit author to explain the creative process behind his previously published novel, *Jacobo el mutante* (2002). It constitutes a rewritten version of yet another novel, this time by Austrian-Jewish author Joseph Roth (1894–1939). In this palimpsest, the implicit author (Bellatin) metadiscursively explains to the reader (using references) the unusual case of a community rabbi who, during his daily ablutions, experiences a complete metamorphosis, changing not only his gender but his entire self/identity:

> The out-of-the-ordinary fact described by Joseph Roth occurred when Jacob Pliniak submerges into the lake [...] he returns to the surface, having transformed into his own daughter. But not into the girl that we've known until now, but rather into an elderly woman, eighty years of age. Jacob Pliniak has acquired the body of an old woman, in whose memory the existence of a Jacob Pliniak is perhaps logged, a dead man that drowned while performing his ablutions in a lake upon whose shores he built his house. It's important to point out that in the Kabbalah these transformations that entail person, gender, and time are referred to as "Aphoristic Pools." (16)[31]

Similarly, the multiple plots of the novel *Lecciones para una liebre muerta* (2005), composed of 243 narrative vignettes, intersect on various levels or story lines, without any of them taking precedence over the others. In it, the transvestite philosopher (who appears as a character and figures as a friend of the narrator) and the transvestite narrator-protagonist of the intratextually mentioned previous novel, *Salón de belleza* (1994), are the

---

[31] Quotes from the English translation by Jacob Steinberg of Mario Bellatin, *Jacob the Mutant*, Los Angeles, CA: Phoneme Media, 2015.

same character. The chanceful appearance of the philosopher in the plot of *Lessons* … inspires the narrator of this story to write (and include himself in) the previously published novel *Beauty Salon* about a beauty parlor transformed into an asylum for the dying sick.

These inter and metatextual relations between the novels, along with the presence of mutant figures, point to textual/sexual transformism. It constitutes a trope that represents the illusory play of identities and accentuates the fugitive (neobaroque) character of this narrative. Palaversich observes that: "[…] bodies that mutate from male to female constitute the norm. These bodies, it should be emphasized, are disturbing […] because of their tremendous power to destabilize any concept of character unity and transparent narrative meaning" (2005: 11–12; my translation). The destabilizing fragmentation of the narrative structure and of the sexual attributes of the characters entails other mutations, such as that of the space of a beauty salon turned into an asylum for the terminally ill, of the sick body transformed into a healthy one and vice versa, of humans into animals, of men into women.

Bellatin's narrative blurs the boundaries between novelistic fiction and documentary, at times critical and autobiographical essays. The author creates his own narrative logic that is transitively flexible and consciously manipulated by the narrator. With metadiscursive awareness, the narrator of the novel *Jacobo el mutante* admits that the logic he proposes is internal and accommodating. As implicit author, s/he comments the story narrated by Roth on a superior, metadiscursive level: "Maybe that is also why the character, Jacob Pliniak, who in the middle of the narrative transforms into a woman like in Virginia Woolf's *Orlando*, is one of the most curious characters in literary history" (9). An analogy can be established between the implied author's simulation of a character's identity and the representation of the process of writing as an apocryphal simulation of (historical) reality in an act of textual "performance." It is not only a physical but also a conceptual metamorphosis, a leap in narrative time to the characters' future transformed identity.

In Bellatin's novels, metamorphosis occurs in different types of transformations. Human beings change into animals: "The woman told him that her brother had been transformed into a suffering hare" (*Lecciones* 114–15; my translation); intertextual change of narrative space: "The book *Salón de belleza* […] seemed to deal with an aesthetic that is transformed into a place prepared for death" (*Lecciones* 125–26); or, as in the case in *Jacobo el Mutante*, the entire body of the protagonist, including the sexual gender

208   K. A. KULAWIK

and age, mutate into what is stated is his own daughter: "Precisely when the reader assumes […] not just Jacob Pliniak's presence in the text […] our character transforms, with no great leap, into his supposed adopted daughter, Rose Plinianson" (2015: 11). The metafictional author in the novel incorporates the reader and her/his point of view as part of the transformation. The metamorphosed Pliniak character serves as an example of the transformative capability of Bellatin's narrative to articulate mobile and transitive identities in the realm of the neobaroque text-as-performance.

Eugenia Prado
Genders and genres intersect in the multifaceted work of Chilean writer and visual artist Eugenia Prado. According to Juan Pablo Sutherland (2000), Prado's transgressive writing "has generated a suggestive imaginary zone that challenges the symbolic order, the masculine logos […] questioning the centrality of power" (16; my translation). Her elaborate use of language, reminiscent of the Neobaroque, represents cyborgs, or posthuman identities that emerge from the rubble of the traditional categories of "human." Just as Bellatin, Prado resorts to a manipulative metanarrative language to generate a text that is not subordinated to any pure literary genre. With a multidimensional hermaphroditic look of the human body and an androgynous perception of gender, the author explores the posthuman condition as another possibility for nomadic identity.

The presence of posthuman identity in Prado, embodied in the figure of the cyborg, has been addressed by Andrew Brown, who departs from Katherine Hayles' (1999) definition of the cyborg: "a hybrid being of flesh and technological apparatus that, through this hybridity, defies the classifications of traditional society" and "represents the possibility of completing a mutilated and incomplete identity" (2007: 802). The cyborg produces couplings (combinations) that, in its sexual desire, generate pleasure while violating limits and boundaries of defined sexual identity. The concept of the cyborg corresponds to the fragmented character of the protagonists in Prado's works, whose action takes place in the realm of the alienating post-industrial metropolis. It is an automated and posthuman universe in which the combinatory and transitive game of machines and humans begins to degenerate stable binary identities.

The identity transformation of the characters alienated in a hypertechnological world is presented in Hembros (2004). It is a work as hybrid, transgeneric, and multifaceted as the very idea of the cyborg that fluctuates in a constant combinatory movement of plural entities, between human and machine. The text refuses any univocal categorization of sexual, gender, or

3 SUBVERSIONS OF SELFHOOD: TRANSGRESSIVE CHARACTERS... 209

literary genre categories. It constitutes a fluid project of a text-in-gestation, a "performance novel" (novela instalación according to Prado)[32] staged with video and music. The original text, begun in 1999, was conceived to be a continuous work in progress, open to changes, modifications, and reeditions. By 2004, it was reworked with musical accompaniment and staged as a performance of the novel with the title Hembros: asedios a lo post humano ("Fe-Males: Sieges of the Posthuman") which, in the words of Prado, proposes the reading of a novel from other vantage points, that is, taking it out of the traditional format of the book to a stage installation integrated with multimedia and technology (Kulawik 2012: 236–38). Fourteen stagings were held in Santiago's Galpón Víctor Jara Theater of the Colectivo de Artes Integradas as a multimedia scenic installation integrating music, theatrical performance, dance, video, and plastic arts. The soundtrack was composed by Chilean musician and educator John Streeter to accompany declamations of the narrative text written by Prado. The work explores the emergence and ultimate rebellion of dispersed and mobile androgynous subjects—hembros [fe-males]—who prowl the liminal spaces of the feminine and the masculine: "Probable identification: man + woman = hunger" [hombre + hembra = hambre] (Chant 7). [33] Their interaction with technology traps them in subjugating power relations controlled by the master figure of the Father. Despite their attempt to interrelate and free themselves from formulated categorizations, they turn out to be the new subaltern— the cyborg: "We are species of automatons, a sick genre created to place horror" (Chant 3); "animals of what species, beasts that recognize each other, that fuse and confuse" (Chant 15).

Hembros explores dispersed and mobile subjects lost in a technologically advanced world to reveal what the author, in her correspondence, explained as "the interactions between artistic forms and current technological devices." She states that her goal is to capture "the symbols and signs of the forces that, in a technologized and codified environment, act as models imprinting themselves on posthuman minds and bodies" ("Correspondence" 2–3). [34] The multimedia integration of the crafts of

---

[32] In an interview with Kulawik (2012), Prado refers to *Hembros* as an "installation novel that incorporates video, among other artistic disciplines" (236); "*Hembros* is a novel in process. We agreed with John [Streeter] to work the text from different disciplines" (238).

[33] All quotes from *Hembros* are my translations from Chants 1 to 12 of the screenplay of the performance novel included in the booklet of Eugenia Prado, Hembros: Asedios a lo post humano. Santiago, Chile: Beca Fondart Artes Integradas, 2004. DVD

[34] These statements are quoted from the non-published transcription of Prado's correspondence with Krzysztof Kulawik, 2011.

literature, theater, music, dance, graphic design, audiovisual, and digital technologies allows to cross the boundaries of genders and genres. In this context, androgynous subjects (combinations of binary categories) unleash a rebellion against the Father—an abstract figure of authority—and against the whole technocratic institution he represents. The guiding theme is the search for mutual transitioning with the Other. The androgynous protagonist, represented with the neologism hembro ("fe-male"), interprets what we would call a schizophrenic litany of an awakening in a hostile world, a rebellion against the patriarchal system that categorizes, organizes, and oppresses the subject by means of language and technology. The hembro is surrounded by images and signs that bombard hir from all sides, mixing with the corporal acts staged by the actress with her movements, body painting, songs, and dances (Figs. 3.19 and 3.20).

Multiple screens project images that act against the movements of the characters, intervening the words of the protagonist simultaneously from different angles. Multiple voices overlap: "Who, when am I? How, when love does not exist? Hating the father, hating all of them. Hate them by

Fig. 3.19 Hembro levantándose [Hembro arising]. Scene from the staging of Eugenia Prado's Hembros, 2004. Screenshot from video clip by Marcelo Vega, CAIN. (Courtesy of Eugenia Prado)

Fig. 3.20 Novia freak [Freaky Fiancée]. Scene from the staging of Eugenia Prado's Hembros, 2004. Screenshot from video clip by Marcelo Vega, CAIN. (Courtesy of Eugenia Prado)

force of authority with hatreds that cry out their lies [...] Hate all fathers and their institutions" (Chant 1). Among the different voices that speak in sequence or simultaneously, the androgynous female protagonist is distinguished. An oneiric dimension prevails in which dreams merge with the word-text in a linguistic-symbolic reality parallel to the material one, "[...] with the sensation of going through terrifying dreams. Dreams that relate to a state that makes me disappear behind the words" (Chant 3). The character is aware of hir otherness—a sexually and posthumanly ambiguous "otherness"—which distinguishes him/her from hir creator and from the anonymous crowd. S/he situates hirself "behind the word," that is, behind the mask of language that shapes hir as an asexual-textual being. The awareness of being confined to an imposed normative identity incites hir rebellion and the desire for liberation from the categorizations prescribed by the patriarchal system of signs as conventions formulated by the social and technological machinery: "I have this strange appearance, alien and unbearable mixture that excludes me. An ambiguous example in the need to flee, to get out of the fabric, out of one's own fabric, to get rid of I don't know which of all the traps. […] Where did the same identical story trap me? I learned to subdue this feminine and ambiguous form of mine" (Chant 4). The character, fully aware of her androgynous bisexual body, struggles to reformulate hirself, assuming a voice of hir own as a gesture of empowerment, freeing hirself from the imposed word by deconstructing it in the broken morphology and syntax of the text, resembled by the word "hembro." Cyborg consciousness presents a rebellion against submission to the control of the oppressive patriarchal System. It is accompanied by an inherent desire of liberation from the technological control of "an empire of mechanical brains precipitates our images" (Chant 8).

In a dialogue that is triggered between the Creator (the Father) and the protagonist, words are incoherently dispersed in attempts at self-definition, while ideas float freely in new conceptual territories, making new connections, leading to new "nomadic" formations of the self. One of them is precisely the undefinable hembro, phonetically close and semantically related to the word "embryo," to suggest a beginning or a (de-/re-)categorization by inversion of the grammatical gender in the Spanish word "hembra" (female). In the operatic performance, the deconstructive voice of the narrator eventually resounds in the first person as the new re-creator (no longer the Father) to explain: "HEMBRO: name I have given to call species of both sexes, the male female, the female male, as a generic name that defines their condition, moments before placing them in more elaborate concepts that allow me to incorporate both terms in a possible (re-) classification" (Chant 9; capitals in original). The narrator goes on to clarify: "Two opposing forces in the same sign or a new instance that transcends us and allows us to change angles." Its voice appears in Hembros, the continuously evolving "novel in process," metanarratively referring to the hembros figures:

> They are two characters, Yellow and Blue. A woman and a man. Two men. A woman and a woman. I will intentionally omit the gender. I will say: they are two colors that pass like lights between the words. […] Two colors that describe desires, their own, between the lines of the writing. […] communicated through that so resounding and definitive way that words allow, as an insistence in populating intimate scenarios, just at the limit of a communication with another. (n.p.; my translation)[35]

[35] Quote from the unpublished text of Eugenia Prado's "novel in process," titled *Hembros/Asedios/Gestos maquinales*, begun in 1999. This fragment was written in 2023. Text provided by Prado as a courtesy to the author.

3 SUBVERSIONS OF SELFHOOD: TRANSGRESSIVE CHARACTERS... 213

The transitive and nomadic hembro emerging in the text (and on stage) is fluid and mobile, partly human and malleable: "[...] every day the image, even your own image, can be modified" (Chant 9). As a result of the efforts of the characters and the creative intervention of the narrator, a posthuman nomad appears, an androgynous cyborg whose plural identity combines multiple heteronormative categories.

In the novel Lóbulo (1998), Prado presents the story of Sofía, a disoriented adolescent girl who inhabits two worlds: the outside urban environment of the metropolis and the inner space of the house. Sofía is a technology addict (of her computer and phone), bound to the confines of her room. She struggles with her demons: the images of a father she has never met, an invasive mother who manipulates and corrects her in everything she does, and the telephone that rings every night to reveal the voice of an unknown man who hypnotizes her. Gradually, through the telephone, he invades her existential space, virtually violating her body in a cybernetic siege. Sofía's human identity is transformed into that of a cyborg, a human extension of her telephone. The progressive disintegration of her subjectivity first leads to a state of confusion and mutation, then to pregnancy and childbirth, and finally to death. As she is dying, Sofía gives birth to folds of printed paper: her text is "the book" of her existence, her experiences of transformation, disintegration, dissolution of her stable identity, and transit to the posthuman state. The fusion between her body, her mind, and the telephone produces what several theorists such as Deleuze and Guattari, as well as Hayles and Haraway, have explained as a cyborg, or an android being with ambiguous traits between human and machine, between masculine and feminine.

Metaphorically, the novel illustrates the phenomenon of the dissolution of inter-human communicative space amidst the invasion of tele-technology. In a metafictional twist, the narrator's voice abruptly intervenes: "Or don't you think that in this contemporary world the telephone configures an absurd scenario? Take a good look, look at all those people in the streets, with their gaze transferred to the mouths of their cell phones" (71; my translation).[36] From this metanarrative dimension comes a critical observation: "[t]he telephone is a mere instrument to make [you] participate in a process of comunicatransaction that I have imagined [...] in a scenario delimited by hallucinations, a disjointed, anachronistic character,

---

[36] Quotes from the novel are my translations from Eugenia Prado Bassi, Lóbulo, Santiago de Chile: Cuarto Propio, 1998.

even with some baring effects. We are attempts intervened by retouched calls, you and I in an extreme act of incommunicatransaction" (70; emphasis in original). Sofia's identity is transformed to merge with the identities of the "others" on the other end of the line, a multitude of beings desperately seeking contact with "the other" through technology: "Look in that phone, because in the red plastic device is everything you need to look at yourself in the absence of another. We are all absent" (114).

Her behavior yields to the will of a harassing man's voice who uses the power of language as an instrument of domination. The distinction between the two subjects-bodies-voices gradually disappears as the speaking voice splits into two beings: "Sensations fall sharp, my submerged body changes shape, it begins to move almost independently, undulating in the water it separates from my mind. [...] I am another being born from the water" (118). The two become indistinguishable, they con-fuse as they cross the boundaries of one and the other, of female and male, of human and apparatus, resulting in a combined being, a cyborg. A multidirectional metamorphosis occurs in which the distinction between human, animal (snake), and machine (telephone) is erased. The transformation/mutation culminates in a sexual act. Its apparent eroticism points to the material dimension of the transformation that occurs in the body and its extension (also material) of the written text.

It is only through language-writing that Sofia attempts to overcome the full dissolution of her human identity and her transformation into a cyborg: talking to herself and writing on her computer, she does not silence herself, disappear, or perish. Through writing, she persists: "She knows the [textual] trance to the point of seeing herself transformed" (66). In her obsessive search for the other in the virtual space of the telephone, she transforms herself into that *other within* the device, changes her identity, assumes different "foreign" aspects, even changing her ethnic identity: "I have to leave all convention to placate them [men]. I become an Indian. Indian I dance, as if I were one of them, Indian like everyone else, I become part of it, Indian my flesh persists" (136). She reaches a state of such profound mutation that her body acquires the consistency of a hermetic shell of metal or plastic, just like that of a cyborg—a hybrid between human and machine, an extension of the machine within the human: "My body changes, transforming little by little into a resistant shell. [...] From that formless body, other and overflowing, I say: barely a whisper" (148). Her hybrid state reflects the fragmentation and fluidity of her selfhood, which no longer possesses an identity but a flow in otherness: "Going to pieces among the fragments, disintegrating into dismembered images, moving away from fiction. Only fragments, flashes [...] then shadows" (45).

The disintegration of her human identity occurs in the communication and fusion with the other: "Sofia is disappearing, in the equilibrium both of them go through their solitude, both are becoming emptiness. [...] No one will be able to prevent the two from merging through the transfers" (172). The resulting state is a cyborg, the fusion between human and machine, between Sofia and the man on the other side of the line with the telephone their intermediary. The modus operandi of this transformation is an artificial system of sounds and signs that is language, both oral, written, and coded. The fusion is consummated with the "insemination" of the protagonist by the voice on the telephone: "Isn't it ironic that he has no body? don't you think so? You were fertilized in this labyrinth of sounds, he says" (204). From Sofia's fertilized body a baby is born: an immense fold of printed paper coming out of her womb, now transformed into a printer.

The passage of human identity into posthuman is reflected in the disjointed syntax of the sentences, and in the narration which confuses the voices of the characters with those of the multiple narrators who change grammatical person. After months of telephone conversations, Sofia's "cybernetic" body becomes an "organic printer" of paper texts that leave her body and cause her death, at least in the physical sense. The birth of a child-text indicates both an anti-patriarchal rebellion and an existential-symbolic continuity of a new subject through language, her nomadic immortality of a "writing" cyborg. Beyond revolutionary, with her posthuman ambiguity, Sofia is transgressive in her attempt to disidentify from the normative categories of patriarchal logocentrism in her articulation of a hybrid trans-self. She becomes the victim of a virtual, yet dominant male presence through technology. Her rebellion and liberation are achieved through her seditious quest to merge with otherness and transform into the "other"—a cyborg, a hybrid, transitive, and multiform posthuman being seductively embodied in the printer and subversively encoded in the text.

3.2.4 Borderland Nomads of In-Between Spaces

Gloria Anzaldúa
The literary-critical work of this Chicana writer expands borderland theory's intersectional scope to encompass themes of feminism, gender, and ethnicity. It develops the concept of a multicultural identity in movement

216   K. A. KULAWIK

across various borderland spaces. The narrative/poetic voice in her auto-biographical essays and poetry engages multiple dimensions of cultural belonging shaped by the underlying notion of the US-Mexican border. Although the point of departure in *Borderlands/La frontera: The New Mestiza* (1987) is the physical border with the history of Mexican population in Southwestern United States and the Chicane heritage, the book moves beyond to distinguish the multiple symbolic borders of a *"mestiza* consciousness." It addresses gender, sexuality, ethnic, and racial relations in a broader inter-American context. Anzaldúa states that as a homosexual, she is a "supreme crosser of cultures" with a role "to link people with each other—the Blacks with Jews with Indians with Asians with Whites with extraterrestrials [...] to transfer ideas and information from one culture to another" (2007: 107). The author examines the symbolic spaces and cultural signs of the Anglo-Hispanic-Native American borderland area. The book constitutes a multi-genre testimonial treatise, "above all a feminist one" (2007: 2)[37] that refuses any categorization, opening a new genre that Anzaldúa herself describes as "autohistoria-teoría." It combines autobiographical elements with historical facts, cultural criticism, and theorizations. "Her book focuses on the term she coined to describe women-of-color interventions into and transformations of traditional western autobiographical forms. Autohistoriateoría includes both life-story and self-reflection on this story" (2009: 9).[38] As Ricardo Vivancos stated, "Anzaldúa is a metapoetic writer" (2013: 30).

In *Borderlands/La Frontera*, but also in her other two major works *This Bridge Called My Back* (1981) and *This Bridge We Call Home* (2002), Anzaldúa alternates critical prose of academic rigor with a hybrid narrative of anecdotes, stories, and personal reflection. She interweaves this mix with pieces of creative poetic prose, free-verse poetry, linguistic experimentation, and dramatized dialog (including interviews). In this hybrid textual space, the speaking subject reflects on *la historia* of the Chicano people in a serpentine interweaving of cultural history with mental and spiritual states of being. Borderland culture and identity are explained as a combination of converging and diverging traditions that interact in the contact dynamics between two nations and multiple cultural worlds. In

---

[37] Quotes marked with (2007) come from the 3rd edition of Gloria Anzaldúa, *Borderlands/La Frontera: The New Mestiza*. 3rd ed. San Francisco, CA: Aunt Lute Books.
[38] Quotes marked with (2009) are from *The Gloria Anzaldúa Reader*, ed. AnaLouise Keating, Durham and London: Duke UP.

this cross-border dimension, she situates the genealogy of the Chicanos as representatives of a multilayered *Mestizo/a* or mixed identity of a hybrid people interpolated as both Natives of the Americas and heirs of Western—Hispanic and Anglo-Saxon—traditions. Anzaldúa's narrative explores their borderland identity as both a historical and a spiritual formation. Within the frame of a collective Chican*e* identity, the narrator's self-definition becomes a process of articulation passing through inner cycles of the spirit and psyche bound by history, and whose realization is the creative act of writing. This process represents a combinatory movement of outside historical determinants that include pre-Columbian history of the Nahuatl-Aztec populations, the Spanish Conquest, US domination since the nineteenth century, to twentieth-century northbound migrations. Shifting from these collective historical factors that split Chicana identity, her self-definition as a non-binary feminine subject moves through the inner states of identification with Indigenous spirituality of the Nahuatl deities (Coatlicue) in a syncretic combination with Catholic religion (the Virgin of Guadalupe) and other feminine cultural icons (La Malinche). This combination of outer and inner determinants emerges in what she calls a "new knowledge," or *conocimiento*, and a new state of consciousness that she calls the "new *mestiza*"—a multiple and transitive self that embodies a feminine perception of openness and an attitude of resistance. More importantly, in her proposal of this "new *mestiza* consciousness," Anzaldúa uses gender and sexuality to redefine cultural identity as a borderland condition of transitivity. This allows to further reconfigure existing ideas of an ethnically and racially determined nationalism and Western feminist theory.

From her native borderland Río Grande Valley in South Texas, Gloria Anzaldúa addresses the issue of the historic marginalization of the Chicano people, especially females and LGBTQ minorities of the border areas and contact zones across the United States. Within the Chican*e* ethnic category, she distinguishes female, homosexual, peasant, and middle-class subgroups as formants of a plural identity, split between the two sides of the Mexican-American border. The author-narrator undertakes a textual journey through the symbolic spaces and cultural signs that define this hybrid group sharing two cultures but not fully belonging to either of them. Her criticism focuses on the discriminatory situation of farm workers and laborers, of women (doubly discriminated because of race and sex) and homosexuals (triply discriminated). To explain their marginal situation, she looks to the common cultural determinants in the pre-Hispanic

218   K. A. KULAWIK

Nahuatl peoples of northern Mexico and the modern history of southwestern United States.

AnaLouise Keating describes Anzaldúa's hybrid genre of writing as "shaman aesthetics" to underscore the writer's belief in language's and imagination's transformative power through its experimental game of transiting genres. In her essay "Metaphors in the Tradition of the Shaman" (in *This Bridge We Call Home*), Anzaldúa posits an intimate interrelationship between image, metaphor, and change. She maintains that a writer's words enter and transform their readers: "Like the shaman, we transmit information from our consciousness to the physical body of another" (Anzaldúa 2009: 8). Hence, the prose in *Borderlands* is interwoven with lyrical-poetic forms: free verse, syntactic and lexical experimentation, and figurative imagery charged with symbolism. The narrative adopts a conversational tone of a testimonial account written with the technique of "code-switching" between English and Spanish in a kind of "linguistic cross-dressing"(Kulawik 2009: 292–95). The text is dotted with examples of the linguistic hybrid, Spanglish. These destabilizing elements also indicate Anzaldúa's affinity with neobaroque techniques. By means of mutating literary forms, the text displays an open feminine subjectivity of the narrative voice.

The text's hybridity is also a formal expression of cultural openness and flexibility of passing between multiple cultures. Embodying the rebellious and transformative consciousness of the "new *mestiza*," the female narrator represents a simultaneous dwelling in multiple worlds of gender, sexuality, color, class, personality, spiritual beliefs, and experiences of a Chicana. This open identity constitutes a synergistic combination of multiple contradictory Euro-American and Indigenous traditions into a "*mestiza* consciousness," what Keating describes as "holistic, relational modes of thinking and acting or, as [Anzaldúa] explains in 'La conciencia de la mestiza,' 'a more comprehensive perspective, one that includes rather than excludes'" (2009: 10). At its base is the female "other" with its resistance to masculine hegemony of "one": "woman is the stranger, the other. She is man's recognized nightmarish pieces, his Shadow-Beast" (2007: 39). This plural subject also incorporates the queer and other sexual minorities that are rendered invisible by the heterosexual dominant matrix: "The queer are the mirror reflecting the heterosexual tribe's fear: being different, being other and therefore lesser, therefore sub-human, in-human, non-human" (2007: 40).

Mestiza consciousness is dual-multiple in its openness: it is feminine, decentered, and rebellious, but in its openness, it is still capable of encompassing aspects of hetero-masculine and homosexual identifications. It is willing to accept and adopt elements of any category with the caveat that these forms of subjectivity situate in the horizontal, non-hierarchical psycho-social space of the rhizome in connection with the "other" on the same playing level and with the same "tolerance for ambiguity." A rhizomatic linking allows to move across the rigid formations of Western thought toward non-hegemonic, inclusive, and holistic modes of coexistence. In this regard Anzaldúa states:

> The new *mestiza* copes by developing a tolerance for contradictions, a tolerance for ambiguity. She learns to be an Indian in Mexican culture, to be Mexican from an Anglo point of view. She learns to juggle cultures. She has a plural personality, she operates in a pluralistic mode. [...] Not only does she sustain contradictions, she turns ambivalence into something else. (2007: 101)

The new *mestiza* finds her affinity to queer identity by way of androgyny as ambivalence. It results from combining within oneself, in the manner of yin and yang, the traits of the two traditional genders of male and female, and of the two sexual orientations of hetero and homosexuality, as cohabiting elements that are not contradictory or exclusive. The narrator uses the image of "the half and half" to express her duality and ambiguous queerness: "there is something compelling about being both male and female, about having an entry into both worlds. [...] What we are suffering from is an absolute despot duality that says we are able to be only one or the other" (2007: 41). She overturns the claim that human nature is limited to this duality, with no way of evolving into a more complete self/being. "But I, like other queer people, am two in one body, both male and female. I am the embodiment of the *hieros gamos*: the coming together of opposite qualities within" (41). Even when for some gender is something genetically inherent, she declares her conscious choice to be queer as part of her own identity creation, a process that she compares to a path that continually slips in and out of categorical identifications that she refers to as White, Catholic, Mexican, Indigenous, and other "limiting normative instincts" (41). For Anzaldúa, identity is a process of creating the self in the act of writing. In *This Bridge We Call Home* (2002), she calls it a story of *la búsqueda de conocimiento*, a quest for knowledge, and a spiritual faculty (*la facultad*) that gives her purpose, gives her life a meaning and a sense of belonging (562–63). Queerness becomes a path to this knowledge, to *el conocimiento* as learning of both the history of "our *raza*" (the Chicanxs) and the present state of oppression of minoritarian groups. Adopting a hybrid, borderline, and mobile *mestiza* consciousness is to balance and mitigate the duality of the subject-object position of hegemony in all categories that establish power relations in order to transcend them and eliminate dualistic-discriminatory-hegemonic thinking.

The identity of the new *mestiza* is the result of one's own creative process based on feminist intercultural thought, as stated by the narrative voice of *Borderlands*: "What I want is an accounting with all three cultures—white, Mexican, Indian. I want the freedom to carve and chisel my own face. [...] I will have to stand and claim my space, making a new culture—*una cultura mestiza*—with my own lumber, my own bricks and mortar and my own feminist architecture" (2007: 44). As a procedure of design, identity is in constant movement and passes through various stages of transformation. Forging of identity implies metamorphosis of the mind and body. As a borderland narrative subject, the new *mestiza* character consciously adopts animal incarnations that are "older than gender" such as of *La Víbora*, Snake Woman. Through the body, she incarnates the animal flesh and soul (2007: 48). Her transformations pass through the stages of the "Coatlicue State" in which she assimilates with the serpent. She establishes a bodily connection with the native Nahuatl feminine deities, one of which is Coatlicue, or the Earth Mother goddess of birth and death, the incarnation of cosmic processes. "Simultaneously, depending on the person, she represents duality in life, a synthesis of duality, and the third perspective—something more than mere duality or synthesis of duality" (2007: 68). Coatlicue's headless monster-like image symbolizes life and death together as parts of one existential process. Like in Medusa and Gorgon, she depicts the contradictory dual element, as a symbolic fusion of opposites (Fig. 3.21).

Consumed by an inner whirlwind, the emerging new *mestiza* character experiences painful periods of confusion, mental blocks, symptomatic of a larger creative process of cultural shifts through dismemberment, fragmentation, and rearticulation that she expresses creatively through Writing—the "Path of Red and Black Ink—Tlilli, Tlapalli" (2007: 87). Here, her prose begins to disintegrate into poetic narrative or semi-verse: "She has this fear that she has no names that she has many names that she

Fig. 3.21 Coatlicue (sculpted figure), Mexica, central Mexico. National Museum of Anthropology, Mexico City. (Source: Wikimedia Creative Commons)

doesn't know her names she has this fear that she's an image" (2007: 65; spacing in original).

At the end of the painful "Coatlicue state," a change occurs: the subject emerges in a transformed body that fuses with Text as the culmination of her metamorphosis, a process that also implies dialog. "I am playing with my Self [...] I am the dialogue between my Self and *el espíritu del mundo*. I change myself, I change the world" (2007: 92). Shifts and changes constitute her path "Towards a new consciousness," as the title of Chapter 7 of *Borderlands* suggests, a path that leads to the emergence in the new feminine *mestiza* consciousness, "*una consciencia de mujer*. It is a consciousness of the Borderlands" (2007: 99). It requires the subject to step in and out of one gender or culture into the other in a back-and-forth movement of constant transition or coexistence of two, three, or more genders/cultures. It is a way of being all of them at the same time in a multi-track simultaneity. This transitivity is expressed in a poem titled "*Una lucha de fronteras*/A Struggle of Borders" in which the lyrical subject—the speaking "I" of the *mestiza*—states how she is directed toward all the voices that call her at the same time:

> Because I, a *mestiza*,
> continually walk out of one culture
> and then to another,
> because I am in all cultures at the same time,
> *alma entre dos mundos, tres, cuatro,*
> *me zumba la cabeza con lo contradictorio.*
> *Estoy norteada por todas las voces que me hablan*
> *simultáneamente.*
> [soul between two worlds, three, four,
> my head is buzzing with contradictions.
> I'm turned north by all the voices that speak to me
> simultaneously.] (2007: 99; my translation; italics in original)

As such, *la mestiza* embodies a non-binary, border-crossing subject whose identity forms by shifting to a new transitive consciousness of openness and inclusivity. It proposes to open the paradigms of traditional normative gender and sexual identification, shunning the affirmations of exclusive masculinity and femininity, hetero and homosexuality, racial and ethnic purity and national belonging expressed by an exclusive patriotism. Anzaldúa remarks, again with an intersectional edge: "As a *mestiza* I have no country, my homeland cast me out; yet all countries are mine because I am every woman's sister or potential lover. (As a lesbian I have no race, my own people disclaim me; but I am all races because there is the queer of me in all races.)" (2007: 102). This does not mean the rejection of one's roots or heritage, of one's belonging in terms of gender-racial-ethnically determined identification. Anzaldúa expresses it in "El retorno" or the new mestiza's symbolic return to her homeland, "the Tragic Valley of South Texas" (2007: 110–12). The mestiza subject does affirm a belonging to *all* identities in their multiplicity and simultaneity. However, it is a belonging that is alternative to exclusionary binary power structures of masculinity and heterosexuality, and to the hegemonic institutionalized categories of race, ethnicity, and nationality. Instead, being a *mestiza* woman of color proposes the admission of otherness as an additional element of a multiple identity that is mobile, as it can adapt and adopt

3 SUBVERSIONS OF SELFHOOD: TRANSGRESSIVE CHARACTERS...   223

elements of difference in an effort to create a new hybrid and transitive Mestize culture. It implies adjusting identity to the tenets of nomadism as transformation through movement and adaptation to changing conditions of interaction with "otherness." By embracing differences of otherness that are in contact with oneself, the subject fulfills its selfhood, retrieving it from the void produced by rejection, marginalization, and self-deprecation. Anzaldúa's *new mestiza* subject states the following:

> I am cultureless because, as a feminist, I challenge the collective cultural/ religious male-derived beliefs of Indo-Hispanics and Anglos; yet I am cul-tured because I am participating in the creation of yet another culture, [...] a new value system with images and symbols that connect us to each other and to the planet. *Soy un amasamiento* [I am amalgamated]. (2007: 80–81)

Filling the voids of borderland identity is a (neo)baroque way of elimi-nating the *horror vacui* caused by marginalization with a multiplicity of interchangeable identity markers that come into play in the (*mestiza*—as mixed) consciousness of the new trans-self, as proposed by the narrative-poetic subject-character in Anzaldúa's literary and theoretical works. In *This Bridge We Call Home* (2002), Anzaldúa makes another important critical point about the new mestiza identity. It is not to be perceived as an indiscriminate blending or lumping of all "other" points of view, identi-ties, and traits, but rather a *critical* choice of combining and accepting those elements that are alike in their openness, flexibility, tolerance, and inclusive thinking:

> but sometimes you need to block the other from your body, mind, and soul. You need to ignore certain voices in order to respect yourself—as when in an abusive relationship. It's impossible to be open and respectful to all views and voices. [...] las nepantleras, [the wise women] [...] acknowledge the need for psychological armor (picture un nopal) to protect their open vul-nerable selves from negative forces while engaging in the world. (2002: 573)

Anzaldúa's work comes as both a theoretical and an artistic proposal for cultural studies and philosophy of identity in times of intercultural migra-tion. She calls this moment "a threshold in the extension of conscious-ness," a systemic change across all fields of knowledge, a collapse of the binaries of colored/white, female/male, mind/body (2002: 541). Positioning the new *mestiza* identity in *nepantla*—the border space between different yet overlapping perceptions and belief systems—she foregrounds the intersectional consciousness of changeability of racial,

224 K. A. KULAWIK

ethnic, gender, sexual, and all other categories. The possibility of conceiving this transitive form of selfhood renders the conventional labeling of identities obsolete. "Stubborn, persevering, impenetrable as stone, yet possessing a malleability that renders us unbreakable, we, the *mestizas* and *mestizos*, will remain" (2007: 86).

Guillermo Gómez-Peña

Cross-cultural borderland subjects appear as characters with nomadic identities in the performances, poems, and critical essays of this Mexican-American performer and writer. His life of an itinerant artist moving back and forth between California and Mexico and his career of touring across the globe are themselves examples of a nomadic subject, a border crosser with a plural identity. In the mid-1970s, Gómez-Peña graduated from the UNAM with a degree in Linguistics and Literature. In 1978, he immigrated to the United States and has since lived and worked mainly in California. In his book of essays and diaries *Bitácora del cruce* [Crossing Log], he admits: "My artistic work in the uneven terrain of performance began to take shape with more meaning and weight in the early 1980s, in my condition as an undesirable migrant in the US" (2006: 69; my translation). [39] He further states how performance was his salvation and his personal way of responding, fighting, and affirming himself in an imaginary creative space of freedom and dignity amid the desolate Anglo-Saxon cultural environment he claims to have encountered in the United States (2006: 69).

Gómez-Peña's critical stance on the concept of the border as a space of intercultural transfusions comes from his direct experience as a migrant, someone who was despised by "official" cultures on both sides of the border. In one of his other edited volumes of criticism, the artist describes the itinerant, migratory, and nomadic nature of his activity:

> I first left Mexico City in 1978. Since then, I've spent almost 20 years traveling from South to North and back—from city to city, country to country, English to Spanish. I travel from myth to social reality, always returning to my origins (by now mythical as well), retracing the footprints of my biological family and revisiting the many overlapping communities of which I am part: the diasporic Latin Americans, the deterritorialized citizens of every-

---

[39] Quotes and references marked with (2006) are my translations from Guillermo Gómez-Peña, *Bitácora del cruce*, México: Fondo de Cultura Económica.

where and nowhere, the habitants of these so-called 'margins' and crevices, *los vatos intersticiales*, the hybrids, exiles, and renegades. (2000: 9) [40]

Whereas he identifies with the marginalized, the hybrid *vato* [dude or guy] of the in-between interstices has always been an artist on the move, reaching different cultural spaces: "this partly conscious desire to retrace the footprints of these peoples and communities is precisely what compels me to keep moving" (2000: 9). His trajectory is probably the most compelling illustration of a nomadic identity of a transitive subject in perpetual motion. The nomadic-transitive effect of performance art exerted on the reader/viewer is described in the preface to *Dangerous Border Crossers*: "Through the performance ritual, the audience vicariously experiences the freedom, cultural risks, and utopian possibilities that society has denied them" (2000: ii). Gómez-Peña explains the interactive and haptic (sensorial) dimension of this aesthetic experience in which "audience members are encouraged to touch us, smell us, feed us, defy us. In this strange millennial ceremony, the Pandora's box opens, and the postcolonial demons are unleashed" (2000: ii). He defines performance as an artistic genre in a constant state of crisis, an ideal medium for articulating the permanent crisis occupying our society. "Performance is a disnarrative and symbolic chronicle of the instant which focuses mainly on the 'now' and the 'here'" (2000: 9). Performance's focus on presence, and not representation, differs from classical theories of theater which would suggest performing is only a mirror representation, an indirect copy of something distant. For a critical purpose, performance deforms reality in a transformative happening of the instant, "the actual moment in which the mirror is shattered" (2000: 9).

During his four-decade career, Gómez-Peña has transited the border South to North, back and forth. With his troupe "La Pocha Nostra"[41] and teaming with other artists, he has taken his performance around the world: "Touring the overlapping cartographies of Anglo- and Latino-America, Europe, Asia, and North Africa, my performance accomplices [Roberto Sifuentes, Coco Fusco] and I have crossed many dangerous borders. In

---

[40] Quotes and references marked with (2000) are from Guillermo Gómez-Peña, *Dangerous Border Crossers*, London–New York: Routledge.

[41] The word *pocho* may be derogatory when referring to a culturally assimilated Mexican-American living in the United States. Etymologically, it derives from Mexican Spanish, where it literally means "discolored, faded" (Wiktionary). Here, it is used in the feminine as a pun, playing with the name *La Cosa Nostra* of the Italian Mafia organization.

226   K. A. KULAWIK

doing so, we have risked our identity, our dignity, and occasionally even our lives" (2000: 8). Gómez-Peña's career of performance includes interventions in the form of happenings, installations, interactive theatrical dramatizations in public spaces, both indoor and outdoor, like museums, galleries, art centers, libraries, universities (as invited speaker/performer), street corners, parks, plazas, beaches, and in the backlands of the very US-Mexican border zone. Some of his most notable works were "Border Walk," "Border Brujo" ["The Border Witchdoctor"], "El Naftazteca," "1492 Performances," part of which was the "World Tour of the Guatinaui" (with Coco Fusco) that included the artists as Native Americans displayed in a cage representing Columbus' "exotic exhibits" from the New World.

Gómez-Peña has also been active in the realm of cyber space, resorting to digital internet technology as a medium of diffusion, after initially having to use radio (talk shows), TV, and analog video in the predigital era of the 1980s and early 1990s. In his works, he has adopted many *alter egos* as artistic incarnations of performance personae with aliases that represent his transient nomadic identity as an artist. They illustrate the nomadic trans-identity that Gómez-Peña emulates in his work. Some of them, contained in his "Criminal Identity Profile" (2000: 21), include El Existentialist Mojado,[42] Border Brujo, El Warrior for Gringostroika, El Untranslatable Vato [guy, dude], El Mariachi Liberaci, El Naftazteca, El Mad Mex, El Mexterminator, El Web-back. Most of them correspond to the titles of his most famous performances, of which he was also the main character. They reflect the parodic nature of his work and his areas of interest: the plight of Hispanic migrants, immigration and politics, economy, current world affairs, especially as they pertain to cultural contact, and the exploration of technology in cyber media.

A feature of his characters is their permanent condition of deterritorialization as they transit a jagged terrain of transnational cultural exchanges between hybridized identities originating in Latin American countries that are undergoing an accelerated process of political fragmentation, economic polarization, and cultural hybridization, and whose citizens are displaced to the second largest (after Mexico) Spanish-speaking country in the world, the United States (2000: 72). In his earlier book of essays, poems, and scripts, titled *The New World Border: Prophecies, Poems &*

---

[42] The literal meaning of *mojado* is wet, but it has been metonymically translated as "wetback," a derogatory term for Mexican farm workers in the United States.

Loqueras for the End of the Century, Gómez-Peña explains how his work in performance "explores the notion of a growing third world culture within the shrinking first world" (1996: 85).[43] He addresses issues of nostalgia, memory, language, homeland, nationality, and "the interactive role that these factors play in the formation and continuous (re)creation of transitional and multiple identities" (1996: 85). Affirming himself as "a member of a culture of resistance," he defines his art in relation to the border by saying: "I make art about the misunderstandings that take place at the border zone. But for me, the border is no longer located at any fixed geopolitical site. I carry the border with me, and I find new borders wherever I go. [...] My America is a continent (not a country) that is not described by the outlines on any of the standard maps" (1996, 5). Regarding the problematic relationship that often occurs between history, geography, economy, border politics, and art, the artist-author defines his position in the parodically titled essay "The Free Trade Art Agreement/El Tratado de Libre Cultura," stating the following:

> Artists and writers are currently involved in the redefinition of our continental topography. We see through the colonial map of North, Central, and South America, to a more complex system of overlapping, interlocking, and overlaid maps. Among others, we can see Amerindia, Afroamerica, Americamestiza-y-mulata, Hybridamerica, and Transamerica—the "other America" that belongs to the homeless, and to nomads, migrants, and exiles. We try to imagine more enlightened cartographies: a map of the Americas with no borders; a map turned upside down; or one in which the countries have borders that are organically drawn by geography, culture, and immigration, and not by the capricious hands of economic domination and political bravado. (1996: 6)

The political bravado that has defined conventional maps of the American continent, from Independence to NAFTA and other free trade economic pacts that define today's neocolonial Latin America, is replaced in his work by a concept map that Gómez-Peña calls "Art-America." Along with the other hybrids that he calls Hybridamerica and Transamerica, Art-America is no longer based on avid disputes between nations, but on cultural groupings of ideas and artistic productions:

---

[43] Quotes and references marked as (1996) proceed from Guillermo Gómez-Peña, *The New World Border*, San Francisco: City Lights Books.

Personally, I oppose the outdated fragmentation of the standard map of America with the conceptual map of Arte-América—a continent made of people, art, and ideas, not countries. When I perform, this map becomes my conceptual stage. Though no one needs a passport to enter my performance continent, the audience is asked to swallow their fears and to question any ethnocentric assumptions they might have about otherness, Mexico, Mexicans, other languages, and alternative art forms. (1996: 7)

The new conceptualization of the political and cultural map of the American continent is complemented here with a postcolonial inversion of the notions of center and periphery. Similarly to Pratt, who had already stated that "in a contact perspective, borders are placed in effect at the center of concern while homogeneous centers move to the margins" (Pratt 1993: 88), Gómez-Peña parodically relocates the subject to the "New World Border" space, a "duty free" zone of two-directional transits, "free" trade, and enslaving *maquiladoras*, and in which the displaced subject loses allegiance to any center:

I oppose the sinister cartography of the New World Order with the conceptual map of the New World Border—a great trans- and intercontinental border zone, a place in which no centers remain. It's all margins, meaning there are no "others," or better said, the only true "others" are those who resist fusion, *mestizaje*, and cross-cultural dialogue. In this utopian cartography, hybridity is the dominant culture; Spanglish, Franglé, and Gringoñol are *linguas francas*. (1996: 7)

Moreover, Gómez-Peña replaces the anachronistic colonial dichotomy of First and Third World with the notion of a mobile Fourth World (as in Diamela Eltit's novel), a conceptual space of the philosopher, writer, and artist, a place in which Indigenous (aboriginal) peoples from around the world meet with the diasporic communities of the displaced, exiles, refugees, etc.:

In the Fourth World, there is very little place for static identities, fixed nationalities, "pure" languages, or sacred cultural traditions. The members of the Fourth World live between and across various cultures, communities, and countries. And our identities are constantly being reshaped by this kaleidoscopic experience. The artists and writers who inhabit the Fourth World have a very important role: to elaborate the new set of myths, metaphors, and symbols that will locate us within all these fluctuating cartographies. (1996: 7)

Along with its politically charged content, Gómez-Peña's work is highly eclectic in its form, displaying elaborate and complex elements of hybridity and saturation with cultural referents. He admits that "(according to critics) the style of my performance work is 'excessive' and 'neobaroque'" (2000: 81). The accumulation of the visual element (artifacts, altars, statues, cages, screens, electronic devices, and dense imagery) often saturates the space in a neobaroque manner of excess. It recreates a mobile cross/inter-border space, visible in the installation of "BORDERscape 2000." The artist was called by interviewers a "hunter of images," which suggests his use of a visually and technologically hybrid space of surplus.

> I think that one of the many jobs of an artist is to look for new, fresh metaphors and symbols to help us understand our ever-changing realities and fragmented cultures [...], we create composite images. [...] Then we begin to do nasty things to these images. We begin to layer them as a kind of palimpsest. We add layers of contradiction or complexity, or we begin inserting details and features from other sources until these "traditional" images implode. (2000: 167–68)

These techniques point to the neobaroque combination of avant-gardist formal experimentation with technology and discursive saturation, resulting in a subversive political effect that this arrangement intends to produce.

An example of this type of visual intervention is "The Virtual Barrio@ The Other Frontier (or the Chicano interneta)" (1997) that included a "techno-placa" sign distributed on the Internet: "We are wetbacks/we are web-backs/we defy your sense of belonging/to a world you can't even understand/despite your claims of discovery and ownership" (2000: 247). In this virtual Web-performance, on one of the "conceptual billboards" that the artist posted (also on real-world billboards), a poem called "Web-backs" (playing with "wetbacks") appears accompanied by critical and theoretical writing and culturally hybrid images of Hispanics, Texan-Anglos, virtual "gamer warriors," Aztec warriors, and cross-dressed Mexican supermachos. Gómez-Peña ventures into what he calls "the terra ignota of cyberlandia without documents, a map or an invitation at hand" (248), becoming a self-proclaimed visionary of a contagious virus of cultural dissidence. In this space of intersecting identities, the combinations of images and texts present a transitioning of haphazardly mutating personalities. The main character is a cross-dressed cross-cultural hybrid, a mutant monster of multiple cultures who defies any categorization. Its shifting identities are displaced in the text by mobile grammatical subject positions, shifting from "I/he" to "we" (referring to fellow performers Sifuentes and Fusco, other Chicanos, and all the marginalized). Referencing to his critical writing, Gómez-Peña states that "like most of my theoretical writing, it suffers from an acute crisis of literary identity—partly because it reflects my ever-shifting positionalities as a mexicano/chicano interdisciplinary artist and writer living and working between two countries and multiple communities, but also because the text attempts to describe fast-changing realities and fluctuating cultural attitudes" (2000: 247–48). The figure of Gómez-Peña as the Mexterminator—a cross-dressed "ethno-cyborg"—creates a composite image that saturates the meaning of identity in multiple categories by layering them on the body of the performer in order to parodically implode the stereotypical vision of the "other" (2000, 252–53, 256–57). In his techno-ethnic virtual performances on the Web, the artist introduces into cyberspace a transcultural Chicane character as a persona-agent who intends to "brownify" virtual space, "Spanglishize" the Web, and infect the English lingua franca.

The divided subject, with dual (yet transitive) identity (going back and forth), is visible in the poem "El half & half" which Gómez recited at an academic event at Stanford University in front of a crowd of scholars who took to intellectually examine his "authenticity": "me dicen el half & half/half-Indian/half-Spaniard/half-Mexican/half-Chicano/half-son/half-father/half-artist/half-writer [...] (*busco a alguien en el público*)/y tú my dear jaina/te atreverías a amar/a un ser tan incompleto?" ["(*I look for someone in the audience*)/and you, my dear jaina/would you dare to love/such an incomplete being?"], sarcastically adding at the end: "the Spaniards, the gringos & the art world/left me all angry and fractured" (2006: 153).

Cross-dressing is a major theme in Gómez-Peña's performances. Working with the primary inversion of gender categories, the artist incorporates inversions of other binary, two-sides-of-the-border, identity roles. His appearances as cross-dressed (not always in drag, but in more ethnic or conventional and elegant feminine apparel) are notable in several photoshoots, for example, in the more recent photo-portrait, *La Loca*, displayed in Oregon's Portland Art Museum in 2022; also in "El emperador del Tate" in London's Tate Modern Gallery in 2004, and in the series "Border Brujo" where he incarnated one of his long-standing avatars of the "cultural transvestite" (Fig. 3.22).

Fig. 3.22 *La Loca* [*The Drag Queen*], classic photo portrait of Guillermo Gómez-Peña by Juan Carlos Ruiz Vargas, Mexico City, 2019. (Courtesy of La Pocha Nostra Living Archives)

Like a painting canvas, his elaborately tattooed body carries multiple marks of superimposed ethnic, racial, and national distinctions that overlap with inversions of gender categories. His multi-identitarian incarnation of the posthuman-ethno-cyborg figures of Aztec High-Tech, Naftazteca, and Mexterminator sometimes included an underlayer of the cross-dressed male using subtle and vivid elements of female attire and makeup (Fig. 3.23). This was visible in his 2018 performance "The Most (un) Documented Mexican Artist" in Los Angeles, in "The Three Fridas: GP and his alteric selves" solo tour, and the "GP as Native American" photo displayed on the web page of the National Museum of Mexican Art in Pilsen, Chicago.[44]

Making a direct reference to the transitive borderland "spaces in between," Gómez-Peña identifies with and recreates in his performances

[44] https://nationalmuseumofmexicanart.org/artists/guillermo-gomez-pena

Fig. 3.23 Guillermo Gómez-Peña as "Naftazteca." (Photograph by Lori Eanes, 2004. Source: Wikimedia Creative Commons)

subjects who correspond to the outcast, marginalized, exiled, and hybrid "cultural criminals," cross-border nomads whom he calls *vatos intersticiales* ["interstitial buddies"] (2006: 69). Their transitive identity corresponds to a multicultural borderland self that Gómez-Peña presents in his own assessment of the performance artist: "In this sense, when we present a performance, we are not 'actors,' we are not even human beings with a fictitious individuality. We are more like post-Mexican Frankensteins, or what I call 'ethno-cyborgs'. We are 1/4 part human, another 1/4 part products of technology, another 1/4 part cultural stereotypes, and a final 1/4 part psychological projections of the audience itself" (2006: 260). This statement sums up the performative borderland character created to

3 SUBVERSIONS OF SELFHOOD: TRANSGRESSIVE CHARACTERS... 233

represent the highly complex, hybrid, syncretic, transitive nomadic self of the "New World Border." As Border Brujo, "I assumed myself as I am: a transcultural hybrid and an orphan of two states/nations" (2006: 263).

The (cyber)performance of Gómez-Peña represents the destabilization of official cultural categories by transgressing the borders between art and the "mined political territories, meaning interracial relations and immigration" (2006: 138). The formal and conceptual opulence of his distinctively neobaroque style combined with avant-garde formal experimentation allows the spectator to visualize a transitive borderland subject embodied in the nomadic cross-dressed "ethno-techno" characters of his performances.[45]

Washington Cucurto
In an outlandish caricature of the Argentinian Independence Wars, the novel *1810: La Revolución de Mayo vivida por los negros* ["The May Revolution as Lived by the Blacks"] (2008) by Argentine novelist, poet, and editor Washington Cucurto (artistic name for Santiago Vega, b. 1973) presents an apocryphal version of history using a technique that he calls *realismo atolondrado* ("bewildered realism"). It reveals affinity to classic Latin American magical realism in the vein of Gabriel García Márquez and Isabel Allende in its plausible cartoon-like blending of fantasy with reality. The novel depicts a supposed "Argentine Revolution" of the common people instead of the official historic version of the White Creole uprising against the Spanish Crown, driven by the Primera Junta Libertadora de Gobierno (the first independent government of the Río de la Plata). The comical tone of sheer parody and caricature, and the profusion of exuberant narrative, linguistic, and stylistic forms make this probably one of the most neobaroque works engaged in our study.

Crossings and transits between racial, ethnic, social, and sexual categories of nomadic—inverted, displaced, and shifting—identities appear in this fantastical satire about 1810's popular uprising in Buenos Aires against both the Spanish colonial and the liberal Creole authorities. Notwithstanding its historical undertones, it becomes a carnivalesque sexual revolution of gay and queer characters from the entire LGBTQ spectrum, fought by an army of freed Blacks and their Native-American allies

---

[45] I borrow the term "ethno-techno" from the title of Gómez-Peña's book of essays, *ethno-techno. Writings on performance, activism, and pedagogy.* New York and London: Routledge, 2005.

234 K. A. KULAWIK

from the Andean province of Upper Perú, all led by a gay and Africanized general, none other than José de San Martín. Along with Simón Bolívar, he is historically one of the two most important leaders of the Latin American Independence struggle. Cucurto's depiction of San Martín's passing identity makes the novel highly provocative and iconoclastic.

In the historical context of the Wars of Independence, Buenos Aires was crisscrossed by multiple mixed (Mestizo) registers of races and ethnicities, which Cucurto relates to today's presence of immigrant groups of mainly Bolivians, Paraguayans, and North Argentinians in that city. On top of this, the identity of the main character—the gay, cross-dressed, and multiethnic San Martín—is inverted and hybridized. This is carried out textually in the most opulent neobaroque style, using ultra-detailed and outrageously ornate descriptions. While recruiting soldiers (still then called "slaves") in Africa, the General parodically (cross-)dresses as an effeminate (admittedly gay) sovereign of the African tropics:

> The General came out of his room, dressed like a king. [...] The dress coat that covered his knees was made of blue velvet with bright-colored flowers embroidered in silver. More than two thousand eyelets of gold cloth crossed it from top to bottom and formed dizzying psychedelic arabesques. The jacket he wore had pockets full of black roses freshly cut from the Mozambique River. Three roses were tied to the end of his saber. Tight-fitting crimson velvet-striped silk panties revealed the lushness of his sex. (63–64)[46]

The transgressively exuberant neobaroque style used in this novel produces a destabilizing effect. In his study of Cucurto's work, Oscar Martín Aguierrez states that "he does not retouch a little, he disfigures everything: San Martín is nothing more than a repressed homosexual [...] the distortion is so exaggerated that it provokes morbidity and the complete desacralization of the institution. [...] The writing, then, becomes erotic and burlesque" (2016: 58).[47] Eroticism plays a key role in the configuration of characters that, in their sexual excess of irrepressible enjoyment, unbalance any notion of sexual and racial fixity. Their fluid identities germinate from the opulence and excess of the popular carnival and the creole

[46] All quotes from this novel are my translations from Washington Cucurto, *1810: La Revolución de Mayo vivida por los negros.* Buenos Aires: Emecé, 2008.

[47] All quotes from Aguierrez are my translations from *Palimpsesto profano: La escritura de Washington Cucurto,* Universidad Nacional de Tucumán, 2016.

banquet of the Cabildo Palace as distinctive marks of a rebelliously hybrid American identity, represented by the figure of the *Señor Barroco* (Lezama 1957: 32–34). As Aguierrez points out, "In the narrative of *1810... sex* can be analyzed as a great banquet, understood as that overabundance no longer of food, but of pleasure. [...] This banquet acquires special characteristics: it is stripped of hierarchies and rituals" (2016: 59). This leveling of social and racial strata can be associated with the Carnival explained by Bakhtin (1981) as a form of subversion through the inversion of roles. This is attained in the text by means of exuberance (of bodies and food), "a leavening that the author places to make pleasure and eroticism grow and swell. [...] raising the sexual scene to totally excessive climaxes" (60). Aguierrez emphasizes the role of the hyperbole as a reflection of erotic enjoyment and bodily transformation, carried out in the words that textually mold the characters' bodies and identities. "The levels of hyperbolization are so great that they produce surprise in the reader and the sensation that the writer uses and abuses language" (60).

San Martin's contact with Africa, where he was sent to capture slaves for the lucrative colonial business, led to his double transculturation stemming from, on the one hand, his alleged Amerindian and *Mestizo* origins in the subtropical north of Argentina and, on the other hand, the affection for his multiple lovers and offspring in Africa:

> The General loved Africa as much as he loved his beloved Yapeyú, there in the province of Corrientes, the subtropical paradise, [...] so different from that Pampean hamlet, the axis of struggles that was Buenos Aires. [...] What was there in Africa? What did this continent, the distributor of blood, hold for this distant South American dreamer? Would the answer be love, Olga? [...] What was there that brought him sweet remembrances of the lost paradise: [...] the Indianade speaking a musical Guaraní, [...]? We will never know what Africa was like and what color it was painted in the eyes and soul of this dreamer of *brown America*, but *we hope* that it was the same as *we dream* of it two hundred years later. (63; emphasis added)

Here the narrator identifies himself and the transformed General—dreamer of a dark-skinned America—with the American "other": the marginalized of color, the Indigenous, the *Mestizo* and Mulatto groups, marking a historical continuity from the apocryphal ethno-racial and social Revolution of 1810 to today's Trans-American waves of immigrants. The present context of intercultural contact and cross-racial, ethnic, and

236   K. A. KULAWIK

national migration is reminiscent of San Martin's motley army that set out to reclaim not only its independence from Spain, but its emancipation from socio-economic oppression.

In Chapter 52, "Unity is strength," the narrator reveals the revolutionary enthusiasm sprouting from the union and intermingling of people: "Long live the true revolution!—shouted the Black [and Amerindian] soldiers of both armies. And they mixed and a new revolutionary army was created, yes now, a mixed army, salad, *mezclita* [a little blend], of sons of the earth and excluded humans, Blacks and Indians or Indians and Blacks, embraced [...] they went out to reconquer Buenos Aires, with all their anger they rode to destroy the bourgeois revolution" in a "diluvian and apocalyptic army of free beings of America" (2008: 193). Cucurto's textually contrived Revolution of 1810 becomes an alternative intersectional revolution of categories, border crossings, and authentic changes taking place in a fantastical social, racial, and sexual emancipation of America at the dawn of the twenty-first century. The transgressive characters portrayed in *1810* ... cross all boundaries of normative (and historical) selfhood and situate themselves in a mobile, transitive, in any case, nomadic space of in-between from which Cucurto's neobaroque narrative forges a new vision of an American trans-self.

WORKS CITED

PRIMARY SOURCES (CORPUS OF ANALYZED TEXTS)

Anzaldúa, Gloria. (2007 [1987]). *Borderlands / La Frontera: The New Mestiza*. San Francisco: Spinsters / Aunt Lute.

Bellatin, Mario. (2000 [1994]). *Beauty Salon*. Trans. Kurt Hollander. San Francisco: City Lights Books.

Bellatin, Mario. (2002). *Jacobo el mutante*. México: Alfaguara.

Bellatin, Mario. (2005). *Lecciones para una liebre muerta*. Barcelona: Anagrama.

Bellatin, Mario. (2014). *Jacobo reloaded*. Illus. Zsu Szkurka. México-Madrid: Sexto Piso.

Bellatin, Mario. (2015). *Jacob the Mutant*. Trans. Jacob Steinberg. Los Angeles: Phoneme Media.

Casas, Francisco. (2004). *Yo, yegua*. Santiago, Chile: Seix Barral—Ed. Planeta Chilena.

Cucurto, Washington. (2008). *1810: La Revolución de Mayo vivida por los negros*. Buenos Aires: Emecé.

3 SUBVERSIONS OF SELFHOOD: TRANSGRESSIVE CHARACTERS... 237

Echavarren, Roberto. (2000). *Performance: género y transgénero*. Buenos Aires: Eudeba.

Echavarren, Roberto. (2005). *El diablo en el pelo*. Buenos Aires: El Cuenco de Plata.

Echavarren, Roberto. (2007). *Ave Roc*. Buenos Aires: Mansalva.

Eltit, Diamela. (1983). *Lumpérica*. Santiago de Chile: Onitorrinco.

Eltit, Diamela. (1997). *E. Luminata*. Transl. Ronald Christ. Santa Fe, NM: Lumen.

Eltit, Diamela. (1995). *The Fourth World*. Transl. Dick Gerdes. Lincoln: U of Nebraska P.

Gómez-Peña, Guillermo. (1996). *The New World Border: Prophecies, Poems & Loqueras for the End of the Century*. San Francisco: City Lights Books.

Gómez-Peña, Guillermo. (2000). *Dangerous Border Crossers: The Artist Talks Back*. London-New York: Routledge.

Gómez-Peña, Guillermo. (2005). *Ethno-techno. Writings on performance, activism, and pedagogy*. New York and London: Routledge.

Gómez-Peña, Guillermo. (2006). *Bitácora del cruce (Textos poéticos para accionar, ritos fronterizos, videografitis, y otras rolas y roles)*. México: Fondo de Cultura Económica.

Hilst, Hilda. (1993). *Rútilo nada. A obscena Senhora D. Qadós*. Campinas, Brasil: Pontes.

Hilst, Hilda. (2012). *The Obscene Madame D*. Trans. Nathanaël. Callicoon, New York: Nightboat Books.

Kulawik, Krzysztof. (2009). *Travestismo lingüístico: el enmascaramiento de la identidad sexual en la narrativa latinoamericana neobarroca*. Madrid, Frankfurt am Main: Iberoamericana-Vervuert.

Lemebel, Pedro. (1995). *La esquina es mi corazón*. Santiago de Chile: Ed. Planeta.

Lemebel, Pedro. (2001). *Tengo miedo torero*. Santiago de Chile: Ed. Seix Barral Planeta.

Menstrual, Naty. (2008). *Continuadísimo*. Buenos Aires: Eterna Cadencia.

Prado Bassi, Eugenia. (1998). *Lóbulo*. Santiago de Chile: Cuarto Propio.

Prado Bassi, Eugenia. (2004). *Hembros: Asedios a lo post humano. Installation–Performance. Novel-screenplay booklet*. Santiago, Chile: Beca Fondart Artes Integradas. Chants 1–12. DVD.

Santiago, Silviano. (1994 [1985]). *Stella Manhattan*. Trans. George Yúdice. Durham and London: Duke UP.

Sarduy, Severo. (1970 [1967]). *De donde son los cantantes*. México: J. Mortiz.

Sarduy, Severo. (1975). *Cobra*. Trans. Suzanne Jill Levine. New York: E.P. Dutton.

Sarduy, Severo. (1981 [1972]). *Cobra*. 2nd ed. Barcelona: Edhasa.

Sarduy, Severo. (1984). *Colibrí*. Barcelona: Argos Vergara.

Sarduy, Severo. (2000 [1994]). *From Cuba with a Song*. Trans. Suzanne Jill Levine. Los Angeles: Sun and Moon Press.

Shock, Susy. (2011). *Poemario Trans Pirado*. Buenos Aires: Nuevos Tiempos.

238 K. A. KULAWIK

SECONDARY SOURCES (CRITICAL AND THEORETICAL REFERENCES)

Aguierrez, Oscar Martín. (2016). *Palimpsesto profano: La escritura de Washington Cucurto*. Tucumán, Argentina: Universidad Nacional de Tucumán.

Anzaldúa, Gloria and AnaLouise Keating, eds. (2002). *This Bridge We Call Home: Radical Visions for Transformation*. New York: Routledge.

Anzaldúa, Gloria E. (2009). *The Gloria Anzaldúa Reader*. Ed. AnaLouise Keating. Durham and London: Duke UP.

Araujo, Kathya, ed. (2007). *Cruce de lenguas: Sexualidades, diversidad y ciudadanías*. Santiago de Chile: LOM Ediciones.

Aruquipa, David, Paula Estenssoro, and Pablo Vargas. (2012). *Memorias colectivas. Miradas a la historia del movimiento TLGB de Bolivia*. La Paz: Conexión Fondo de Emancipación, Serie Estudios e Investigaciones 5.

Aruquipa Pérez, David. (2016). "Placer, deseo y política: la revolución estética de La Familia Galán." *Bulletin de l'Institut Français d'Études Andines*. 45.3: 451–61.

Aruquipa Pérez, David. (2018). "La Familia Galán: Una historia sobre zancos." *Diario Página Siete*. La Paz, Bolivia. May 20, 2018, 23–26. https://issuu.com/revistarascacielos/docs/rascacielos_17/26. Accessed November 20, 2022.

Bakhtin, Mikhail. (1981). *The Dialogic Imagination. Four Essays*. Austin: U of Texas P.

Brown, J. Andrew. (2007). "Identidad poshumana en *Lóbulo* de Eugenia Prado." *Revista Iberoamericana*. LXXIII. 221 (2007): 801–12.

Burgos, Fernando. (1992). *Vertientes de la modernidad hispanoamericana*. Caracas: Monte Ávila.

Cervantes, Miguel de. (2004 [1605]). *Don Quijote de La Mancha*. Edición del IV Centenario. Madrid: Real Academia Española–Alfaguara.

Echavarren, Roberto. (2008). *Arte andrógino: estilo versus moda*. Santiago de Chile: Ripio.

Echavarren, Roberto. (2010). "Resistance." *The Journal of Natural and Social Philosophy*. 6. 2: 20–26.

Ellis, Albert and Albert Abarbaniel. (1961). *The Encyclopedia of Social Behavior. Vols. 1, 2*. New York: Hawthorn Books.

Flores, Juan. (2004). "The Latino Imaginary: Meanings of Community and Identity." *The Latin American Cultural Studies Reader*. Eds. Ana del Sarto, Alicia Ríos, and Abril Trigo. Durham and London: Duke UP. 606–19.

Halberstam, Jack. (2018). *Trans*: A Quick and Quirky Account of Gender Variability*. Oakland, CA: U of California P.

Hayles, N. Katherine (1999). *How We Became Posthuman: Virtual Bodies in Cybernetics, Literature, and Informatics*. Chicago, London: U of Chicago P.

Jeftanovic, Andrea. (2000). "El cronista de los márgenes. Entrevista con Pedro Lemebel." *Lucero*. 11.2: 74–78.

3 SUBVERSIONS OF SELFHOOD: TRANSGRESSIVE CHARACTERS... 239

Jones, Nicholas, Rachel Marks, Roberto Ramírez, and Merarys Ríos-Vargas. (2020). "Census Illuminates Racial and Ethnic Composition of the Country," US Census Bureau. August 12, 2021. https://www.census.gov/library/stories/2021/08. Accessed 25 September 2022.

Kulawik, Krzysztof. (2012). "Asediar la literatura, la política y la cultura: conversación con la escritora chilena Eugenia Prado Bassi." *Revista Nomadías*. 16 (2012): 227–46.

Lezama Lima, José. (1957). *La expresión americana*. La Habana, Cuba: Instituto Nacional de Cultura.

Maíz-Peña, Magdalena. (1997). "Diamela Eltit: Chilean Prose Writer." *Encyclopedia of Latin American Literature*. Ed. Verity Smith. London, Chicago: Fitzroy Dearborn. 293–94.

Malamud, Carlos. (2010). *Historia de América*. 2nd ed. Madrid: Alianza Editorial.

Martínez, Ariel and Ana Sabrina Mora. (2020). "The Scenic Performance as Subversive Negativity: radical alterity and *trava sudaca* performance in the voice of Susie Shock." *Revista Brasileira de Estudos da Presença - Brazilian Journal on Presence Studies*. Porto Alegre: 10.3: 1–24. http://seet.ufrgs.br/presença. Accessed 15 October 2022.

Masiello, Francine. (2001). *The Art of Transition: Latin America and Culture and Neoliberal Crisis*. Durham and London: Duke UP.

Ortega, Julio and Lourdes Dávila, eds. (2012). *La variable Bellatin: Navegador de lectura de una obra excéntrica*. Xalapa, Veracruz: Universidad Veracruzana.

Palaversich, Diana. (2003). "Apuntes para una lectura de Mario Bellatin". *Chasqui: Revista de Literatura Latinoamericana*. 32. 1. 25–38.

Palaversich, Diana. (2005). "Prólogo" to: Mario Bellatin. *Obra reunida*. México: Alfaguara. 11–23.

Peralta, Jorge Luis. (2010). "La narrativa travesti de Naty Menstrual." *Lectora*. 17 (2010): 105–22.

Pratt, Mary Louise. (1993). "Criticism in the Contact Zone: Decentering Community and Nation". *Critical Theory, Cultural Politics, and Latin American Narrative*. Eds. Steven, M. Bell, Albert H. Lemay y Leonard Orr. Notre Dame: U of Notre Dame P, 83–102.

Quinlan, Susan. (2002). "Cross-dressing: Silviano Santiago's Fictional Performances." *Lusosex: Gender and Sexuality in the Portuguese-Speaking World*. Eds. Susan Canty Quinlan and Fernando Arenas. Minneapolis and London: U of Minnesota P. 208–32.

Richard, Nelly. (2001). *Residuos y metáforas (Ensayos de crítica cultural sobre el Chile de la Transición)*. Santiago de Chile: Editorial Cuarto Propio.

Sutherland, Juan Pablo. (2000). "*El cofre*, la extraña tonalidad del lenguaje tránsfugo de Eugenia Prado." Prologue to: Eugenia Prado. *El cofre*. 2nd ed. Santiago de Chile: Surada Gestión Editorial. 2000. 7–16.

Vaggione, Alicia. (2009). "Literatura/enfermedad: el cuerpo como desecho. Una lectura de *Salón de belleza* de Mario Bellatin." *Revista Iberoamericana.* LXXV. 227 (2009). 475–86.

VivancosPérez, Ricardo F. (2013). *Radical Chicana Poetics.* New York: Palgrave Macmillan.

Wayar, Marlene. (2019). *Travesti / Una teoría lo suficientemente buena.* Buenos Aires: Muchas Nueces.

Williamson, Edwin. (2009). *The Penguin History of Latin America.* 2nd ed. London and New York: Penguin Books.

Zarranz, Luis and Franco Ciancaglini, eds. (2019). *Trans Formaciones.* Buenos Aires: Lavaca Editora.

CHAPTER 4

One-T(w)o-Many: Neobaroque Articulations of Nomadic Identity

We enter a neobaroque labyrinth that invites us to walk
through an enclosure that operates by association of species,
of organic bodies, plants, flowers [...] to configure an
artificial universe of association of species and forms that
circulate through the closed body [...].

—Eugenia Prado, "Resistencia neobarroca" (2015; my translation)

This chapter explains how categorical identities are decentered and rearticulated as trans-identity by means of neobaroque mechanisms of representation. To this effect, we will apply concepts from the theories of Neobaroque, semiotics, and gender-queer studies to illustrate *how* transgressive characters-subjects, in their literary and artistic depiction, destabilize normative categories of identity and facilitate the perception of "transentity" as embodiment of transitive selfhood. Conceptual devices from these theories will help explain how the use of transgressive modes of representation associated with neobaroque stylistic techniques (that include exuberantly ornate, parodic, metadiscursive, and experimental narrative and visual forms) achieve the destabilization of identity and the figuration of an alternative—nomadic—mode of personal and cultural becoming. The deconstructive techniques of the Neobaroque are further explained with semiotics—specifically applying Peirce's mobile triadic sign—to demonstrate the fracturing and opening of meaning conveyed by

© The Author(s), under exclusive license to Springer Nature
Switzerland AG 2024
K. A. Kulawik, *Visions of Transmerica*, Literatures of the Americas,
https://doi.org/10.1007/978-3-031-42014-6_4

241

the neobaroque sign/artistic work. The transgressions involved in neobaroque figuration of meaning pave the way to articulating the nomadic transitivity of the trans-self using concepts generated by poststructuralism, queer, Chicana, feminist, and border theories. These concepts include "*devenir*" or "subject-as-becoming" (Deleuze 1977, 1980), "trans*" (Halberstam 2018), borderland identity (Ruiz-Aho 2011) in its forms of transvestism (Sarduy 1987c [1982], 1990; Garber 1997 [1992]), androgyny (Echavarren 2000, 2008), and queerness (Jagose 1996, 2015). They situate the "nomadic subject" (Braidotti 1994, 2002) in transitional "spaces of in-between" (Santiago 2001) in its transit through "points of passage" (Perlongher 1997) to ultimately experience the transformative effects of "nepantlism" (Anzaldúa 2007 [1987]; Moraga 2011; Vivancos 2013). In this chapter, we articulate these and other concepts related to metamorphosis introduced in Chap. 2 and apply them to the examples of transgression analyzed in Chap. 3, with the ultimate aim of demonstrating the viability of a transitive selfhood embodied in the nomadic trans-self. The chapter ends with an assessment of the socio-political implications of Neobaroque art and literature in the hybrid space of Transmerica.

4.1   The Neobaroque as a Style of Instability and Excess: In the Footsteps of Sarduy and Bataille

Analogically to the transgressive characters described in the previous chapter, Neobaroque discourse operates as a destabilizing, yet also transformative, force in the configuration of a nomadic trans-identity. A distinguished practitioner and theoretician of the Neobaroque in Latin America, Severo Sarduy constitutes a prime example of the level this style attained by the 1990s and of the influence it has exerted not only in the Caribbean but throughout Latin America. The narrative and poetic mechanisms perfected by Sarduy lend themselves to the representation of the end-of-the-century crisis of normative identity categories. The presence of these "neobaroque" techniques in Latin American Boom, Post-Boom, and Postmodern ("New") narrative has also been noted by literary critics, ranging from Chiampi (2000), Zamora (2006), Arriarán (2007) to Figueroa (2008), Kaup (2012), and Baler (2016). The most prominent facet of both baroque and neobaroque poetics pointed out by these critics is *exuberance*, exhibited in form by profuse ornamentation and artifice, and in content by conceptism, illusionism, simulation, and satire. Exuberance appears in the title of the translation of Zamora's *The Inordinate Eye* (2006), *La mirada exuberante* (2011), to refer to a series

4 ONE-T(W)O-MANY: NEOBAROQUE ARTICULATIONS OF NOMADIC... 243

of inter-artistic relationships between the visual arts and literary structures enabled by the baroque aesthetic modality. Zamora explains baroque exuberance as "overflowing abundance, from Latin *uberare*, being fruitful, with the prefix *ex-* to mean an extravagant, extraordinary, disproportionate abundance" (2011: xxx).[1]

Formal exuberance and conceptual decentering are related respectively to the two typically baroque stylistic categories of *culteranismo* and *conceptismo*, as we read in *Cuestiones gongorinas* by Alfonso Reyes. He brings forth these two terms when he refers to Spanish literary Baroque (which he calls *barroco gongorino*, named after its greatest representative, Luis Argote y Góngora) as the basis for American Colonial Baroque.[2] *Culteranismo* corresponds to an elaborately ornate use of language through contrived forms of expression, while *conceptismo* to an intricate use of elaborate conceptual devices such as illusionism, anamorphosis, simulation, and parody in a playful representation of thematic content. The common denominator of both is artifice. Cristo Figueroa explains how these two elements of formal and conceptual exuberance of the historical Baroque find their place in the Neobaroque poetics of instability:

> The artificiality of the historical Baroque—manipulation based on standardized rhetoric, illusionism, allegorical resources, decentering of perspectives, exacerbated metaphorisms, enervating polychromies, etc.—constitutes an obligatory point of reference for the end of the twentieth century, also fascinated by simulacra, hyperrealities, labyrinthine textualizations or heterodox narratives and poetics. (50–51; my translation)

---

[1] Here, I use my own translation of this fragment of Zamora's Spanish version of *The Inordinate Eye* because the English original does not render the same meaning of "exuberance." However, in the original, we find the following explanation of the eccentric character of the Baroque, which relates to exuberance: "The figurative meaning of 'inordinate' parallels its literal sense: 'inordinate' structures are *not* normative, *not* predictable, but eccentric, disparate, uneven. The Baroque passion to increase and include [as forms of exuberance] characterizes much of contemporary Latin American fiction, and this passion frequently follows from (and may result in) disproportion, disjunction, and their accompanying narrative energies" (2006: xxii; emphasis in original).

[2] Alfonso Reyes includes a precise classification of the terms that define the Spanish literary baroque: "cultismo" (better known as "culteranismo") and "conceptismo" in the essay "Savoring Góngora," part of his book *Cuestiones gongorinas*. Cf. in *Baroque New Worlds*. Eds. Zamora and Kaup (2010), 170–71.

In the Neobaroque, *culteranismo* and *conceptismo* are combined with a new content of ambiguous disidentifications of categories (such as queer sexualities) and trans-/intercultural displacements. For instance, we see that the action of Sarduy's novels is situated in spaces dispersed between multiple locations in the West and the East, as when sexually ambiguous Cobra moves from Cuba to Europe, Morocco, and Tibet. This formal and conceptual "wastefulness" produces a conceptually disconcerting effect which, from the point of view of pragmatic analysis, is the intention of the Neobaroque as a radical style of destabilization and subversion of the capitalist-neoliberal economic order subjected to consumer culture, what Sarduy calls "the stingy administration of goods" (Sarduy 1987b: 209). On the other hand, it aims at destabilizing the patriarchal, heterosexual, and logocentric order, on which the socio-economic and political establishment is founded, by opening meaning and displacing it at the level of language, the basis of that order. Sarduy expands in this regard:

> On the contrary [to the historical], the current baroque, the neo-baroque, structurally reflects inharmony, the rupture of homogeneity, of the logos as absolute, the lack that constitutes our epistemic foundation. Neobaroque of imbalance, structural reflection of a desire that cannot reach its object, a desire for which the logos has organized nothing more than a screen that hides the lack. (1987b: 211–12; my translation)

In Chap. 2, we defined the Neobaroque as a transposition of four historical stylistic elements (formal sophistication, profusion of ornamentation, pessimistic existential attitude, and affinity to the disproportionate or spectacular) to the context of twentieth-century literature and the arts, in their combination with more recent contents and experimental forms that are achievements of the historic Avant-garde of the 1920s–1930s, as well as the more recent (sometimes referred to as postmodern) Neoavant-garde appearing in Latin American literature since the 1960s. This combination results in Neobaroque's discursive capability to decenter and ambiguate meaning, to question stable identities determined by logocentric and patriarchal categories of belonging. This is the potential that neobaroque discourse makes effective in its use of rhetorical procedures of artifice, parody, metafiction, and simulation in combination with the element of eroticism. All these components lead to the destabilization of the ideas of "identity" and selfhood as seen in the transgressive characters and their ontological disunity, as well as in their dispersed identities, undefinable in terms of traditional and normative categories.

4.1.1 Techniques of Transgression: Artifice, Parody, and Simulation

Exuberance, as one of the most characteristic elements of neobaroque discourse, masks and destabilizes meaning on the textual surface of narrative, performative, or visual representation. It should be understood as the effect of a conscious and intentional action of the speaker (the author/performer) carried out in the text/work. According to Sarduy (1972), this effect is achieved by means of three discursive modalities, or three stylistic operations characteristic of neobaroque discourse: artifice, parody, and simulation, with eroticism as the primary creative drive. In each of these modalities of neobaroque representation, several specific mechanisms or techniques are employed which, in sum, produce the desired effect of neobaroque exuberance that is the destabilization, transfiguration, or "cross-dressing" of meaning, in what I propose to call "linguistic transvestism" (Kulawik 2009). It ultimately leads to perceive a decentering of identity, as we observed in Chap. 3 with the represented characters.

Artifice
Demetrio Estébanez Calderón's dictionary of literary terms defines artifice (from Lat. *artificium*, a "work of art") as "a product in which artistic elaboration predominates over spontaneity or naturalness" (1996, 62; my translation). This definition coincides with the analysis of poetic language in general made by Russian formalists Sklovski, Medvedev, and Jakobson in the first half of the twentieth century. According to them, artifice is linked to the "deautomatization" of language, an attempt to free words from the automatism resulting from the functional use of language by speakers, from its mere use as a "reference tool" (Estébanez 62). This approach emphasizes the poetic (rather than utilitarian, communicative) value of the word, highlighting the *form* of the message by means of procedures called "verbal artifices," or literary figures that draw the attention of the listener or reader to that verbal form. Besides achieving the effect of "de-automatization," it produces "estrangement" (остранение— *ostranenie*, a term introduced by the Russian formalist Pavel Medvedev) of the artistic or literary word, poetically and imaginatively constituted on

246   K. A. KULAWIK

the basis of the conscious and creative use of the linguistic system, a system of conventional signs.

Perhaps the most focused study of this artistic procedure was carried out by Guy Scarpetta (1988, 1992), who rescued the concept of "artifice" in its historical and current meaning, highlighting its aesthetic value in all areas of artistic production. He relates artifice to a "baroque sensibility," historically present in the arts of the seventeenth and early eighteenth centuries, as well as in the second half of the twentieth century, in the form of a "neo-baroques," or what he calls the "art of seduction" (1988: 22–27; my translation). Among the multiple traits highlighted by Scarpetta, some are consistent with baroque artifice. In terms of content, these include movement, metamorphosis, inconstancy, change and decentering, the play of reflections and illusions, and spectacle (hence the predilection for theatrical forms); in poetic forms, he lists paradoxical punctuation, metaphorical and surprising expansion, insistence on ellipsis and oxymoron (1988: 24). In the context of film, Scarpetta mentions overcodification (*surcodage*) as a contrived procedure of conventionality (restrictions, playing with limitations), hypertheatricalization, the subjection of the work to an established code, and the denaturalization of the narrative with theatrical codification (1988: 192). It is the unproductive, non-functional squandering of formal and technical resources by way of constant supplementation of an absent and illusory meaning (1988: 192–95).

These elements, deemed by Scarpetta as proper to artifice, correspond to those presented by Sarduy as neobaroque when referring to the element of quantitative disproportion of the signifier over the signified within the process of signification, or "overcoding" of discourse.[3] According to his appraisal, artifice presents, above all, a waste of signifiers, a "decorative luxury" whose function is not to be what it was supposed to do at first sight, that of ornamenting the story, but one that constitutes the story itself. It is a playful use of the constitutive material of the discourse. All the above leads us to understand that the decorative overload and fancy stylization, as preferred over functional communication, produce in the reader an enjoyment of reading (*jouissance*), an enjoyment that does not refer to

---

[3] Scarpetta explains artifice as part of Neobaroque discourse, "[…] where the narrative is 'overcoded,' invaded by a luxury (decorative) or a gratuity (technical), submerged by a waste of signifiers which make it constantly drift […], [a discourse] in which the decoration, the digression, the technical overload, the interlacing of the non-functional elements are not satisfactory in covering the narrative, but which literally constitute it" (1988: 211; my translation).

the nature or authenticity of communication but to deliberate, self-conscious play conceived as a game of unleashing of consciously conventional and ostentatious forms (Scarpetta 1988: 310).

In his essay "El barroco y el neobarroco" (1972), Severo Sarduy presents artifice (along with parody) as a constitutive element of a "semiology of the baroque" (1978 [1972]: 167–68). He explains artifice as a denaturalization or "the ironic derision of nature," a masking by means of a progressive envelopment of discourse with verbal and imaginary matter, as metaphor and metalanguage taken to the square, that is, to "metametalanguage," which is a phenomenon also mentioned and present in works by Haroldo de Campos (1978 [1972]: 169). Sarduy distinguishes multiple discursive techniques in the achievement of artifice proliferation based on the use of verbal material (linguistic elements).[4] The text provides a space for experimentation and transgression of language's communicative function in the process of achieving a figurative dimension by means of metaphor, metonymy, anamorphosis, and metamorphosis. What is striking here is the analogy between this denaturalization of language and the denaturalization of gender identification of the subjects appearing in the literary and performance/visual works. At a deeper level of interpretation, the eroticism of ambiguating sexual attributes parallels the wasteful imagery and linguistic squandering observed in Sarduy's narrative representation of the characters Cobra, Colibrí, and the duet Auxilio and Socorro. Artifice, combined with eroticism, attains a non-(re)productive and, at the same time, destabilizing effect on language and the established system of administering discourse.

Once again, a functional relationship between exuberant language and intricate content is perceived. In Sarduy's novel *From Cuba with a Song* (1994 [1967]), an example of this is the playful usage of the phonetic configuration of chained syllables, perceptible in the cacophonic sound of the vowels [a] and [o], of the liquid consonants [r], [l], and [ll], and of the dentals [t,d], velars [k,h], and sibilants [s], in the Spanish original. This playful caricature of language also appears in the contrastive and fragmented syntactic structure of the sentences themselves or their fragments, as in this description of cross-dressed Auxilio (Help) and Socorro (Mercy)

---

[4] Providing a detailed analysis of the constitutive elements of the baroque style, Sarduy distinguishes artifice with its three mechanisms: substitution, proliferation, and condensation (1978 [1972]: 168–73). He also includes parody with its mechanisms of inter and intratextuality (174–80).

248   K. A. KULAWIK

in one of their figurative, animal-like incarnations of squirrels and moles looking for food in a restaurant of a post-industrial metropolis: "—¡Metafísicas estamos y es que no comemos! ¡Vámonos al Self-Service! [...] Papa por papa, papa por papa las recoge [...] tras un tomate que rueda, el vaso de cartón, la copa de remolacha rallada—hilillos morados sobre los zapatos" (Sarduy 1970 [1967]: 15). ["—My, we're metaphysical, we must be hungry! Let's go to the Self-Service! One potato, two potato, one by one they pick up the potatoes [...] behind a rolling tomato, the paper cup, the bowl of grated beets—little purple strands on somebody's shoe"] (Sarduy 1994: 15). The arbitrary use of pronouns creates ambiguity of sexual gender. Other resources likewise contribute to obfuscating meaning. As in *From Cuba...*, internal rhyme, frequent use of Anglicisms, and repetitions also appear in *Cobra*, which is observable in the Spanish original: "—la seguían la mucama, los doce negritos y el macaco—después de tanto sofoco, de tanto break-down, de tanto quítate tú para ponerme yo" (Sarduy 1978 [1972]: 72) ["—the maid, the twelve little black boys and the macaque followed her—'after all that running out of breath, all those break-downs, all that move aside you so that I can sit down"] (Sarduy 1975: 46).

The syntactic structure of the sentences in Sarduy's novels is complex, convoluted, and often inverted. In *Cobra*, frequent interruptions with additional information produce an effect of anti-naturalness, confusion, decentering, and ambiguation of meaning: "Ivory with sashes—the purple reflections of the sofa—bones striped like peppermint candies, gay-colored skeleton, yes, even the Wretch's support is pretty, [...] From the above-mentioned bundle of darts, and with the delicacy of one who selects the best pastry from an overflowing tray, the Transformer—ex-champion of chopsticks—picked up between his fingers a slightly curved needle, which ended in a small sphere" (1975: 45). The (parodic) experimentation with the syntactic-textual conformation of the sentences goes to the extreme of representing various events and characters' transformations in the story by means of mathematical-logical formulas that sometimes appear in footnotes: "^{1}[Sra + Cobra (+/=) Pup = (3/2)]" (1981: 85, appears as footnote); "Cobra = Pup^2," "la √de Señora" [the square root of Madam] (53–55).

The neobaroque texts presented in Chap. 3 are laden with elements of artifice, such as metaphors and substitutions. In *From Cuba...*, instead of "his body" we read "his venerable somatic vehicle" (1994: 33). Metaphorical substitution also operates in *Cobra* where it combines with

4 ONE-T(W)O-MANY: NEOBAROQUE ARTICULATIONS OF NOMADIC... 249

the use of similes, characteristic of poetic language: "The bilious lady rushed against the spasmodic bundle as if she were putting out a fire; she launched forth with the devotion of one who flagellates a penitent brandishing a cat o'nine tails with ball-bearings on the tips" (1975: 11). All this linguistic squandering is to illustrate the cosmetic operations aimed at dwarfing Pup's feet.

When substitution operates in a more comprehensive way on a totality, an allegorical image forms as in the following example in *Cobra* with religious connotations. Its meaning is rendered difficult due to the disfigurement and strident juxtaposition of elements in a peculiar distribution of the tex:

> She went   /barefoot, dragging incensories,
> /smeared with crosses of black oil,
> /in a Carmelite cassock, a yellow rope at her waist,
> /wrapped in damasks and White cloths,
> with a wide-brimmed hat and a staff,
> /naked and wounded, beneath a dunce cap. (1975: 11–12)

This overabundant use of artifice is also characteristic of the novel *Colibrí*, in which the identity of the characters is blurred and their appearance is caricaturized in excessive ornamentation. The proliferating artifice in the form of exuberant description reaches its peak when the gender of the characters, apparently transvestites, swaps between masculine and feminine features, as do their ambiguous sexual orientations in the course of the plot. In the following two fragments, the use of poetic figures, the hyperbole and simile, are added to general artifice that blurs the gender attributes of the cross-dressed characters. They are, in fact, two incarnations of one, La Enana [The Dwarf]:

> Then the Enanota [Huge Dwarf] appeared in high heels, violently blushing with makeup, her raspberry-colored mouth flashing. She was armored in red taffeta, pot-bellied and dense; on her head, like a peddler of drunken panettone, she wore a round white cushion, and leaning on it, a huge cage, which gathered all the birds in a motley bellicose colony. (1984: 52; my translation)

Behind such artifice flowing from metonymic proliferation is the distinctly baroque drive to fill every possible space of signification, avoiding ("like the death") any empty space without a possible (erotic) meaning; all blank spaces are filled with potential associations, charged with tension created in the surrounding referents. It is the typically baroque *horror vacui* mentioned by Sarduy: "The ceremony [of writing] has no other meaning than the horror of emptiness, the disordered proliferation of signs, the reduction of a body to a baroque fetish" (1987a: 239; my translation). The original sense is obliterated, which now "works on nothingness," eroticizing the referent—character or body—reifying it into a fetish. The Strange ornaments and adornments are embedded in the body, preventing it from any natural movement; they schematize it, reduce it to a doll, a objectified statue. Writing is related to the inscription of the body with painting-makeup, tattooing, or goldsmithing-inlaying in a process that Sarduy describes as "[...] the metallization of the flesh, the aurification [... of] the bodies tattooed with arabesques, incrusted, millimeter by millimeter, with stones, feathers, birds' heads [...] with flower-sexes" (1987a: 241). In its relation to eroticism, this metonymic artifice can be considered as the "rhetoric of the accessory becoming essential, the multiplication of the adjectival turned noun, the excessive ornament, the contortion, the stylized vegetal element, the statues and swans, the cosmetic as a mediatized instrument [that] situate us [...] in a well-oriented eroticism: the one celebrated in its borders, as metaphors of bodies, the art of 1900" (1987a: 240).

Lois Zamora and Monika Kaup (2010) also remind us of the essentially baroque idea of *horror vacui*, the philosophical and existential fear of emptiness, the impulse to fill every possible space with excessive ornamentation, however simulative it may be.[5] Therefore, artifice may be seen as one of the ways this emptiness is filled given the all-encompassing character of baroque discourse. Kaup points to "the inclusive baroque position of 'both/and' as an alternative to the exclusive 'either/or.' Facing the modern epistemological crisis, the baroque opts for the strategy of abundance, excess, and contiguity of the dissimilar, which is also expressed in the baroque topos of *horror vacui*, the horror of the void" (2012: 33). As

[5] In their introduction to *Baroque New Worlds: Representation, Transculturation, Counterconquest*, Zamora and Kaup adduce the following observation by Carlos Fuentes regarding the importance of the concept of *horror vacui* (the horror of emptiness) for Baroque art: "The *horror vacui* of the Baroque is not gratuitous—it is because the vacuum exists that nothing is certain. The verbal abundance of Carpentier's *The Kingdom of This World* or of Faulkner's *Absalom, Absalom!* represents a desperate invocation of language to fill the absences left by the banishment of reason and faith. In this way, post-Renaissance Baroque art began to fill the abyss left by the Copernican Revolution" (2010: 25).

another component of neobaroque discourse, simulation is a technique of hiding or masking a hidden content behind a vast array of apparent semblances and lavish ornamentation. In Sarduy's narrative, the baroque procedures of artifice and simulation procure to fill the void left by the transformations and dismemberment of the subject-protagonist Cobra with the heterogeneity of the character's incarnations and *hir* chameleonic sexualities. Perhaps it marks a (postmodern?) crisis of the exhausted Manichean categorizations within the framework of dualistic distinctions of masculinity-femininity, blackness-whiteness, or West-East. As seen in Fig. 3.1, an illustrative example of this destabilizing "overcoding" is the opulent description of cross-dressed Cobra in a Paris subway car:

> Cobra appears at the back of the car, standing against the tin wall, bird nailed against a mirror. Her makeup is violent, her mouth painted with branches. Her orbs are black and aluminum-plated, [...] powdered paint and metal, to her temples, [...] instead of eyebrows, fringes of inferior precious stones hang from the rims of her eyelids. Up to her neck she is a woman; above, her body becomes a kind of heraldic animal with a baroque snout. Behind, the curve of the partition multiplies her ceramic foliage, repetition of pale chrysanthemums. (Sarduy 1975: 81)

As a result of profuse ornamentation of the body, the identity of cross-dressed Cobra fades in the plethora of masculine, feminine, and animal identifications that multiply the subject's metamorphic incarnations of a trans*subject. This (neo)baroque procedure of proliferation seeks to fill the existential void with a multiplicity of new identities, embodied by Sarduy's fragmented and fluctuating characters Cobra, Colibrí, Pup, La Enana, Enanota, Auxilio and Socorro. Their transformations are set in a plethora of shifting (destabilizing) transcultural referents, arbitrarily progressing from the American rainforest and tropical Cuba to Paris, Morocco, and Tibet.

The semantic opening of meaning to non-binary modes occurs thanks to the abundant use of artifice, which is also related to the technique of simulation. In *Simulacra and Simulation* (1994), Jean Baudrillard explains two interconnected concepts: "To dissimulate is to pretend not to have what one has. To simulate is to pretend to have what one doesn't have. One implies a presence, the other an absence" (3). Figueroa Sánchez makes a direct association between simulation and the baroque work, which he explains with the visually (spectacularly) transformative character

252   K. A. KULAWIK

of the baroque image and its play with multiple perspectives (52).[6] We reason with Baudrillard that social convention (as obedience to a norm) in sexual differentiation plays a key part as a hegemonic model (artificial, by convention) that imposes itself and precedes the tradition that sanctions this model. Here, the neobaroque simulating (non-realistic and distorting) text or image, by being playful and preceding any model by going beyond it, becomes satirical and rebellious, subverting the traditional representation of sexual, gender, racial and ethnic, social, national, and even posthuman distinctions.

In Bellatin's novels, narrative artifice is employed as an inter- and intra-textual game of cross-dressed and metamorphous characters. It aims at the dissimulation (concealment) of a "naturally"—masculine, old age, even human (as not animal)—appearance, and the simulation (pretense) of an equivocal difference: the feminine, young, animal. This follows the model of distinctive and conventional marks of externalizing sexual gender using clothes and makeup, and of the whole body as human/animal, old/young. Artifice allows to dissimulate being "one" in otherness (because there really is no other without one) and to simulate the unnoticed presence of the other in one (because there is no one behind the mask if it is not an other). Bellatin himself admits: "Everything to make the other enter and from that complicity, to be able to generate a writing. Then a reader comes to talk to me about the masks, about the external part" (Rodríguez 2006: 66; my translation). Regarding this transitivity between subjects, we agree with Silvia Vaggione when she states that "*Salón de belleza* works in that intermediate point, in that space 'between' light and shadow, life and death, to delimit a transit, to design a passage that shows the stripping of some bodies" (2009: 485; my translation). Similarly, Francisco López Alfonso's interpretation of the novel *Lecciones...* is well aimed when referring to the indefiniteness of the "I": "There is no certainty to hold on to. Not even to the 'I.' The cognizable always refers to what is other and always moves from self to others. No matter how much

---

[6]Figueroa points to the visual aspect of baroque aesthetics in relation to simulation: "In turn, from a Baudrillardian perspective, the baroque image is exciting in our times, because more than dissimulating a presence, it is a simulation of an absence; more than a mere visual distortion, it is a true *anamorphosis*, revealing the conventional character of normal spectacularity. Consequently, the baroque image, reread from this perspective, presents itself as a variable visual possibility based on its contradictory relations between surface and depth. [...] it is a reflection on two central categories of modern aesthetics: *language* and *image*" (52; my translation, emphasis in original).

the identity with the other as neighbor is envisaged, the place of the self remains blank, cloudy" (2008: 138; my translation). This place is left for the filler, and if not as decorative as Sarduy's descriptive preciosity, in Bellatin it will be narrative and conceptual, but equally "baroque."

The combination of these artificious procedures relates to the same objective: the dissimulation and concealment of coherent meaning in the narratives and the simulation of the sexuality (and all identity) of the characters. This masking is a common procedure in the works analyzed in Chap. 3 and has a pragmatic function. Mary Ann Gosser-Esquilín explains it referring specifically to the use of artifice in Sarduy's narrative,

> [...] the stacatto rhythm and the elliptic terms are significant components of the style and lexicon Sarduy utilizes to present a being hiding behind many masks. By using such techniques, Sarduy insists on diminishing the importance of knowing what the gender, and by extension, what the sexual inclination, of a character may be. Bodies, and not only those of transvestites, often appear lavishly decorated, inscribed or tattooed, amid the accumulation of trite details of the neobaroque—in other words, simulated. (1991: 415)

The inordinate use of artifice produces a destabilization in terms of especially sexual identity of the subjects. On the other hand, the deconstructive philosophical intentionality of the works in relation to decentering normative cultural categories of identity may be best expressed by an antimimetic style, like the neobaroque, that lends itself to such transgressions and facilitates identity-destabilizing operations. As we observe in *Cobra*: "—'who made me squander my savings in order to restructure you, pull out your scalp with wax and electricity, [...] until you achieved the imposture: canary yellow contact lenses?'" (Sarduy 1975: 47). Paired in a humorous and caricatural way with artifice, here parody appears as the second constitutive element of neobaroque technique.

Parody

The masking of univocal sense in the analyzed works is achieved by means of another discursive method that is part of neobaroque wasteful exuberance of signifiers and meanings. Parody, as a rhetorical technique and discursive mode that uses imitation, is comparable to a humoristic mask placed over the narrative. Its remote, tragicomic origin and its permanence in contemporary literature have been pointed out by analysts ranging from

254   K. A. KULAWIK

Bakhtin (1981) and Kristeva (1969) to Sarduy (1972). A brief and operative definition that situates parody within the neobaroque framework of exuberance would be that of David Kiremidjian who considers "parody to be a work of art which retains the form but alters the contents of the work or tradition of works it imitates" (1985: 36). It points to the satirical character of parody, which uses certain forms to express varying tonalities. Its character of "double artifice" is observed in its re-elaboration of or insertion of irony into another work of art. In Kiremidjian's words,

> Parody [...] imitates another work of art [...] and thus becomes a reflection of the character of art itself. Parody is thus conditioned from the outset by the substitution of artifice for nature in its contents, the same substitution which primary art reaches in the self-mimetic state. Parody is thus a phenomenon in which artifice imitates artifice, performing from the outset that which primary art forms do only eventually. (1985: 31)

From Kiremidjian's definition we infer that parody is a "metaform," superior to "primary" representation, since it is elaborated on the basis of it. It is important to highlight the introverted and metadiscursive character of parody as a procedure that reveals the semiotic relationship between content and form; by means of derision, it forces the receiver to reflect on the conventionality (artificiality) of the constitutive form of the work: "[...] parody embodies the opposition between the artificial and the natural" (1985: 17). This discursive procedure, related to humor and artifice, is frequently carried out in a direct and open manner in most of the analyzed works.

In general terms, several of the texts appear as parodies of the novelistic genre itself. Literary critics had already noted the fact that the novel *Colibrí* constitutes a parodic re-reading of the Latin American "novel of the land" of the early twentieth century.[7] In the novel *Cobra*, there is a number of characters whose transgressive identities are parodied, almost caricatured: the perverse and despotic mistresses of brothels, transvestites (the Flemish pugilist in *Cobra* 1972: 27 and Eustace the Greek 27), "dermal

---

[7] Critics consider *Colibrí* as a work of intertextual-parodic reinterpretation of the Latin American "novel of the land" (*la novela de la tierra*) tradition and Alejo Carpentier's novel *Los pasos perdidos* (1953). These positions are explained by Roberto González Echevarría in *La ruta de Severo Sarduy* (1987: 211–42), in Adriana Méndez-Ródenas' review of *Colibrí* in *Revista Iberoamericana* v. 51 (1985: 399–401), and by Emilio Bejel in *Literatura de nuestra América* (1983: 106).

goldsmiths" (such as "the Indian" 27), impostor surgeon doctors (Ktazob in *Cobra* and Karaxim in *Qadós*), slave traders, and drug dealers (*Cobra* 1972: 96; *1810...*: 43, 59). The parodic relationship of the novel *Lumpérica* with the experimental film novel *Cagliostro* by the Chilean Avant-garde poet Vicente Huidobro is also notable. It is possible to point to the parodic character of the internalized discourse of Hilst's two novels as condensed miniature versions of the works of European Modernism in the Joycean or Proustian vein of the *bildungsroman* or, possibly, a double ("squared") parody of Clarice Lispector's (itself parodic) novels belonging to New Brazilian narrative of the 1960s and 1970s.

Diamela Eltit mentions the high level of artifice and parody in the performance of the Bolivian Galán Family. She refers to the collective of cross-dressed transformists as a "carrier of diverse identities […] composed of men and women who maintain diverse gender options" (Araujo 2007, 122; my translation). These options are achieved through a transgressive artificiality that attributes them an attitude of an artful, performative activity. Its parodic relationship to language and the semiotic process indicates a form of neobaroque expression. According to Eltit, transformism presents "a jumbled and convulsive model of extreme and parodic complexity of its signs" (Araujo 123). She observes that the Galán collective is a compilation of differences and identities that refuse any classification. The members define themselves only as bio-males and bio-females, leaving any other identities as unclassifiable. Cultural referents become arbitrary and conventional, mobile and modifiable. The Galán Family renounces establishing fixed classifications, rendering the idea that identities are social constructions in constant movement and, as such, cannot be permanent. "Thus, their apparent un-belonging is assumed to allow their multiple identities to float, overlap, and contaminate among themselves […] as they allow signs to flow and overrun their bodies, decentering official mandates of normalization and standardization" (Eltit in Araujo 123). Its potential as a "family" destabilizes the heteronormative model with the alternative of the *rhizome*, introduced by Deleuze and Guattari (1980). As a proliferation of connections that are not hierarchical but horizontal, the rhizome does not have a beginning or an end; it is always the middle element that playfully positions in the "in-between." This ritual play of in-betweenness (mentioned by Silviano Santiago) renders all identities to be mobile semiotic simulations, performances of social conventions. In the Galans' performance, the signs proliferate in their artifice, superficiality, and excess, providing a strategy of perforating and destabilizing identity.

Parody is used as the sustaining technique of structuration and tonality in Silviano Santiago's *Stella Manhattan*. It puts a humoristic tone to the novel, managing to ridicule official discourse of Cold War politics and official government rhetoric within the Brazilian diplomatic circles of New York City in its presentation of three destabilizing transvestite characters: Stella (Eduardo), the Black Widow (Coronel Viana), and Leila (wife of Aníbal, a Columbia University professor). With a game of double identities and alliances, these characters give the novel its unexpected twists and produce dramatic tension. With the parodic simulation of the transvestite, embodied in a double persona, Eduardo/Stella, represents the relativity of identity marks on the body and of fluctuating narrative roles in the plot. Reality and fiction meet in artistic representation and the written/performative act relativizes its double status of performance (acting) or "real" self (authentic behavior). Similarly, in a metatextual interlude between Chaps. 2 and 3 of Part I, the novel leads the reader to a higher level of representation when the narrator is arguing with the very author of the book. The narrator's intervention in the writing process of the novel shows both the metafictional and the parodic features that characterize Santiago's narrative style and technique as partly neobaroque and confer on it certain performative attributes. This corresponds to the way the identity of the characters is construed in the text as fragmentary and shifting, but also theatrically performative. The distancing that laughter produces (as an element of parody) corresponds to the artificiality that all linguistic constructs and categorizations display, including those of gender and sexuality. The narrator ironically remarks to the author:

> (You can't stand my silence any longer): […] For a brief instant—you give me no time—I try to imagine how the narrator's silent moments of explosive laughter might be inserted into the novel you are writing. The narrator's laughter is after all as important for the novel as his words or as a character's farts. And it's what the reader continually asks about. Aren't novels really made of boisterous and hysterical laughter! (1994: 58)

Art, fart, and literature (especially the novel) are presented as expenditure of the excessive, unproductive part of human activity, which includes the somatic and the erotic. This becomes evident in the "intermission" section of the novel, when the narrator discusses philosophical topics with the author:

I rebel against that energy which was originally economized for the easy transit of the body through a hostile world. It ended up becoming a form of accumulation. I rebel against it and that's why I look for examples of energy which, like vomit, overflow the world of work and commerce. In today's society, whether it is capitalist or communist, the only way to rebel against regimes of work, against the praise of work at any cost, against competitiveness or meritocracy is to create an art based on the waste of energy. (55–56)

By parodying official mimetic discourse, this complex structuring of metatextual narrative becomes a radical political statement against the rational and measured logic of capitalistic production and accumulation in the supply/demand market chain. Neobaroque becomes a platform for squandering that accrual. Semantic ambivalence and lexical-syntactic overabundance reach the excess of emptiness and exhaustion, both philosophical (postmodern) and communicative. This parodying polyphonic aspect of Sarduy's work was pointed out by Biagio D'Angelo:

If polyphony or dialogue is also an act of knowing the other and—according to the bakhtinian reading of Dostoyevski—a recognition of one's own mysterious Other, in Sarduy it is reduced to an empty, useless, and sterile dialogue. If parody is both challenge and artistic creation, an unchained competition in which the imitated master is recognized, in Sarduy it is an artifact that is emptied of the codes of knowledge, a "blank parody," as Jameson would suggest. It is a sign that is only simulation [...]. (2007: 291)

Rather than telling the characters' story, Sarduy's novels simulate, exposing the very process of their discursive figuration reflected in the metatext from the positions of multiple narrative subjects.

Sustaining her argument for a transformative idea of subjectivity through multiplicity, situated against all binarism, Rosi Braidotti builds on Judith Butler's idea of "parodic repetition, that is politically motivated exposure of the masquerade" (2002: 36–37) in a radical sense that brings us again to two of the basic tenets sustaining Neobaroque poetics: exuberance (through excess and proliferation) and parody (through copy and caricature). Braidotti's appraisal of the political implications of parodic repetition as the "exploding of categories" follows Butler's concepts of "proliferation of genders" in a "politics of parody," in which:

we explode the category 'women' by letting many other alternative genders proliferate: not one, not two, but as many genders as there are individuals.

258   K. A. KULAWIK

> Not just lesbian, the ex-woman will be trans-sexually dislocated in many possible directions: if biology is not destiny, if the body is construction, then any sex goes. Butler concludes in a more cautious tone, speaking in the conditional tense about the politics of the parody, and asking what feminist politics *would* look like if genders *were* allowed to proliferate so as to explode the classical binarism. (2002: 37)

With its incisive and corrosive effect of proliferation in the analyzed texts and performances, parody becomes the key player in the articulation of a transitive identity that positions itself as a discourse of political resistance and cultural subversion. The mechanism of parody is constitutive of Neobaroque poetics, as it is one of the operative elements of experimental performance art. Neobaroque literature and performance present the potential and the site for such an "explosion" of identities in its transformative, flexible, and open method of representation, combined with a satirical edge of political engagement.

4.1.2   Nomadic Deterritorialization as a Neobaroque Semiosis

Speaking of the seditious effect caused by the assemblages of rhizomatic segments in the philosophic discourse dealing with logocentric and colonializing systems, Gilles Deleuze and Claire Parnet (1977) point to the crucial role that movement plays in these segmentary assemblages of conceptual decentering, as part of any cultural formations, including selfhood and identity. The two authors refer to "movements of deterritorialization and the processes of reterritorialization" (1987a: 134). Discussing animal and human anatomical structure's adaptability to the environment, they explain that bodies and environments are traversed by differing rates of deterritorialization in differential speeds in complementarities that form continuums of intensity, but also give rise to processes of reterritorialization: "At the limit, it is the Earth itself, the deterritorialized ('the desert grows…'), and it is the nomad, the man of earth, the man of deterritorialization—although he is also the one who does not move, who remains attached to the environment, desert or steppe" (134). Movement and change, stages of stillness as complementarities in mutably adaptable states of being are the underlying forces behind transiting nomadic subjects in their territorial/conceptual transgressions represented in the deterritorializing semiosis of the Neobaroque.

4 ONE-T(W)O-MANY: NEOBAROQUE ARTICULATIONS OF NOMADIC... 259

The fugue-like parodic workings of this style have been amply theorized by Severo Sarduy, whose criticism touches on concepts related to the displacement of the subject and its resulting fragmentation. In his appraisal of modern Spanish novelist Juan Goytisolo's *Juan the Landless* (1975; the last installment of a trilogy that includes *Marks of Identity* and *Count Julián*), Severo Sarduy conceives a conceptual triad of nomadism, expulsion, and parody as the centerpiece of his encompassing idea of *deterritorialization* as the underlying force behind the (neobaroque) literary text. Following Deleuze's "Pensée nomade" in *A Thousand Plateaus...* (1987b), he discerns in Goytisolo's text a centrifugal force situated "out on the periphery [where] communities take on another kind of adventure, another kind of unity, this time a nomadic one, within a nomadic war machine, and instead of letting themselves be supercodified, they decodify themselves" (1984: 104; trans. Lindstrom). This "decodification" occurs through the neobaroque text's use of style, usually based on semiotic overabundance, linguistic excess, and the heightened use of parody. The text acquires a mobility that is akin to nomadism as displacement of signifiers, also achieved in the complex and decentered narrative structure of the novel. As Sarduy states:

> Periphery, nomadism: Goytisolo's work, his extraordinary centrifugal force [...] always toward the exterior, toward the outside that beckons, far from the sedentary group and its codes, far from the despot and his administrative machine. It's the power of an ex-centric discourse, a runaway, the opposite of instituted law, in complicity with someone waiting across the border, [...] from the moment a territory is delimited, that is, from when the narrator sets himself up as producer (and victim) of codes and the unity of the State comes into the picture with its inherently despotic workings, the nomadic machine intervenes with its mechanism of movable warfare. (104)

Sarduy emphasizes the starting point of that endless centrifugal displacement toward the "beyond limits" as point of reference for the nomad. Sarduy compares Goytisolo's nomadic narrative to a "V. Medina-Text [...] with meandering paths, tortuous alleyways [...] [in which] [i]t will be time to leave again" (108). The text becomes an interwoven fabric of threads, a maze of alleyways of the jumbled medieval city (مدينة or *medina*), or today's urban jungle of endless streets and intersections; a place of deterritorialization of the subject, a dystopia.

The discursive techniques of deterritorialization achieve the liberation of the nomadic subject from the constraints of the body-text contained in language. Sarduy's is no longer a writing of the "I," but of the annihilation and dispersion of the "I" in "you/he/she/it," a writing of the word-as-mask, invertible and replaceable, a simulation of the self that unveils the emptiness that exists behind each (pro)noun. "I" is nothing more than a sign, a mask. Sarduy explains nomadic writing as a "[n]eobaroque of imbalance, structural reflection of a desire that cannot reach its object, a desire for which the logos has organized nothing more than a screen that hides the lack" (1978 [1972]: 183; my translation). It is interesting to note that the word "person," which relates to "subject," in Latin originally meant "mask."[8] Rather than characters or closed and coherent discursive functions ("fastened" or "tied," as the Latin etymology of the word "subject" indicates), in Sarduy's (and Bellatin's) novels we find nodular and layered subjects, like marionettes or painted Russian dolls.

The neobaroque text holds an autonomous status of the imaginary (as fiction), licensed to transgress, displace, and deterritorialize, be it by formal means or with ambiguous sexuality and unbridled eroticism. It assaults the normative system—bourgeois and capitalist—of calculated, rational, and controlled distribution and administration of bodies and goods, but also words, all aimed at attaining (re)production (Sarduy 1987c [1982]: 99–100). In a similar fashion, the nomadic cyborg's flows of energy "reconfirm the joy of creative wastefulness and resist the negative passion of greed" (Braidotti 2002: 266).

Likewise, in Hilst's narrative, deterritorialization as linguistic expenditure is carried out through parody and grotesque as a ridiculous and deformed image that destabilizes meaning: "the grotesque becomes a tool for the displacement of determined roles, immersing itself as a means of social and literary transgression" (A-mi 2016, 295; my translation). Tatiana Rodrigues Franca (2012) proposes to see in Hilst's exuberant word an incessant search for understanding: "[...] the main concern is the desire for self-knowledge that, however, is only attainable through verbal representation. It is through the signification given by the word, through

---

[8] Edward A. Roberts, in *A Comprehensive Etymological Dictionary of the Spanish Language* (2014), vol. 2, indicates that the Latin word *persōna* originally meant a character in a dramatic play or the mask that the actor put on to represent this character. Latin borrowed it from the older Etruscan *phersu* which literally meant "mask," and possibly combined it with the Greek *prosōpon*, meaning "face" or "countenance." This combination resulted in what would be the original meaning of "person" as "a masked face" or "mask over the face" (346).

the ability to name, that one arrives at an identity" (85). As such, the search for "transidentity" as a form of transcendence surpassing the limits of life and death by way of the word is visible in the Brazilian's verbal vulgarity and "multiplicity of strange and contradictory terms. [...] Insofar as the doubt about the word irremediably incurs on the idea, this multiplication of the verb results in the fragmentation of the unity that constituted the idea" (Moraes 1999, 118). This fragmentary proliferation of discourse constitutes Hilst's (characters') deterritorializing search for the transcendental Being. As our analysis shows, there are multiple possibilities to interpret this waste of vital force in the overflowing language, in its relationship with play as performance of identity, visible in her novels as the erotic drive toward death.[9] One of its manifestations in Latin American Neobaroque is eroticism as a performative act of playing out one's desire of the Other through transgression of normatively established categorical limits; eroticism as the ultimate drive to reach the limits of life and death is played out, enacted, and embodied, in the process of writing and creation—an aesthetics of deterritorialization of the nomadic trans-self.

4.1.3 Eroticism and the Exuberant Word

Georges Bataille introduced several concepts that help to explain the relationship between eroticism and representation in neobaroque discourse. In *La limite de l'utile*, he introduced the concept of "unproductive expenditure" (*dépense improductive*) (1976: 191), and in *La part maudite*, those of "unproductive use" (*usage improductif*) and "squandering" (*gaspillage*) (1967: 66, 71, 75) to establish a symbolic relationship between expenditure and eroticism. All four terms are associated with the idea of surplus that Bataille coined as "the cursed part" (*la part maudite*), a form of waste in the "immense confusion of the party" (1967: 65), "*potlatch*, economy of vainglory" (1976: 202–03; my translations),[10] and in the tradition of the Carnival with its reversal of roles, dating to the Middle Ages. His concept of *dépense improductive* [unproductive expenditure] refers to the loss of accumulated energy in both the physical and symbolic dimension. The latter is concretized through cultural forms, among which he mentions the different forms of sacrifices, including human (as among the

---

[9] "In fact, the erotic experience and that of death are two forms of excess that allow man to become more than he is" (Hawley 296; my translation).

[10] "immense confusion de la fête" (65), "le *potlatch*, économie de vaine gloire" (202–03).

262 K. A. KULAWIK

Aztecs) (1976: 53–56), *le surplus* of the feast (1976: 64), and the exuberant, excessive offerings made to the enemy in the form of the potlatch, common among the Natives of the American Northwest (1976: 52–56, 66–72). Likewise, Bataille perceived the activity of amorous play as surplus to all utility (as reproduction): "The highest form of play is erotic activity, which is the very antithesis of work. Erotic activity, as fundamentally opposed to the fact of reproduction, is for Bataille an example of pure expenditure in which no return is expected and in which we surrender ourselves to the moment" (Richardson 1998, 95).

The playful dimension of eroticism coincides with what we defined earlier following Sarduy as the first constitutive element of neobaroque discursive exuberance: artifice as a useless, unnatural, concealing leftover (or surplus) destined only for the pleasure that remains in its purest form of eroticism. The transgressive aspect of the ambiguity and sexual transitivity of the analyzed characters relates to what Bataille pointed out as an infraction of the patriarchal (by extension—capitalist) law of vital growth because it is not (re)productive, but rather suicidal: "Eroticism is distinguished from the sexual activity of reproduction in the quality of being an infraction of the law, in the quality of being a refusal of life in the very act which creates this life" (Hawley 296; my translation). Bataille refers to eroticism as an unproductive "loss," devoid of reproductive intent (procreation), and thus of its utilitarian function, pointing to "'eroticism,' that is to say of human sexual behavior diverted from its procreative purpose, from its useful purpose" (Hawley 292; my translation). Similarly, Sarduy translates eroticism to the language of the Neobaroque, in which artifice and exuberance in writing are constitutive unproductive elements, but still pleasurable and gratifying, wasteful but playful.[11] The element of artifice in the neobaroque text is configured in the apparently unproductive erotic dimension as the workings of language-discourse without its utilitarian function of communication. The erotic word becomes playful and acquires a joyful, festive dimension. We could even say, after M. M. Bakhtin (1981), that eroticism "carnivalizes" the discourse of the novels. Through erotic force, the narrative subjects transcend binary heterosexual determination and become homoerotic subjectivities on the run, fugitives in fugue,

---

[11] Sarduy explains: "In eroticism, artificiality, the cultural element, is manifested in the game with the lost object, a game whose purpose is in and for itself, and whose purpose is not the conveyance of a message—that of the reproductive elements in this case—but its waste for the sake of pleasure" (1978 [1972]: 182).

adopting transitive and transient identities that are deterritorialized and banished.

As we noted earlier, Bataille relates eroticism to the transgression of the forbidden in the space of inner experience mediated by writing; he associates it with all vital experience in its extreme, liminal form that is death. The ulterior realms of vitality manifest themselves in eroticism: the excess and exuberance of vital energy that, in addition to being *un*reproductive, is exteriorized in the uncompromised sexual act, in violence, in war, in human sacrifice, in everything that constitutes the expenditure (*la dépense*) of accumulated excessive energy that materializes in writing and in all aesthetic creation (1976: 187–94).

The subversive effect of erotic transgression is also visible in eroticism's proximity to violence. In the analyzed texts, the idea of the body as a surface for physical or symbolic inscription is reaffirmed in the personal, social, or cultural sphere, as proposed by Elizabeth Grosz with "the notion of the body as a surface of libidinal and erotogenic intensity, a product of and material to be further inscribed and reinscribed by social norms, practices and values" (1994: 138). The symbolic value of the characters' bodily marks, such as tattoos, cuts, or burns on the skin, is perhaps not limited to abstract, intellectual or aesthetic pleasure, but, going radically beyond the textual denotation, it constitutes a physical space of erotic pleasure as pain, metonymically extended to the physical (corporal-as-textual) space of the page/stage and, by metonymical extension, the writer's hand and the reader's eyes. Grosz sees the erotic dimension of bodily inscription in its signifying intensity of a text:

> Instead of being read simply as messages, that is, as signifiers of a hidden or inferred signified which is the subject's interiority, these incisions function to proliferate, intensify, and extend the body's erotogenic sensitivity. Welts, scars, cuts, tattoos, perforations, incisions, inlays, function quite literally to increase the surface space of the body, creating […] places of special significance and libidinal intensity. (1994: 139)

The inclusion of blank spaces in Chaps. 6 and 8 ("General Essay") of Eltit's *Lumpérica*, and the inclusion of photographs to illustrate the self-mutilating cuts made on the skin, represents additional examples of the erotic dimension of the text as a symbolic act of political resistance to the violence of the Chilean dictatorship (see Fig. 3.18 in Ch. 3). The erotic excess of bodily inscription-makeup, frequent in Sarduy's, Eltit's, and

264   K. A. KULAWIK

Bellatin's novels and visible in the performed bodies of Guillermo Gómez-Peña, the Familia Galán, Susy Shock, and Francisco Copello (1999), is extensive to the transgression of sexual limits and identity altogether. The pain of injection/incision on the skin metonymically expands to the inscription of ink on the surface of paper or to the direct imprint of photographic images of the lacerated body on the surface of the text (as in *Lumpérica*) or of calligrams reminiscent of passion and suffering (as in *Cobra*). The neobaroque text, as a "speech act," assumes a subversive function: it transgresses literary and social conventions in its search of transcendental meaning. Referring to Hilst, Moraes notes that "the writer exceeds her own measure, which results in a remarkable expansion of the concept of transcendence" (117). The overflowing neobaroque word surpasses categorical sexuality in Hilst's exuberant and contrived, erotically driven word in search of transcendental meaning (of self). In the Brazilian author's case, this is achieved in an experimental narrative in which the erotic experience of the sexual-physiological body is transposed and transcribed onto the textual "body." The focus of interest for this narrative is the discursive conformation of the subject and, in the case of novels such as *Qadós, A obscena Senhora D* (1993), and *Estar sendo. Ter sido* (2006), the erotic body corresponds to an androgynous, trans or homosexual drive, indeterminate or fluctuating in terms of his/her sexuality, as observed in the main characters Qadós, Hillé, Ehud, and Vittorio. Their erotic excess and sexual ambiguity destabilize the phallocentric model of binarism. Susanna Busato associates the self-referential, metadiscursive character of Hilst's text with the function of eroticism as transgression of the word, taking it to another dimension by stripping, un-/cross-dressing it: "Eroticism in Hilda Hilst's work inhabits language, in its linguistic, almost carnal play with the word that goes undressing and experiencing itself, being self-referentialized by discourse" (Reguera and Busato 2015, 11).

Sexual transgression acquires Bataille's sense of "the surpassing of the self, the point of the spirit where limits no longer make sense. It is the coincidence of opposites in which life and death, presence and absence, merge together, where wo/man, in losing her/himself, discovers in his own annihilation the meaning—or the meaninglessness—of life" (Hawley 309). An opportune association of eroticism with the ultimate transgression—death—appears in the French concept of *la petite mort* [the little death], referring to the moment after orgasm. In *L'érotisme* (1957), Bataille explains the erotic phenomenon as a lost and undifferentiated intimacy between subject and object, a transgression that tends to suppress the differences between beings and destroys One as the particular being. He associates eroticism with a violation of the existence of particular bodies, a fusion in which two beings that mix reach the point of dissolution together. "What does the eroticism of bodies mean if not a violation of the being of the partners? a violation which borders on death? which borders on murder? [...] it prepares a fusion where two beings mingle, in the end reaching together the same point of dissolution" (1957: 22; my translation; lower case after interrogations in original).

Hilst's discourse reveals this erotic dimension as a form of dissolution of being in the transgression of the stable boundaries between sexed bodies sanctioned by patriarchal, heterosexual, and reproductive law and parallelly of the boundaries of literary genres in the representation of the transgression. Hilst's discourse ventures to extreme reaches of language, posing a challenge to the reader. As A-mi notes, "the character [in Hilst] draws attention to an erotic mystique that makes her dialogize with life and rebel against any finite and limited idea of God (as unknown) and death (as limit)" (298; my translation). This rebellious dialogue occurs in a process of erotic fusion, in an eroticism "that passes through body and soul, through the instances of the sacred and the profane, the sublime and the grotesque" (298). The fusion of absolute categories (man/woman, human/divine, life/death) is achieved thanks to the exuberant forms of artifice, parody, and eroticism that, according to Sarduy, are the three main elements of neobaroque discourse. Sarduy notes that the Baroque (and, by extension, its Neobaroque counterpart) exteriorizes in three symbolizations: eroticism, the mirror, and revolution (1978 [1972]: 181–84). He states that "Like baroque rhetoric, neobaroque eroticism presents itself as the total rupture of the denotative, direct and natural level of language, as the perversion implied by every metaphor, every figure" (182; my translation). The Neobaroque structurally reflects disharmony, the rupture of homogeneity, of the absolute Logos in the manner of "a pulverized reflection of a knowledge that is no longer closed in on itself" (183, my translation). Eroticism enhances the text's possibilities in the representation of transgressively transitive identities.

Likewise, linguistic exuberance acquires a pragmatic function in Hilst's narrative as "the Hilstian work performatizes the word in its images, making one believe that there is no place for an 'end point'" (A-mi 296–97). The performative word takes place in "eroticism as vitalizing and creative energy" (A-mi 298). In a kind of "eroticism of the word," the word unravels in its profuse meaning as the characters disidentify themselves from binary terms, destabilizing and questioning heteronormative categories of sexuality. Similarly, in her review of *Qadós*, Coelho points out in Hilst "the total experience" originating in "its character of a search for doubts and contradictions"; "language of a consciousness or perhaps a consciousness of language and of writing" (1973: 88).

In *L'érotisme*, Bataille described erotic-bodily transgression as "the ultimate self-transcendence, the point of the spirit where limits no longer have any meaning" (Hawley 1978: 309). In the novels by Hilst and Eltit, the dissolution of the "I" coincides with the sexual-erotic act in a social, political, but also intimate sense. The decentered discourse in these narrative and visual works uncovers this erotic dimension as a form of transgression of stable limits between sexed bodies, limits of the law, of representation, of discourse and language itself. It also represents the fusion of bodies, beings, and identities that is achieved in an exuberant form through the operation of artifice, parody, and erotism. A catalyzing feature that unites the operation of these three mechanisms of the Neobaroque, and that marks the continuity between historical Baroque and its contemporary counterpart, are baroque's "the senses of distortion" analyzed by Pablo Baler (2016). The concept of distortion, as presented by Baler, "points to an epistemological problem that includes [...] perspectivism, skepticism, the limits of identity, the trustworthiness of the senses, and the efficacy of language" (1). Distortion explains the textual operation of artifice, parody, simulation, and eroticism. It also describes the functioning of the three-dimensional sign that holds the potential for the displacement of meaning through distortion of the interpretative process, as we proceed to explain in the following section.

4.2   Articulation of Trans-Identity and the Mechanisms of Nomadism: From Peirce to Deleuze and Beyond

Figurations of decentered identities are the result of a semiotic process of distorting meaning through the displacing operation of a triadic sign. The destabilizing potential of the three-part "open sign" allows to perceive Neobaroque's relativization of logocentrically (normatively) instituted identity categories as a reflection of a general crisis of Modernity's Manichean and homogenizing discourse of dualistic distinctions such as masculine/feminine, Black/White, Western/Eastern, liberal/conservative, capitalist/communist, good and evil, upon which Western cultural thought relies. The flexibility of the three-way operating sign seeks to fill in the void left by the crisis of legitimizing metanarratives (or "master-narratives"[12]) of Modernity with a multiplicity of transitive alterities representing "otherness" and exemplified by characters and narrative voices in the analyzed works. As a communicative act—thus social and political—the Neobaroque literary and performative text constitutes the expression of a postmodern social and cultural position that is associated with the relativization of values and fixed references, symptomatic of the "postmodern condition" indicated by Lyotard (1984).

The transformations taking place in the characters presented in the works of the Neobaroque can be referred to as processes of dis-subjecting the subject in a first stage of figuration of a mobile trans-self. Our earlier reference to the writings of Severo Sarduy and Judith Butler leads us to Julia Kushigian (1999), who provides the following definition of the dispersion and successive reformulation of sexual and cultural identity carried out in an intersectional dimension: "it is a kind of action that goes past the binary opposition between masculine and feminine genders. It produces an erotic struggle in order to create new categories born out of the ashes of the old ones, of finding a new mode of (re)creating the body in the cultural field" (1614; my translation). These new modes of recreating the body and articulating the trans-self are conjured by "mechanisms of nomadism," which involve the open (triadic) sign, *devenir*, queering, trans*itivity, disidentification, cross-dressing, androgyny, metamorphosis, and the posthuman cyborg. These concepts or mechanisms of identification allow us to explain how trans-identity articulates as selfhood incarnated in the figure of the trans-self.

4.2.1 The Open Sign: A Semiotics of Transgression

The literary/artistic work (text) becomes a discursive space for decentering the notion of identity. Neobaroque works represent a textual and visual dis-/rearticulation of an intersectionally perceived transitive

---

[12] In *The Postmodern Condition: A Report of Knowledge* (1979), Jean François Lyotard defines "*postmodern* as incredulity toward metanarratives" to which he includes, first and foremost, the meta-legitimizing discourse of Science as expression of technological progress, along with other truth-legitimizing discourses of History, Religion, and Philosophy. To these "grand narratives" of Modernity, Lyotard counterposes "postmodern" language-based options of "the narrative function" and "legitimation through performativity" as alternative methods of "postmodern" legitimation (1984: xxiii–xxv).

nomadic identity of characters/voices. The process of "identity-as-becoming" can be associated with discursive operations and the very communicative process that takes place in the realm of language, and neobaroque style provides a mechanism for the figuration of a nomadic selfhood. Its transitive flexibility is the result of a meaning-making process of an open sign—the neobaroque sign. In its three-part (triadic) functionality, this sign has a destabilizing effect on the meaning of identity.

The theory of the sign formulated by American philosophers and semioticians Charles S. Peirce (1839–1914) and Charles W. Morris (1901–1979) emphasizes the dynamic, three-way (not binary) relationship between the components of a sign which enhances the flexibility of the meaning-making process. It allows us to see textual and cultural meaning as determined contextually by the reader's situation, competency, and intentionality. In contrast to the binary and deterministic one-to-zero/zero-to-one model of the sign, formulated by Ferdinand de Saussure (1955) and based on the relationship of the "signifier" to the "signified," Peirce's triadic sign includes a third element of the "interpretant," adding an unstable, flexible, and mobile dimension to the sign in the semiotic cultural meaning-making process. As a decentering semiotic tool, the triadic sign offers the potential for decentering, mobility, and displacement of meaning that, in neobaroque representation, applies to the fluidity of the nomadic trans-selves intersectionally articulated as borderland identities in the interstices of normative categories. Peirce's model explains the flexibility and movability of meaning in this creative and interpretive process of transitioning. It underscores the relativization and decentering of meaning resulting from the key role of the "interpretant" and, consequently, the reader in the production of meaning.

The fundamental premise on which Peirce builds his theory of the sign is its triadic structure or the "semiotic triad." Three components of the sign enter a relationship that produces meaning. They are the "representamen," or a materialized symbolization (written/spoken word, symbol, icon) that signals meaning of something to someone. It "represents" (carries) an idea by creating in that person's mind an equivalent image or idea of what is represented by way of association. This "interpreted" or projected version of the representamen (as the symbolic/iconic vehicle of meaning) constitutes the "object" of meaning to which it refers in some respect. It is an object of an external-projected entity and a point of reference. The projected object of meaning (based on the "representamen") becomes possible thanks to the associative and interpretative capacity of the third component in the sign mechanism that is the "interpretant." It is the potential capacity or competency to associate the representing, transporting material (the "representamen") to a signified "object" or concept, and connect/associate them to produce meaning. In Peirce's words:

> A sign, or *representamen*, is something which stands to somebody for something in some respect or capacity. It addresses somebody, that is, creates in the mind of that person an equivalent sign, or perhaps a more developed sign. That sign which it creates I call the *interpretant* of the first sign. The sign [*representamen* or signifier = SGFier] stands for something, its *object* [signified-SGFied[a]]. It stands for that object not in all respects, but in reference to a sort of [context and competency-based] idea, which I have sometimes called the *ground* of the representamen. (Peirce, cit. in Pharies 1985: 14, emphasis in original)

What follows is an illustration of this semiotic mechanism of the triadic sign and the relationship among its three parts in the semantic transformation of the decentered (non-binary) meaning-making process that is mobilized and shifted by the "third" element, the "interpretant." It facilitates the understanding of the aesthetic representation of subjects and borderland identities that are transgressive in their shifting meanings. It also illustrates the rupture and displacement of meaning involved in the unstable and mobile identity of the nomad. The "interpretant" works as an opening element of the sign within the bounds of contextual and cultural competency of the meaning-making agent: the listener, reader, or viewer of the represented sign. Thanks to that meaning-making capacity, the interpretant is able to displace the association of the representamen from an assigned SGFied-A object to a new, alternate SGFied-B object.

According to this model, the functioning of the sign is founded on a dynamic (movable and shifting) relationship within the triadic complex formed by the representamen-object-interpretant interaction. The unique and most significant element in this model, which is not binary (as Saussure's two-part model), is the *interpretant*. It is an active element of semiosis (meaning-making) that establishes a "living"—experiential and contextual—connection between two "material" entities: the *representamen* (what we call in Fig. 4.1 "signifier" = SGFier, as the carrier or vehicle of meaning, yet meaningless without the other two components) and the *object* ("signified" = SGFied-A) as a socially-determined idea of the external referent to which the sign points. This relationship would not be

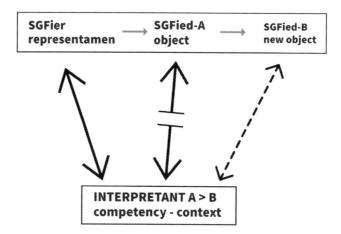

Fig. 4.1 The triadic sign according to Peirce with the addition of displaced meaning—SGFied-B.
(Note: The figure represents semiosis based on the triadic (or three-part) relationship of elements taking place within the sign and, more broadly, the literary/artistic work; based on the explanation by Peirce (1987, 1991), with my addition of "displaced meaning—SGFied-B")

possible without the element of someone/something—another "tool sign" at a metalevel—by whom the relationship between the representamen-signifier (SGFier) and object-signified (SGFied-A) acquires a meaning or some relevance worthy of interpretation and, possibly, reaction. It is the third component of the sign, the "interpretant" (activated by the interpreting agent) that opens the otherwise two-way relationship between the representing "thing" (SGFier) and its object-referent or "idea" (SGFied) by including the semiotic "decoding" competency of the interpreter into this process, thus making the entire relationship possible. The relationship of SGFier SGFied appears in the upper level of Fig. 4.1. The interpretant is placed in the lower level.

To show the displacement of meaning, we added a second "signified" object marked as SGFied-B. The interpretant displaces SGFied-A (the original or "official," socially ascribed association) toward that new ("created") SGFied-B object to the right. The primary association of the representamen to the first SGFied-A object *can* be severed by the interpretant and projected, in a new meaning-making association, to a secondary

SGFied-B object, as observed with the dotted arrow. The interpretant is the operative element of the semiotic process in which the meaning of categories of gender and other identities is opened, displaced, or ambiguated.

This dynamic and displacing relation of the traditional binary pair of "representamen" and "object" (Saussure's "signifier" and "signified") is now mediated through the "interpretant," allowing for a decentering shift of meaning. It also constitutes the key phenomenological element of *intentionality* in the perception of reality. As we recall, in phenomenology there always has to be an *object* of perception for it to acquire meaning through the *intention* of the perceiver. It is important to note that, in Peircean terms, the relation to the object of signification cannot be made effective, explicit, or complete without reference to a "collateral experience" of the interpreter that is incorporated to the sign in the interpretant mechanism. This experience can also be defined as the "store of knowledge" accumulated during the life or the actual real-time experience of the interpreter; it can also be the effect of the contextual, social, political, or cultural situation of the interpreter, of their contextual information-as-situation.[13] These contextual factors of intentionality find their place in the pragmatic dimension of the work that is considered in itself a "macro" cultural sign. In terms of pragmatics, the work of Charles Morris, complied in *Foundations of a Theory of Signs* (1972), reveals the sign's contextual variability (50–67). The most relevant aspect of Peirce's and Morris's approach is the open-endedness of the sign for interpretation, which contributes to the development of a context-based pragmatic dimension of meaning making, as pointed out by Morris:

> Because, in semiotics, the sign is considered to be addressing somebody in a real situation, the system has at its disposal premises from the interpreter's entire body of collateral knowledge, including [...] purely contextual information. This would provide the means of accounting for important context-dependent phenomena such as irony, humor, lies, allusions, puns, metaphor, and all kinds of semantic phenomena based on cultural expectations. (20)

---

[13] Socio-critical theories of literature easily relate to the semiotic model in highlighting the role of the socio-cultural context and competency of the interpreter. The school of "sociocriticism" was initiated in France by Lucien Goldman (tracing back to Georg Lukács) and continued by Pierre Zima and Edmond Cros, further evolving in the work of Pierre Bourdieu. It emphasizes socio-cultural determinants of the interpretive process.

In the examination of transgressive discourse, as the neobaroque, and its representation of sexual, racial, ethnic, national, social, and (post)human subjects, the ideas formulated by Peirce acquire methodological value when considering that the meaning of identity is realized within a fluid semiosis of the triadic relation mobilized by the interpreter (or "the sign" of the sign that makes interpretation possible through cultural competency). In accordance with Peirce's ideas, Barend van Heusden agrees that the complexity of a work of art does not lie in its structure, but in the possibilities of interpretation that this structure creates. The work of art and literature, through aesthetic devices, tries to "postpone" the fixation of beliefs, ideas, prejudices and favors the freedom of semiosis (1996: 246).

The borderland subjects that appear in neobaroque texts and performances are the result of a semiotic displacement of (institutionalized or official) meaning. The representamen, as the carrier of the sign's meaning (the image of the character or voice or performer), holds an attribute of an object that acquires significance (creates meaning, for instance femininity, homosexuality, queerness, etc.) through the interpretative competency of the interpreter facilitated by the sign's third element, the interpretant. Identity and its changing attributes ("objects") are fluid, shifting, and transitive, as the interpretation of textual characters ("representamens") such as Socorro, Auxilio, Cobra, Colibrí, Lumpérica, María Chipia, Qadós, Senhora D, Jacob Pliniak, the Galán Family, Susy Shock, the narrators, performers, and painted subjects is made possible for the reader/spectator. Thus, interpreted meaning may be displaced (to SGFier-B), decentered, and "decolonized" from the imposed, official, and normative precepts of logocentrism (corresponding to "SGFier-A").

4.2.2   Devenir *or the Rhizomatic Subject-as-Becoming*

Real-world transitive identity articulation can also be conceived as any individual's subjective process of dynamic self-formulation enabled by the subject's discursive-symbolizing capacity of semiotic interpretation of cultural signs, combined with desire, affection, and openness to the "other." In the textual realm of the literary and artistic works, it is perceived in the transgressive characters who, with their transformed bodies and voices, portray a decentered and transitive selfhood in its textual figurations of cross-dressing, androgyny, metamorphosis, racial and ethnic mixings, and posthuman-cyborg states. To explain this process of selfhood, Gilles Deleuze presents the concept of *devenir* (which from French and Spanish translates as "becoming"). It is an identity-formative process based on sets of "orientations, directions, entries and exits," "packets of segmentarized lines" of direction indicating "molecular fluxes with thresholds" of passage (1987a: 2, 124). *Devenir* corresponds to a self-formative process of "minoritarian becoming" (at the individual level), based on transitive multiplicity of "passing in between" all (collectively or majority-defined) dualisms in the mode of a *rhizome* (1987b: 6–8, 25, 30). The concept of *devenir* was further developed by Argentine writer Néstor Perlongher who, in *Prosa plebeya* (1997), speaks of "a subject without center, drifting away from the model of individual [unitary] behavior," of a subject undergoing "dynamic subject-less [instant] individuation*s* [...] minorization*s* and marginalization*s*, movements from the periphery, from the margin" (68; my translation and emphasis). Departing from Deleuze's base, Perlongher goes on to affirm that "becoming" does not imply completely transforming into an "other," but rather forming subjective alliances by contagion and immersion with the other's differences. These formations occur in the "in-between" spaces of contact situated on the "borders" of states (of being). Thus, Perlongher defines "becoming" as a process of "entering into (aberrant) alliance, contagion, *inmistión* [roughly 'immersion,' 'soaking,' or 'insertion'] with (the) different. *Devenir*—Becoming does not transit from one point to another, but rather *enters* the 'in-between' of the middle, it *is* that 'between,'" situated in the "points of passage" between the "identificatory polarities (sexual, racial, social, national)" at the "molecular" level of micro/local positions (68; my translation and emphasis).

Devenir (as becoming by *dis*identification) is "a process of desire" in continuous movement that does not fixate in any end. This molecular transformation un-situates in a place of transition in continuous movement, without assigning its identity to an affirmation of a specific "alternative identity" of the Other (or even transforming into any single Other). As such, the labeling of difference into new categories is avoided, as is situating them in an appropriate discursive site of the postcolonial neoliberal establishment: on the homogenized minoritarian margin of multicultural diversity.

The rhizome, as presented by Deleuze in its dimension of a *cartography* effectuated in writing, and as verbal combinations "not amenable to any structural or generative model [...], a *map and not a tracing*" (1987b: 12, emphasis in original), becomes a conceptual tool of creating any transitive identity or trans* selfhood in its multiplicity of horizontal combinations and displacements of categorical logocentric meaning. Following Deleuze's strategy, Braidotti emphasizes the way rhizomatic and intersectional thinking leads each subject to empower him- or herself in a multiplicity of categorizations along multiple axes of classification:

> Resonances, harmonies and hues intermingle to paint an altogether different landscape of a self that, not being One, functions as a relay-point for many sets of intensive intersections and encounters with multiple others. Moreover, not being burdened by One, such a subject can envisage forms of resistance and political agency that are multi-layered and complex. It is an empirical transcendental site of becoming. (2002: 75)

The process of becoming acquires a "feminine" aspect of fluidity and openness. In line with Deleuzian, feminist-based poststructuralism, it moves along horizontal (rhizomatic) lines of deterritorialization that operate in a nomadic subject going through the stage of "becoming-woman," a state of open transitivity that is the key precondition and necessary starting-point for the entire process of becoming. Its political implications will be discussed in more detail in Sect. 4.4. This opens the terrain for other "minoritarian becomings" as transgressions of power structures embedded in normative categorical discourse:

> In this perspective, 'subjectivity' names the process that consists in stringing together—under the fictional unity of a grammatical 'I'—different forms of active and reactive interaction with and resistance to these conditions. The subject is a process, made of constant shifts and negotiations between different levels of power and desire, constantly shifting between wilful choice and unconscious drives. (Braidotti 2002: 75–76)

In the works considered in Chap. 3, various transitive and movable identities emerge. Following Deleuze and Perlongher, I prefer to call them "becomings" (Spn., *devenires*). Androgyny and cross-dressing are just two forms of this fluid state of transitioning into trans-identity. With a notable presence in Latin American art and literature, they signal a conceptual space of decentering of the totalizing discourses of Modernity, as well as the oncoming of a new, more open, originally Latin American form of postmodern thought. I propose to call this a "Transmerican cultural androgyny," an ambiguation of fixed, defined, and instituted identity categories by which individuals live. It signals the transformation of the concept of identity into a movable consciousness, a becoming, in a site of transition, or a contact zone, as defined by M.L. Pratt (1993). It does not affirm itself as "one" new, alternative minoritarian identity, like the typically postmodern tendency of affirming oneself part of a specific minority that is categorized, labeled, and controlled by the neoliberal cultural discourse of homogenizing globalization.

The subject's "oneness" intersects with "otherness" in the social setting of the collectivity that allows for such differentiations. This happens on a level that is still in the "specific singularity of immanent interrelations among subjects collectively engaged" in the expression and actualization of what Braidotti call *potentia* (2006: 182), the virtual force or positive energy to forge one's own identity, as opposed to *potestas*, the force or negative energy that is authoritarian, imposing, and imposed. Braidotti calls the intersubjective space a "laboratory of becoming" (2006: 182) and proposes a model of alternative ethics based on "radically immanent philosophies of nomadism" (2006: 183). It involves applying a non-hierarchical idea of transcendence and a non-binary model of interrelation of subjects that engages the notion of desire as (positive, affirmative) *potentia*. Feminist cultural criticism (Irigaray 1984; Richard 1993; Braidotti 2006) considers this vitalistic, anti-essentialist power of affirmation as coded with the "feminine" without regard to who the agent is or where s/he positions her-/him-self. However, Braidotti warns against affirming the feminine as a new essence and suggests opening up "fields of multiple becomings" to other categories, or positions of identity: "What is at stake in sustainable ethics [of nomadism] is not the feminine as codified in the phallogocentric code of the patriarchal imaginary, but rather the feminine as project, as movement of destabilization of identity and hence of becoming" (2006: 183–84).

The role that creative (literary and artistic) activity plays in the realization of this nomadic subject is evident when subsuming "the potency and relevance of the *imagination*, of myth-making, as a way to step out of the political and intellectual stasis of these postmodern times. Political *fictions* may be more effective, here and now, than theoretical systems" (Braidotti 1994: 4; my emphasis). The realization of the nomadic subject on the social level in a "hypothetical" mode of *potentia*—its possibility for self-accomplishment through contacts that create a network of interconnectedness with otherness—is carried out, in our case, in the textual/performative space of the Latin American Neobaroque. This figurative mode of aesthetic representation relates the subject to the concept of *devenir* as rhizomatic becoming. Braidotti refers this mode to the technique of "as if," a figurative form of "make-believe" representation: "In some cases, the figurative mode functions according to what I have called 'the philosophy of <<as if>> [...]. It is *as if* some experiences were reminiscent or evocative of others; this ability to flow from one set of experiences to another is a quality of interconnectedness that I value highly. Drawing a flow of connections need not be an act of appropriation" (Braidotti 1994: 5; emphasis in original). The role of literature in nomadic becoming is best illustrated by Braidotti when referring to the process of writing as paralleling "the process of becoming-minority and of becoming-woman. Indeed, it is consequently in literature and the arts that Deleuze finds the most significant illustrations for this process" (2002: 94).

4.2.3 Queering Identity: Trans*, Travesti, and Disidentification

The nomadic movement of transitive identity flows constitutes the axis for the enactment of gender identity in sexual and textual embodiments. The characters and personae in the mentioned works incarnate fragments of "otherness" (or "alterity") in transformations that, as a result of their transgressions of normative gender categories, highlight *queerness* as the common denominator of gender-sexual identity. The discursive mechanisms of queer becoming involve concepts that will facilitate our interpretation of transitive identity, a "transentity" emerging in the literary and visual works set in the hybrid cultural context of "Transmerica."

"Queer" has been defined by Annemarie Jagose as an identity option and a self-defining practice of refiguration of sexuality by using a non-heterosexual and non-binary discursive horizon resorting to an alternative and diverging way of thinking the sexual (2015: 26). Whereas "queering" can be understood more amply as an active process of attaining sexual ambiguity in uncategorical "otherness" by diverging from defined gender/sexual categories, it stands for a departure from a binary, heteronormative model of gender/sexual identity. Relating to queerness and relativizing the concept of sexuality through performative transgression, transvestism (cross-dressing) and androgyny divert the attention of the beholder from the fixed center of the "I" as subject to the transition zone between the two genders that make up the transitive (trans-)self. They point to the intermediate space between (binary) categories of masculinity and femininity, and conceptually or symbolically extend onto the gray zone between "I" and "you," "he" and "she," One and Other.

The definition adopted by Jagose follows Teresa de Lauretis in pointing out queer theory's distinctness from strictly and purely lesbian and gay approaches. Queerness broadens the scope of gender/sexuality toward more intersectional perspectives on identity. De Lauretis considers queer's role "as holding open space attentive to 'the respective and/or common grounding of current discourses and practices of homo-sexualities in relation to gender and to *race*, with their attendant differences of *class or ethnic culture*, generational or geographical, and *socio-political location*'" (de Lauretis in Jagose 2015: 28; emphasis added). Joining de Lauretis, Jagose proposes transgressing and transcending, in any case problematizing, any defining or labeling terms of sexuality founded on heterosexual binarism and expanding the concept to the oblique forces of class, ethnic, and racial difference in "coordinates of what is now called *intersectionality*" (28; emphasis in original). What is more, "de Lauretis insists that queer theory, unlike lesbian and gay studies, is a critical [antinormative] enterprise foundationally interested in race and, through the master term *race*, in all the taxonomic classes by which social subjectivity is differentiated" (Jagose 2015: 29; emphasis in original). From this definition of queer as a theoretical concept, it is possible to mark the terminological shift toward understanding queerness "in relation to a complex mapping of majoritarian and minoritarian forces that cannot easily be captured by the antagonistic and unidirectional energy of antinormativity" (30). In other words, it is not solely queer's anti-establishment political resistance to heterosexual binarism that determines its outreach, but the wider scope of creatively combining in multiple identity-forming alliances. This cross-referentiality of categories that form combinations that are not binary but multidirectional and multitemporal constitutes the conceptual foundation of our endeavor of envisioning a trans-identity based on queerness-as-otherness.

As one of queering's alternative modes of reinventing sexualities by means of a different ("another") discursive horizon (Jagose 2015), the concept of trans* introduced by Halberstam (2018) allows us to consider "*trans*identity" as inclusive of *trans*gression: *trans*genderism, *trans*vestism, and, ultimately, *trans*cendence. According to Halberstam, "trans can be a name for expansive forms of difference, haptic relations to knowing, uncertain modes of being, and the disaggregation of identity politics predicated upon the separating out of many kinds of experience that actually blend together, intersect, and mix" (5). It constitutes an open-ended visualization of identity represented in the disheveled, exuberant, and erotic discourse of the Neobaroque.

278   K. A. KULAWIK

It is important to recognize the fragmented, segmented, and multiple nature of the trans* "that, according to Halberstam, can only emerge as an inclusive fluid category and not an attribute (2018: 88). The open-ended concept of "trans*" renders the relationship of subjectivity with the material body and its representation, namely as: "not a matter of whose gender is variable and whose is fixed; rather, the term 'trans*' puts pressure on all modes of gender embodiment and refuses to choose between the identitarian and the contingent forms of trans identity" (2018: xiii). The queer theorist focuses his project not only on looking for trans people (those who have legally changed their sex) as examples, but on discerning "a politics of transitivity" (xiii), as a process of transformation of identity in a general sense, of "becoming" as part of human subjectivity potentiated to any being's ability of *creating* selfhood.

Halberstam's usage of the term "trans*" is motivated by the will to open conceptual possibilities organized *around* but not confined *to* forms of gender variance (5). The asterisk ending the word opens its semantic field to the emergence of an ambiguous, fluid "trans-identity" that avoids any labeling in its attempt to visualize a transitive subject:

> [...] the asterisk modifies the meaning of transitivity by refusing to situate transition in relation to a destination, final form, a specific shape, established configuration of desire and identity. The * holds off the certainty of diagnosis; it keeps at bay any sense of knowing in advance what the meaning of this or that gender variant form may be, and perhaps most importantly, it makes trans* people the authors of their own categorizations. [...] trans* can be a name for expansive forms of difference, haptic relations to knowing, uncertain modes of being, and the disaggregation of identity politics predicated upon the separating out of many kinds of experience that actually blend together, intercept, and mix. This terminology, trans*, stands at odds with the history of gender variants, which has been collapsed into concise definitions, sure medical pronouncements, and fierce exclusions. (4–5)

The author brings forth the notion of "haptic" as related to con-tact (Vacarro), the architectural (Crawford), and the somatic (Hayward) to be able to lay out a new model of embodiment that is both queer and transitive. Another idea that the critic uses is Eva Hayward's concept of "neighborhood rather than home" in the elaboration of such a theory of transition in not only the individual sphere but also in the context of the community. Halberstam pushes us in different directions in the considerations of gender variability, social change, and new political formations, proposing to

Fig. 4.2 Lego DNA. (Source: Wikimedia Creative Commons)

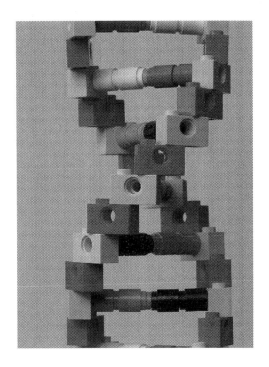

use this malleable frame to rethink the meaning of identity, body, politics, and movement, but with the caveat that "it is certainly well within the bounds of the non-serious. My terminology comes from Lego and uses the movable parts and freestyle building processes associated with Lego to think seriously about new body architectures, component parts of embodiment, and structures of becoming" (129–30) (Fig. 4.2).

With the concept of "trans*," Halberstam is "leaning more toward a Deleuzian understanding of the body as a liquid set of dynamics" (30), placing emphasis on the ideas of motion, transition, flight, precariousness, and in-betweenness (40). The category of trans* is embedded in the notions of fragmentation, segmentation, and multiplicity through "an optic that recognizes trans* as a capacious and fluid category rather than a diagnosis" (88). It supplements the Deleuzian concept of *devenir* as "becoming."

From the perspective of queer theory, the discursive constructivism of sexuality mobilizes categories while questioning their social determination. In the assignment of identity, the word always leaves the expression of subjectivity as a blank space. As Vittorio states in Hilst's novel *Estar sendo. Ter sido* (2001; "To be. To have been," n.t.): "upstairs I was a rooster. then I was a humiliated man, a choleric woman wrapped in a towel" (75; my translation); "no. I'm nobody no. I'm just dust [...] looking for Father. I'm just a dust bitch" (112). Vittorio's initial change into a woman and his subsequent metamorphosis into animals results in a shifting and unstable identity. His shattered self and inverted sexuality, unbridled in all libidinous eroticism, lead to conceiving subjectivity in terms of transitivity. Vittorio's identity shifts to transentity if we apply Halberstam's concept of "trans*" to envision a fragmented and fluid un-category of self-articulation, without determining an identity. Applying a trans* reading to the protagonist Vittorio, we can see the opening of the Hilstian text to a representation of transgenderism as an "art" of embodiment, not only of changing body forms but of the "imagination" of roles in relationships that *may* be homoerotic, bisexual, or just queer. "Trans* bodies represent the art of becoming, the necessity of imagining, and the fleshly insistence of transitivity" (Halberstam 136).

The transvestite's process of (self)identification highlights one of the main ideas emerging from queer theory—transitivity. The sexually ambiguous body of Hilst's Qadós passes through stages of transformation to (transiently) reach a higher state of reconciliation (and fusion) of opposites of masculinity and femininity that coexist in androgyny and transvestism. This coexistence has been pointed out by Kulick in the context of cross-dressed prostitutes in Brazil: "This sexual flexibility allows them [the transvestites] access to the entire spectrum of sexed and gendered behavior and subjectivities" (193). In the same study of transgender in Brazil, Kulick notes: "*Travesti* subjectivity is thus not that of a woman nor that of a man, but that of an effeminate male—a homosexual. 'I'm neither a man nor a woman, [...] I'm a faggot'" (222). The titles of the sections of Kulick's text illustrate well the identification of the transvestite: "Feeling like a Woman" (210), "Males, Not Men" (214), and "Perfectly Homosexual" (*viado*, 221). In Hilst, sex is exchangeable, inverting, transiting, and becoming ambiguous, as the characters search for a God parallelly to the writer's search for the Word in a metonymic extension of being-existing-writing. Trans-identity denies itself of attribution to a fixed meaning or category, as Kulick explains when observing the Brazilian cross-dressers: "If we understand masculinity and femininity not as adhering to or arising from male and female bodies but instead as signs or processes that are invoked and enacted through specific practices, then we are in a much better position to begin to understand transvestite subjectivity" (232).

The same attitude of *not* belonging to any binary categorization, but not denying them either, is noted in the testimonial discourse of Argentine cross-dressers that Marlene Wayar addresses in *Travesti / Una teoría lo suficientemente buena* (2019): "I am not a man, I am not a woman, today I *am being* a transvestite. This gerund explains my *just for today* but does not close it to crisis and transformation" (25; my translation, emphasis in original). Wayar provides further examples of "disidentification" of binary gender categories in the testimonies of transvestites in Buenos Aires: "in the *travesti* experience, it is not so necessary to affirm what I AM, whether I am a transvestite, transgender, transsexual or binary gender; what drastically matters is what I AM NOT" (24; capitalization in original); "It would not be of interest in the transvestite experience WHAT I AM and to close it at some point; rather [it matters] that I go about being the best version of me today. And it matters more what I AM NOT" (Wayar 24; capitals in original). "'We are not women enclosed in the body of a male.' To be able to break that was important. Today, if you ask the girls what they are, they answer 'We are transvestites'" (115). In her testimonial work, Wayar elaborates a *sui generis* theory of *travesti* in which she points to the fluid *entendimiento* (understanding) of sexuality: "So, then, can amorous play take other sensitive and eroticized forms that do not have to do with the dichotomy of being penetrated or penetrating? [...] none of us [here 'nosotr*os*' with a masculine ending], men and women, have the body constructed in a univocal way. Sexuality is a sensibility and not a genitality" (116; my translation). In an etymological note, she adds that the first-person plural pronoun *nosotros* in Spanish literally expresses both "us" [*nos*] and "others" [*otros*], or "us" and "them" fused into a composite one-in-many. Her proposal is to build a third option, alternative to the dichotomy inherent in Identity/I and Otherness; she phrases it as "the possibility of power to construct Ourness [*Nostredad*]" (25).

In his presentation at the Universidad Academia de Humanismo Cristiano in Santiago, Chile in 2007 (moderated by Diamela Eltit), Bolivian transformist cross-dresser Danna Galán makes the following assessment of the voluble *travesti* effect:

> The Galán Family does not seek origins, it is not interested in identities. Now as you say, the transvestite issue looks like an identity, "the transvestite identity." Some transvestite friends told me, "I am a transvestite, that's my

282   K. A. KULAWIK

identity." In that case, I am a transvestite and I do gender performance, so at this moment you see me like this and then you see me different, you see me with other clothes, other makeup, doing other activities, etcetera. I have been in five or six photographs with different clothes, so maybe you don't recognize me in some of them. Being a transvestite is one thing, and looking like one is another, at this moment I am being Danna, it is a performance. (Araujo 136; my translation)

Another mechanism related to transvestism and originating in queer theory is "disidentification," introduced by Butler (1993: 4) and developed by José Esteban Muñoz in *Disidentifications* (1999). It highlights the process of transformation occurring in transvestism as a way to disown categorical assignment of gender traits. For Muñoz, identity is a process of enacting socially codified roles generated by (a dominant) culture, and of negotiating from a fixed disposition of identity, from among the roles or traits available to the minority subject who is bound by heteronormative discourse. Minority subjects are especially determined, or "coded" by the discursive control of heteronormativity. Muñoz defines disidentification as a purging, eliminatory process of reading "oneself and one's own life narrative in a moment, object, or subject that is not culturally coded to 'connect' with this identifying subject. [...] Rather, it is the reworking of those energies that do not elide the 'harmful' or contradictory components of any identity" (12). He further expands his definition with reference to Foucault's theory of the polyvalence of discourse, as it

informs the theory of this identification being put forth here and as much as this identification is a strategy that resists a conception of power as being a fixed discourse. This identification negotiates strategies of resistance within the flux of discourse and power. It understands that counter discourses, like any discourse, can always fluctuate for different ideological ends and in a politicized agent must have the ability to adapt and shift as quickly as power does within discourse. (19)

This definition of "disidentification" contributes to a mobile, fluid, and decentered conception of transitive identity and the trans-self because of its self-critical, purging, and negotiating capabilities that eliminate the stigmatized negativity of any marginalized identity category.

Muñoz refers to disidentification as "a hermeneutic, a process of production, and a mode of performance" (25), which brings us to consider performance as an artistic form that provides the ground for the disidentificatory (as negative, critical, and eliminating) process of subjective figuration and decentered articulation of selfhood. This process of "identity invention" takes place at the "collision points" of discursive perspectives that cultural critics call essentialist and constructivist. Performance exemplifies a negotiation of categorical discourses in the mode of "disidentificatory reception." Identities are "deviated" from (hetero)normativity in artistic representation in "a reconstructed narrative of identity formation that locates the enacting of self at precisely the point where the discourses of essentialism and constructivism short-circuit" (Muñoz 6).

The process of (self)identification of the decentered mobile subject in Hilst's *Qadós* illustrates all three mechanisms of transitivity that are hitherto represented by the concepts of trans*, *travesti*, and complemented by Muñoz's "disidentification." Applied to the transforming (occasionally cross-dressed) figure of Qadós, the idea of disidentification as a negotiation (rejection and adoption) of binary identity fragments allows us to understand the construction of trans-identity in Hilstian characters as a textual process in search of transcendence. Qadós' sexuality becomes uncertain, blurry, and tainted in the fragmented perception of *hir*self: "my whole being of secrecy and fear DOES NOT BELONG, it is this, I am neither this nor that, dark strangeness [...] what an effort to belong (110); [...] BELONGING. TO BE PART OF. TO FIT" (111–12; my translation, capitals in original). One notes here the desire to overcome this fragmentation and "fit" into some entity, to transcend or transition identity. This inconstancy of Qadós can be explained with the concept of transitivity expressed in Halberstam's "trans*" as a term that points to the mobility (passage) of any fixed category that is not specified after the asterisk, holding the transitive potential to change. It signals the modality of indeterminate identity, in a "rendering of transgenderism as a desire for forms of embodiment that are necessarily impossible and yet deeply desired all at once" (Halberstam 20). The opposites of masculinity and femininity coexist in Qadós' androgyny, but also in transvestism, as Kulick observed in the context of Brazilian transvestites. Such sexual flexibility allowed the cross-dressers to adopt multiple sexed behaviors and conceive various gendered subjectivities (1998: 193). The fluctuation in the identity process, distinguished with the term "trans*," allows to perceive the different avatars of the cross-dressed and androgynous character.

Mario Bellatin's construction of queerness becomes visible in what Vek Lewis called a "discourse of identity fracture" (140), in which multiple signifiers are dispersed. Bellatin's narrative focuses on the discursive process of constructing and deconstructing the trans body in the textual dimension. The relationship established in Bellatin's and other writers' work between transvestism and writing also finds part of its explanation in the concept of artifice and in the techniques of masking. Bellatin's narrative (in this case, as Barthes' "writable" literature[14]) barely suggests but does not offer a closed meaning by including unstable and dialogic characters, and by leaving blank spaces of uncertainty. This mode of presenting the content resorts to techniques of deconstruction, concealment, and simulation, what Bellatin himself called the "un-writing" or de-coding of socio-cultural roles assigned by tradition and their aesthetic (un)representation as transitive identities. The undefined, untouchable, and formless constitutes writing's space of the "unsaid." Bellatin opts to "un-write" (or "de-compose") reality and, by extension, the identity of his characters, and to leave out what is stable, fixed, and "true." The motifs of androgyny and transvestism are part of a mobile terrain, a mutant and un-/deformed space, open to the process of re-defining the self in multiple ways with infinite possibilities that the work creates for the reader. He states in an interview: "The aura of the undefined sustains the work and opens the spaces for its self-constitution in the process of reading" (my translation[15]). In another interview, he adds: "It seems to me more interesting to feel, both from the point of view of the writer and the reader, to be transiting all the time in a terrain about which one has no idea" (Bosch 2007: 91; my translation).

Metafiction implies an alteration of the narrative flow to create awareness of the discursive construction of identity on multiple levels, analogous to the transvestite's fluidity of gender identification while crossing the binary categories of the systemic pair. We could say that it constitutes a sort of "discursive transvestism" that resembles the queer discourse of the trans artist, Susy Shock: "from [the point of] the Latin American Trans Theory [...] we try to get out of the systemic pair" (Wayar 2019: 25; my translation). When applying a trans*/*travesti* reading to fictional characters, we see the openness of the text to represent transgenderism as an

---

[14] This idea was introduced by Barthes in his classic *Le plaisir du texte*, 1973, as the idea that a challenging non-mimetic text can be recreated (or "rewritten") by the capacity of the reader's interpretative competency.

[15] My personal interview with Mario Bellatin in Mexico City, July 2009. Digital recording and transcription in Spanish, unpublished.

"art" of embodiment; not only of varying body forms but of the "imagination" (or imaginary forms) of roles in relationships that may be homoerotic. The androgynous disidentification of the heteronormative binary leads to transcending the categorical subject, as Muñoz proposes: "Finally, this self, fashioned through strategic disidentifications with dominant discourses of 'selfness,' presents the potential to ultimately 'cultivate that part of oneself that leads beyond oneself, that transcends oneself'" (Muñoz 178–79). This process operates in language, as observed in Judith Butler's structural relationship between language (discourse) and gender situated on "the limits of a discursively conditioned experience" (1990: 13). The role of language in destabilizing culturally instituted categories of gender/sexuality relates to mobilizing such categories through "disidentification" from the regulatory norms of heterosexual discourse. Discourse and its realm of the symbolic conform one space in which identity can be both constructed and deconstructed (Butler 1993: 4).

4.2.4 Transgressing Normative Categories: Transvestism, Androgyny, Metamorphosis, and Posthuman Cyborgs

As a form of boundary crossing and gender category inversion, cross-dressing is one of the most recurring themes in neobaroque literary and artistic works. This gender-bending procedure can be explained as the desire to or the act of wearing the clothes of the "other" (than assigned) sex. The word derives from Latin *trans* as "opposite" and *vestis* as "clothes" (Ellis and Abarbaniel 1961; ref. Ch. 3). It can be a performative activity of external representation of gender identity carried out by means of personification, acting, pretending, or simulating. Its purposes can be theatrical, humorous, and parodic, as in *drag*, or a way of "passing" to disguise and conceal true gender identity, or to show the arbitrariness of the social constructs of gender categories, such as the gender-bending mixture of feminine and masculine elements (Hogan and Hudson 1998, 159). With its origins in the Roman saturnalias, transvestism sometimes takes on the form of mockery, parody, and play in theatrical arts, particularly on such occasions as the Carnival (Randell 1976, 51). It attracts the element of ambiguity, but it does not necessarily imply a determined hetero, homo o bisexual orientation. As such, transvestism ought not to be confused with "transexuality," or a complete inversion of gender with a psicosomatic identification with the opposite-to-biological sex. For the transvestite, "pleasure comes from wearing the clothes of the other sex rather than in physically becoming a member of that sex" (Garber 3). Cross-dressing differentiates itself in that it has an external and performative character in which the normative categories of gender and sexuality (as orientation or preference) come into play through simulation and inversion.

In his study of transvestism in Latin American literature, Ben. Sifuentes-Jáuregui (2002) defined it as a "performance of gender," "a process always evolving [...] of what historically and culturally gets labeled as 'femininity' and 'masculinity'" (3). It is as much about representing the other and taking his/her place as it is about representing oneself and becoming oneself in an act of self-realization in/through otherness: "transvestism is an operating strategy that deconstructs a specific 'normality' in a gender binary hierarchy. [...] Transvestism inaugurates an epistemological shift that locates, defines, performs, and erases the fundamental dichotomy: Self / Other. This [...] manifests an anxiety that could be called 'the denaturalization of genders'" (4). Similarly, Josefina Fernández (2004) points to the challenge that transvestism poses to the binary notion of gender by questioning the categories of masculine and feminine, and by deconstructing the very concept of gender (58). As she states, "*transvestism questions the principles of classification and recognition of socially legitimized gender identities*" (16; my translation; cursive in original). One of her definitions of transvestism is "performative"—transvestism as a parodic repetition of "ordered" genders in order to subvert their meaning in the cultural context: "The cross-dresser's gesture deconstructs thinking in terms of categories [...] to install a discursive order based on staging of images and representations" (63). This performative modality undermines, from a political position, the dichotomy of an assigned body/gender relationship in appearance expectations. It exposes irreverent, antinormative desires of the body-psyche relation, causing male/female identities to explode into a diversity of combinations and possibilities of self-determination. More importantly, Fernández focuses on the cross-dresser's claiming a subjectivity that is nomadic, as it transits between the modalities of masculine and feminine (64).

In her comprehensive study of transvestism in *Vested Interests: Cross-Dressing and Cultural Anxiety* (1992), Marjorie Garber establishes a relationship between cross-dressing and theatricality, explaining how simulating modes of external appearance, such as the specific use of clothing and accessories, contribute to both constructing and deconstructing the categories of gender and sexuality. Transvestism's modulation of appearance correlates to racial, social, and power structures of identification, and are constitutive of the articulation of culture itself (Perlongher 1997: 3). The discursive, language-based nature of cross-dressing lies in its "status as a sign of the constructedness of gender categories" (9) and in the reversibility, artificiality, and dissociation of signs from their allegedly "natural" referents (151). As such, transvestism offers a critique of reversible binary distinctions in the way it denaturalizes, destabilizes, and defamiliarizes sex and gender *signs*. Its presence indicates that the signs encoding heterosexuality have been detached from a "natural" referent with which, as transvestism further reveals, they have always been in a conventional rather than natural connection (147).

According to Garber, transvestism constitutes a "vestimentary code" in Barthes' sense of a rhetorical system of signification that, as a code, operates in "a secret or private language that must keep changing in order to avoid being broken, or broken into, by those whom it seeks to elude or escape" (157–58). In this sense, transvestism functions as an encoding mechanism of identity founded in eroticism and desire, in its dynamic and flexible meaning potential. Its performative realization operates from a continuously shifting borderline of categories that allows its encoded and mobile parameters of gender and sexuality to avoid detection, as fixation of meaning. The presence of the cross-dresser points to the dissolvable nature of the fictional character, as our analysis of literary and performance works demonstrates in the rupture of the illusion of a character's defined identity. Just as in Barthes' description of the illusive character of fashion and simulating nature of the discourse of clothing (1983: 254–55), the interchangeable accumulation of signifiers on the transvestite's body makes any characterization of the cross-dresser ungraspable and illusive. Like the fashion system based on external appearances made-up of "an accumulation of signifying 'essences,'" the transvestite "also changes 'characters,' becomes, as s/he has always been, unknowable, unknown" (Garber 250).

Garber's semiotic approach to transvestism is innovative in the sense that it moves away from looking *through* the cross-dresser (to attribute an underlying meaning) to looking *at* him/her without subsuming its character within the gender-sex binaries. This avoids appropriating transvestism for specific political and critical objectives. As Garber states:

> For me, therefore, one of the most important aspects of cross-dressing is the way in which it offers a challenge to easy notions of binarity, putting into question the categories of "female" and "male," whether they are consid-

288 K. A. KULAWIK

> ered essential or constructed, biological or cultural. The current popularity of cross dressing as a theme in art and criticism represents, I think, an undertheorized recognition of the necessary critique of binary thinking, whether particularized as male and female, black and white, yes and no, Republican and Democrat, self and other, or in any other way. This critique often takes shape [...] as the creation of what looks like a third term. (10–11)

Garber relates the presence of the cross-dresser on the binary gender spectrum as the "third sex" in a similar way as Peirce locates the third element of the sign in the "interpretant"—the producer or displacer of meaning. Contextually situated, it is relatable to either the male or the female pole of the binary gender spectrum, becoming mobile or disappearing altogether. The "third" element questions binary thinking and introduces a crisis of categories, as it does not represent a category or a term: "the 'third term' is *not a term*. Much less is it a *sex* [...] the 'third' is a mode of articulation, a way of describing a space of possibility. Three puts in question the idea of one: of identity, self-sufficiency, self-knowledge" (11; emphasis in original), just as the "interpretant" of the triadic sign opens the institutionalized meaning of the sign, relativizing the 1:1 relationship between the "representamen" and the "object" of reference and displacing it according to the context and the cultural competency of the meaning-producing agent—the listener, viewer, or reader. Nevertheless, it does not represent *a* third *one*, as a separate category. The "third" deconstructs the complementary, commutable, yet controllable binary relationship of self and other, placing it in the dangerously destabilizing zone of uncertainty (is it a man or a woman?) and "challenges the possibility of harmonious and stable binary symmetry" (12).

Transvestism constitutes a mode of interruption in the normative spectrum or course of things as it reconfigures binary relationships and questions stable, unchallengeable, and instituted identities. It represents a disruptive act of putting in question the "known." Moreover, its deconstructive analogies extend to racial, ethnic, and social relations. Garber claims that the transvestite's most effective function in culture is to indicate what she calls a general "category crisis" with an extraordinary power to disrupt, expose, and challenge, put in question the very notion of the "original," of any stable identity:

> By "category crisis" I mean a failure of definitional distinction, a borderline that becomes permeable, that permits of border crossings from one (appar-

4 ONE-T(W)O-MANY: NEOBAROQUE ARTICULATIONS OF NOMADIC... 289

> ently distinct) category to another: black/white, Jew/Christian, noble/bourgeois, master/servant, master/slave. The binarism male/female, one apparent ground of distinction [...] between "this" and "that," "him" and "me," is itself put in question or under erasure in transvestism, and a transvestite figure, or a transvestite mode, will always function as a sign of overdetermination—a mechanism of displacement from one blurred boundary to another. (16)

As is visible in many of the works that we have examined, the spontaneous or unexpected entrance of the transvestite figure acts as a decentering, gender-bending force in the text, indicating a more general category crisis of a conflictual epistemological nature that leads to destabilizing "comfortable binarity" (Garber 17). That decategorizing force is incarnated in art and in life by the marginal or minoritarian figure. Such gender category crises (inversions) carry over to multiple other axes of class, race, ethnicity, nation, posthumanity. The possibility of crossing the boundaries of gender instills social apprehension of the possibility of crossing racial boundaries, and vice versa. The "transvestite effect" produces a general cultural anxiety in its challenging what Garber refers to as the "vested interests" of patriarchal postcolonial discourse. It becomes a sign and symptom of the dissolution of boundaries, and of the arbitrariness of social law and custom. According to Garber, "transvestism is a space of possibility structuring and confounding culture: the disruptive element that intervenes, not just a category crisis of male and female, but the crisis of category itself" (17). This idea is constitutive of cultural nomadism as transitivity of identity and is the cornerstone of trans-selfhood that foregrounds the inviability of any fixed taxonomy.

Transvestism's mark of excess and hyperbolization in its ultra-convincing desire of passing as the other (female or male) is indicative of its affinity with (neo)baroque forms of parodic figuration. Excess as overflow of a boundary conforms the space of the transvestite. In a transgression of vestmental codes, the cross-dresser violates expected boundaries of gender identification or decorum by going beyond the expected limits of representation, marking the arbitrariness of these limits. This excess is also what provokes its stigmatization and rejection, as it brings about a destabilization of not just the gender category, but of *category* as a pillar of the established system of colonizing patriarchal normativity. The cleavage in dress codes as regulated forms of appearance brought about by the cross-dresser puts all determinate categories of class, gender, sexuality, race, and ethnicity in a state of suspension and "the transvestite is the figure of and for that crisis, the uncanny supplement that marks the place of desire" (Garber 28).

The semiotic reading that Garber makes of the transvestic effect coincides with our interpretation of the cross-dressed, drag queen characters in the performances of La Familia Galán, Lemebel and Casas, and Susy Shock, as a foregrounding of illusion and falsehood, unmasking the sign and symbol as arbitrary constructs in the representation of material reality. This happens in the drag queen's constant assertion of the body as text, of representation as illusion. But the question that these artists raise is "which body"? Garber answers explaining the drag queen's position: "paradoxically, the body here is no body, and nobody, the clothes without the Emperor" (374), just as the "blank sign" of the Baroque voided by its exuberance and depleted of meaning, "a 'blank parody,' as Jameson would suggest. It is a sign that is only simulation" (D'Angelo 291). For the cross-dresser makes the realization that instead of a "natural" referent, the ground of reference of its act/representation of identity should be the figure itself, a mere sign of convention (and hegemony); the referent (as concept or category) is itself a symbolization, it is artifice. The transvestite makes the viewer aware that gender exists only in representation: "But this is the subversive secret of transvestism, that the body is not the ground, but the figure" that repeats itself as a copy of the "natural" by an act of will and artifice taking on an uncanny, transgressive life of its own, and becoming "the fascinating dramatization of the transvestite effect that underlies representation itself" (Garber 374).

In Naty Menstrual's stories, categorizations are deconstructed in the cross-dresser's *travesti* identity by adopting fluctuating binary categories of male and female. Menstrual voiced her view of transvestism in an interview: "The transvestite is what this person wants to be, if I want to have a macho voice, more macho than you, I can have it and be a transvestite" (Peralta 109; my translation). As one of the most notable trans activists in Argentina, the late Lohana Berkins once stated: "What we are saying is that we are neither a man nor a woman. I am a transvestite, a person who has a genitality and who can live perfectly constructed under another identity or under another gender, which is the feminine one" (Berkins quoted

4 ONE-T(W)O-MANY: NEOBAROQUE ARTICULATIONS OF NOMADIC... 291

by Peralta 109).[16] This, again, is reminiscent of Garber's notion of the "third sex"—the cross-dresser occupying Santiago's "entre-lugar" or "space in-between," an intersection of the categories of male and female. As Peralta observed, in Menstrual's stories,

> Her characters oscillate permanently between the poles of the feminine and the masculine, without establishing themselves definitively in either of the two. While their names and external signs establish identifications with women, other characteristics, such as the use of physical strength and the assumption of an active role in the sexual relationship, refer to what is conventionally interpreted as masculine [...]. [T]he images projected by the transvestites in *Continuadísimo* dialogue with these paradigms, recreate them and combine them with references to popular culture, producing a series of tensions between the real and the imaginary, from which emerge the [narrative] *personalities* [...]. (110; my translation)

The mutant identities of the characters undergo further transformations. As marginal, abject, and victimized, the cross-dresser is inverted through metamorphosis, but also by means of *hir* active role of the disobedient, protecting *hir* integrity in violent situations, struggling to get by in a hostile world, as frequently occurs in Menstrual's *Continuadísimo*. Such disparity between appearance, behavior, and attitude situates transvestism in the transitive space of gender ambiguity, conferring it a subversive dimension.

According to Roberto Echavarren, cross-dressing both relates and contrasts with androgyny in its status of a cultural sign representing "twists of appearances and fugitive identities [*identidades tránsfugas*]" (2008: 5). He depicts these external mutant appearances as friction sites of identity positions that interrogate the heteronormative regime of categories. The figure of the cross-dresser and the androgyne are for him the two fundamental, yet differing in technique, figures, or modes of normative category transgression. Added to the transformation of sexual appearances is the drive for the total transformation of the subject into a different being in the process of metamorphosis. In its form of Transvestism, it depicts the transformative use of the body and the space it occupies, with explicit political purposes, as noted by Sarduy:

---

[16] Peralta quotes from Lohana Berkins (2000), "El derecho absoluto sobre nuestros cuerpos," *América Libre*, September 10, 2010. http://www.nodo50.org/americalibre/. Accessed October 5, 2022.

> The human transvestite is the imaginary appearance and convergence of the three possibilities of mimicry: *cross-dressing* as such, imprinted in the unlimited drive of metamorphosis, of transformation, it is not reduced to the imitation of a real, determined model, but rather it rushes in pursuit of an infinite unreality, which right from the start of the "game" is accepted as such, an unreality ever more elusive and unattainable—to be more and more woman, until surpassing the limit, going beyond woman [...]. (1987c [1982]: 56)

As Sarduy points out, this transformation is not merely a mimetic copy of a model in order to appear/take possession of it, but a transgression of limits imposed by the model to the point of parodically de-naturalizing its conventionality—the basis of its existence. By observing the exuberance of language, visible on the textual surface of the works, an analogy can be made with the concept of a simulating "textual mask" that is writing itself. Sarduy defines the mask as the apparent exteriority of the text, the surface that deceives us because there is nothing behind the surface of the mask. It only hides itself and makes us suppose that it is the essence, the substance itself (1990: 224). Transvestism becomes a metaphor for writing—an act of simulating in the coexistence, in the same body, of antagonistic masculine and feminine signifiers (224).

Androgyny is interpreted both as an erasure or blurring and as a fusion or blending of the distinctions of gender-binary forms of masculinity and femininity. While usually associated with gender, this blurring or blending, may apply to other categories that undergo neutralization of distinctive traits that results in hybrid-syncretic forms. Androgyny is associated with queerness and, as an ambiguation and relativization of categories, it represents a defining trend of the current cultural condition: "This blurring of the boundaries of sexual difference, in the sense of a generalized androgynous drive, is characteristic of post-industrial societies. Lyotard (1988) singles it out as one of the defining features of the postmodern condition: queering identities is a dominant ideology under advanced capitalism" (Braidotti 2006: 49).

In *El andrógino sexuado* (2018), Estrella de Diego focuses on indefinability as one of the driving forces that motivate androgyny, besides desire, mobility, and political action, as "an open struggle for the right not to have a permanent gender or sex in a world of characters representing beauty and ambulatory sexuality that is never detained [...] that grants belonging in the LGBTQ-I community" (16; my translation). She situates androgyny as one of the most ancient manifestations of desire—as an exorcism, as replenishing a void inside the Self by means of the Other, as overcoming fear inspired by the Other—in its ultimate form that is love. It is a form of fusion of One with the Other and a drive toward an ideal state of totality or completeness, "the most dramatic form of the impossibility of liberation" (31). Diego also explains the etymological origin of the word in its compound form of *andro* (man) and *gyne* (woman) that extends to any pairing of opposites, "those polarized concepts that unforgivably and hopelessly attract each other: Heaven/Earth, Light-Darkness, Life/Death" (33; my translation). Yet, the components of femininity and masculinity are the two most determinant ones in the conformation of a dual totality.

In Diego's terms, androgyny is that precipitated encounter with another being in a conciliatory mood, a union that can be interpreted as a fusion of traits and appearances in an image of men looking feminine and women looking masculine (34). Thus, it is also a highly visual procedure, like transvestism, yet with a different, more subtle objective of neutralization of traits rather than their hyperbolization. In the physical aspect of an individual, it is associated with the condition of hermaphroditism, or the presence of masculine and feminine traits within a single body. However, "the purest form of androgyny does not symbolize a state of sexual totality, but rather the perfection of a primordial state, that state in which *autonomy*, *force* and the *feeling of totality* take precedence" (42; emphasis in original). From the perspective of religious studies (Eliade 1969), androgyny is seen as acquiring the meaning of Totality in an ancient and universal formula of *coincidentia oppositorum*, or the coexistence of opposites in a single subject that represents the drive toward the regaining of a Cosmic Unity (originating in the Absolute) from which beings were separated in a subsequent process of decadence (the Biblical Fall), as Diego explains following the theories of Jung and Eliade (41). Mircea Eliade perceives the desire to regain a lost (divine) unity as the motivation for humans to consider opposites as complimentary aspects of a single reality that pulls them toward androgyny (156). He tracks this perception from ancient Greece and the Bible through nineteenth-century Romanticism and *fin de siècle* Modernism, when the idea of androgyny took on a sexual meaning that brings it closer to its modern perceptions, and whose presence we observe in contemporary art and literature. As Eliade explains:

> For the decadent writers, the androgyne means only a hermaphrodite in which the two sexes coexist anatomically and physiologically. It is not any-

more about a plenitude achieved in the fusion of both sexes, but the over-abundance of erotic possibilities. [...] Not the appearance of a new type of humanity [...] but a supposed sensual perfection as a result of the active presence of the two sexes. (126; my translation)

Another approach to androgyny, taken by José Ricardo Chaves in his study of Romantic literature (2005), brings the concept closer to the element of the "third," as we previously exemplified with the ideas of Peirce's "triadic sign" and Garber's "third sex." Chaves situates androgyny "not in a network of differing ideas, but within an opposition of masculine/feminine, in which the androgyne would be set in the middle of the two poles, *between* the sexes, as the late 19th century English poet and reformer Edward Carpenter presents it with his postulation of an 'intermediate sex,' a new version of a 'third sex'" (27; my translation, emphasis in original). Diego stresses the desire of fusion and reunification at any cost that, in its literary-artistic depiction, has taken two fundamental paths: totality by means of love (as union with the ideal being) and emancipation by means of sexual and social equality (Diego 43). Both dimensions stand out in the works that we have addressed in this study, as we could observe in Chap. 3 with the most salient examples of characters in Roberto Echavarren's novels *Ave Roc*, *Diablo en el pelo*, and *Yo era una brasa*, and in Eugenia Prado's *Hembros* with the liberated "divine hermaphrodite."

In the essays *Arte andrógino* (2008) and *Performance* (2000), Roberto Echavarren focuses on the figure of the mutant which he describes as close to the cyborg, "a creature beyond man and woman" (2008: 12), "as a third way to generic classifications" (2000: 16), "a possibility of escape from stable identities, which allows the production of specters and monsters" (2000: 358; my translation of all passages from Echavarren). Superseding the cross-dresser's exaggerated marking of gender, Echavarren describes mutants as those who evade reclassification or any labeling in terms of alternative sexualities or cultural categorizations, as they represent change, mutation, and metamorphosis, but leading to no endgame. However, these changes are based on selective appropriation that maintains a hesitancy that shuns from the extreme poles of masculinity and femininity: the total woman (the cross-dressed *superhembra*) or the total man (the gay *supermacho*). The mutant as androgyne maintains a certain touch of the assigned (original) gender mark and never attempts to conceal a "different" gender underneath the surface. Unlike the cross-dresser, s/he is not parodic in *hir* simulation of the feminine or the masculine, which constitutes just the touch of the indefinite, the feminine "opening" of signification toward ambiguity.

Moreover, it is the transitive incorporation of these elements, their non-static co-presence and actively transformative coexistence in the space of a single body, that characterizes the decentered androgynous identity of the postmodern era. Calling it a mutant identity beyond defined gender, Echavarren explains: "A creature beyond a man or a woman emerges—some will say: it is neither man nor woman—and it embraces N [infinite] sexes" (2008: 12; my translation). Mutant identity is not a simple union of genders or other states, but involves entering a relationship with other individuals; it implies transitions that include the metamorphosis of human into animal, organic, or cosmic: "It is not a myth, it is not the union of Adam and Eve. It is a mutant who, by breaking down differences into itself, can relate to other individuals, to a plant, an animal, the sky but, above all, results in a rig of artificial appendages that impress by their per-plexing combination" (2008: 12–13). This mutant self is not just search-ing for an inexistent complement of what it doesn't possess, it is incorporating the "other" element into *one*self, as part of its hybrid self: "An androgyne is not in search of another half […] it is an accretion of power by a plural attraction. Accretion escapes from conventional territo-ries and implies confusion" (2008: 13). The mutant evades a fixed identity because s/he is in the dynamic process of becoming, transiting conven-tionally defined identity options in a spectrum found within him or her-self, and enters a combinatory game that transforms *hir*self into something else: "If we lose sight of this spectrum, we will fall into new classifications, gender prisons and oppressive postures like the previous ones" (2008: 13).

Gender roles acquire a performative dimension and, in combination with the poetic word incorporated in Echavarren's works, result in the staging of trans* gender-sexuality-identity within the subjects that embody it. The enactment of identity also occurs in the text by way of crossings and short-circuits of elaborate prose, essayistic reflection, and poetic figuration. The identities in fugue-like movement, represented in the novels by Jim, Julián, and Lágrima Ríos,[17] are trans(-itive/-gressive) identities that embody a transformative drive for multiplicity, or "meta-morphosis of the multiple into the multiple" (Panesi in Echavarren 2000:

---

[17] The protagonist and first-person narrator of the novel *Yo era una brasa* (Montevideo: HUM, 2009) about the intercultural/-sexual transits of an Afro-Uruguayan dance vedette. Due to lack of space, we omit a more detailed analysis of this character.

167; my translation). The reading of *Ave roc*, *El diablo en el pelo*, and the poetic-critical collection *Performance* detaches us from any categorization in a feeling of "hatred for identity and for identifications: movement and turmoil preserve from fixity; there is no arrest of the image nor capture of any subject" (Panesi in Echavarren 168). There is rather a rejection of the exclusive poles of binary sexual identities and of their identifying reinforcements of hetero and homosexuality. Mobility and transitivity imply, in a baroque way, the excess of multiplicity's loss of limits and the *horror vacui* as an aesthetically (and conceptually) exaggerating impulse to fill any space (corporal, conceptual) to the point of an immeasurable surplus: the excrement, the golden bath of the ornament, of the jewel, of the work of art, as both Lezama (1957) and Sarduy (1987b) worded it. The indeterminacy of the androgynous nomadically wanders along the fluctuating paths of borderland indeterminacy, the no-man's-land of empty spaces to be filled, contrasting with exaggerated gender polarization of the transvestite's proliferating baroque supplementation of distinctive signs on the surface of the body, the artwork.

Echavarren's novel *El diablo en el pelo* exemplifies the androgyne with the figure of Julián, the queer, non-conformist, and, above all, Uruguayan emo. As a *Mestizo*, s/he falls outside the ethnic-racial and sexual molds shaped by the uniformizing majority of White-Hispanic Uruguayan society (Fig. 4.3).

In the novel *Ave roc*, the main character-Jim's rebellious and androgynous figure, attire, and performance, contrived with ornate language and intricate narrative devices, points to both masculine and feminine elements, transforming him into an androgynous icon of sixties' pop culture. The frequent "points of passage," (as seen in Bellatin's novels [2000, 2015] and Perlongher's) essays [1997], overlayered intersectionally in the domains of the sexual and ethnic-racial, produce feedback between Western pop culture and Amerindian traditions, in the manner of Ortiz's transculturation. In both novels, ethnic, racial, and cultural miscegenation takes place with transitions between Western culture and the marginalized (and disappearing) Indigenous elements of the Mojaves in California and the Charrúas in Uruguay. Here, the reference is Rincón's simultaneity and García Canclini's hybridization. The cross-cultural interaction of diverse elements within the body of the same subject, be it emo Julián, mutant Jim, or Afro-Uruguayan Lágrima, characterizes the multiple, rhizomatic androgyne. As Juan Pablo Sutherland explains in the Introduction to *Arte andrógino*:

Fig. 4.3 Arturo Pozo, an androgynous emo. (Photo by José Miguel Serrano, Ecuador, 2007. Source: Wikimedia Creative Commons)

Here, there is an identity, but there is an elopement [*fuga*]. Echavarren reminds us that "the emo is a punk adolescent, feminized, softened (…) Gender identity is something that is not raised here, it is denied; it is not raised at all." […] Echavarren constructs an androgynous epic that interrogates the politics of representation of the masculine and the feminine, proposing new cultural readings to inhabit the body, reinvent gender or evaporate it to extinction. […] Echavarren proposes a nomadic transit accompanied by dandies, mutants, androgynes, emos, katoeys, glam rockers, fetishes, all of them vanishing points of a politics of style. (Echavarren 2008: 8–9; my translation)

The androgyny that populates Echavarren's narrative points to a philosophical questioning of any stable, closed notion of sexual and, by extension, ethnic, racial, national, social, or cultural identity. Echavarren creates a fugacious trans-self that escapes gender, sexual, and ethnic categorizations whose remnants transit the trans-self, momentarily injecting it with elements of otherness. Adrián Cangi refers to the "baroque soul" of both Perlongher and Echavarren's work as having made a "libidinization against the self," breaking with the notion of fixed identities that are instituted under crystallized and polarized forms, adding that: "Echavarren, in particular, opened a surface of magnetization of the desiring mobilities encoded in the figure of the androgynous, as a third way in the midst of generic classifications" (Echavarren 2000: 16; my translation). In his works, the androgynous subject is conceived as a mutant or spawn, close to a cyborg, that opens a line of flight in the constitution of subjectivity. As a self beyond man and woman, embracing both or infinite sexes, the mutant breaks out from binarism in the open space of writing, but also in the space of music or any art. Echavarren states in *Performance* that a work of art opens "a possibility of escape from stable identities, which allows the production of mutants and monsters" (2000: 358). To illustrate such "identities on the run," he prefers to speak of mutants like Jim (Morrison) and emos like Julián, who go against the fixedness of identity, because they are in the process of becoming, impossible to apprehend. Androgynous rock music styles are neither masculine nor feminine and do not fail to produce monstrous images of mutants, as the Japanese rock band Tokyo Hotel illustrates. Echavarren's aesthetic appreciation is a starting point for formulating a theoretical proposal for a transitive *un*-identity of a trans-self that emerges in the gray spaces of the fissures of normative identity, the "in-betweenness" of established categories of gender, race, ethnicity, nationality, social group, or even humanity. Cangi states that: "As an anti-identity, the androgynous is reborn in every hiatus of history in which desire, condemned to dissatisfactions, ordered in a framework and subject to norms, is unleashed" (Echavarren 2000: 17). Androgynous desire sets off a sort of "style war" waged by the lower classes of society against the officialized, market-driven fashion imposed by the establishment of capitalist power in the hands of the elite. Style is individual and can be contentious, unlike fashion which is collective and conformist. It is the analogy that Echavarren makes when speaking of Elvis Presley "who determines something like a 'trumpet blast,' a style that makes the status quo of the empire collapse like the trumpet of Jericho and that declares itself a national danger" (2000: 322; my translation). In Sutherland's words, "Echavarren once again unveils the strategies, the devices of dissolution, an identity in fugue escaping the classic politics of representation of the masculine and the feminine" (2008: 8; my translation).

As we pointed out in the works of Echavarren, Bellatin, Hilst, Eltit, Sarduy, and Lemebel, the semantic proliferation and condensation of the androgynous character, alongside the exaggerated opulence of the transvestite's permutation, situate these subjects in the borderlands of identity, where they nomadically cross the bounds of categorical normativity. The transvestite, who assumes otherness by inversion of the masculine and feminine, does not completely leave behind the traces of the original self. Likewise, the androgyne's neutralizing adoption of both genders and sexual orientations in a combinatory mode is a search of something encompassing, not abandoned in the performance, or rather transit, of multiple identities as alternating forms of selfhood. In the neobaroque text, or in its performative staging, we again observe an analogy between the transvestite's and androgyne's simulation of sexuality and ethnicity, and the process of writing/staging as enactment of selfhood in a process of nomadic identity figuration.

Metamorphosis

Another transformative operation within the nomadic subject is metamorphosis, or the subject's mutation in terms of genders, sexualities, and identities, as well as texts with interchanging literary genres. This transformative effect opens the subject marked by difference of gender, sex, race, ethnicity, or literary-artistic form to change, to be "one" *and* "other." As contrastive references in the constitution of the subject, categorical differences need *not* be eliminated by merely inverting or completely mutating into an other "one," a socially enforced role. Instead, Rosi Braidotti proposes "metamorphoses" as in-depth transformations to be enacted *within* the nomadic identity process of constituting the self (2002: 38). She relates it to an "instability at the heart of the self" (2002: 40). Metamorphosis would imply, therefore, a mutual, multidirectional transformation, a transfusion of sorts, of two or more gender, racial, ethnic, national, or social categories into a mutated self that incorporates multiples, but does not get rid of its base identity, nor that of any of the "others." The mutating subject is not fixed into categories, but rather represents the ongoing *process* of ex- or inter-changing them, while transforming into something else, a trans*self, made up of fragments that are mutated by mutual influence.

Metamorphosis is related to queerness in that it involves a transformative process of subjectivity resulting in a departure from imposed normative categories, and the formulation of differing variations of selfhood. In *Metamorphoses* (2002), Braidotti refers to the *process* of transformation more than to the resulting outcome that this process produces. It is not the transformed *identity* that matters as much as the very procedure of mutating and reforming it. Queerness, in its destabilizing mobility of dis-/un-identifying in fluid movement, an open, ongoing, and feminine shift in subjectivity, represents an instance of metamorphosis in the realm of sexuality: "Whether in the queer or the radical heterosexual way, I think that a subversive approach to sexual identity and to sexuality is one of the legacies of a feminist, nomadic becoming-woman process. In other words, the object-choice (homo/hetero/perverse) or the choice of sexual lifestyle is far less important than the structural shifts entailed by this process in the structures of the desiring subjects" (2002: 60).

In the process of metamorphosis, the transformation of appearance is motivated by the drive for a total transformation of the subject into a different being. In terms of sexuality, this phenomenon can be related to the transsexual alteration by means of surgery and hormonal modification in the subject's body; the transgender person mutates by a complete subjective identification with the other gender through bodily (or textual) transformation into otherness. But, as Sarduy points out, in this transformation, it is not merely a matter of *copying* a model of otherness to resemble it (mimesis, *trompe-l'oeil*), but to transgress the limits that the model imposes until un-naturalizing it in the very base of its existence, stripping the conventions that govern it, or simply going beyond the model. The mutant transforms into something *unreal* (imaginary and created) that surpasses the limits of the model (the shunned category):

> The human transvestite is the imaginary appearance and convergence of the three possibilities of mimicry: literally *cross-dressing* as imprinting [on the body] the unlimited drive of metamorphosis, of transformation that is not reduced to the *imitation* of a real, determined model, but rushes in the pursuit of an infinite *un*reality, which from the beginning of the "game" is accepted as such, an unreality increasingly elusive and unattainable—to be more and more woman, until surpassing the limit, going beyond the woman. (Sarduy 1987c: 56; emphasis in original)

In the production of simulative artifice, especially in the literary context, by means of such techniques of mimicry and transformation as illusion, *trompe-l'oeil*, and metamorphosis, the aim is not the mimetic copy of something, of another being, by way of mere imitation. Whereas it conserves a suggestion of verisimilitude, it aims at surpassing the model in a

4 ONE-T(W)O-MANY: NEOBAROQUE ARTICULATIONS OF NOMADIC... 301

complete transgression by means of its hyperbolization (parody and exaggeration) to strip the artificiality of the copy participating in the game of linguistic and artistic conventions. It does not imply making a mimetic (realistic) copy, exact and plausible, but going beyond the original, as in the exaggerated copy made by the transvestite:

> The butterfly turned into a leaf, the man turned into a woman, but also the anamorphosis and the *trompe-l'oeil*, do not copy, do not define and justify themselves within the true proportions, but produce, using the position of the observer, including him in the imposture, the verisimilitude of the model; as in an act of predation, they incorporate its appearance, they simulate it. (Sarduy 1987c [1982]: 60)

The incorporation of the reader/spectator and their point of view within the text is one of the defining features of the work of art, as can be perceived in the fragmented metafictional narrative of Bellatin, Eltit, and Anzaldúa, and in Susy Shock's performance. The metanarrative opens the work to the reader's/viewer's creative intervention in perceiving the metamorphosis of the characters.

Several examples from the analyzed works demonstrate the role and operation of metamorphosis in these works by means of such simulating and metanarrative mechanisms. Mario Bellatin reveals in his novels a particular sensitivity to transformative techniques, particularly the narrative fugue, visible in the construction of his mutating characters. The narrative, undergoing metamorphosis parallelly to the characters, contains "vanishing points" or fugues of the plot that flow in multiple directions, analogically to the transformations of the characters and their stories. In an unpublished interview, Bellatin explained the alteration of his characters and the "transformist" nature of his narrative. He emphasized the importance of these "vanishing points" that multiply as the story progresses in order to avoid any kind of realist or logical-normative schematism. By including several levels of metadiscourse in *Salón de belleza* and *Lecciones para una liebre muerta*, the narrator himself unfolds as a transvestite character and enters the narrative as a writer "Mario Bellatin" in a polyphonic and metafictional manner, opening up possibilities for the realization of the story by a second, subordinate narrator, and for its final recreation by the reader turned co-author. Bellatin prefers the illusive and mutating form of the "novel-as-process." By including playful and sexually fluctuating characters/narrators along with the reader, and by

302   K. A. KULAWIK

rupturing arbitrarily established literary genres, the unstable narrative form allows him to transcend to the level of metafiction, a feature of both neobaroque and postmodern narrative. The boundaries between novelistic fiction and documentary discourse (e.g., in frequent footnotes) or of palimpsestic rewriting of existing literature (e.g., Austrian Joseph Roth's novel) are also blurred by means of numerous historical and "documented," but ultimately apocryphal, references: "One of the most surprising discoveries for literature, not just for that of Joseph Roth but for all of twentieth-century literature, seems to be in the mechanism for how a role assigned to a particular character drifts, quite suddenly, into another, completely different one" (2015: 11). The logic of Bellatin's fiction is completely internal, autonomous, and malleable, as expressed in another metanarrative comment in the novel *Jacobo el mutante*: "Precisely when the reader assumes, quite plausibly, not just Jacob Pliniak's presence in the text but, especially, his right to remain in its structure, our character transforms, with no great leap, into his supposed adopted daughter, Rose Plinianson" (11). The metafictional author in the novel suggests that the incorporation of the reader and her/his point of view is a defining feature of the work. In other interviews, Bellatin highlights the importance of "the text itself creating the mechanisms to be decoded" (Bosch 2007: 88); he also affirms that "[a]ll my books are a kind of textual puns or devices seeking to make the reader not read what he or she is reading" (Hind 2004: 200). The logic that Bellatin proposes launches the text into a space of open possibilities of realization by the reader incorporating her/his point of view as part of the metamorphosis process involving the characters' ever-changing avatars.

The mutant identities of the characters in stories by Naty Menstrual undergo various forms of transformation. Marginal, abject, and victimized, the cross-dresser's identity is altered through metamorphosis—an invertible transformation of gender and sexual categories—but also by means of *hir* assumed active role of the disobedient *loca*, determined to seek pleasure, protecting her integrity in situations of aggression and surviving in an antagonistic milieu of prostitution and homophobic violence. Sometimes this happens by animalization, adopting animal traits, or monstrous forms, which represent the abject (thus shocking and subversive) element in heterosexual convention, as observed by Peralta:

> The reappropriation of figures and words used from the discourse of heteronormative/transphobic tenor, allows Menstrual an inversion of the mean-

ings conventionally attributed to them. If, following Judith Butler (2008: 26), we understand transvestite bodies as abject, trembling on the border of the human and the animal, Naty Menstrual will make of that abjection a style, will turn those animalized bodies into examples of a subversion to the established order. (110–11; my translation)

Abjection, accompanied by humor, places the transvestite character in the neutral "in-between" space of gender categorizations of "trans-subversion" or the "subversion of the trans" represented by the transvestite character in a "crude and eschatological language" (Peralta 118). As we have seen in the performance of Susy Shock's monstrous identity, the trans(-gressive) character she adopts is part of the metamorphous transformation intended to destabilize the viewer/listener's perception and subvert heteronormativity in the established order of cultural signs, as instituted categories. The abject imagery of the mutant is a destabilizing element of the symbolic range. Let us recall the examples of Menstrual's La Mr. Ed mutating in the bathtub into a plant that takes over her entire apartment, of the cross-dresser whose entrails transformed into a man-eating monster in "Amada Kombucha," and in cross-dressers Sissy Lobato, Sabrina Duncan, Minita, and multiple anonymous narrators in ambiguous states of transitivity and fluidity between human, animal, and monster. As stated by Peralta: "Julia Kristeva (2006: 11) relates abjection to 'that which disturbs an identity, a system, an order. That which does not respect the limits, the places, the rules'" (118; my translation). According to Kristeva, the abject is sublimated through artistic and literary forms, as well as sexual behaviors that the society rejects. It forms a part of cultural discourse by way of art, literature, philosophy, and religious ritual. In metamorphosis, as boundaries are crossed, the abject is dignified. The multiple identities of the cross-dresser are inverted yet sublimated through the artistic form, as seen in the linguistically exuberant and dynamic narrative of Menstrual.

The metamorphic process of change that Gloria Anzaldúa's new *mestiza* undergoes through the stages of the serpent-woman involves sacrificing one's body, "for only through the body, through the pulling of flesh, can the human soul be transformed. And for images, words, stories to have this transformative power, they must arise from the human body— flesh and bone—and from the earth's body" (2007 [1987]: 97). As Anzaldúa explains in the chapter "*La conciencia de la mestiza*" of

Borderlands... (2007 [1987]: 99–113), the transformation of the body and spirit in the passage through the border zone of *nepantla* implies "a more whole perspective, one that includes rather than excludes'" (2009: 10). Its foundation is the female "other" as the "stranger" that faces the male in opposition to masculine hegemony; she stands as man's nightmarish appendage, "his Shadow-Beast" (2007 [1987]: 39). As a plural subject, she also incorporates queer and all minoritarian identities that are subaltern in the neocolonial hierarchy. Queerness reflects the dominant heterosexual's fear of difference as otherness and is therefore marginalized to the "inferior state of the sub-human, in-human, non-human" (2007 [1987]: 40). To acquire resilience, the new *mestiza* (as queer) passes through stages of the Serpent—Coatlicue, the Nahuatl Earth Mother goddess—metamorphosizing into the Shadow Beast and acquiring traits of the monstrous, hybrid, queer, feminine mutant, the other of masculine normativity, and, again, reminiscent of Argentine Susy Shock's monstrous self.

Forging identity implies a metamorphosis of the mind and body. Situated in the borderlands, the narrative subject of the new *mestiza* character consciously undergoes different animal incarnations that are "older than gender [...] I think of *La Víbora*, Snake Woman. Forty years it's taken me to enter into the Serpent, to acknowledge that I have a body, that I am a body and to assimilate the animal body, the animal soul" (Anzaldúa 2007 [1987]: 48). In her many transformations, the narrative I-subject passes through stages of assimilation with the animal, the beast, the snake, in a "Coatlicue State of the Mother-Serpent." She searches for her otherness, her mark of difference in what she calls "the mark of the beast," comparable to Susy Shock's Monster identity: "the secret I tried to conceal was that I was not normal, that I was not like the others. I felt alien, I knew I was an alien. I was the mutant stoned out of the herd, something deformed with evil inside" (2007 [1987]: 65). Metamorphosis plays a crucial role in this process based on shifting from one entity to another and assuming oneself in the Other: "My 'awakened dreams' are about shifts, thought shifts, reality shifts, gender shifts; one person metamorphoses into another" (2007 [1987]: 92). Her path "towards a new consciousness" leads to the emergence of a new feminine *mestiza* awareness, "*una consciencia de mujer.*" Also for Echavarren, it is a morally sensitive, socially aware "consciousness of the Borderlands" that is determined by metamorphous shifts and changes (2010: 25).

Posthuman Cyborgs

Feminist/feminine discourse envisions alternative imaginaries or forms of representation of selfhood that are estranged from the dominant figure of the Human and its symbolization in the Logos. Those alternative imaginaries include posthuman states. Braidotti emphasizes the limitations of a logocentric approach in the constitution of identity and the possibility of other modes of reasoning:

> [Haraway] proposes instead the figure of the cyborg, that is to say a high-tech imaginary, where electronic circuits evoke new patterns of interconnectedness and affinity [...] committed to the radical task of subverting conventional views and representations of human and especially female subjectivity. [...] [They] rely on alternative figurations as a way out of the old schemes of thought. (1994: 3)

Braidotti points to Haraway's preference of multiplicities as multiply displaced identities that are the result of a non-linear, non-fixed, non-unitary subjectivity that is "situated in close proximity to woman, the native, the dispossessed, the abused, the excluded, the 'other' of the high-tech clean and efficient bodies sponsored by contemporary culture" (2002: 139). In "A Cyborg Manifesto," one of the chapters of *Simians, Cyborgs, and Women* (1991), Haraway defines the cyborg as "a cybernetic organism, a hybrid of machine and organism, a creature of social reality as well as a creature of fiction. Social reality is lived social relations, our most important political construction, a world-changing fiction. [...] Contemporary science fiction is full of cyborgs—creatures simultaneously animal and machine, who populate worlds ambiguously natural and crafted" (149). The cyborg's presence also extends to medicine, where its power of intimacy as a coded device, a coupling between organism and machine, was not fully considered in the history of sexuality before Foucault's early premonitions of technological domination. The cyborg's unsettling presence is explained by Haraway in its genderless, category-free, and disjointed nature: "The cyborg is a creature in a post-gender world; it has no truck with bisexuality, pre-oedipal symbiosis, unalienated labour, or other seductions to organic wholeness through a final appropriation of all the powers of the parts into a higher unity" (150). As "an ultimate self untied at last from all dependency," the cyborg is beyond categorizations, and cannot be claimed by any binding definition (thus, domination and control). In this sense, the cyborg is undefinable and "resolutely committed to partiality, irony, intimacy, and perversity" (151).

As a menace for the political and cultural establishment, Haraway's cyborg "is about transgressed boundaries, potent fusions, and dangerous possibilities which progressive people might explore as one part of needed political work" (154). That work Haraway sees in the cyborg's at least partial acceptance of the inevitable symbiosis with the technological, without totally rejecting any parts that might serve humanity's transitional state of technological transformation and "silently" resisting the negative aspects of dehumanization and domination that comes with technology. As an opening toward such a clandestine opposition is the experience of "fractured identities." As the cyborg does not identify with any patriarchally or logocentrically established category, its mere fact of non-identifiability in itself is a subversive ("perversive") political statement. The "needed political work" mentioned by Haraway indicates a dynamic and mobile direction of identity displacement in a "slightly perverse shift of perspective [that] might better enable us to contest for meaning, as well as for other forms of power and pleasure in technologically mediated societies" (155). Fractured identities mark out a technologically neutralized space that self-consciously incapacitates the subject's acting on the basis of "natural" or hegemonically imposed identification, enabling its acting only in conjunction with conscious coalitions of affinity and political kinship outside normative cultural patterns. This political-subversive aspect of the cyborg is represented in Eugenia Prado's *Hembros* ("*Fe-males*"), which we established in our previous analysis as an example of post-human identity fracturing.

For N. Katherine Hayles, the construction of the cyborg is centered on informational pathways connecting the organic body to its prosthetic extensions. The non-identity of this posthuman (because non-unitary and not fully organic-based) entity is explained in the centrality of the information flow between carbon-based organic and silicon electronic components in a single system constituting the cyborg and its posthuman character. According to Hayles, "the posthuman subject is an amalgam, a collection of heterogeneous components, a material-informational entity whose boundaries undergo continuous construction and reconstruction" (1999: 3). The fluid and disembodied nature of information that constitutes the cyborg undercuts its unitary will and sense of belonging to a single self, "for the posthuman's collective heterogeneous quality implies a distributed cognition located in disparate parts that may be in only tenuous communication with one another. [...] the distributed cognition of the posthuman complicates individual agency" (3–4). Lacking the universal human subject's unified, consistent identity, the posthuman cyborg accentuates hybridity and "the liberatory potential of a dispersed subjectivity distributed among diverse desiring machines" (4) that Hayles calls, after Deleuze and Guattari, "bodies without organs," in the sense that posthumans represent more sets of informational processes than fully (or only) organic wholes, "because information had lost its body" and "embodiment is not essential to the human being" (4). It involves a particular cybernetically (digitally and informationally) fluid construction of subjectivity based on flows of information.

The posthuman does not exclude the human, but rather "'human' and 'posthuman' coexist in shifting configurations that vary with historically specific contexts" (6). An additional feature of the posthuman condition represented by the cyborg is its collective orientation of a "posthuman collectivity," an "I" transformed into a "we" of multiple autonomous agents that operate jointly to articulate the self in impulses of dialogical connections. "The infectious power of this way of thinking gives 'we' a performative dimension" (Hayles 6), as observed in Prado's *Hembros*.

In her assumption that otherness includes the posthuman element of the cyborg as one of its minoritarian or subaltern articulations, Braidotti points to multiple "counter-figurations" that function for the non-Oedipalized (not sexually predetermined) unconscious and "trace a sort of becoming-animal: the cyborg, the coyote, the trickster, the onco-mouse [and] produce alternative structures of otherness" (2002: 139). Posthuman-cyborg identity enters the parameters of a non-linear and non-unitary subjectivity that displays proximity to Deleuze's rethinking of becoming-animal "as a figuration for the humanoid hybrids we are becoming" (139). Nomadic body-machines correspond to anti-representational, non-profit assemblages that encourage us to think about the in-depth transformations of post-industrial culture as a spectrum of changes carried out through "firm feminist interventions" within philosophical nomadism "in order to re-inscribe the politics of location and of sexual difference" within a context of techno-industrial and cybernetic "meta(l)-morphoses" or processes of "becoming machine" (212–13). These constitute a set of mutations, released in our times with a negative connotation of the monstrous and grotesque imaginary inherited from the nineteenth century. Literary and artistic representation, such as sci-fi, posthuman speculative fiction, and, in our case, neobaroque fiction and performance, proposes to de-pathologize these new mechanical/cybernetic elements affecting current transformations of the human (267).

Alongside *Hembros'* depiction of the cyborg, Eugenia Prado's novel *Lóbulo* offers an example of how the human-cyborg boundaries emerge and operate, thanks to discursive devices forming or transgressing the intersections of human and posthuman identity. Nicolás Poblete (2000) and J. Andrew Brown (2007), who draw on the concepts of earlier theorists such as Deleuze and Guattari (1980) and later studies by Haraway (1991) and Hayles (1999), address the symbiotic operation of the cyborg in Prado's novel. On his part, Poblete refers to Deleuze and Guattari in observing the binary-combinatory character of machines and devices, since they wish to couple with another, not by fusing but as coupling of co-presences: "schizophrenia is the universe of productive and reproductive desiring machines. […] Desiring-machines are binary machines, obeying a binary law or set of rules governing associations: one machine is always coupled with another" (Poblete 3; my translation). The cyborg produces couplings or combinations of supplements, in the presence of a "one" and an "other." In their mutual desire, they generate pleasure while violating limits and boundaries of sexual identity. In their transitivity, they disrupt the structures not only of the traditional family but also of any conventional categorization in terms of binary gender. Cyborgs reflect "an automatic and posthuman universe" in which "spaces begin to be overwhelmed by external encounters that start to degenerate identities" (3).

In his study of the novel *Lóbulo*, J. Andrew Brown points out the relationship between the decomposed subjectivity of the character and the fragmented text of the novel: "Prado accentuates the electrical (and metaphorical) changes of Sofía's body with a division of identity where the narrator vacillates between third and first person, along with the electrical power that also causes abrupt changes in the narrative itself" (808). The critic observes and comments on the appearance of the cyborg that progressively invades and merges with the protagonist. This reasoning follows Katherine Hayles's line of thought on the configuration of posthuman identity: as "seamlessly articulated with intelligent machines" without significant differences or demarcations between bodily existence and computer simulation (Hayles 3).

Prado confirms that mutation and the accompanying adaptability of Sofía's character, as openness to technological supplements, are key elements in this novel: "For many, the human experience is crisscrossed with machines; we are technological animals. I'm telling you, without my computer, I am nothing; I almost live *in* my computer, connected to the Web all the time in front of a screen" (Kulawik 2012: 233; my translation and emphasis). These ideas of penetrability and openness point more forcefully toward the theme of fusion of living bodies with machines, noted earlier by Haraway: "the cyborg is a hybrid being of flesh and technological apparatus who, by that hybridity, defies the classifications of traditional society" (Brown 802). Generally, critics highlight this double—physical-*bodily rooted* and borderland—aspect of posthuman nomadic subjectivity.

4.3 On the Borders of Identity: In-Between Flows of the Trans-Self

The works of contemporary Chicane artists and writers display a new perception of the concepts of the border. Visual artist Guillermo Gómez-Peña asserts in *The New World Border* (a book of essays he calls "a disnarrative ode to hybrid America," 1996: i) that "his" America is a whole continent and not just a country; it is not traceable on geopolitical maps. Both in his performance and his essays, he proposes "to open the matrix of reality and introduce unsuspected possibilities" (1996: 6) that he represents in his performance in the form of cross-ethnic transvestism. In a more figurative dimension of the poetic testimonial *Borderlands/La Frontera* (1987), Gloria Anzaldúa proposes a symbolic transiting of the border between the United States and Mexico through the intermediary nomadic figure of the new *mestiza* whose borderland experience constitutes an intersexual transcultural self. She portrays it as a "third being" situated between opposing binary powers: "In attempting to work out a synthesis, the self has added a third element which is greater than the sum of its severed parts. That third element is a new consciousness—a *mestiza* consciousness—and though it is a source of intense pain, its energy comes from continual creative motion" (2007: 101–02). Similarly, Bolivian critic Silvia Rivera Cusicanqui proposes the Aymaran term of *ch'ixi* as a liminal state of thirdness set in between (binary) categories of selfhood, an intermediate condition of indefinite yet conciliatory in-betweenness. The term enters Western cultural discourse as a decolonizing device of Indigenous origin. These "unsuspected possibilities" of thirdness are akin to Silviano Santiago's idea of *entre-lugar* and Néstor Perlongher's *puntos de pasaje*. Together, they confirm a vision of "in-betweenness" as a state of transitive flows across the borders of identity. Borders appear as transitional spaces

310   K. A. KULAWIK

and zones of transit of subjectivity and trans-identity formation. While the articulation of a transitive selfhood has its foundation in the traditional concepts of hybridity, *mestizaje*, and heterogeneity that we presented in Chap. 2, its nomadic dimension is fully perceived with the Indigenous concepts of *nepantla* and *ch'ixi*. In the following subsections, these concepts will reveal the mechanisms that operate in the nomadic state of mind and body occupying the intermediate zone of political and categorical boundaries.

4.3.1 Borderland Spaces of In-Between: From Nepantla to Ch'ixi, from "dangerous beasts" to Border Crossers

Gloria Anzaldúa and Cherríe Moraga, among other Chicana authors, have used the Indigenous concept of "nepantlism" to describe a transitory and transformative state of inhabiting an intermediate state of subjectivity (soul, mind, and body) experienced in the spiritual dimension of the mythical *nepantla*, a space-in-between existential categories of being, of selfhood, of life and death. Extending the scope of the term, they apply it to the Chicana experience shifting between multiple cultural values determined by hegemonically established categories. According to this approach, Chicane identity is formed in a "feminine" process of transitioning between subjective categories and, by extension, between cultural values. The space of these spiritual-symbolic transits corresponds to a mystical transitive zone of in-betweenness that Chicana theorists refer to, using the Nahuatl term, as *nepantla*. Translated as "the land in the middle," the term has been used by Chicana scholars to name the transitional space inhabited by the border subject.

According to Anzaldúa, it is possible to achieve an inner transformation (opening) of one's identity by assuming a "tolerance for ambiguity" when sharing elements and signs of the opposite (to one's) identity, and by adopting and transcending, deconstructing and reconstructing them. One shifts from being "one" to becoming the "other" by embodying a *nahual*—the shape-shifting ancestral spirit of the Nahuatl peoples. This implies becoming vulnerable to "strange ways of thinking," being able to transform oneself into a tree, a coyote, into another person, into another sex, resulting in an *amasamiento* ("kneading") that Anzaldúa presented as constitutive of the multiform and mobile identity of the new *mestiza* (2007: 103). This transformative interaction of beings brings Anzaldúa's proposal close to neobaroque aesthetics that rely on the *par excellence*

4 ONE-T(W)O-MANY: NEOBAROQUE ARTICULATIONS OF NOMADIC... 311

transformist techniques of the American Colonial Baroque style: metamorphosis, anamorphosis, and *trompe l'oeil*. As Severo Sarduy pointed out (1978 [1972], 1990), a prominent example of such neobaroque strategy is transvestism as a simulating transformist technique of illusionism. Assuming a deconstructive stance on cultural identity, Anzaldúa's writing incorporates neobaroque techniques of transformism, proliferation, decentering, shape shifting, and metamorphosis embodied in her transitive character-figures. Her "new *mestiza*" is the incarnation of an intercultural and transitive consciousness that is also feminine and nomadic as it emerges from the borderlands.

Anzaldúa's fragmented, centerless, and nomadic new *mestiza* constitutes a rebellious feminine trans-identity that is still inclusive of only positively masculine, homosexual, trans*, and any other "outsider" minorities. It operates in an openly divergent mode that situates transversally (both horizontally and vertically) its relation to the Other. It possesses a character that is resilient in withstanding conflicts through a "tolerance for contradictions." The flexible dynamic of its horizontal and vertical psychic coordinates allows it to transgress obliquely the formations of Western thought and move toward a more divergent, yet inclusive, holistic mode of becoming that is characterized by an equivocal ambiguity of self. She learns to adopt multiple and divergent points of view while constantly changing perspectives between Hispanic, Indigenous, and Anglo-European points of view, in what she calls "juggling of cultures." She lives with a multiple personality that operates in a pluralistic mode using "ambivalence as a tool and a weapon" (2007: 101). The *mestiza* consciousness resembles an androgynous (or polyvalent) identity, one that the author explains as combining, in the manner of yin and yang, multiple binaries such as feminine and masculine, Hispanic Mexican and Anglo-American, European and Indigenous.

The new *mestiza* character that emerges from *Borderlands* is a subject that operates in intersectional combinations of categories that conform a transitive coexistence of identities. Other identities cross intersectionally in the formative process of the Self: "The struggle is inner: Chicano, Indio, American Indian, *mojado, mexicano*, immigrant Latino, Anglo in power, working class Anglo, Black, Asian—our psyches resemble the border towns and are populated by the same people" (2007: 109). In a characteristically bilingual poem that resorts to code switching, titled "To live in the Borderlands means you," the lyrical subject expresses the interstitial character of "in-betweenness" of the *mestiza* figure and summarizes the

312   K. A. KULAWIK

non-essential character of the plural borderland self that, like a nomad, transcends the notions of a single unitary identity to show the multiplicity and mobility of the minoritarian identifications that make it up:

> [you] are neither *hispana india negra española*
> *ni gabacha*,[18] eres mestiza, mulata, half-breed
> caught in the crossfire between camps
> while carrying all five races on your back
> not knowing which side to turn to, run from. (2007: 216; cursive in original)

Identifying with both sides is also suffering rejection by either or both for trespassing and "betraying" traditional categories. The poem ends with the verses: "in the Borderlands/you are the battleground [...]/to survive the Borderlands/you must live *sin fronteras*/be a crossroads" (216–17).

For Anzaldúa, identity is a creation of the self through the process of writing that situates in the in-between space of *nepantla*. In *This Bridge We Call Home* (2002), she calls it a story of *la búsqueda de conocimiento*, a quest for knowledge and a spiritual faculty (*la facultad*) that gives her purpose, her life a meaning and a sense of belonging. This ability and knowledge lead her writing, not without distress, to a *mestiza* self-awareness (562–63). They situate the Self at the interstices of the in-between state of *nepantla*, where it transitorily assumes multiple identities and connects them from the "home" vantage point of a bridge: "For you writing is an archetypal journey home to the self, *un proceso de crear puentes* [a process of creating bridges] to the next phase, next place, next culture, next reality. You realize that 'home' is that bridge, the in-between place of nepantla and constant transition, the most unsafe of all spaces. [...] And nepantla is the only space where change happens" (2002: 574).

In *Radical Chicana Poetics* (2013), Ricardo Vivancos Pérez explains the meaning of *nepantla* as a subjective process of transitional and concurrent positioning of cultural values in the identity articulation process of becoming (81). It involves movement in the dimensions of both space and time. *Nepantla* is associated with the spiritual space of the subject's situation in a transitional state of in-betweenness "that is not only geopolitical, but also psychological" and that relates to "situational moments of

---

[18] In current usage, this is a Chicano term for an Anglo White woman (Anzaldúa 2007: 217). The Spanish word originally referred to a French or Spanish woman in the Americas, and was used especially in colonial times.

4 ONE-T(W)O-MANY: NEOBAROQUE ARTICULATIONS OF NOMADIC... 313

identity crisis" (81). It also forms the basis for Anzaldúa's rearticulation of her early definition of "borderland" as a state of blockage or frozenness, of "her encounter with Medusa in the mirror" in her poetry from the 1980s, "symbolic for her recognition of the mark of the beast in her" (Vivancos 81). In Anzaldúa's later thought, explains Vivancos, "nepantla becomes the term for an abstract, impossible state, virtual but never fixed. It is a state that is defined by its movability and mutability." This borderland condition enables the performative enactment of a continuous becoming that defines the subject's spiritual and physical quest, as well as *hir* individual and collective struggle.

Cherríe Moraga defines *nepantla* as a psychological and intuitive, almost visionary state of mind and body situated in the interstitial space between sites of perception, in the "fissure between vision and lived reality" (Vivancos 82). What Anzaldúa and Moraga describe as a consciousness of a *nepantlera* refers to the feminine ability of seeing "between worlds." In the drawing *Nepantlera*, Chicana artist, performer, and educator Celia Herrera Rodríguez depicts the transformative state of in-betweenness of *nepantla* in the positionings and fragmentation of the female body (Fig. 4.4).

Strategically set in Moraga's text, it is one of seven drawings by Herrera that connect Moraga's essays in *A Xicana Codex of Changing Consciousness* (2011) as if they were separate parts of one rhizomatic body of writing incarnating the Chicana consciousness. Herrera's illustrations are the artistic connecting tissue in Moraga's theoretical work that in several essays presents the different elements flowing across Chicana consciousness. As Vivancos observed, "[t]he statement is clear: art and theory must come together. The *Xicana codex* cannot be shaped only by one kind of artistic representation. The stuff of Xicana writing cannot be fully envisioned through a single univocal or unilateral artistic representation" (83–84). Vivancos explains Herrera's representation of the *nepantlera* as a dismembered visualization of the Aztec goddess Coyolxauhqui adorned with common symbols of Aztec cosmology that serve as junctures linking her body parts. She is a half dis- and "half re-membered" feminine figure that joins multiple states of consciousness into a single and complex transitive identity: "Her body parts are at different stages in the process of being connected" (84). Of note is the skull that floats on her side, apparently talking to the writer—a *nepantlera* herself—who establishes connections with "otherness." It reflects the moment of transformation (also from life

Fig. 4.4 *Nepantlera* by Celia Herrera Rodríguez. "Drawings from *A Xicana Codex of Changing Consciousness.*" Handprinted screen-print on Mohawk birch archival paper, 2011. (Courtesy of the artist)

to afterlife) in the process of remembering and conversing with the other (the dead), occurring in that transitional space/state of *nepantla*.

Herrera's depiction of the *nepantlera* as a dismembered interpreter of the in-between zone, a mediator between worlds, dimensions, and categories, is a polycentric visual figuration illustrating the effects of passing through *nepantla*. The strategic in-between position gives the feminine figure the "capacity to see beyond surface phenomena; […] the awareness of changeability and lack of closure; the capacity for self-reflection and repositioning" (Vivancos 84–85). This vantage point entails a strategy of making viewers aware of "the dismemberments involved in any process of transformation" (85). According to Moraga, Herrera's work uncovers spiritual knowledges that underlie all Indigenous cultures before any claiming of territory, borders, and new categories that occurred during

Spanish colonization. She uncovers the *ánima* ("spirit") contained within the major symbols explored by radical Chicana writers, with *nepantla* being one of them. Herrera's *Nepantlera* relies on symbols derived from Nahuatl-Aztec mythology, one of them being the dismembered goddess Coyolxauhqui who was cast out and thrust down from the heavens by her vengeful brother, the god of war, Huitzilopochtli. The dismembered body of the *Nepantlera* is symbolic of the fragmentation of interconnected existential elements, while academic discourse that interprets it, for Moraga "is simply 'making the connections between things'" (207). We can observe *Nepantlera's* connection with neobaroque poetics in that both rely on the decentered, open, and visual symbol. It also connects with twentieth-century semiotics that proposed the opening of meaning, as illustrated by Peirce's three-part sign that includes the transformative role of the interpretant.

According to Moraga, nepantlism's significance is to forestall the real-life loss of knowledge of our Indigenous forebears that current generations of Native Americans experience. The passage through *nepantla* is a spiritual and physical return (by bodily transformation) to that space and that life knowledge that is lost in the consumer-driven materialism that is imposed on Western society by the universalizing-uniformizing neocolonial liberal system of capitalist globalization. In one of her critical and autobiographical essays from *A Xicana Codex* titled "Indígena as Scribe: The (W)rite to Remember," Moraga refers to herself—a writer and educator—as the intermediator in a process of conscientious awakening and a guide in a journey of returning to the lost origins of a people—the "MeXicanos," referring to all Mexicans, Indigenous, and Chican@s. In a setting of liberal multicultural diversity, propagated by official political discourse and the intellectual academia, Moraga criticizes the neutralizing weakness of the terms "hybridity" and *mestizaje*, as they uniformize subjects under a blanket of "monocratic definition" of categories that define allegiances of identity by geopolitical borders that colonialism and modern imperialism have constructed (87–88).

Hence, Moraga's proposal of a "return journey" home. This is also a path of *conocimiento* (echoing Anzaldúa) that leads to a deeper state of knowledge and spiritual awareness, wisdom of the integral self. The path leads through *nepantla*: a passage point, a borderland zone, and a gateway. It is a dual zone of differentiations between one and other, life and death, body and mind. Thus, it is a state of one's contradictory consciousness confronting otherness. For Moraga, this means to return to the "preliterate oppositional consciousness, derived [not from books but] from brutal physical labor, displacement, and profound want." It is an alternative to modern-day Western education that has "made us stupid, forgetful, and even further entrenched in our colonization" (84). She describes the passage through *nepantla* as a will to transit, to return, to change: "so if we are willing to go through the broken places first, through our own acts of self-sabotage and cultural amnesia, we will find our own authentic way home. We may have to borrow or invent along the way, but we have the right to remember. [...] The profound project of transgression can only be achieved by return. We know more than we know we know: the aboriginal mind at work" (84–85). Passage through the borderland space of *nepantla* opens the subject to other ways of knowing, the Native American being one of them:

> At the turn of the century, our divergent identities—indigenous and mixed-blood, transnational and transgender—provide critical approaches to knowings that open roadways to radical transformations in our collective progressive thinking. My own queer and mixed-blood identity resides in the crux of contradictory meanings, where I have suffered the homelessness of queer colored womanhood within the constructs of nationalisms that deny us our female bodies, our desires, our renegade spirits. (88)

The idea of "returning home" that emanates from Moraga's vision is not only to transform *oneself*, but to make progressive social change specific to one's historical and cultural conditions. The return, also by way of *nepantla*, involves the educator, the artist, and the writer. Experiencing nepantlism gives the writer an insight to our *relative* truths, what Moraga refers to as "the social constructions of identity" that lie on the way to the only absolute truth—our ever-impermanence in this world. "We live with a kind of necessary 'double consciousness'—wherein both truths remain in our awareness as we arrive at each obstacle, each opportunity for change in our lives. This is how I understand Gloria's 'Nepantla,' that interstice between both sites of consciousness. She was a nepantlera because she saw between worlds" (126–27).

The figuration of the Chicana as *nepantlera* is part of what Vivancos calls "dangerous beasts poetics," referring to a creative educational undertaking of raising self-awareness of the minoritarian subject from a transitional position of otherness that builds tolerance for ambiguities and contradictions. It is also a poetics of bringing in the reader-viewer "to participate in the active process of re-membering" the many selves that make up the complex (Chican*e*) identity, "a process that involves constant repositionings" (85). Vivancos rightly observes that Chicana poetics are based on the concept of "polycentricity," which is fundamental in the Baroque according to Sarduy's focus on the polycentric oval shape as opposed to the classical monocentric circle. Additionally, they involve the idea of an infinite plurality which, in its amalgamation (like Frankenstein), is the base for imaging the "dangerous beast" as the monster, the mutant, a composite of many fragments. The dismembered *nepantlera* occupies the middle ground of *nepantla* to lead the subject through the interstices of the border zones that make up the fragmented nomadic self. Vivancos explains "dangerous beasts poetics" as a style of consciousness based on "schizoid polycentricity," that he cites from James Hillman: "'This style thrives in plural meanings, in cryptic double talk, in escaping definitions, in not taking heroic committed stances, in ambisexuality, in physically detached and separate body parts'" (Vivancos 26).

Norma Alarcón's explanation of the "mark of the beast" within the other—the marginalized and the outcast, particularly the maligned and abused Indigenous woman—invokes the presence of the "dark Beast" within any male or heterosexually dominated culture. This presence leads to its eventual denial and invisibility, its cultural and psychic marginalization and dismemberment. Vivancos explores the appropriation and reshaping by Anzaldúa and other Chicanas of the "dangerous beast" figure as a discursive position of difference and otherness that are stigmatized from the outset. This "mark of the beast" is engraved especially on women of color, Native American women, and most women writers, artists, and intellectuals (2). As a radical, risk-taking process, dangerous beasts poetics of these Chicana writers construct new subject positions "that are initially preconceived as those of impossible monsters" (Vivancos xiv); as a continuously evolving figuration of identity through otherness, it constitutes a "performative process of altering, discarding, adding, and reshuffling that has no end, and in which looking for ends, definite outcomes, or fixed truths should be a mistake" (xv). Overall, the figurations of monsters and dangerous beasts point to a destabilizing process of a radical revision of identity and reformulation of the subject occurring in the borderland space of *nepantla*.

The *mestiza* consciousness that is situated in the intermediate zone of *nepantla* is this "something else" that Anzaldúa mentions, or the new "third" (hybrid and indefinite) element in our proposal for a new

318   K. A. KULAWIK

transitive, queerly androgynous identity that deconstructs, combines, conjugates, inverts, or diverts the two traditional genders—the feminine and the masculine—by way of mutual and transient exchanges, temporary flows of sexual (and other cultural) traits.

Silvia Rivera Cusicanqui presents *ch'ixi* as a critical concept of identity deconstruction within a logic of decolonizing discourse emerging from Andean Indigenous philosophy. It stands as a critical alternative to the historical colonial fracture of American identity initiated by the Iberian Conquest and continuing in contemporary discourses of progressive "modernization" accompanied by Western academia-based discussions of *mestizaje* and hybridity. Rivera's theoretical option refers to the possibility of constructing a transitive, multi-component *ch'ixi* world of deep transformation of thought, knowledge, and selfhood. In *Un mundo ch'ixi es possible* ["A *Ch'ixi* World Is Possible" n.t. (2018)], Rivera Cusicanqui asks the question, valid not only for Bolivia but other parts of the world, if it is viable, or at all meaningful in the minoritarian struggle, to achieve the destitution of established neocolonial and hegemonic categories of cultural belonging by using any "new" categories (including *mestizaje* and hybridity) that only restitute the old ones in a continuing game of power wielding (2018: 112; 2020: xxiii, xxiv, xxviii). Thus, as an alternative to hierarchical structures like majority-minority, center-periphery, male-female, pure-hybrid, she proposes using combinatory models of thought, incorporating autochthonous, Indigenous, but also Western (modernizing) paradigms that acknowledge a necessary and constructive dialog between diverse human and non-human (nature-based and environmental) subjects, between the past and the present, between subaltern communitarian-based microstructures and dominating state, corporate-based macrostructures. The concept of *ch'ixi* represents a motley mixing of differing elements in a logic of something that "is" and at the same time "is not," as an appendix of the "third" to any binary opposition, similarly to Anzaldúa's and Garber's "third element" or the dynamic and movable "interpretant" as the third component in Peirce's triadic model of the sign.

Rivera Cusicanqui utilizes *ch'ixi* as a Native-American talisman concept to express an undefined and open "motley mix" of any state or entity. The word, originally referring in Aymara to gray color that at first sight appears as a conceptual unity, renders a meaning of multiple elements (as black and white) that are combined as "one" with "other-multiples" of "third" and beyond; *ch'ixi* is at the *same time* "one and multiple" or "multiple-one" (Gómez-Muller 2019: 311). As Rivera states: "*Ch'ixi* entities exist; […]

4 ONE-T(W)O-MANY: NEOBAROQUE ARTICULATIONS OF NOMADIC... 319

they are indeterminate, neither white nor black, but both at once" (Rivera C. 2018: 79; 2020: xxi). The idea of an undetermined, transitive, and mobile "third" complements the traditional cultural lexicon of *mestizaje* and hybridization (that imply a fused unity) by presenting the idea of something that exists not only in a differential two-fold manner or co-exists as one with the other, but includes *within one* the presence of a third element in the "combined" experience of multiplicity. It is also all elements coexisting, but none completely as "one": "The notion of *ch'ixi*, like many others (*allqa, ayni*), reflects the Aymara idea of something that is and is not at the same time. It is the logic of the included third. A *ch'ixi* color gray [...] is both white and its opposite, black" (Rivera C. 2020: xxi, 65). The Bolivian cultural theorist considers herself as an example of *ch'ixi* and proposes "motley mix" as the most appropriate modern translation for this Aymaran word, as it also refers to a collectivity, "a 'we,' who are called *mestizas* and *mestizos*" (Rivera C. 2020: 64–65). Since the word originally referred to the product of the juxtaposition of opposed or contrasting colors in their "imperceptible mixing [...] confused by perception, without ever being completely mixed" (65), Rivera highlights the possibility of a transformative coexisting of opposites but precluding their fusion. Inasmuch as they have the potential to (at least partially) fuse and join, they are never irreversibly mixed, conserving their original traits so as to be able to restitute them after a temporary intermingling. This differentiates *ch'ixi* from "this fashionable notion of cultural hybridity lite [sic] conforming to contemporary cultural domination" of neoliberal multiculturalism (65).

Another meaning Rivera Cusicanqui ascribes to this concept is "undifferentiation" (as "motley mixing") taking place in a borderline *ch'ixi* state. It is a mental/spiritual process in which differing traits are temporarily joined, fused, or blended in an illusory (fleeting) double perspective from two opposite vantage points that actually never erase or extinguish their original traits but simulate or project a "third," subsuming the potential for a subsequent return or reversal of the transformative operation: "And so as *allquamari* combines black and white in symmetrical perfection, *ch'ixi* combines the Indian world and its opposite without ever mixing them" (2020: 65). Shying from the infertile—in the sense of unreproducible—metaphor of the hybrid, used as a mainstay of García Canclini's "hybrid cultures" theory, however still maintaining proximity to Cornejo Polar's "cultural heterogeneity," Rivera proposes *ch'ixi* as a distinctly Indigenous term that, in the broader cultural context, refers to a "motley [*abigarrada*] society" inhabited by "the parallel coexistence of multiple cultural differences that do not extinguish but instead antagonize and complement each other" (66; my translation). She presents a method of overcoming the disjunctive of "being either pure modernity or pure tradition. Maybe we are both things, but the two not molten, because melting privileges only one side" (2018: 153). Being both at once in a state of *ch'ixi* transforms the way of thinking about modernity and tradition, about micro and macro politics, about community versus nationhood, and finally about racial, ethnic, and gender belonging. The Bolivian sociologist-historian defines it as a project of Latin American cultural reinvention that, by decolonizing thinking, may lead to overcoming the globalizing neoliberal multiculturalism that confines, stereotypes, and neutralizes the cultural subject, and to creating an alternative ("our own," i.e., Indigenous; 2020: 69) project of modernity through the *feminine* practice of "weaving the fabric of the intercultural" while "seducing the other" (68).

4.3.2   *Santiago's* entre-lugar *and Perlongher's* puntos de pasaje

The configuration of sexuality and gender in relation to postmodern discussions of otherness in the figuration of Brazilian identity occupy a central locus in Silviano Santiago's critical and fictional work. Most notably, he is known for adapting the Deleuzian concept of the "space in-between" (*entre-lugar*) to the Brazilian context, as he deftly combines it with cultural hybridity, but more as a *supplement* of otherness than a fusion with it. This space is defined by Santiago as a place of transit, with movement becoming a large part of his dynamic perspective that points to overcoming binarity of the "I" and the "other," and of the colonial and the colonized as relations of power that exercise authority across several other categories such as race and gender. He compares modern-day travelers to the colonial quest to dominate with language and cultural categories, imposing "a meaning on the Other in the very place of the Other" in an operation carried out through language (2001: 3). Another key concept taken from the poststructuralists, "the supplement," as the trait of the Other, of Difference grafted onto One's Sameness, serves for the Brazilian context as a counterpart to the imposition of the traveling visitor, whether scientific, academic, or tourist who is being "offered [material] by the so-called New World for the constitution of a new regime of alterity" (3). According to Santiago, America is the site where excess of mixtures and the resulting cultural expressivity define a "force field" that displaces hegemonic centrality with a "happy and affirmative copy" (3), as much as it is a simulation. Here, Santiago's deconstruction of the notions of the original (Old World) and its copy (New World) can be related to parody and artifice as constitutive elements of the Neobaroque. But it is the in-between space of the queer that for Santiago is the deconstructed space of decategorizations that rejects Manichaean oppositions in any cultural theories of national identity and multicultural globalization.

The "third" space of "in-between," as exemplified in Santiago's novel *Stella Manhattan*, is related to Santiago's own vision of the *entre-lugar*, theorized in his essay "Latin American Discourse: The Space In-Between" (2001: 25–38).[19] In an ingenious combination of the political, cultural, and sexual spheres in this novel, as well as with his theorization of in-betweenness, Santiago challenges static and exclusive notions of sexuality, gender, culture, and politics:

> The Latin American artist accepts [neocolonial] prison as a form of behavior, and transgression as a form of expression. [...] Somewhere between sacrifice and playfulness, prison and transgression, submission to the code and aggression, obedience and rebellion, assimilation and expression— there, in this apparently empty space, its temple and its clandestinity, is where the anthropophagous ritual of Latin American discourse is constructed. (37–38)

Santiago proposes a Latin American discourse whose transgression lies in its "cannibalistic" assimilation of dual, mutually exclusive, traits and identities (like Black or White, male or female, Native or European, self or other) in a fluid transitivity of self-devouring hybridized forms. As Susan Canty Quinlan observed "It [the text] is a place that speaks to the infinite ability to change and to know the other and, through the process of change, to manipulate the power structure that e[a]ffects the politics of who we are in relation to ourselves and others" (Quinlan and Arenas 2002, 212). The unique dimension of Santiago's work (both essay and narrative) becomes the "third" space that shapes his narratives "as he cannibalizes not only his own culture, but others as well, in his process of constructing identities" (212). According to Quinlan, the cross-dresser as the "third sex" (as defined by Garber 1992) represents the "space of in between,"

---

[19] Originally published as "O entre-lugar do discurso latinoamericano" in Silviano Santiago, *Uma literatura nos trópicos*, São Paulo: Editora Perspectiva, 1978.

322   K. A. KULAWIK

transiting the binary categories of space, time, and sex in the creation of "the 'third' as, perhaps, the essence of constructing identities" (211). It is a space that is overlooked by society, invisible from a hegemonical point of view. The examples of characters like Paco, with his mother-like protectiveness, Eduardo/Stella's chameleonic transformations and transiting relationships, and the author-narrator's questioning of the veracity of literature, point to what in Santiago's novel Quinlan expressed as "the stage for constructing the identities of the 'third' way of knowing" (222).

An example of this queer "in-between" space is the sexual mobility personified in the transient homosexual and cross-dresser, present in the novel *Stella Manhattan* (1985). Its array of queer characters constitutes a critical space of transit that brings any fixed categories to a state of crisis redeemed by the performance of identity configurations. In regard to the cross-dresser, Quinlan follows Marjorie Garber's idea of "category crisis" as "a failure of definitional distinctions, a borderline that becomes permeable, that permits of border crossings from one category (apparently distinct) to another" (Garber in Quinlan 209).

Quinlan provides a meaningful explanation of Santiago's theorizations on identity and cultural difference using as a point of departure his novel *Stella Manhattan*, in which transgressions of gender and sexuality play an essential role:

> Santiago's fictional work is filled with disruptive notions of history and political processes that form part of conscious choices to mark a plurality of visions […] that investigate the forms of figurative and linguistic exile or linguistic order, subjects that are often masked, but they are paramount to any study of identity politics that tries to read for differences. Santiago defines his quest as his *entre-lugar* (space in-between), a "third" space […] that challenges static notions of sexuality, gender, and politics and that is at the center of much of his fictional work. (212)

Santiago's novels follow Sarduy's ideas about "performing" sexual-gender roles to reaffirm transvestism as coexistence of masculine and feminine signifiers in a single body and the ensuing tension as the basic force that drives writing itself. This exemplifies the aforementioned concept of the "baroque ethos" introduced by Echeverría. As a silent strategy of resistance and drawing attention, the character vanishes into multiple alternatives, and as typically happens in these novels, the character either dies or disappears. As in many of the texts that we examined in Chap. 3, the spaces change but the character's performance and reinventing of him/herself in all *hir* disguises and multiple cross-genders continue in different settings across cultures. "The text, the images, and the characters are all masked in order to question identity. They epitomize Santiago's own struggle for gay space, the 'third' space of his *entre-lugar*" (Quinlan 229).

Santiago's concept of *espaço dentre* is related to the ideas of Néstor Perlongher, particularly his concept of "passage points" [*puntos de pasaje*], which are analogous to Bellatin's "vanishing points" (*puntos de fuga*). The wiles of performative writers and artists reflect Néstor Perlongher's ideas, as well as Sarduy's concepts of the neobaroque "creative leprosy" that produces borderline beings in transit and nomads in a constant process of movement as becoming, in intermediate spaces of in-between. This Argentine writer, poet, and essayist provides us in his book of essays *Prosa plebeya* (1997) an explanation of these processes. He humorously calls the Argentine resurgence of baroque poetics the *neobarroso* (literally, "neo-muddy" instead of neobaroque) (97–99). Bringing back Deleuze's concept of "minoritarian becoming," in "Los devenires minoritarios" (65–76), he explains identity as a point of subjectivation, a becoming without any center: "there are no longer subjects, only dynamic individuations without a subject that constitute collective agencies [...] instantaneous individuations" (66; my translation). They form a map of "processes of marginalization and minoritization, of mobilizations of 'non-guaranteed' subjects" (67). Self-constitutive movements of the "I" take place from the periphery, from the margin. Perlongher explains that

> [t]hese processes of marginalization, of escape, in different degrees, release *devenirs* (molecular particles) that throw the subject adrift along the edges of the conventional behavioral pattern. [...] To become is not to transform oneself into another, but to enter into (aberrant) alliance, into contagion, into *inmistión* [roughly 'immersion'] with (the) different. Becoming does not go from one point to another but enters the 'in-between' of the medium, it is that 'in-between'. (68)

Perlongher locates "points of passage" between sexual, racial, social, and national "identificatory polarities in the conformation of becoming of the self-constitutive process of the subject" (68). These transitive points offer a hermeneutic device in the examination of the chameleonic sexual identifications of Sarduy's classic characters Cobra, Colibrí, Auxilio, Socorro, Luis Leng, and Cocuyo. Their unstable sexuality becomes a site of transgression and transition of the identificatory polarities of the subject

324   K. A. KULAWIK

that are in constant flow. The points of passage create an opening of identity in a deconstructive postcolonial critique of Modernity from the angle of a contemporary stylization of historical discourse. This critical dimension of the Neobaroque has been supported by Irlemar Chiampi (36–37), Lois Parkinson-Zamora (2011: xxvi), and Gonzalo Celorio (in Zamora and Kaup 487–507). With its emphasis on non-heteronormative sexuality and displays of formal exuberance, the Neobaroque becomes a modern critical tool for the decentering and deconstruction of normative categories in the unstable context of postmodernity and the hybrid cultural setting of the Americas. Cobra, Colibrí, Stella, and the New Mestiza avoid being bound a fixed sexual or national identity. They constantly transform in dialogical flows of alterities that transitorily conform them.

4.3.3   Nomadism as Transformative Flows of Identity: Braidotti's Point

Transitive identity, as a form of subjective and cultural nomadism, is determined by movement and displacement, by a migratory flow that leads to crossing, mixing, and coexistence of distinctions in the shared, in-between borderland space of *nepantla*. The trans-self positions its subjectivity in multiple simultaneous social, political, cultural, and desiring perspectives that are mobile and fluid in their transits. They are propelled by Desire in the affective (also erotic) drive toward otherness that is substantiated in writing and artistic creativity, in the driving force of (neobaroque) aesthetic representation.

Movement, shifts, and flows of identifications experienced by changing characters, voices, and bodies, are key features of the many contemporary Latin American literary and artistic works. As Rosi Braidotti opportunely pointed out, "[t]he only constant in today's world is change, but that is neither a simple nor a unilinear process. It rather operates with web-like sets of simultaneous shifts and contradictory trends" (2002: 264). The fluidity and mobility of the nomadic subject, in all its transitivity, metamorphoses, and displacements, is best illustrated by the figures of the cross-dresser and the androgyne.

Nomadism as cultural, social, and sexual fluidity is well represented in Echavarren's novel *Ave Roc* through the mutant figure of Jim (Morrison), an exemplary model of the nomadic in transit between genders, sexes, ethnicities, and cultures. This novel aspires a cultural juxtaposition of Western Modernity, seen through the excesses of Jim and his band Del Otro Lado (The Doors), with Indigenous cultures of the Hopi, Gabrielinos,

Mojaves, Tehuelches, and Charrúas. It produces a space of cultural feedback between Western pop culture and Amerindian traditions that illuminates the fissures within the North American cultural paradigm. The frequent references to Indigenous rituals (the dances, the use of hallucinogens such as the peyote) with the presence of the androgynous shaman, "neither man nor woman," result in a hybrid and transitive cultural space for envisioning transentity. The cultural intersection of Western values with Native Americans of the U.S. Southwest in *Ave roc* and the virtually extinct Charrúas of Uruguay, which Julián embodies in *El diablo en el pelo*, indicate Inter-American transitivity, co-presence, or simultaneity (according to Carlos Rincón), and hybridization (in García Canclini's terms) that characterize the Western hemisphere. The multiple and decentered sexual, national, and ethnic identities presented in the mutant figures of Jim and Julián derive from the transitive and translative incorporation of elements of otherness and their transformative coexistence (not only co-presence) in the space of a single androgynous/ *Mestizo* body.

Nomadic identity articulation through transitivity of categories occurs in fluid webs of intersectional connections and alliances that form the basis for a refiguration of subjectivity, one that is founded on multiple belongings and flexible forms of cross-border citizenship. Braidotti affirms that nomadism "allows for complex allegiances and multiple forms of cultural belongings" (2006: 79). It dismantles the us/them binary and replaces a fixed notion of citizenship, and nationality with a flexible and movable concept of transitory identifications. The historic miscegenation of Latin America reflects the current hybridization of Europe: "These effects boil down to one central idea: the end of pure and steady identities, or in other words, creolization and hybridization producing a multicultural minoritarian Europe" (2006: 79).

Latin American Neobaroque aesthetics become the discursive space for the nomadic subject's strategies of identity deconstruction, carried out through alternative feminine subject positions (2002: 64). The notion of a dynamic subjectivity is founded on a consciousness that is unstable, transient, and in constant movement, in continuous change and transformation. The *process* of change and *movement* toward it matter more than any specific objective, concept, or result; what matters is the *transit* of the nomad in a fluid state of passage across borders and categories: "Transformations, metamorphoses, mutations and processes of change have in fact become familiar in the lives of most contemporary subjects. [...] If the only constant at the dawn of the third millennium is change, then the challenge lies in thinking about processes, rather than concepts" (2002: 3). The process of becoming is reflected in the slippage taking place in deterritorialization—the exile of the nomad and the minoritarian mutant—more than the nomad's point of destination (as there is no destination, only movement); the movement never ends, only flows in the figurations of One in Two or many Others. Nomadic identity, in whatever form its avatars appear, wander, or terminate, is never a given, but a constant flow in the dissolution of momentary incarnations, figurations, representations, appearances. We coincide with Braidotti in procuring a new mode of representation or a conceptual map, a philosophical reconfiguration of identity as an ongoing process of transformation and change of the nomadic trans-self.

It is the transitory and fluid nature of transformative identity, as movement—crossing, transiting, trespassing, moving to and fro, one way or back and forth—that has relevance, as does the in-between space of *nepantla* with its fissures, interstices, and borderlines. "The definition of a person's identity takes place *in between* nature-technology, male-female, black-white, in the spaces that flow and connect in between. We live in permanent processes of transition, hybridization and nomadization, and these in-between states and stages defy the established modes of theoretical representation" (Braidotti 2002: 2).

The fluid and mobile nature of identity articulation in the nomadic mode involves affectivity and desire in a momentary intersubjective relation of one to other. As an "identity transfusion," we have seen it in the performance (and photo) of Lemebel and Casas' *The Two Fridas* and in the bodily transfusions of María Chipia and her twin brother in Eltit's *The Fourth World*. "That capacity to endure is collective. It is a moment in a process of becoming [...] 'I' is rooted, but 'I' flows" (Braidotti 2006: 199–200). A nomadic subject functions in transformative flows that do not lead to an ultimate destination. It represents a transitive way of becoming in its multiplicity, relationality, and its dynamic of transiting and crossing boundaries. The point is that nomadism is less about *being* a nomad than about *becoming* nomadic (2002: 86). Becoming is a process, not an entity; the open non-teleological nature of becomings points to processes without beginning or end, origin or destination. It is not necessarily the result that matters (blackness or whiteness, femininity or masculinity, human or machine, etc.) but the very transformation of self as openness to otherness and change, the very movement toward it; trans-self in a movement of trans-"it."

Deleuze's process of subjective becoming is grounded in the feminist stance acknowledging the indispensable presence of the material body as open and fluid, and of which our cross-dressed, androgynous, metamorphosized, trans*, and posthuman characters are examples. As we have seen in the works analyzed in Chap. 3, these subjects represent the material body that undergoes a series of processes that Braidotti calls translations, transactions, transplants, and transits.

In line with our observations about the Neobaroque is Braidotti's reference to non-fixity of identity and the constant flows of the borderland transiting process. Nomadic identity becomings are fully conscious and predictable in their flexibility and mobility, zigzagging in and out of one another, entering multiple combinations of subjectivity. The key to nomadism is perceiving the process of becoming in its movement and trajectories as more important than the identity formations to which it leads. "The flows matter more than steady roots" (2006: 62). Nomadic subjectivity does not to reach a fixed objective or return to any point of departure; it does not stop on any one side of the boundary, and does not operate with a clear, monologic vision of the past, but rather conceives cultural intermixture as an opportunity for creating new posthuman, ethno-racial, intersexual landscapes, as it takes advantage of the possibilities for bonding and community building (2006: 66). Transitive identity is not about fortuitous role reversals as momentary adoptions of a defined "other" for the purposes of entertainment. It is about continuous meaningful contacts resulting in mixing through contagions and transmissions. Trans-identity is articulated in round-trip transits across fluctuating borders as markers of difference that are mere points of reference.

Comparably to the horizontal interconnections of a rhizome (Deleuze and Parnet 1977; Deleuze and Guattari 1987b), the process of becoming trans-self implies a non-hierarchic *fluidity* and openness at the root level, which are attributable to feminine and non-binary writing (as creation). In a state of mental transitivity, "becoming woman" is the first opening to other forms of becoming or being minoritarian. As Braidotti observes, nomadism has the potential of a transformative and destabilizing power of the underprivileged minoritarian subject that does not have to be oppositional or confrontational:

> [T]he nomadic subject signifies the potential becoming, the opening out—
> the transformative power of all the exploited, marginalized, oppressed
> minorities. Just being a minority, however, is not enough: it is only the

starting point. What is crucial to becoming-Nomad is undoing the opposi-tional dualism of majority/minority and arousing an affirmative passion for and desire for the transformative flows that destabilize all identities. [...] Becoming nomadic means that one learns to re-invent oneself and one desires the self as a process of transformation. It is about desire *for* change, for flows and shifts of multiple desires. (2002: 83–84; emphasis in original)

The nomadic trans-self does not stop at one-time role reversals or one-way boundary crossings. S/he goes about repeating these inversions in constant flows, like repetitive cross-dressing and undressing, or the gender-erasing transformations of the androgyne. It is about deterritorialization of any and all established categories, a self-exile of the trans*self from the territories of categorical heteronormative logocentrism, past the boundary-limited cultural structures of neocolonialism.

This specifically feminine morphology of transition involves fluidity and fluid mechanics, hence Braidotti's emphasis on some key elements that she borrows from Luce Irigaray, one being the "mucosity and inter-stitional humidity such as the placenta, blood and other bodily fluids, [which] expresses the creation of alternative figurations of the self—and the necessity to find expressions for them," the other "feminine sex as not-one, that is to say, as multiple within itself," combined with the concept of "an open whole, a flux" (2002: 112). Transiting (and transgressing) categories of selfhood requires a process of nomadic flows of subjectivity in "the poros-ity and mucosity of a female desire that can open to a desire and wander between the sexes" (2002: 113). This feminine morphology of one's sub-jective transformation allows for an affirmative, inclusive, and affective bor-derland fluidity for transitioning with and *within* the "other," and assuming difference affirmatively. Braidotti re-asserts the flowing presence of "'femi-nization' of the sensibility of nomadic subjects, in terms of affectivity, fluid-ity, porosity of boundaries and constant interrelations" (2002: 260).

4.4　The Neobaroque Strategy: From Self to Other, from Seduction to Sedition

The final dimension of the Neobaroque that we wish to address is the political. The aesthetic representation of categorical identity transgressions exerts a subversive effect on the reader in its quality of a literary/artistic work and on society in its capacity of a cultural artifact. Not to be over-looked is the subliminal presence of a "baroque ethos" within Neobaroque's aesthetic function. Neobaroque rewriting of identity as transitivity in the nomadic mode acquires a political sense of resistance that Braidotti so pointedly expressed with regard to the desire-driven relationship of individual transformations of the self (as the local) to politics (as the global): "Our politics begins with our desires to enact positive transformations on the environment we happen to inhabit. We need to think, resist and act the same way we live, that is to say, g-locally" (2002: 267). Politics begins in the (inter)personal One-Other(s)-Many relationships and moves to the social level of the gender-sexually, ethnically, racially, nationally, posthumanly defined group. Subject and identity remain, but in a multiplicitous, flexible relationship within oneself and among other selves, in a nomadic transit that affects the political and social *status quo*.

In *Gender Trouble*, Judith Butler establishes the relationship between language/discourse and sexual gender: "the boundaries of analysis suggest the limits of a discursively conditioned experience. These limits are always set within the terms of a hegemonic cultural discourse predicated on binary structures that appear as the language of universal rationality" (13). Identity formation, as a discursive experience, enters the political dimension of power relations that resemble the dialogical relationship between the two hierarchic positions of speaker/listener, grammatical subject/object. The political dimension of the identity-formative process as intersubjective communication can be intersectionally related to the concepts defined by postcolonial criticism, referring to the "center" and the "margin" developed by Gilles Deleuze, Homi Bhabha (1990), Gayatri Spivak, and Mary Louise Pratt (1993), which have helped to visualize the marginal and peripheral place of Latin America in the political-cultural sphere of the postcolonial (subaltern) peripheral West. Identity conceived from a linguistic and philosophical, but also cultural and subaltern point of view, becomes a discursive relation of "one" with "other" operating through the hegemonical signs of linguistic representation. From this intersubjective point of view, Latin American identity, instead of being perceived as a hybrid fusion of multiple racial, cultural, social, and personal elements into one entity, could and should be perceived as an ongoing process of "cultural becoming" through a web of interweaving elements of "otherness."

4.4.1 *Politics of the Neobaroque*

The neobaroque text, as a transgressive literary-aesthetic space, forms a site of contestation and political dissidence. Referring to its links with the historical Baroque, Severo Sarduy considered the Neobaroque as a radical discourse, a "style of discussion," a "revolutionary style," contentious with the bourgeois capitalist order in its destabilizing of the dominant Western heterosexual-binary gender order and categorical formulations of cultural identity.

The discursive modes of the neobaroque can be perceived as a way in which literature aims at destabilizing power structures, parodically "infecting" language—the indispensable gears of the patriarchal-masculine, logocentric, and neocolonial order. Sarduy stated that "[t]he current baroque, the neobaroque, structurally reflects the lack of harmony, the rupture of homogeneity of the logos as the absolute, lack which constitutes our epistemic foundation. A neobaroque of imbalance, a structural reflection of a desire which cannot attain its object, desire for which logos has not organized more than a screen which hides the lack" (1987b: 211–12; my translation). In a similar way, Nelly Richard explains the intentionality of the neobaroque text as "an extreme word" set between an anti-globalizing harshness and a refinement of the literary-figurative mechanisms that dote language with signifying intensity (2002: n.p.). With its exuberant, transgressive, and erotic modes of seductive figuring of the self and its seditious transgression of normative categories of the logocentric postcolonial order, the narrative works of the analyzed authors weave a text of resistance to the established order's in-/e-vasion of minoritarian spaces. These spaces appear in Bellatin's (and Jacob Roth's) Austrian Galicia and Mexico City's suburbs, in Lemebel's and Eltit's margins of the socio-economically polarized metropolis of Santiago, the underworld of Buenos Aires, Bolivia's and Uruguay's marginalized areas lying on the outskirts of neoliberal economic interests. These works create voices and figures—transgressive nomadic subjects—that represent marginal spaces by using the transgressive poetic word combined with performance and image as a political tool, a weapon of resistance; the word-image as artifice, parody, and simulation becomes radically difficult and useless due to its alienation from the mimetic and numeric profitability of super production and (re) productive communication. In the parodic representation of sexually mutating characters, eroticism aims at the economizing, calculated, and rational mentality of postcolonial capitalist (re)productivity. It ironically proposes a squandering exuberance of signs in its excess of ornamentation and meaning. Its best example is the cross-dresser's and the androgyne's eroticized representation of ambiguous sexuality.

The fragmented and fluid nature of the nomadic subject forms a site of contestation and political agency through its outlandish metamorphic presence in the neobaroque text. As Sandra Garabato (2003) argues, there is "a relationship between transvestism and subversion which extends beyond the laws of sexuality to situate itself in the terrain of political and economic affiliations" (49; my translation). The analyzed authors and artists express an antipatriarchal and antiphallocentric attitude of dislodging the all-powerful Logos, which translates in their texts to transgression of the word/image/sign in the representation of cross-dressed, androgynous, and mutant characters. This sumptuous style becomes a tool of condemnation by *not* limiting itself to language's purely communicative function. The Neobaroque plays with a saturated discourse that utilizes decorous language in a deceptive, anti-mimetic, and politically subversive mode. The striking combination of stylistic procedures such as metaphors, neologisms, the juxtaposition of registers, and parody, all characteristic of the historical Baroque, produces a destabilizing effect on a new content of modernity, technology, commerce, fashion, and sex. According to Sarduy, the Neobaroque is a radical style, rebellious of the parsimonious economic order of calculated capitalism (1987b: 209). It destabilizes at the level of language, at the structural basis of the functioning of the *bourgeois* economic order and the patriarchal, compulsorily binary, heterosexual establishment.

Similarly, the experimental acrobatics of Eltit's early novels indicate her affinity with the Neobaroque avant-garde. Also, in Lemebel and Casas, the opulently rich and poetic language is in stark contrast with the crude reality of their socio-economic testimony. The elements of style and technique form part of a "neobaroque literary strategy," mentioned by Gálvez Acero (1987), Bustillo (1990), and Ortega (1984). Addressing the form and language of Eltit's novel *Mano de obra* (2009), Chilean critic Nelly Richard describes the subversive, non-conformist character of Eltit's narrative:

> From the swearword as an extreme word in its antiglobalizing rudeness to the refinement of the other extreme word: the literary word, the hypertextual word undoes and redoes itself thanks to the figurative machineries which dote language with signifying intensity [...] to display those "brilliant stylized shreds" is a strategy which only literature can design to oppose itself to the communicative technologies of the mass media society. (2002: n/p; my translation)

332 K. A. KULAWIK

Alongside Lemebel's and Casas' chronicles, Eltit's novels weave a text of resistance made of, as Richard proposes, "the literary word—as artifice and ceremony of a slow, difficult and useless word because of its distancing from the numeric profitability of superproduction" (2002: n/p). Sexual agency comes into play as a broader signifier of cultural belonging and nationhood, as Garabato points out: "If Sarduy reads in the sexuality of the transvestite a gesture of daring at the utilitarian morality of capitalism, Lemebel situates that gesture in the national difference. By placing the accent on the 'Latin American body,' his work seems to suggest that sexual difference is not necessarily established before the nationality of a given subject" (49; my translation). The aforementioned cross-dressed *sudaca* children in Eltit's novel *The Fourth World* are reflective of Lemebel's "demos-gracia" ["let's-give-thanks" as a play on "democracy"] in the "habitat of poverty" (34), questioning the formation of sexual, national, and cultural identities assigned to Third World countries as an economic *status quo* by foreign centers of power. This radical strategy of the subversive word is described by Gisela Norat (2002), in her analysis of Eltit's narrative, as a political act of social conscience: "Revolutionizing language in writing is one weapon Eltit wields in her struggle to insert the margins into the Chilean literary mainstream" (110). The posture represented by Eltit, Lemebel, Casas, and other non-Chilean writers, such as Néstor Perlongher, Carlos Monsiváis, and Cristina Peri Rossi, is that of a radically queer political agency. The extreme neobaroque word of Richard's "brilliant stylized shreds" emerges beyond the textual realm with political overtones of parody in Susy Shock's, the Galán's, Guillermo Gómez-Peña's, Coco Fusco's, and Nao Bustamante's satire-laden performances.

According to Nelly Richard (1993: 86–89), feminist criticism proposes to see identity as a mobile and dynamic construction, a "multipositionality of the subject" represented by means of changing and mobile, feminine cultural symbolizations to question the integrity of the classic masculine subject and the stability of genders in their relation to heteronormative power (79). Richard states that "[t]his relativization of the categories of man and woman, thought of not as fixed substances but as mobile constructions, is perhaps one of the theoretical postulations of feminism that best synchronizes with certain postmodernist approaches: those related to the pluralization of meaning, the fragmentation of identity and the dissemination of power" (1993: 86). Bellatin's novels reflect Richard's idea of a "feminine writing" carried out from a "female position." Like Barthes' (1973) "writerly" (open) text, it has the power to articulate the text's active and dynamic mechanisms of meaning-making, and to stimulate the reader to take a critical stance toward imposed categorizations and to formulate new interpretations of identity favorable to the emergence of alternative and dissident subjectivities (Richard 1996: 744). In Bellatin's randomly mutating or transformed by illness bodies, Vek Lewis observes a "discourse of identity fracture" operating with multiple and dispersed signifiers (2010: 140). It is one example of how literature and art provide the freedom for such new interpretations of the self.

With the "death of the (determined and unique) author,"[20] feminine writing and literature of *jouissance* revives, as an open and "writable" literature. The neobaroque work opens to a plurality of positionings of the subject that coalesce in antinormative feminine gestures. Richard calls it "the gesture of continuing to mobilize gender as a platform for social vindication based on the signifier 'woman,' with the other gesture of confronting the codes of symbolic and interpretative power from a mobile plurality of positions-postures of critical subjectivity that displace and make the constellation of 'minority becomings' of the 'feminine' turn" (1993: 87; my translation). Sexuality and textuality interact with narrative transformations and sexual transgressions, indicating the multipositional, polyphonic, and dialogical character of writing at the limits, but without limits.

Aesthetic creation, as an act of political resistance and sedition, is most visible in Eugenia Prado's staging of *Hembros*. The theme of negotiation of power between the two opposing poles of outside negative constraint (*potestas*) and inside positive empowerment (*potentia*) is observed in the loss of unity and stability of the emerging posthuman subject (Braidotti 2006: 196–98). Its splitting and dispersion are reflected on multiple occasions throughout the work. The chanting voice expresses the growing opposition and ultimate rebellion against the creator figure of the Father and the technocratic, capitalist, and mercantile system that He represents and controls by means of a logocentric, categorizing, and oppressive language:

> Illusions of desires multiply our schizophrenic identities, illusions unleashing schizoid revolutionary processes, sinister and profound signs, paranoid

---

[20] Foucault explains this idea in his lecture "Qu'est-ce qu'un auteur?" ["What Is an Author?"]. Published in Michel Foucault. *Dits et écrits*. 1954–1988. Vol. I 1954–1969. Paris: Gallimard, 1994. 789–821.

procedures, the quoted "plastic beings" in the official language of marketing, productions of desires executing actions, as decomposed masses traversed by flows, we mutate, we adapt to everything [...] exploded bodies, crossed by an infinity of flows that pulsate us [...] sexuality is now our greatest offer, starting where do we start to be cut off from cultural and mechanical bases? [...] as meanings of this world of possibilities, between mobile roles [...] uncertain muse, beautiful fierce hermaphrodite, responding to the imposed representations of familiar landscapes. (Final Chant, "Scenes for an ending"; my translation)

A desire for liberation accompanies the rebellion. However, this rebellion has two dimensions. On the one hand, what remains of militancy is the adaptation from within (as silent sabotage of a "baroque ethos") to the prevailing commercialized system, when the subject assumes a sexuality that eventually "sells out" ("our greatest offer") on the market of institutionalized diversity. On the other, it adopts mobile, inapprehensible roles that, as simulacra, not only quietly adjust to the symbolic market but also exert resistance through the "beautiful fierce hermaphrodite," who equivocally responds to its imposed (official) representations with *hir* best weapon—ambiguity. Overcoming their incommunicability and inability to coexist as cyborgs, these sexual beings strive to liberate themselves from the categories imposed by the System-Creator. Their emancipatory breakout is what gives the work a sense of certain optimism.

4.4.2 Cross-Dressing and Androgyny as Destabilization of Heterosexual Hegemony

Our considerations have led us to consider with Marjorie Garber "that the specter of transvestism, the uncanny intervention of the transvestite" manifests a space of cultural anxiety aroused by unstable identities, what she calls "commutable or absent 'selves'" (32). Transvestism situates at the intersection of multiple categories, of which gender turns out to be commutable along multiple categorical axes (race, ethnicity, social group). When one set of boundaries is transgressed, the inviolability of any one of them, and of the social codes that regulate these boundaries, is questioned. "The transvestite in this scenario is both terrifying and seductive precisely because s/he incarnates and emblematizes the disruptive element that intervenes, signaling not just another category crisis, but—much more disquietingly—a crisis of 'category' itself" (32).

4   ONE-T(W)O-MANY: NEOBAROQUE ARTICULATIONS OF NOMADIC...   335

In theoretical and philosophical terms, the experimental neobaroque narrative portrays a rejection of binarism, be it hetero or homosexual. The possibility of a mobile and transitive sexuality (and identity in broader intersectional terms) has not been recognized by social or scientific discourses based on a heterosexual, patriarchal, and logocentric matrix. Eltit's textual "cross-dressers" E. Luminata, María Chipia, and Coya (in the novel *Por la patria*), with their transgressive identities and androgynous transcultural characters, attack from the margins the bourgeois order of heterosexuality, patriarchy, and centralism of power. The experimental metanarrative procedures and linguistic exuberance aim at destabilizing the system from within the very foundations of its normative discourse— the novel.

In Lemebel's *La esquina...* and in Casas' *Yo, yegua*, transvestism is adopted as a strategy of a decentered and hybrid identity with all the transitivity of unstable masculine and feminine attributes. In Gilles Deleuze's words, transvestite identity would be a "minority becoming" that is based on a relation of transitive multiplicity, of passing "between" all dualism (1987a: 8, 40–43). The neobaroque "crazy cartography" of the Chilean city that Lemebel and Casas offer us is comparable to the works of other Latin American urban essayists-chroniclers of the end of the twentieth century, such as Argentine Néstor Perlongher, Mexican Carlos Monsiváis, and Puerto Rican Edgardo Rodríguez Juliá. Again, it is sustainable to speak here of a "trans-Latin American Neobaroque." Ángeles Mateo del Pino (1998) points to the encompassing capacity of the critical eye of the two Chilean transvestite authors and their projection from the particular and local perspective of Santiago to a more universal dimension. She refers to the chronicles of *La esquina* as "a social macro-criticism, a puzzle of stories that offer a panoramic view of the spirit that hovers over the city of Santiago today. They also have the gift of reflecting the mood that hovers over all large cities. Hence, one of the successes of these chronicles is the fact that, settling in the local particular, they build a vision of the universal" (23; my translation). The figure of the sexual/ethnic "other" is disguised behind a thickly embroidered curtain, trammeled with exuberant language. It is placed at the level of "what the text does not want to say and says" and, in the words of Dino Plaza Atenas (1999), "accounts for the functioning of *différance* described by Derrida [...] as the author succeeds in making his chronicles speak with the language of the Other and for the Other about the marginal" (134; my translation). In the manner of the Derridean "supplement" of what one is *not* and simulates by the element of otherness, the (Trans) American metropolis presents itself as a "queer" denial of the System. The transvestite's discourse, besides being *Mestizo* and *Mulatto*, Chilean and Latin American (Lemebel highlights his Indigenous origins in an interview with Blanco and Gelpi 1997, 96), threatens the racist heteronormative system, and enters the spaces of "in-between" (White-Colored, light-dark, male-female, etc.) that fissure the imposed socio-political system; it invades and opens new areas of subjectivity along the edges of the established order.

Similarly in Bolivia, the Familia Galán attempts to find new strategies of destabilizing the system with mutant appearances and provocative behavior. The Galán Family's performance engages Bolivian cultural history from the perspective of a political practice based on aesthetic provocation and interpellation. The emblematic figure of the China Morena, a female dancer in popular folk celebrations, now exemplified by cross-dresser Danna (see Fig. 3.9), caught on in Bolivian mentality and, as David Aruquipa observed, modified the political perception of popular culture in Bolivia: "We have transformed ways of seeing and understanding sexualities and possible genders, constantly questioning the binary and essentialist views of the sex-gender system using the body as a political discourse, a space of struggle, as a current and historical challenge to conservative views" (2016: 459; my translation). This representation marks a continuity in time, building a bridge between the traditions of the Indigenous Andean cultures and the present strife of Bolivian LGBTQ groups, and recovering the element of queerness from vernacular culture of the Andes. More importantly, it opens a road of possibilities for the emergence of new characters with identities that are not fixed in binarism. They have produced a nomadic, because mobile and transitive, figure of the transformist as transformer of identity and culture. This political action, paired with the Galans' artistic work, crossed into the territory of academic discourse with the publication of *Memorias colectivas* (2012), coedited by Aruquipa with Pablo Vargas and Paula Estenssoro (Fatal Galán). It is a testimony of how La Familia Galán was able to use transformism as a tool of political struggle and transformation of views on sexuality and gender in their transit through uncharted territories of Bolivian Postmodernity in a coupling of cultural resistance and neobaroque eccentricity. Aruquipa meaningfully states: "We continue reflecting on ourselves and theorizing about our actions. We are not victims of the system, but rather we are transforming it" (2016: 460). Maybe that is the point after all; let us recall the words of Néstor Perlongher: "*A la sedición por la seducción*" [To sedition through seduction] (96).

4.4.3 Transformative Impact of Nomadic Subject Positions and the "Baroque Ethos"

Nomadic theory has brought to our attention new figurations of identity that account for transformative processes of selfhood defined by states of in-betweenness, transits, and flows. The presence of nomadic subjects leads us to approach the sphere of political engagement in an effort to develop more empowering methods of deconstructing categorical identities, "so as to enable a radical shift of perspective within the subject and to lay the foundations for new interconnections and alliances" (Braidotti 2006: 78). The challenge is to find the mechanisms and forms to represent these processes. One way that we found effective is through aesthetic representation by means of a style recognized as the Neobaroque, given that it assumes the risk of bold creativity and experimentation.

Braidotti points to the transformative impact of nomadism as "one's political process" veered toward a positive change of oneself in a desire-driven affectivity for otherness (2002: 169). Openness, freedom, and continuity further describe the ongoing process of nomadic self-definition: "These alternative subject positions express the transformation they embody and act as the free-floating affectivity, which Massumi describes as a tendency without end, or a non-self-consuming, non-capitalizing process" (169). Braidotti argues for understanding gender differentiation as part of a transformative process that implies uncertainty and displacement of sexual identification: "My claim that the on-going transformations of our times do not erase sexual difference, but merely displace it, is simultaneously a conclusion and a new start" (169). Hence, transitivity, as both differentiation and ambiguity, suggests the two-sidedness of the transformative process. Its two facets are exemplified by the gender-reinforcing inversion process of cross-dressing on one end, and androgyny as an erasing process of undifferentiation in the traditional duality of categories, on the other. In both cases, identity rearticulation is circumscribed by the political impact of one's positionality in the networks of power that determine the discursive spectrum of logocentric heteronormativity of the post-colonial *status quo*.

Braidotti's theory of the nomadic subject and, in particular, her "ethics of nomadism" (2002: 260–261) lead us to envision the nomadic trans-self as a collectively oriented multiple subject that constantly re-negotiates with a variety of forces—its "cross-vested interests."[21] Its feasibility requires re-adjustments in patterns of desire, hence reconfigurations of sexualities along multiple, potentially contradictory axes of power and mutual influence. As an open and inclusive process of becoming, it implies a "feminization" of sensibility that relates it to affectivity, fluidity, porosity of boundaries, and constant intermingling.

Roberto Echavarren's narrative and critical writings on gender mutations also make incursions into the Latin American philosophical-political sphere by giving a voice to marginal mutant identities. The unsettling textual operations, which correspond to the defiant and rebellious behavior of his novelistic characters Jim, Julián, and Lágrima Ríos, question values imposed by hegemonic discourse that controls the administration and interpretation of meaning. Intersectional deconstructing of cultural categories of gender, sexuality, race, and ethnicity at their discursive roots certainly has a political effect. It aims at destabilizing the "politically correct" multicultural neoliberal order of "affirming" oneself as either Black or White, Anglo or Latino, gay or straight. As we have attempted to demonstrate in this analysis, determined labels do not apply in textual and performative world of neobaroque ambiguity populated by androgynous characters such as Jim, Julián, or Lágrima. Categories are not operative in the transgressions of the transvestite (Kulick 1998), nor in the androgyny of other mutant (or monstrous) characters emerging from the works of Shock, the Galans, and Menstrual. When speaking of the role of writing and artistic creation, Echavarren remarks: "We know that any label is provisional and responds to a complicated but unquestionable strategy, and we go about deflowering words to touch what surpasses and overtakes us" in our effort to define the undefinable, an identity beyond genders, sex, nation, race, or humanity. Echavarren attributes to *art* the transformative role of change, extending his view of the arts to "the creation of alternative edges of perception" (2008: 13; my translation).

Adrián Cangi highlights Echavarren's role in the aesthetic subversion of identity as a political act (Echavarren 2014: 179). Even in the progressive cultural process of Latin American hybridization, canonical literature has usually stood in the service of traditional humanist techniques of suiting and appeasing the spirit of colonizing heteronormativity. In its traditional forms, it has leaned toward the reproductively oriented domestication of men and

---

[21] We credit Marjorie Garber and the title of her book, *Vested Interests* (1992), as the inspiration behind this formulation.

women, of ethnic and racial groups, within their categorical roles set by a discourse in the service of (post)colonial European logocentrism. Meanwhile, Echavarren and the voices of other Neobaroque writers pursue, in the combat of transitive bodies and identities, a transgression and subversion analogous to the socio-political revolutionary undertakings endemically emerging in the conflictive history of Latin America. The aesthetic representation of a nomadic trans-self traces a decentered outline of a subversively hybrid selfhood that supplements the queer theorizations of subjectivity analogously to the postmodern questioning of logocentric neocolonialism.

In the realm of the visual arts, the message relayed by the excessively saturated cyber-performances by Gómez-Peña seems to be that there is no utopian and genderless, ethnic-free, or nationless reality beyond the parody of cyberspace, and that identities must (co)exist, interact, and cross over the "real" world. As "a terrorist intellectual" representing cyber-immigrants in his performance *Webbacks*, Gómez-Peña reads his "First Draft of a Manifesto: Remapping Cyberspace," in which he claims for a better use of digital Internet media: "—re-map the hegemonic cartography of cyberspace, politicize the conception of cyberspace;—develop a multicentric, theoretical understanding of the cultural, political [...];—exchange different sorts of information—mythopoetic, activist, performative, imagistic" (2000: 258–59). Cultural hybridity in an era of transborder crossings and mass migrations caused by economic and political displacement is a reality of the American continent. The disarticulation of normative postcolonial cultural labels and the articulation of a hybrid multicultural subject is the intent of Gómez-Peña's politically engaged artistic activity in the context of intercultural transits and crossings. The traditional idea of the West (referring to the United States and Western Europe) is being redefined and the maps are being redrawn in the face of multidirectional intercultural mingling in a plural, multicultural America:

> The South and the East are already installed within the West. Today, being "American" in the broadest sense of the word implies participating in the drafting of a new cultural topography and the invention of a hybrid artistic language capable of recognizing and incorporating multiple cultural sources and interdisciplinary languages. [...] This plural "other" America within the United States is located in the Indian reservations and Chicano neighborhoods of the Southwest [...] and although it still lacks a name and geopolitical configuration, we—as border artists—have the responsibility to reflect it. Our work in the realms of performance [...] serves as a sketch of a new cartography. (2006: 149–50)

Gómez-Peña's cartography includes an array of alternative subject positions overlayered in the performative personae of the cross—racially/ethnically/sexually—dressed Border Brujo, Naftazteca, and Mexterminator, among the many incarnations of Indigenous, Chicane, *Mestize*, Hispanic, Anglo, White, and Colored trans-selves. Their politically transformative impact lies in their staged multipositionality of the nomadic border crosser.

The politically transformative impact of neobaroque representations of alternative subject positions can be explained as an "ethos," a set of cultural values governing the collective cultural behaviors of a group. Gloria Anzaldúa used its more traditional form of "mythos" to refer to a combination of traditional beliefs that work into the transformation of the self as a new *mestiza* consciousness. Anzaldúa accurately transfers the Western ethos of progress to a more hybrid mythos of nepantlism in a new *mestiza* ethics, as a cross-cultural and transborder combination of traditionally Native American and modern Western values. As a plural subjectivity combining both masculinity and femininity, hetero and homosexuality, the *mestiza* character offers an identity model for (not only) the migrant subject exposed to cultural contact, transiting and adapting to multiple agencies of economic and social hegemony. Referring to the future of this borderland subject, she admits that: "*En unas pocas centurias*, the future will belong to the *mestiza*. Because the future depends on the breaking down of paradigms, it depends on the straddling of two or more cultures. By creating a new mythos—that is, a change in the way we perceive reality, the way we see ourselves, and the ways we behave—*la mestiza* creates a new consciousness" (2007: 102).

Roberto Echavarren refers to the ethical dimension of violence and oppression exerted by the categorizations of gender, intersectionally crossing with ethnicity, that is reminiscent of the triple discrimination of the lesbian *mestiza* woman portrayed by Anzaldúa (2007: 102–03). Cultural oppression endows Chicana literature with a political meaning. "To hit a woman is gender violence. But we have to realize that the matrix of gender is violence in itself. It oppresses us. We are bound to adjust to normal expectations having to do with gender codes, dress codes, coded attitudes and behavior, in conformity with dominant heterosexism" (Echavarren 2010: 22). In even more political terms, Cherríe Moraga refers to this violence as a "cultural war" waged virulently and disingenuously by the dominant majority with the marginalized minority in a struggle for cultural appropriation of "difference." However, Moraga warns that the very tools of cultural resistance become appropriated by hegemonical discourse with a neutralizing effect of meaningless multiplicity of "anything goes" and of superficial "political correctness" that hide the real issues at stake. Moraga reflects and asks:

> both hybridity and mestizaje intend to address the cross-cultural collisions of multiple identities (queer, transnational, gender, etc.) requisite of a post-modern world. But as metaphors, are they brave enough to counter the insidiousness of the U.S. project of a global empire, whose cultural agenda is to erase our awareness of the bitter realities of social difference? Do the terms not assume and succumb to the loss of our aboriginality with no hope for recuperation? (87–88)

The Baroque Ethos

Bolívar Echeverría (1994) presents the idea of a collective disposition of cultural resistance to governing socio-economic and political systems by introducing the universally encompassing concept of the "baroque ethos." It can be related to Louis Althusser's (1970) concept of "interpellation" as the process of encountering and internalizing cultural values that are imposed within the ideological context of a socio-cultural order. The "baroque ethos" represents a critical collective attitude (or consciousness) in cultural behaviors that constitute a reaction to the systemic *status quo*. Echeverría's term is motivated by the insufficient explanation of the "state of crisis" that seventeenth century (Baroque) and, in part, modern and postmodern philosophies have attempted to address. The "baroque ethos" is one of four ethoses that Echeverría uses to describe civilizational modes of cultural consciousness, alongside the realist, the romantic, and the classical. "Baroque" refers to a mode of interiorizing ("ethos") the condition of Modernity, as distanced from the all-empowering transcendence of capitalism and of considering it an inacceptable and alien necessity. As Elizabeth Ginway (2020) explains, the baroque ethos "has been developed by subaltern classes in Latin America as an attitude that enables them to survive and prosper in the face of the historic injustices and economic difficulties that have been imposed on them by colonialism and capitalism" (10). It stands as a "conflictive combination of conservatism and nonconformity" as it contests capitalism's view of profit and negotiates social reality in a way that avoids direct confrontation with hegemony in its pursuit of social and economic advantage (11). Stressing the importance of *mestizaje* [miscegenation] of cultural forms since the seventeenth century, Echeverría describes the baroque ethos as a strategy of survival, of "life after death, in the behavior of the subjugated 'natives,' that is, of the Indigenous and African descendants integrated in civil existence" (34; my translation). Their "silent" resistance carried on in the persistence of idiosyncratic modes of symbolization of reality in which defeat was relegated to a second level and the defensive creation of a new (imposed) culture was discreetly forged with the subversive trademark of the Other. Ginway further explains Echeverría's baroque ethos "as a set of strategies and attitudes forged by subalterns and their allies as a way of surviving on the margins of capitalism" (11). In line with the political dimension of neobaroque figurations of the nomadic subject, she explains that "[t]he emphasis on the body and survival are in harmony with Echeverría's baroque ethos of resistance while surviving within capitalism" (13). From a political perspective, the concept "forms an overarching approach to non-normative sexualities, in the sense that those who flouted societal norms were forced to find ways around the increasingly punitive attitudes toward their behavior" (15). In relation to Latin American speculative fiction, Ginway uses "baroque ethos" to illustrate ways of "negotiating sexuality" by the non-heterosexual subject in a less confrontational mode, and even as a method of "resistance through sexuality and gender" that, borrowing the term from Nemi Neto, she describes as "baroque queer" (15).

As much as this ethos—a cultural state of mind—admits capitalism as a "natural and inevitable form" of civilization, it "resists in accepting it," proposing a "silent [secret] resistance" through imaginary forms of cultural creation and eroticism. In George Bataille's terms, this means an "approval of life even in death" (Echeverría 1994: 20–21; my translation). Therefore, the "baroque ethos" is a lurking consciousness of resistance and a "will for form" (24). In this form, the old reencounters its opposite—the modern. It synthesizes rejection with fidelity as two aspects in one eclectic whole of cultural awareness of multiplicity and contradiction that we propose to link (following Echeverría) to the Neobaroque state of mind. Its artistic forms are in unconformity with the mercantile (realist and classical) vision of the world and art, but the (neo)baroque recycles and subjugates them in a "game of transgression that refunctionalizes [redefines] them" (1994: 26–27).

This tacitly subversive attitude is reflective of the previously mentioned postmodern crisis and decentering of the unitary Subject present in the grand (meta)narratives of Modernity (Lyotard 1984). It relates to a more generalized critique of the canonical humanist subject in light of the decentering vision of philosophical posthumanism that is influenced by posthuman theory's radical vision of the hybrid cyborg figure. For example, the unitary agency of an autonomous controlling human is rejected by Katherine Hayles who takes a firm stand in favor of a radical redefinition of the subject in a more flexible posthuman condition of bodily materiality fused with artificial intelligence. This position attacks "the classical humanistic notion that subjectivity must coincide with conscious agency, [...] an autonomous subject whose 'manifest destiny is to dominate and control nature'" (Hayles in Braidotti 2002: 256).

The Neobaroque work configures a fluid migratory space of Trans-American cultural nomadism that transforms the concept of identity into a consciousness of difference. Nomadism is a projection of one's becoming in otherness in the transitive border zone of contact that is *nepantla*. Trans-identity does not crystallize into any *one* alternative identity, but rather, in a dimension of trans-it, it acquires political meaning by questioning exclusive binarism and other Manichean forms of duality. By giving a voice to mobilized trans*identities, it destabilizes the heteronormative and logocentric system of power, the neocolonial hegemonic discourse of socio-economic establishment. It relativizes the *status quo* of imposed cultural tradition. As part of the hybrid postcolonial context of Latin America, the literary and artistic works of the Neobaroque carry a political meaning of parodic dethronement of bourgeois economy, as stated by Sarduy (1987b: 209). The *neobaroque of transgression* "cross-dresses" cultural categories with its strategy of opulent figurative language and exuberant performance to articulate a *sui generis* Latin American (sub-/per-) version of the variegated postmodern discourse. With its eccentric common denominator of cross-border *nomadism*, it calls for the subject's authenticity (in flexibility) and emancipation from the dominant neocolonializing and commercialized neoliberal Western cultural paradigm.

Today sexuality, race, ethnicity, and nationality are politically questionable categories in the multicultural, yet conflictive American (and global) context marked by social upheaval, crises, and revolts that oppose the totalizing and oppressive discourses of neofascist populism. However, many young people search for perhaps less combative, more creative, and inclusive ways to live out their versions of selfhood. One need only to observe the presence of the multiple urban cliques in the first decades of the 2000s, particularly emos, punks, and Pokémons, with their "alternative," androgynous, and mutant look to see how jaded the new generation is with the outdated categories of gender, sexuality, nationhood, ethnicity, and race. They are intent on finding other, more alternative, forms of

344   K. A. KULAWIK

identity marked by transitivity and nomadism. Notwithstanding the political intentionality of trans-identity, maybe it is worthwhile to perceive the philosophical rewards of nomadism with a more aesthetically focused approach based on Neobaroque's "insubordinate exuberance" (Zamora 2006). Another path is to focus on subjectivity with a peaceful return to the original concept of yin and yang. The possibilities are endless. The transformist flexibility of the cross-dresser and the coalescent value of the androgyne's fusion of binaries provide alternative routes for Oneness to complement with and transit into Otherness. Let us leave the matter here to future speculation about the philosophical interpretations and political implications of the nomadic trans-self as one-t(w)o-many selves in transit.

WORKS CITED

A. PRIMARY SOURCES (ANALYZED WORKS)

Anzaldúa, Gloria. (2007 [1987]). *Borderlands / La Frontera: The New Mestiza*. San Francisco: Spinsters / Aunt Lute.

Bellatin, Mario. (2000 [1994]). *Beauty Salon*. Trans. Kurt Hollander. San Francisco: City Lights Books.

Bellatin, Mario. (2015). *Jacob the Mutant*. Trans. Jacob Steinberg. Los Angeles: Phoneme Media.

Echavarren, Roberto. (2009). *Yo era una brasa*. Montevideo: Ed. HUM.

Gómez-Peña, Guillermo. (1996). *The New World Border: Prophecies, Poems & Loqueras for the End of the Century*. San Francisco: City Lights Books.

Gómez-Peña, Guillermo. (2000). *Dangerous Border Crossers: The Artist Talks Back*. London-New York: Routledge.

Gómez-Peña, Guillermo. (2006). *Bitácora del cruce (Textos poéticos para accionar, ritos fronterizos, videografitis, y otras rolas y roles)*. México: Fondo de Cultura Económica.

Hilst, Hilda. (1993). *Rútilo nada. A obscena Senhora D. Qadós*. Campinas, Brasil: Pontes.

Hilst, Hilda. (2006). *Estar sendo. Ter sido*. São Paulo: Ed. Globo.

Menstrual, Naty. (2008). *Continuadísimo*. Buenos Aires: Eterna Cadencia.

Prado Bassi, Eugenia. (2004). *Hembros. Performance-installation of novel with screenplay booklet*. Santiago, Chile: Beca Fondart Artes Integradas. Chants 1-12. DVD.

Sarduy, Severo. (1970 [1967]). *De donde son los cantantes*. México: J. Mortiz.

Sarduy, Severo. (1975). *Cobra*. Trans. Suzanne Jill Levine. New York: E.P. Dutton.

4 ONE-T(W)O-MANY: NEOBAROQUE ARTICULATIONS OF NOMADIC... 345

Sarduy, Severo. (1981 [1972]). *Cobra*. 2 ed. Barcelona: Edhasa.
Sarduy, Severo. (1994). *From Cuba with a Song*. Trans. Suzanne Jill Levine. Los Angeles: Sun and Moon Press.

B. SECONDARY SOURCES (CRITICAL AND THEORETICAL REFERENCES)

Althusser, Louis. (1970). *For Marx*. New York: Vintage.
A-mi, Jo. (2016). "Do sublime e do grotesco: a obscenidade em Hilda Hilst." *Acta Scientiarum. Language and Culture*. 38.3: 291–99.
Anzaldúa, Gloria and AnaLouise Keating, eds. (2002). *This Bridge We Call Home: Radical Visions for Transformation*. New York: Routledge.
Anzaldúa, Gloria E. (2009). *The Gloria Anzaldúa Reader*. Ed. AnaLouise Keating. Durham and London: Duke UP.
Araujo, Kathya, ed. (2007). *Cruce de lenguas: Sexualidades, diversidad y ciudadanías*. Santiago de Chile: LOM Ediciones.
Arriarán, Samuel. (2007). *Barroco y neobarroco en América Latina: Estudios sobre la otra modernidad*. México: Ítaca.
Aruquipa Pérez, David. (2016). "Placer, deseo y política: la revolución estética de La Familia Galán". *Bulletin de l'Institut Français d'Études Andines*. 45.3 (2016): 451–61.
Bakhtin, Mikhail. (1981). *The Dialogic Imagination. Four Essays*. Austin: U of Texas P.
Baler, Pablo. (2016). *Latin American Neo-Baroque: Senses of Distortion*. Trans. Michael McGaha. New York: Palgrave.
Barthes, Roland. (1973). *Le plaisir du texte*. Paris: Du Seuil.
Barthes, Roland. (1983). *The Fashion System*. Trans. Matthew Ward and Richard Howard. New York: Hill and Wang.
Bataille, Georges. (1957). *L'érotisme*. Paris: Éditions de Minuit.
Bataille, Georges. (1967). "La notion de dépense." In: *La part maudite*. Paris: Minuit. 29–64.
Bataille, Georges. (1976). "La limite de l'utile." In: *Oeuvres complètes*. Paris: Gallimard. Vol. V, VII. 185–18.
Baudrillard, Jean. (1994 [1981]). *Simulacra and Simulation*. Trans. Sheila Faria Glaser. Ann Arbor: U of Michigan P.
Bhabha, Homi. (1990). "DissemiNation: time, narrative, and the margins of the modern nation." *Nation and Narration*. Ed. Homi Bhabha. New York: Routledge. 290–315.
Blanco, Fernando and Juan Gelpi. (1997). "El desliz que desafía otros recorridos: entrevista con Pedro Lemebel." *Nomadías*. 3 (1997): 93–98.
Bosch, Lolita. (2007). "Mario Bellatin: Tumbado en la cama y mirando el techo." *Quimera*. 284 (2007): 88–91.

346   K. A. KULAWIK

Braidotti, Rosi. (1994). *Nomadic Subjects: Embodiment and Sexual Difference in Contemporary Feminist Theory.* New York: Columbia UP.

Braidotti, Rosi. (2002). *Metamorphoses: Towards a Materialist Theory of Becoming.* Cambridge, UK: Polity Press.

Braidotti, Rosi. (2006). *Transpositions: On Nomadic Ethics.* Cambridge, UK: Polity Press.

Brown, J. Andrew. (2007). "Identidad poshumana en *Lóbulo* de Eugenia Prado". *Revista Iberoamericana.* LXXIII. 221: 801–12.

Bustillo, Carmen. (1990). *Barroco y América Latina: un itinerario inconcluso.* Caracas: Monte Ávila.

Butler, Judith (1990). *Gender Trouble.* New York: Routledge.

Butler, Judith. (1993). *Bodies That Matter: On the Discursive Limits of Sex.* New York: Routledge.

Chaves, José Ricardo. (2005). *Andróginos: Eros y Ocultismo en la literatura romántica.* México: UNAM.

Chiampi, Irlemar. (2000). *Barroco y modernidad.* México: Fondo de Cultura Económica.

Coelho, Nelly Novaes. (1973). Review of *Qadós* by Hilda Hilst. *Colóquio Letras* 8 (1973): 87–88.

Copello, Francisco. (1999). *Fotografía de Performance: Análisis autobiográfico de mis performances.* Santiago de Chile: Ocho Libros Editores.

D'Angelo, Biagio. (2007). "Neo-Baroque Poetics: A Latin American Affair." *Caribbean Interfaces.* Ed. Lieven d'Hulst. Amsterdam: Rodopi.

Deleuze, Gilles and Claire Parnet. (1987a [1977]). *Dialogues.* Trans. Hugh Tomlinson and Barbara Habberjam. New York: Columbia UP.

Deleuze, Gilles and Félix Guattari (1987b [1980]). *A Thousand Plateaus. Capitalism and Schizophrenia.* Trans. Brian Massumi. Minneapolis: U of Minnesota P.

Diego, Estrella de. (2018). *El andrógino sexuado: Eternos ideales, nuevas estrategias de género.* Madrid: La Balsa de la Medusa.

Echavarren, Roberto. (2000). *Performance: género y transgénero.* Buenos Aires: Eudeba.

Echavarren, Roberto. (2008). *Arte andrógino: estilo versus moda.* Santiago de Chile: Ripio.

Echavarren, Roberto. (2010). "Resistance." *The Journal of Natural and Social Philosophy.* Vol 6, no. 2, (2010): 20–26.

Echavarren, Roberto. (2014). *Fuera de género: Criaturas de la invención erótica.* Buenos Aires: Ed. Losada.

Echeverría, Bolívar, ed. (1994). *Modernidad, mestizaje cultural, ethos barroco.* México, D.F.: UNAM-Equilibrista.

Eliade, Mircea. (1969). *Mefistófeles y el andrógino.* Madrid: Ed. Guadarrama.

4 ONE-T(W)O-MANY: NEOBAROQUE ARTICULATIONS OF NOMADIC... 347

Ellis, Albert and Albert Abarbaniel. (1961). The Encyclopedia of Social Behavior. Vols. 1, 2. New York: Hawthorn Books.

Estébanez Calderón, Demetrio. (1996). *Diccionario de términos literarios*. Madrid: Alianza.

Fernández, Josefina. (2004). *Cuerpos desobedientes: Travestismo e identidad de género*. Buenos Aires: Edhasa.

Figueroa Sánchez, Cristo Rafael. (2008). *Barroco y neobarroco en la narrativa hispanoamericana. Cartografías literarias de la segunda mitad del siglo XX*. Bogotá-Medellín: Pontificia Universidad Javeriana-Universidad de Antioquia.

Franca, Tatiana Rodrigues. (2012). "A compreensão é uma grande porca acinzentada—Uma leitura sobre a busca da linguagem em *A obscena senhora D* de Hilda Hilst." *Brasiliana—Journal for Brazilian Studies*, 1.1: 84–102.

Gálvez Acero, Marina. (1987). *La novela hispanoamericana contemporánea*. Madrid: Taurus.

Garabato, Sandra. "Lemebel: políticas de consenso, masculinidad y travestismo." *Chasqui* 32. 1 (2003): 47–55.

Garber, Marjorie. (1997 [1992]). *Vested Interests: Cross-dressing and Cultural Anxiety*. 2nd ed. New York: Routledge.

Ginway, M. Elizabeth. (2020). *Cyborgs, Sexuality, and the Undead: Body in Mexican and Brazilian Speculative Fiction*. Nashville: Vanderbilt UP.

Gómez-Muller, Alfredo. (2019). Book review of Silvia Rivera Cusicanqui. *Un mundo* ch'ixi *es posible. Ensayos desde un presente en crisis*. Buenos Aires: Tinta Limón, 2018. In *Ciencia Política*. 14.28: 309–13. https://doi.org/10.15446/cp.v14n28.82650

González Echevarría, Roberto. (1987). *La ruta de Severo Sarduy*. Hanover, N. H.: Norte.

Gosser-Esquilín, Mary Ann. (1991). "*Cobra*: Writing Is the Art of Ellipsis and Digression." *Critical Essays on the Literatures of Spain and Spanish America*. Eds. Luis T. González-del-Valle and Julio Baena. Boulder, Colorado: Society of Spanish and Spanish American Studies. 111–20.

Grosz, Elizabeth. (1994). *Volatile Bodies: Toward a Corporeal Feminism*. Bloomington & Indianapolis: Indiana UP.

Halberstam, Jack. (2018). *Trans*: A Quick and Quirky Account of Gender Variability*. Oakland: U of California P.

Haraway, Donna J. (1991). *Simians, Cyborgs, and Women: The Reinvention of Nature*. New York: Routledge.

Hawley, Daniel. (1978). *L'oeuvre insolite de Georges Bataille: une hiérophanie moderne*. Geneva–Paris: Slatkine–Champion.

Hayles, N. Katherine. (1999). *How We Became Posthuman: Virtual Bodies in Cybernetics, Literature, and Informatics*. Chicago, London: U of Chicago P.

348 K. A. KULAWIK

Heusden, Barrend van. (1996). "Aesthetic and artistic semiosis: A Peircean perspective." In *Peirce's Doctrine of Signs. Theory, Applications, and Connections.* Eds. Vincent M. Colapietro and Thomas M. Olshewsky. Berlin, New York: Mouton de Gruyter. 239–50.

Hind, Emily. (2004). "Entrevista con Mario Bellatin". *Confluencia.* 20.1: 197–204.

Hogan, Steve and Lee Hudson. (1998). *Completely Queer: The Gay and Lesbian Encyclopedia.* New York: Henry Holt.

Irigaray, Luce. (1984). *L'éthique de la différence sexuelle.* Paris: Minuit.

Jagose, Annamarie. (1996). *Queer Theory. An Introduction.* New York: New York UP.

Jagose, Annemarie. (2015). "The Trouble with Antinormativity." *Differences: A Journal of Feminist Cultural Studies.* Brown University. 26.1: 26–47.

Kaup, Monika. (2012). *Neobaroque in the Americas. Alternative Modernities in Literature, Visual Art, and Film.* Charlottesville and London, U of Virginia P.

Kiremidjian, David. (1985). *A Study of Modern Parody.* New York and London: Garland Press.

Kristeva, Julia. (1969). *Semeiotiké. Recherches pour une sémanalyse.* Paris: Seuil.

Kristeva, Julia. (2006). *Poderes de la perversión.* México: Siglo XXI.

Kulawik, Krzysztof. (2009). *Travestismo lingüístico: el enmascaramiento de la identidad sexual en la narrativa latinoamericana neobarroca.* Madrid, Frankfurt am Main: Iberoamericana-Vervuert.

Kulawik, Krzysztof. (2012). "Asediar la literatura, la política y la cultura: conversación con la escritora chilena Eugenia Prado Bassi." *Revista Nomadías.* 16 (2012): 227–46.

Kulick, Don. (1998). *Travesti: Sex, Gender and Culture among Brazilian Transgendered Prostitutes.* Chicago: U of Chicago P.

Kushigian, Julia A. (1999). "Severo Sarduy, orientalista posmodernista en camino hacia la autorrealización. *Une ménagerie à trois: Cobra, Colibrí y Cocuyo.*" In *Sarduy. Obra completa.* Eds. Gustavo Guerrero and Francois Wahl. Madrid: Galaxia Gutenberg, Colección Archivos. 1605–18.

Lewis, Vek. (2010). *Crossing Sex and Gender in Latin America.* New York: Palgrave Macmillan.

Lezama Lima, José. (1957). *La expresión americana.* La Habana, Cuba: Instituto Nacional de Cultura.

López Alfonso, Francisco José. (2008). "Modernismo y nihilismo en *Lecciones para una liebre Muerta.*" *Studi di letteratura ispano-americana.* 39–40 (2008): 125–42.

Lyotard, Jean-François. (1984 [1979]). *The Postmodern Condition: A Report on Knowledge.* Trans. Geoff Bennington and Brian Massumi. Minneapolis: U of Minnesota P.

Mateo del Pino, Ángeles. (1998). "Chile, una *loca* geografía o las crónicas de Pedro Lemebel." *Hispamérica.* 27. 80: 17–28.

Méndez-Ródenas, Adriana. (1985). Review of *Colibrí* by Severo Sarduy. *Revista Iberoamericana*. 51 (1985): 399–401.

Moraes, Eliane Robert. (1999). "Da medida estilhaçada." *Cadernos de Literatura Brasileira*. 8 (1999): 114–26.

Moraga, Cherríe L. (2011). *A Xicana Codex of Changing Consciousness*. Durham, NC: Duke UP.

Morris, Charles. (1972). *Fundamentos de la teoría de los signos*. Madrid: Taurus.

Muñoz, José Esteban. (1999). *Disidentifications: Queers of Color and the Performance of Politics*. Minneapolis and London: U. of Minnesota P.

Norat, Gisela. (2002). *Marginalities: Diamela Eltit and the Subversion of Mainstream Literature in Chile*. Newark: University of Delaware Press.

Ortega, José. (1984). *La estética neobarroca en la narrativa hispanoamericana*. Madrid: José Porrúa Turanzas.

Peirce, Charles S. (1987). *Obra lógico-semiótica*. Madrid: Taurus.

Peirce, Charles S. (1991). *Peirce on Signs: Writings on Semiotic by Charles Sanders Peirce*. Ed. James Hoopes. Chapel Hill: U of North Carolina P.

Peralta, Jorge Luis. (2010). "La narrativa travesti de Naty Menstrual." *Lectora*, 17 (2010): 105–22.

Perlongher, Néstor. (1997). *Prosa plebeya*. Buenos Aires: Colihue.

Pharies, David A. (1985). *Charles S. Peirce and the Linguistic Sign*. Amsterdam, Philadelphia: John Benjamins.

Plaza Atenas, Dino. (1999). "Lemebel o el salto de doble filo." *Revista Chilena de Literatura*. 54 (1999): 123–35.

Poblete, Nicolás. (2000). "Engendrando el texto posthumano en *Lóbulo* de Eugenia Prado." *Crítica.cl. Revista Latinoamericana de Ensayo*. http://www.critica.cl/html/poblete_01.html. Santiago de Chile. Vol. 4. 20 July, 2000. Engendrando el texto posthumano en Lóbulo, de Eugenia Prado. – Critica.cl Accessed 30.

Prado, Eugenia. (2015). "Resistencia neobarroca en *Claustro Cordillera* de Álvaro Castro, una épica, una poética." Essay presented at Cierre del Taller Avanzado de Moda y Pueblo, dir. Diego Ramírez, Santiago de Chile, June 2015. Accessed in Academia.edu: https://www.academia.edu/13798136/Resistencia_neo-barroca_en_Claustro_Cordillera. June 10, 2020.

Pratt, Mary Louise. (1993). "Criticism in the Contact Zone: Decentering Community and Nation." *Critical Theory, Cultural Politics, and Latin American Narrative*. Eds. Steven, M. Bell, Albert H. Lemay y Leonard Orr. Notre Dame: U of Notre Dame P, 83–102.

Quinlan, Susan Canty and Fernando Arenas, eds. (2002). *Lusosex: Gender and Sexuality in the Portuguese-Speaking World*. Minneapolis and London: U of Minnesota P.

Randell, John. (1976). *Sexual Variations*. Westport, Conn.: Technomic Publishing Company.

Reguera, Nilze Maria de Azeredo and Susana Busato, eds. (2015). *Em torno de Hilda Hilst.* São Paulo: Editora UNESP.

Richard, Nelly. (1993). Masculino/Femenino. *Prácticas de la diferencia y cultura democrática.* Santiago, Chile: Francisco Zegers.

Richard, Nelly. (1996). "Feminismo, experiencia y representación." *Revista Iberoamericana.* LXII.176–77: 733–44.

Richard, Nelly. (2002). "Tres recursos de emergencia: las rebeldías populares, el desorden somático y la palabra extrema." Proyecto Patrimonio: Escritores y Poetas en Español. Letras.mysite.com; http://www.letras.mysite.com/eltit091202.htm. Accessed November 26, 2022.

Richardson, Michael, ed. (1998). *Georges Bataille—Essential Writings.* London: Sage.

Rivera Cusicanqui, Silvia. (2020 [2010]) *Ch'ixinakax utxiwa. On Practices and Discourses of Decolonization.* Trans. Molly Geidel. Cambridge, UK and Medford, MA: Polity Press.

Rivera Cusicanqui, Silvia. (2018). *Un mundo ch'ixi es posible. Ensayos desde un presente en crisis.* Buenos Aires: Tinta Limón.

Roberts, Edward A., ed. (2014). *A Comprehensive Etymological Dictionary of the Spanish Language with Families of Words Based on Indo-European Roots.* Vol 2. Thorofare, NJ: Xlibris.

Rodríguez, Fermín. (2006). "Mario Bellatin" (entrevista). *Hispamérica.* 35.103 (2006): 63–69.

Ruiz-Aho, Elena. (2011). "Feminist Border Thought". Eds. Delanty, G. and S.P. Turner. *Routledge International Handbook of Contemporary Social and Political Theory.* London: Taylor and Francis.

Santiago, Silviano. (2001). *The Space In-Between: Essays on Latin American Culture.* Ed. Ana Lúcia Gazzola. Trans. Tom Burns, Ana Lúcia Gazzola, and Gareth Williams. Durham and London: Duke UP.

Sarduy, Severo. (1978 [1972]). "El barroco y el neobarroco." *América Latina en su literatura.* 5th ed. Coord. César Fernández Moreno. México: Siglo XXI. 167–84.

Sarduy, Severo. (1984). "Deterritorialization." Trans. Naomi Lindstrom. *Review of Contemporary Fiction.* 4 (1984): 104–09.

Sarduy, Severo. (1987a [1969]). Escrito sobre un cuerpo. In *Ensayos generales sobre el Barroco.* Buenos Aires: Fondo de Cultura Económica. 225–67.

Sarduy, Severo. (1987b [1974]). Barroco. In *Ensayos generales sobre el Barroco.* Buenos Aires: Fondo de Cultura Económica. 143–224.

Sarduy, Severo. (1987c [1982]). La simulación. In *Ensayos generales sobre el Barroco.* Buenos Aires: Fondo de Cultura Económica. 51–142.

Sarduy, Severo. (1990). "Writing/Transvestism." *Modern Latin American Fiction.* Ed. Harold Bloom. New York: Chelsea House. 221–24.

Saussure, Ferdinand de. (1955 [1916]). *Cours de linguistique générale.* Paris: Payot.

Scarpetta, Guy. (1988). *L'artifice*. Paris: Grasset.

Scarpetta, Guy. (1992). *Le retour du Barroque*. Paris: Gallimard.

Sifuentes-Jáuregui, Ben. (2002). *Transvestism, Masculinity and Latin American Literature*. New York: Palgrave.

Vaggione, Alicia. (2009). "Literatura/enfermedad: el cuerpo como desecho. Una lectura de *Salón de belleza* de Mario Bellatin." *Revista Iberoamericana*. LXXV.227 (2009): 475–86.

Vivancos Pérez, Ricardo F. (2013). *Radical Chicana Poetics*. New York: Palgrave Macmillan.

Wayar, Marlene. (2019). *Travesti / Una teoría lo suficientemente buena*. Buenos Aires: Muchas Nueces.

Zamora, Lois Parkinson. (2006). *The Inordinate Eye. New World Baroque and Latin American Fiction*. Chicago and London: U of Chicago P.

Zamora, Lois Parkinson and Kaup, Monika, eds. (2010). *Baroque New Worlds: Representation, Transculturation, Counterconquest*. Durham: Duke UP.

Zamora, Lois Parkinson. (2011). *La mirada exuberante: Barroco novomundista y literatura latinoamericana*. Frankfurt am Main and México: Iberoamericana-Vervuert, UNAM, Bonilla Artigas.

CHAPTER 5

Conclusions: At the Crossroads of *Nepantla*

What we are suffering from is an absolute despot duality
that says we are able to be only one or the other.

—Gloria Anzaldúa, *Borderlands / La Frontera* (2007: 41)

5.1 Latin America and the Transformative Potential of Neobaroque Nomadism

The transgressions of boundaries that we have observed in the works of the Latin American Neobaroque carry aesthetic, political, and philosophical implications of a larger cultural order. They reveal the presence of borderland nomadic subjects, which unfolds the possibility for the reader, viewer, and critic to reenvision the normative categorical concept of Identity, bound by a hegemonic heterosexual neocolonial system of the Logos, and to conceptualize an alternative model of selfhood in transidentity. Approaching identity transformations and boundary crossings of established categories from the vantage point of Latin American literature and visual arts, particularly narrative and performance, allows us to conceive selfhood as transitivity and mobility, as flexible subjectivity. The neobaroque works' inclusion of gender-bending themes of cross-dressing, androgyny, and queerness leads us to consider boundary crossings, transits, and broader cultural and political transformations taking place in the

© The Author(s), under exclusive license to Springer Nature   353
Switzerland AG 2024
K. A. Kulawik, *Visions of Transmerica*, Literatures of the Americas,
https://doi.org/10.1007/978-3-031-42014-6_5

354   K. A. KULAWIK

hybrid and heterogeneous spaces of a decolonizing transcultural America. In the first decades of the twenty-first century, the Americas still represent a crossroads of cultures transited by shifting minoritarian and peripheral voices, some of which have found a form of expression in the exuberant style of the Neobaroque. These voices are the embodiment of a nomadic selfhood that shapes in the multiplying borderland spaces of migratory contacts, transits, and transgressions that conform the Trans-American crossroads of *nepantla*.

Any reflection on art and literature in Latin America at the dawn of the twenty-first century is bound to include references to migration, displacement, and nomadism often beset by violent confrontations, but also to cultural (trans)fusions and mixings (*mestizaje*) epitomized in hybrid identity transformations resulting from historical contacts. Racial, ethnic, and social variability appears analogous with transgression of gender binarity and heterosexual normativity in the multiple "queer becomings" and gender-sexual variations of cross-cultural, inter-racial/-ethnic, and post-human subjects. The dialogic dimension of the novel (recalled earlier with Bakhtin), extending to other neobaroque textual and visual forms of performance and painting, provides an aesthetic platform to the polyphony of a culturally mobile and unstable American continent. Carmen Bustillo aptly sums it up: "It could be argued that Latin America has never ceased to be in crisis, to be historically dislocated [...] a continent in formation, aware of its exogenous location and its own exoticism" (1990: 94; my translation). Its multiple, hybrid, and fragmented identities are the product of a complex intercrossing and overlapping of heterogeneous elements of the three major world races and countless ethnicities, and whose interaction (as coexistence or fusion) does not preclude elements of friction and violence. The particularly diverse context that is America is prone to such historical violence, as Chilean novelist and critic Ariel Dorfman remarked:

> The aggression has long since begun: America is the fruit of prolonged violence, of continuous plundering, of civil and fratricidal war throughout its geography. The novel itself, the aesthetic act, is a protest against a world that tries to deny that violence, hoping perhaps that in the bombardment of linguistic slaps someone will wake up to ask fundamental questions in order to critically look at reality itself and become an integral human being. (1972: 41; my translation)

The narrative, essays, poetry, performance, and visual works that we have presented offer precisely that "bombardment of linguistic slaps" and critical awakening carried out by the aesthetic act of the neobaroque work with its transgressively unstable and mutant trans*(-sexual, -ethnic, -racial, -cultural, and -/post-human) subjects.

Neobaroque's functionality in aesthetic representation is that of destabilizing any fixed notions of identity determined in politically and culturally established normative categories. The decentering of selfhood is symbolized in a series of Latin American works by the borderland nomad— an ambiguous and transitive self. To this effect, the dynamic and mobile "triadic" sign, based on Peirce's model, serves as the carrier of unstable meaning in the neobaroque work and acts as a semiotic mechanism in the interpretation of transgressive characters in the works, and subsequently in our articulation of a trans-identity and figuration of the trans-self.

In philosophical and literary terms, neobaroque narrative overtakes social convention and science, fields that conceive sexuality in definable binary categories, whether hetero or homosexual. Considering that many of the works examined here represent it in ambiguous terms of transvestism, androgyny, and queerness, it is viable to conclude that neobaroque aesthetics advance a distinct intersectional vision (or even theory) of identity. It results in the notion of trans*-identity (or transentity) embodied by a mobile trans-self that transgresses the heterosexual and logocentric framework of institutionalized selfhood.[1] To the extent that they do not fall within the parameters of mimetic realism, Sarduy's, Bellatin's, Eltit's, Echavarren's, and Hilst's neobaroque novels, as well as the performance works mentioned in the analysis, acquire a radical political resonance, as well as a feminist and queer one. In addition to the long list of names included in this study, we would be remiss not to mention, for the lack of space, Chilean performer Francisco Copello, Peruvian visual artist Christian Bendayán, Czech-Peruvian writer Mirko Lauer, Puerto Rican novelists Luis Rafael Sánchez and Mayra Santos-Febres, and Cuban narrators Jesús Gardea, Ezequiel Vieta, María Liliana Celorrio, and Ena Lucía Portela who, in the vein of Sarduy, continue to spread Lezama's neobaroque "creative leprosy."

There is also the Neobaroque vein of the Río de la Plata where, before contemporary Uruguayans Roberto Echavarren, Cristina Peri Rossi, and Argentine Luisa Valenzuela, there was an Osvaldo Lamborghini and a Héctor Libertella in Buenos Aires, and where, more recently, Washington Cucurto, Naty Menstrual, Susy Shock, Camila Sosa Villada, and Gabriela

---

[1] With all due credit to Jack Halberstam for introducing the term "trans*" (2018).

Cabezón Cámara continue cultivating this exuberant style with interracial and transsexual themes. Probably the most significant neobaroque mark was left by Néstor Perlongher, who built a stylistic bridge linking the Río de la Plata with Brazil. There, the neobaroque line emerging in the 1960s is associated with Haroldo de Campos and Paulo Leminsky in literature and Hélio Oiticica in visual-plastic arts; in narrative, the list includes the radical neo-vanguardism of Clarice Lispector and her epigone, Hilda Hilst, as well as novelists and essayists Silviano Santiago, João Gilberto Noll, and Osman Lins, all of whom continued in the neobaroque mood.

As transgressors of normativity, the displaced transcultural mutants and nomads of neobaroque works attack from the margins, and with experimental linguistic exuberance, the established discursive order and its mimetic-logocentric system of representation, particularly the traditional novel as a nineteenth-century and bourgeois form *par excellence*. They attack a system of neoliberal capitalist order that conceives language in terms of the economy of effective communication (as mimetic-realistic representation) and savings (as accumulation of wealth). The neobaroque text bursts into and unmasks the arbitrary nature of linguistic representation and of language as a communicative system beset with underlying power relations that hold normative categories in place. By questioning the stable boundaries in sexual, racial, ethnic, and cultural distinctions, the neobaroque unbalances the system of values considered indisputably "natural," determined not only by Western scientific discourse, as Thomas Laqueur explained in *Making Sex* (1990), but also by the Eurocentric neocolonial cultural discourse. Moreover, it is legitimate to suppose that the presence of the neobaroque discursive mode is also the result of what Lyotard pointed out in *The Postmodern Condition* (1984) as the crisis of the totalizing and uniform discourse of identity, a crisis that leads to the emergence of a fragmented, malleable, if anything, open discourse and ontology, as explained by Alfonso de Toro (1997: 13, 17), Steven Best (1991: 3), and Samuel Arriarán (1997: 27–28).[2] This "postmodern condition" is portrayed by the neobaroque texts mentioned in this study. The

---

[2] Alfonso de Toro makes the following observation: "Postmodernity can be understood as the search for new identities, not by means of exclusion or discrimination, but by means of integration, 'habitation.' Lyotard's metaphor referring to 'modernity pregnant with postmodernity' amounts, on the one hand, to the creation of a new language that seeks the constitution of new systems of signification in the deep structures of thought, exactly where it is born and constructed, and on the other, to the production of discontinuity, diversity, and difference in the surface structure. There is a tendency to reconcile both structures, as this line of thought pursues a universality and totality in multiplicity and fragmentation" (17; my translation).

Neobaroque presents itself as the bearer of a decentered intercultural dialog that, in its heterogeneity, is characteristically Latin American. It also constitutes an aesthetic proposal of a particularly Latin American (postmodern) condition, voicing the fragmented and mobile subject of a non-binary, hybrid cultural identity.

By relativizing the concepts of heteronormative sexuality, transvestism and androgyny divert attention to the "contact zone" (Pratt 1993) of both sexes and genders that situates in the in-between zone of the binary categories of masculinity and femininity at the intersections of other cultural categories. They point to the gray zone of transition—*ch'ixi* and *nepantla*—and to the "spaces in between." In the words of José Ismael Gutiérrez, "[t]his roaming across spatial and identity borders presupposes a vertiginous dynamic full of transversal experiences" that emerge from the linguistic displacements of the neobaroque text (2013: 21; my translation). The works of Sarduy, Bellatin, Echavarren, Anzaldúa, and others lead to the deconstruction of defined sexualities and totalizing definitions, offering a springboard for the formulation of a new theory of a transcultural nomadic subject.

Sarduy's classic, *Cobra*, presents avenues for the study of other more recent novels that do not fit the confines of this inquiry, yet contain cross-dressed, androgynous, and mutant protagonists, such as Pedro Lemebel's *Tengo miedo torero*, Dani Umpi's *Aún soltera*, Mayra Santos-Febres's *Sirena Selena vestida de pena*, Roberto Echavarren's *Yo era una brasa*, and Hilda Hilst's *Fluxo-Floema*. The ambiguous characters sketched out in these works manifest an impossibility of apprehending identity in any sexual or cultural belonging. Again, Gutiérrez states that "his/her [the transvestite's] displacements intensify the formation of a nomadic, transitive consciousness, which lies in the opposition to dressing up in a kind of permanent national and personal identity" (2013: 21). The works presented here intonate a "baroque fugue" that escapes categorization in the open narrative, performative, and artistic forms of the postmodern neobaroque text, laying bare the very mechanisms of representation. They assume a posture of political dissidence in opposition to the system of authoritative administration of meaning, imposed by the colonializing White-masculine logos. Neobaroque discourse chooses to parodically stylize the stilted artistic language of the baroque tradition of the Spanish Golden Age and of nineteenth-century French and Hispanic Modernism. At the end of the twentieth century and the beginning of the twenty-first, it does so for risibly playful and deconstructive purposes, as a voice from the peripheries of the multicultural Western world, as a form of expression of a nomadic Trans-American selfhood.

358   K. A. KULAWIK

The Neobaroque enters the broader picture of what Braidotti criticizes as "the imaginative deficit of our culture, that is to say our collective inability to find adequate representations of the kind of embodied nomadic subjects we have already become –multiple, complex, multi-layered selves" (2002: 258). Conditioned by desire, affectivity, movement, and inclusiveness, this destabilizing style illustrates conceptual shifts (or deterritorializations) taking place at the depths of subjectivity. The Neobaroque opens the field to philosophical inquiry that approaches selfhood from the three angles of ontology, epistemology, and axiology (aesthetics), by presenting (the) "trans*it/self" as a positive deconstruction of identity by way of the transitive, mobile, and nomadic subject. A nomadic approach has the potential to make a lasting impact on the social and cultural discourses of the yet to be defined postmodernity, as much as it is claimed they are in a state of crisis. Ultimately, the explorations of nomadic trans-its (or selves) allow us to broaden the vision of the border as not a limiting space, but as a point of contact and opening to otherness. Borderland identities connect with the Neobaroque in that both effectively express and represent the breadth of Latin American cultural heterogeneity experienced through cross-border contacts and migrations. The potential of neobaroque expression founded in baroque devices is truly border-breaking. Concluding Chapter 5 of *The Inordinate Eye*, "Baroque Illusionism of Borges," Lois Zamora states: "If, suddenly, we see the *retablos* [altar pieces] of Tepotzotlán and San Luis Potosí as Borgesian Alephs, as parts of Borges's 'unimaginable universe,' then we have amplified our understanding of both Borges and the Baroque." More significantly, she describes Neobaroque's self-reflecting capacity in constituting its heterogeneous self in a genuinely New World form: "This double discourse of Baroque and Neobaroque, grounded in the cultural awareness of the New World Baroque, is essential to the ongoing process of self-reflection and self-construction in Latin America" (2006: 284), adding that "[f]or this reason, the Neobaroque is pertinent as an attitude rather than a style" (295).

The formal intricacy of neobaroque works, as seen in the analyzed examples of artifice, parody, simulation, and erotic excess, combines with the conceptual mobility of trans*—transvestism, mutation, and disidentification—to reformulate identity in terms of nomadic transgression. This process implies becoming as *devenir*, metamorphosis, *mestiza* consciousness of border crossers, *ch'ixi*, figurations of dangerous beasts, monsters and cyborgs, of becoming in the in-betweenness of *nepantla*. With the idea of erotic surplus—Bataille's "cursed part"—the transgression of sexual gender and literary genre in these works acquires the sense of an epistemological quest of the unknown, of liminal understanding. It becomes a quest of the fragmented self in search of a transcendental self-hood through or with otherness. Likewise, complementarity underlies the idea of *yin* and *yang* and of the androgyne as the complete (albeit fragmented but fluid) being. Perhaps it is a futile search, as evidenced by the imploring and eventual demise of characters such as Qadós and Hillé in Hilst's novels and of Cobra and Colibrí in Sarduy's. But perhaps the process is worth the effort. For these characters and the narrators, authors, performers, and painters who lead them, the nomadic quest is an unattainable territory that they traverse by means of an opulently ornate, figurative, and experimental discourse. Even without ever reaching anything, they are bound to a constant transit, and it is the movement, the process, that matters more than the result. The Neobaroque is that nomadic transit through language, a discourse that attempts to reach the limits of representation in what shapes to be an epistemology of the borderland. It is the foundational discourse for an epistemology of nomadic transitivity embodied in the trans-self.

5.2 From Identity to Alterity: Mappings of the Trans-Self in a Nomadic Cultural Theory

Nomadic subjects are symptomatic of postmodern relativism, a deconstructive decentering of cultural categories. Reformulating the concept of identity with trans-identity (or transentity) is meaningful in the context of a postmodern crisis of the subject. Rather than speaking of identity, the focus ought to be placed on "alterity" (as otherness), represented by the trans-self as a subject propelled by desire (of otherness). While referring to the expressive force of poetry, Roberto Echavarren states: "Each person is not an I, much less an identity. In the poem, the alternative use of all the personal pronouns, carrying on the verbs and actions, does not accord with an identity. One writes to become different; one plays with words to become other. The Buddhist intuition of the insubstantiality of the I opens a flux of impressions, starts a motor, undergoes a trajectory, changes the horizon" (2010: 22). Echavarren points to a transformation that can take place in the nomadic consciousness of the trans-self experiencing not a *new identity* but an *ongoing process* of becoming, a transentity achieved through alterity in the transformative transit of the nomad.

360   K. A. KULAWIK

Nomadism represents a shift from identity to lived alterity in a new conceptual cartography of selfhood. Such cartographies are needed (just as maps are on any good trip) to track the fluctuations of our nomadic cultural becoming in the twenty-first century. They situate transitive identities in the already partially posthuman (mechanical and cybernetic) New World of cultural (dis)order marked by fragmentation and displacement. A mapping of selfhood should determine the starting point for formulating adequate accounts of transiting nomadic identities that emerge, first through literature and art, in the culture of Transmerica. The ultimate aim of this cartographic account of the trans-self is to visualize the possibility for change, a transformation of selfhood by means of cultural mobility and border-zone transits between self and other. Our map of trans-selfhood establishes a pathway of resistance to hegemonic categories of the instituted (and static) Self, categories which are none other than normative impositions of power, of hidden power structures operating within an imposed order of Identity. Cartographies are also creative and qualitative theoretical leaps across the uncertainties of a fluid selfhood. They will locate nomadic rearticulations of identity in the territories of philosophical and cultural thought, as they draw out alternative pragmatic solutions for contemporary cultural politics with sustainable models of nomadic subjectivity, "in the hope that their vital structure will not be homologized into the system of commodification" (Braidotti 2002: 265).

The dichotomy of the subject in terms of "I" and "you," "man" and "woman," "Black" and "White" is dismantled in neobaroque works, as the characters confuse the voices they represent or assume in roles of the "other." Authors and performers undertake the quest of trans*it beyond the limits of the rational and known through language, an aesthetic resource in the expression of the depths of subjectivity. Neobaroque discourse displaces selfhood from the limiting bounds of (hetero)sexuality and any instituted categories, and from the systemic structures that hold them in place. It transposes subjectivity to the gray zones of contact and transition, to the spaces of "in between" binaries of masculinity and femininity, to the interchangeable gender boundaries of cross-dressing and androgyny, to *nepantla*. The nomadic self stands between "I" and "you," between "he" and "she," "one" and "other." The androgynous disidentification of the heteronormative binary leads to transcending the categorical subject, as José Esteban Muñoz proposed with the idea of detaching

5 CONCLUSIONS: AT THE CROSSROADS OF *NEPANTLA*   361

the self from categorical markers of identity.[3] Yet, this search for the trans-(cendental)-self that the analyzed authors and artists attempt to figure in their novels reveals the partiality of all discourse and the limitations of human understanding.[4] In fact, language exposes the mobility (thus arbitrariness and relativity) of the categories that define our understanding of sexuality, and all identity. The pursuit of language through the discursive forms of prose, poetry, performance, film, and painting has led these creators to achieve, if only to some extent, opening selfhood to an array of possibilities of experiencing otherness and opening categorical borders and boundaries to borderland transits of the migrant nomad.

Braidotti argues that "philosophical nomadism is not a heterogeneous brand of monism, but the actualization of multiple differences" (2002: 265). The process of nomadic becoming involves the coexistence of differences that do not need to be nulled. Nomadic identity rests on (a flexible) maintaining (of) sexual, racial, ethnic, national, social difference with the principle of "not-only-oneness" at the heart of subjectivity, as plurality. However, it is not just a quantitative plurality within a one-dimensional vision of "one" *or* "other," nor a unidirectional passing from "one" *to* "other," but a qualitative transformation in an open-ended series of *two-way* complexities. Nomadism is not in any way determined by one-way essentialist instinct *for* or drive *to being* something. Its qualitative value rests in not being but *becoming*. According to Braidotti, it is rather a vitalist tendency without an aim or an end, a non-self-enforcing and non-capitalizing entity. "It is my conviction that this non-unitary, nomadic subject is the prerequisite for an ethics of complex but sustainable subjectivity in the age of the posthuman" (2002: 265).

Transiting between identity and alterity, Braidotti asks relevant questions: "'So what, then?' What if the subject is 'trans,' or in transit, that is to say no longer one, whole, unified and in control, but rather fluid, in process and hybrid? What are the ethical and political implications of a non-unitary vision of the human subject?" (2006: 9). Looking for answers,

---

[3] "Finally, this self, fashioned through strategic disidentifications with dominant discourses of 'selfness,' presents the potential to ultimately 'cultivate that part of oneself that leads beyond oneself, that transcends oneself'" (Muñoz 1999: 178–79).

[4] Eliane Robert Moraes observes that "[i]t is in the prose of Hilda Hilst, therefore, that the exploration of the unknown gains unusual poetic violence, without parallel in Brazilian literature. Working on the edges of meaning, she will put language to the test of a confrontation with emptiness in which the eternal is irremediably confused with the provisional, and essence slips completely into the accidental" (118; my translation).

she argues that "a nomadic and post-humanistic vision of the subject can provide an alternative foundation for ethical and political subjectivity" that is inclusive of alterity, understood as the incorporation of different, not necessarily human, forms of existence (2006: 11). Following Deleuze's line of thought, she stresses engendering and sustaining processes of *multiple* "becomings" as central to philosophical nomadism (2006: 27). A theory of nomadic becoming*s* allows to ground the unitary human subject's dissolution in "an eco-philosophy of multiple belongings" (2006: 41). This includes pre-/posthuman or even non-human elements in a network of forces and energies that conform nomadic subjectivity. Transitive identity, being a crucial part of it, acquires the dimension of "the endless vitality of life as a continuous becoming." The nomadic process involves transversal forms of subjectivity in a complex and multi-layered "trans-individuality" (Braidotti 2006: 41). It does not correspond to a dialectical model of opposing traits, but rather follows a more dynamic, non-linear, and complex set of internally contradictory *options*. The "others" of "oneself" are not points of exclusion or marginality, but rather the sites of alternative subject-positions of "one" that, as fluid processes, are consequently and inherently contradictory.

A crucial feature of the relational/transitive character of nomadism is the subject's consciousness of power relations affecting it from its environment, thus making it assume a voice. The nomadic subject expresses these interconnections or hybrid contaminations from others in a "radical non-purity" of self (2006: 57). Nomadic identity becomings are infectious, flexible, and mobile, zigzagging in and out of one another, entering multiple combinations. The key to nomadism is perceiving the process of becoming in its movement and trajectories as more important than any resulting identity formations. "The flows matter more than steady roots" (Braidotti 2006: 62). What matters is not to return to fixed alternative categories, clear boundaries, or visions of the past, but rather to perceive cultural intermixture as an opportunity for creating new post-industrial ethnic and gender landscapes, taking advantage of the possibilities that nomadism offers for bonding and community-building (2006: 66). In this process, writing acquires the necessary role of "the primary vehicle for deterritorialization or becoming-minoritarian [...]. Writing is about transiting the in-between spaces, cultivating transversality and mutations" (2002: 94).

As the outcome of our analysis, a model of transitive selfhood based on trans-(c)end-ing established categories of identity into alterity by experiencing difference is ready to be applied in a queer and feminine cultural theory of nomadism. More than a theory of identity, it should be a theory of alterity that uses the concept of "transentity" based on the ideas of transitivity, movement, and transit. A queer, trans*(-vested) model of the self can be used in both literary and cultural studies in the analysis of the migratory transcultural phenomenon of the Americas and beyond. This nomadic model of trans-it(s) applies to any subject situated simultaneously in the exclusive hegemonic spectrum of One or Other, on *both* sides of the US-Mexico border or any other political border; on both sides of sociocultural boundaries marking the separations of male-female, Black-White, Anglo-Hispanic-Amerindian, high-low income. This model of a transiting self assumes the presence of the self that is here, there, and everywhere. Identity matters everywhere and concerns everyone. Where I am and who I am locally has repercussions globally and the multiplicity of humanity flows into me, constitutes (or should) constitute who I am, as Many in Me and Me in Many. It is a two-way flow, a transit of I into Other, and Others into I-Me in a transitive flow of Me in You and You in Me, and S/He in We. But it is always partial, incomplete, and temporary, just as it is transitory and infectious.

We agree with Jack Halberstam when he establishes that the future can be transgendered (better yet, "multigendered" but not genderless) if the focus of the critic and reader shifts from bodily determinism of gender/sex to the idea of transition as an open and creative space, which he epitomized with the term "trans*." It refers to the body in a creative dimension of an "art of becoming," one that derives from a necessity of imagining, a self-perception governed by "the fleshly insistence of transitivity" (2018: 136). A change of perception is necessary for transformation to occur: "If we shift our focus […] away from the housing of the body and toward the notion of 'transition'—perpetual transition—we can commit to a horizon of possibility where the future is not male or female but transgender" (2018: 131). Similarly, José Esteban Muñoz, quoting David Halperin, proposes that "through strategic disidentifications with dominant discourses of 'selfness'" can we "cultivate that part of oneself that leads beyond oneself, that transcends oneself" (1999: 178–79).

The connection between transgressive text (as genre) and sexuality (gender) that we observed in neobaroque works is established within the represented or performed material body of the subject as a direct empirical referent of a new aesthetics and a new philosophy of the nomadic self. Its presence through the creative process of writing and performance (and

364   K. A. KULAWIK

painting) as the written/performed body and the body of writing/performance is determinant in transiting identity categories and experiencing otherness as difference: "genders only emerge in relation to other bodies and within multiply oriented and complex populations" (Halberstam 11–12). The extratextual, immanently material, and empirical "body" behind the textual mask is a determining factor in the figuration of the nomadic subject. The represented body is a figurative projection of a material entity that entails a real-life experience of a transgender, interracial, transnational, cross-border transiting subject. Along with other cross-border experiences, "a trans* reading could open the sequence up to a new rendering of transgenderism as a desire for forms of embodiment that are necessarily impossible and yet deeply desired, all at once" (Halberstam 20). In the figurative realm of artistic representation, queer characters' desire of transiting between categories, or taking on the mark of ambiguity, represents both the impossibility of fixity and the possibility for all forms of embodiment. Both textual and performative embodiment, in the act of writing or staging the body, is a potentiality but also a realization of trans-identity's becoming in a "real body/world" experience. The work of art accounts for its past, present, and future constitution of a nomadic borderland identity inhabiting the in-between space of *nepantla*.

5.3   POLITICAL IMPLICATIONS: THE SUBVERSIVE EFFECT OF THE NEOBAROQUE

The textual-visual representation of ambiguous and transgressive subjects presents several aesthetic-philosophical implications in the context of postmodernity and does not preclude other political effects in the historically unstable context of the Americas. First, it offers the opening of new conceptual spaces that allow the reader and the critic to formulate a notion of a mobile and flexible selfhood. By extension, it allows to reconceptualize identity in different dimensions that intersectionally relate sexuality to racial, ethnic, national, social, and (post)human belonging. Literary texts, performances, and paintings provide a space to forge a decategorized, mobile, and transitive conceptualization of identity, one that has not yet been considered by social, scientific, and philosophical discourses of normativity, at least not until the official discourse of postcolonial logocentrism relinquishes its monopoly of power defined by heterosexual, masculine-dominated hegemony. In considering the transformative

5 CONCLUSIONS: AT THE CROSSROADS OF *NEPANTLA*   365

potential of both aesthetic and theoretical discourses, Braidotti upholds that "[t]he ultimate aim is the quest for resistance, but also creative and qualitative theoretical leaps across the uncertainties" (2002: 265).

The neobaroque figuration of trans*identity acquires a political dimension. It is an emancipatory quest for self-fulfillment outside the imposed categorizations of a limiting unity. It represents any individual's longing for the free expression and acceptance of an inclusively queer selfhood in multiplicity. An open, unending process of subjective creativity (one's identity trans-formation) implies tolerance and freedom to move, flow, and transit the paths of nomadic self-definition. The literary/visual text and the act of performance are aesthetic venues that provide literary and artistic forms for the political enactment of this desire for experiencing otherness through nomadic transit. Trans-selfhood is a sign of and a sign for cultural transformation, a change of paradigms that is the result of "the transformative impact of one's political processes" (Braidotti 2002: 169). The continuous flows and multiplications of identity do not necessarily delete gender, race, ethnic, national, or (post)human differentiation in the transformative process of intersectional identification. Inasmuch as gender differentiation remains, it ought to position within a range of uncertainty (as non-determination), staying flexible and mobile on the male-to-female spectrum, just as race on the skin color spectrum. Braidotti's claim "that the on-going transformations of our times do not erase sexual difference, but merely displace it, is simultaneously a conclusion and a new start" (2002: 169). As an outtake of this position, we conclude that identity differentiation exists and will remain, but only as a partial and movable point of reference that is less static than tradition's normative prescriptions.

Not denying the existence of gender, race, ethnicity, and nationality and, at the same time, avoiding their diffusion in a multicultural, global hodgepodge of a homogenized hybridity, we perceive the two-sidedness of the transformative process: a simultaneous letting go of the self by assuming the "other" as part of it, but also a holding on to what "one" represents by *not* relinquishing traits of one's now more open, porous, nomadic selfhood. This reflects the two-sided nature of any border or boundary crossing. Cross-border transit implies entering the "other's" territory and accepting its customs, but *not* giving up the part of identity that One brings along and exerts onto the Other. The border, as a zone of transit, constitutes a line that is crossed from one side to the other, but it does not preclude a return and multiple future crossings. However, such crossings of any normative, politically imposed boundaries are illicit within the hegemonic socio-economic and political system without a "passport" determining one's identity. As they are nomadic migrations without a visa or passport, they constitute transgressions. Presumably, there is another way to transit that is not binary or two-directional. There must be more oblique ways of traversing, or even remaining in the borderlands in an encounter with the other, while standing at the crossroads and setting forth in all directions at once. Standing at the border is a transformative experience. In Anzaldúa's and Gómez Peña's works, we witnessed such enlightening sojourns in the borderland spaces of *nepantla*. Emerging from that space is the trans-body incarnating a feminine theory of nomadism that, in the context of artistic representation, lays the foundations for a better understanding of selfhood, enhanced by Latin American literature and performance. Nomadic cartographies tracing queer and feminist theories are that intellectual passport to venture into the territories of the yet undiscovered trans-selfhood. The implications here are not only political.

Seditiously infecting postmodern Latin American narrative, the originally Antillean Neobaroque becomes a Pan-American style of a radical aesthetic and political posture.[5] Due to its broader outreach, we suggest calling it a Trans-American Neobaroque, a transformative style of exuberance and excess, of transgression. In Latin America, it has expressed a progressive stance assumed by writers in regard to the unrestrained capitalist developmental policies of a postcolonial *status quo*. With its marked sexual overtones, it aims at destabilizing phallogocentric discursive forms upon which the neoliberal-colonialist pattern of Modernity is based. It suggests a poetics of irrational squandering of signifiers that relativizes closed meanings and shifts the boundaries of literary expression into new, still uncharted waters. As textual and performative transgressions of genres and genders, Neobaroque works constitute a deconstructive discourse of resistance to the socio-political and economic establishment.

Roberto Echavarren envisions poetry's radical political dimension as a form of resistance to the manipulation the System exerts on all of us: "We must perform and sustain an exercise of resistance, in order not to be eaten by the machine of work and business, family or office" (2010: 20); "The poetic space, as I see it, is a space of resistance. Resistance against the

---

[5] Across the different latitudes of South America, the Antillean (Cuban originated) *neobarroco* has been playfully given different names ranging from *neobarrocho* (Lemebel), in reference to the Mapocho River in Santiago de Chile, to *neobarroso* [neo-muddy] (Perlongher), in reference to the murky waters of the Río de la Plata.

media which do not need poetry" (2010: 22). Selfhood may be fully enacted in the artistic process of writing and performance in a politically defiant mode: "The queer person can opt for his weirdness, his singularity, as Oscar Wilde advocated, when he conceived of his life as a work of art. Freedom requires courage. To build one's life as a work of art is a practice of resistance" (Echavarren 2010: 23).

Referring to the pragmatic dimension of his own writing, Echavarren points to the political effect that fiction, poetry, literary and cultural criticism, performance, and the visual arts wield on our culture: "Through my writing I have tried to deconstruct gender as a matrix of oppression" (2010: 23). Dissidence through art is a human impulse that binds us across cultures: "I see liberation as an intercultural rift. The gap between cultures. Crack, crevice, fissure. A montage effect. It broadens the horizon of our personal experience" (2010: 22). With its wealth of poetic and experimental language and erotic content, the presented works evidence their affinity with a politically engaged neobaroque current flowing in the groundwaters of Latin American aesthetics. Néstor Perlongher used the term "Latin American Neobaroque arch" given the similarity of styles and erotic nature of the works sprouting across the continent (1997: 101). It was the path of an unbridled neobaroque exuberance in a subversive discourse of eroticism, ambiguity, and seduction, that led Hilst's, Sarduy's, Eltit's, Bellatin's, Prado's, Menstrual's, Santiago's, and Echavarren's texts toward political sedition with their seductive transgressions.[6] This was also the trajectory of the performance and visual works of Guillermo Gómez-Peña, Familia Galán, Susy Shock, Alfredo Muller, and Juan Dávila that, in their subversive aesthetic forms, took on the baroque ethos of tacit cultural resistance. The sedition of the Neobaroque, seen in the wastefulness of the overflowing text, represents a liberation from the constraints of the logocentric-heterosexual order of the realist-mimetic word, categorical identity, and normative sexuality. The Neobaroque, as a transgressive style in all its exuberance and opulence, destabilizes the established order and proposes an alternative form of expression of the dissolution of identity. We agree with Sarduy when he states that being baroque today means to threaten, judge, and parody the neoliberal bourgeois economy based on the stingy administration of goods, concepts, and identities (Sarduy 1987: 209). Transitive and transgressive, these writers, performers, and painters emerge in the

---

[6] I borrow this idea from Néstor Perlongher: "*A la sedición por la seducción*" (1997: 96; cursive in original).

Americas as feminine queer voices of otherness, of opposition and resistance to established patriarchal normativity. They emerge as seditiously seductive, exuberantly disheveled, and subversive; as neobaroque.

5.4 Philosophical Openings for a Theory of Cultural Nomadism

With its overflowing language, the destabilizing voice of Latin American Neobaroque unravels identity in a postcolonial relativization and alteration of cultural discourses that determine selfhood. It is a fitting form of representation of a decentering that Deleuze and Braidotti designated earlier as cultural nomadism. The nomadic subject perceived in the literary, performance, and visual works of the Neobaroque indicates a broader phenomenon of postmodern categorical opening. It paves our way toward a proposal of identity decentering in a discourse of nomadism that stems from the cultural transformations taking place in Latin America, the United States, and beyond. This discourse destabilizes the hegemonic neoliberal system of identity assignment by opening a space for self-fulfillment in the nomadic transits to otherness, transits that inevitably lead through the borderlands of *nepantla*. Transmerican cross-cultural androgyny provides a path to reach beyond the exclusivity of heterosexual binarism, ethno-racial nationalism, and anthropocentric humanism while questioning any normatively imposed binarism. The Latin American aesthetic experience of the Neobaroque, within the bounds of Eurocentric neocolonial dependency, offers a liberating conceptual ground for the creation of an alternative mentality of transitivity and cultural mobility.

The transgressions of the cross-dresser, the queer, and the mutant are grounded in an eclectic aesthetics of premodern baroque forms combined with postmodern acrobatics of the Neoavant-garde. The Neobaroque is thus an extensive Latin American (per-)version of Western aesthetics, a critical cultural mode and state of mind at "play with the lost object, a game whose finality is only itself [...] wastefulness grounded in pleasure. [...] like the perversion that all metaphors and figures imply" (Sarduy 1978: 182; my translation). Like the Eastern *yin-yang* dichotomy of joined parts, the trans-self is constituted in the complementarity of contradictions, resembling the cross-dresser's and androgyne's combination of opposites. The categories of gender, race, nation, and social group become invertible and combine in a context of human and cultural migration and technological interconnectivity. The questioning and rejection of normative discourses, particularly of gender and social belonging, are exemplified in the rebellious presence of hippie, punk, and metalhead subcultures in the 1960s, 1970s, and 1980s, and gothic, emo, and Pokémon urban cliques that depict alternative mutant identities surging in mostly urban environments since the early 2000s. Even if, due to cyber-saturation, most of them are not as visible in the 2020s as they were in previous decades, they still seem to disturb the cultural establishment with the marginal presence of their unsettling alternative forms of being—as mutant selves.

Entering an era of the cyber- posthuman, we are locally affected by the global dimension of a diverse humanity. It is difficult and undesirable to remain stagnant in any oneness in an age of increased migration when otherness is all around us. As Echavarren put it:

> In our lives the global and local coexist. [...] still, beyond commonplace identity, I go for change and transformation. So that which seemed to be ours becomes strange. In this sense to pass is to think, to question a certain regime, to marvel that it is still there, to wonder what makes it possible, [...] looking for traces of the movements which formed it and discovering in those stories apparently in ashes, how to think, how to live otherwise. (2010: 26)

The possibility of "living otherwise," also brought up in a postcolonial and postnational context by Homi Bhabha (1992: 207; ref. in Chap. 2), can come about by transiting differences that cultural nomadism proposes. In a world of increasing contacts and intermingling, this becomes a question of living out, through mutability and transitivity of different perspectives, one's desire for experiencing otherness. Everyone is a potential nomad.

The fictional and critical works by authors as varied as Sarduy, Bellatin, Eltit, Prado, Santiago, Hilst, Echavarren, Anzaldúa, Menstrual, Lemebel, and Casas, and by cross-dressed performers Susy Shock, Guillermo Gómez-Peña, and the Familia Galán, constitute the basis for an outline of a Trans-American cartography of a mutant Neobaroque *body* of work that voices marginal and decentering positions in a postmodern discussion on queerness, identity, and transgressive expressions of cultural and political dissidence of early twenty-first-century Americas. Our analytical reading of these literary, performative, visual, and critical-theoretical works, whose recurring theme is nomadic transgression of boundaries by mutant characters, will perhaps allow the reader and the critic to get ahead of social norms and scientific prescriptions in the deconstruction of gender/sexual binarism, racial and ethnic (Euro)centrism, national and social exclusivity, and even anthropocentric humanism, and lead to formulating less restrictive ideas of subjectivity, understood as cross-border transitivity. Perhaps the Neobaroque, as an outrageously exuberant and disruptive literary-aesthetic form, can take us further to the frontiers of knowledge to advance a theory of the hybrid subject that neither society nor science is ready to formulate within the academic discourse of scientific rationalism, still determined by a patriarchal and heterosexual (neo)colonizing of the subject. Experimental neobaroque forms of expression that boost the emergence of trans- and posthuman subjects unveil a "postmodern" (whatever it means) American consciousness of nomadism that points toward the in-between borderland spaces of *nepantla*. Nepantlism represents an Indigenous *Transmerican* spiritual practice of mind and body that is constitutive of the nomadic trans-self. It is indicative of a developing process of an emancipatory self-consciousness that results from the hybrid (Latin) American jumble of crossing, juxtaposing, shifting, connecting, and intermingling cultures. Echavarren explains Latin America's transformative ("nepantlic") uniqueness with the example of poetry: "The Modernists mixed races (crossbreeding) and juxtaposed places (exoticism). [...] Exoticism and velocity were the concerns of [Avant-garde] poets a hundred years ago. I think that today we can use a third term to describe that developing process: connectivity" (2010: 25). That spatial, temporal, and cyber- connectivity is the junction of all inter-subjective circuits in *nepantla*.

The transvestite, the androgynous mutant, and the posthuman cyborg, with their ambiguously changing appearances and chameleon-like mutations into "otherness," question Identity as a systemically and discursively predetermined construct. As transgressively liberating forms of existence, they suggest possibilities of experiencing selfhood other-wise in the presence of other-ness in each individual, of otherness in each id-entity—now transformed into trans-identity or *transentity*. In an attempt to access the cross-border reality of the "other" that lies beyond, but also within the fragmented self, the Neobaroque works that we have presented here trace alternative nomadic routes of a transcultural humanity experiencing selfhood transitively. They do it by means of decentering language and destabilizing the representational function of the sign. These works present a hermaphroditic, ambiguously polyvalent position of a transvestic (transformist and transformative) androgynous trans-self, composed of multiple sexual, ethnic, racial, social, and national identifications. As a posthuman

5 CONCLUSIONS: AT THE CROSSROADS OF *NEPANTLA* 371

nomad, this subject transits a Native-Latin-Anglo-techno-American, transformationally virtual borderland space of *nepantla*; it emerges with (neobaroque) style from the intercultural space of the Americas. From (t) here, the Neobaroque appears as "an art of dethronement and discussion. [...] Baroque, in its swinging action, in its fall, in its *showy*, sometimes strident, jumbled, and chaotic language, metaphorizes the challenge to the logocentric entity that until then structured it and us from its distance and authority" (Sarduy 1978: 183–84; my translation, emphasis in original). By incorporating the theoretical strategies of Braidotti's "nomadic subjects" and Halberstam's "trans*" to the cross-dressed textual body of the Neobaroque, we hope to offer a conceptual tool of postmodern decentering in the form of transitive selfhood, a transentity that evolves from the hybrid and transformative borderland spaces of the American *nepantla*. Let the queer and nomadic border transgressions of the trans-self be an-"other"—strategically neobaroque—vision of Transmerica.

WORKS CITED

Arriarán, Samuel. (1997). *Filosofía de la posmodernidad: Crítica a la modernidad desde América Latina*. México, DF: UNAM.

Best, Stephen. (1991). *Postmodern Theory: Critical Interrogations*. New York: Guilford Press.

Bhabha, Homi. (1992). "Interrogating Identity: the Postcolonial Prerogative". *Anatomy of Racism*. U of Minnesota P. 183–209.

Braidotti, Rosi. (2002). *Metamorphoses: Towards a Materialist Theory of Becoming*. Cambridge, UK: Polity Press.

Braidotti, Rosi. (2006). *Transpositions: On Nomadic Ethics*. Cambridge, UK: Polity Press.

Bustillo, Carmen. (1990). *Barroco y América Latina: un itinerario inconcluso*. Caracas: Monte Ávila.

Dorfman, Ariel. (1972). *Imaginación y violencia en América*. Barcelona: Anagrama.

Echavarren, Roberto. (2010). "Resistance," *The Journal of Natural and Social Philosophy*. 6.2 (2010): 20–26.

Gutiérrez, José Ismael. (2013). *Del travestismo femenino. Realidad social y ficciones literarias de una impostura*. Vigo: Academia del Hispanismo.

Halberstam, Jack. (2018). *Trans*: A Quick and Quirky Account of Gender Variability*. Oakland: U of California P.

Laqueur, Thomas. (1990). *Making Sex: Body and Gender from the Greeks to Freud*. Cambridge, Massachusetts, and London, England: Harvard UP.

372   K. A. KULAWIK

Muñoz, José Esteban. (1999). *Disidentifications: Queers of Color and the Performance of Politics*. Minneapolis and London: U. of Minnesota P.

Perlongher, Néstor. (1997). *Prosa plebeya*. Buenos Aires: Colihue.

Pratt, Mary Louise. (1993). "Criticism in the Contact Zone: Decentering Community and Nation". *Critical Theory, Cultural Politics, and Latin American Narrative*. Eds. Steven, M. Bell, Albert H. Lemay y Leonard Orr. Notre Dame: U of Notre Dame P, 83–102.

Sarduy, Severo. (1978 [1972]). "El barroco y el neobarroco". *América Latina en su literatura*. 5ª ed. Coord. César Fernández Moreno. México: Siglo XXI, 167–84.

Sarduy, Severo. (1987 [1974]). Barroco. In *Ensayos generales sobre el Barroco*. Buenos Aires: Fondo de Cultura Económica. 143–224.

de Toro, Alfonso, ed. (1997). *Postmodernidad y Postcolonialidad. Breves reflexiones sobre Latinoamérica*. Madrid, Frankfurt am Main: Iberoamericana-Vervuert.

Zamora, Lois Parkinson. (2006). *The Inordinate Eye. New World Baroque and Latin American Fiction*. Chicago and London: U of Chicago P.

INDEX[1]

NUMBERS AND SYMBOLS

1810: La Revolución de Mayo vivida
   por los negros, see Cucurto

A

Act of Writing, 96, 110
Affectivity, 15
Africa, 225, 234, 235
African, 36, 39, 41, 43, 54,
   57n6, 62n9
Aguierrez, Oscar Martín, 234, 234n47
AIDS, 144, 165
Alarcón, Norma, 69, 75, 78, 317
Aleijadinho, 127
Allende, Isabel, 133, 233
Alterity, 1, 7, 8, 12, 276,
   320, 359–362
Althusser, Louis, 6, 341

Ambiguity, 68, 69, 83, 87, 88, 92,
   102, 103, 125, 136, 137, 140,
   142–144, 149, 151, 152, 157,
   180, 181, 188–204, 211–213,
   215, 219, 364, 367
Ambiguous genders, *see* Ambiguity
America, 125–132, 134, 149, 173,
   217, 225, 227, 228, 235, 236
American Baroque, 4
   See also Baroque
American Colonial Baroque, 243
   See also Baroque
A-mi, Jo, 92
Anamorphosis, 243, 247, 252n6,
   301, 311
Androgyne, *see* Androgyny
Androgyny, 7, 13, 14, 20, 22, 125,
   137, 180, 189–198, 208–213,
   219, 242, 264, 267, 272, 274,

---

[1] Note: Page numbers followed by 'n' refer to notes.

© The Author(s), under exclusive license to Springer Nature
Switzerland AG 2024
K. A. Kulawik, *Visions of Transmerica*, Literatures of the Americas,
https://doi.org/10.1007/978-3-031-42014-6

374 INDEX

276, 280, 283–309, 311, 318,
324, 325, 327, 328, 331,
334–338, 343, 344, 353, 355,
357, 360, 368, 370
Andrómeda, 183, 184
Anglo-America, 9
Animalization, 302
Annihilation the meaning, 264
Anzaldúa, Gloria, 2–5, 12, 14, 19–21,
24, 69, 70, 72, 75, 77, 78, 83–85,
131, 215–219, 216n37, 216n38,
222, 223, 242, 301, 303, 304,
309–311, 312n18, 313, 315,
317, 318, 340, 357, 366, 369
This Bridge We Call Home, 216,
218, 219
Araujo, Kathya, 255, 282
Arenas, Reinaldo, 133, 137
Argentina, 129, 133, 167, 178, 235
Arguedas, José María, 45, 47
Arriarán, Samuel, 242
Arte andrógino (2008), 294, 296
Artifice, 2, 6, 18, 20, 22, 24, 53, 59,
61, 76, 82, 87, 88, 96, 103, 107,
107n16, 110, 113, 115, 242–258,
246n3, 247n4, 262, 265, 266,
284, 290, 300, 321, 330, 332, 358
Art of seduction, 246
Aruquipa Pérez, David, 174, 174n20,
174n21, 175, 177, 336
As if, 249, 275, 313
Autohistoriateoría, 216
Auxilio and Socorro, 203, 204, 247,
272, 323
Ave Roc (1994), 294, 324
Aymara, 179, 309, 319

B
Bakhtin, Mikhail, 47, 235, 254, 262
The Dialogic Imagination, 47
Baler, Pablo, 16, 56, 242

Banquet, 235
Barba Jacob, Porfirio, 137
Baroque, 5, 7, 16, 17, 23, 48, 54,
55n4, 56, 56n5, 57n6, 58–63,
58n7, 58n8, 65, 66n12, 67, 76,
127, 127n1, 128, 132–134, 157,
158, 166, 172, 182, 185, 204,
242–244, 243n1, 243n2, 246,
247, 247n4, 249–251, 250n5,
252n6, 253, 265, 266, 289, 290,
296, 298, 311, 317, 322, 323,
328, 330, 331, 334, 337–344
colonial Baroque, 66n12
New World, 358, 371
ethos, 6, 18, 20, 23, 36, 48, 68, 75,
76, 322, 328, 334, 337–344
strategy, 76
Barthes, Roland, 284, 287, 332
Barvosa, Edwina, 83
Bataille, Georges, 16, 21, 24,
261–264, 266, 342
Baudrillard, Jean, 251
Bazin, Germain, 54
Beauty Salon (2021), 89
Becoming, 18, 20, 26, 54, 62n10,
63n11, 75, 77–79, 82, 86, 92,
93, 95–97, 105, 106, 109, 110,
117–119, 241, 250, 257, 268,
272–276, 278–280, 286, 288,
290, 295, 298, 300, 307,
310–312, 320, 323, 326, 327,
329, 335, 338, 343, 358–364
Bellatin, Mario, 4, 14, 21, 71, 85, 89,
91, 92, 108, 113, 133, 144–147,
145n6, 205–208, 206n31, 252,
264, 283, 284, 302, 330, 332,
333, 355, 357, 367, 369
Jacobo el mutante, 206, 207
Jacobo reloaded, 206
Salón de belleza, 144, 147,
206, 207
Bendayán, Christian, 355

INDEX 375

Benítez Rojo, Antonio, 5, 10, 19, 29, 47
Berkins, Lohana, 290, 291n16
Bhabha, Homi, 84, 369
Binarism, 169, 174, 188, 257, 258, 264, 277, 289, 298, 335, 336, 343
Binary identities, 208
Bitácora del cruce, 224, 224n39
Body and text, 104
Body of Writing, 21, 24
Bolaño, Roberto, 137
Bolívar, Simón, 187, 188, 234
Boom, 51, 242
Border, 1, 3, 4, 6, 12, 17, 19, 20, 22, 24–27, 29, 34–38, 60, 68–73, 75–78, 84–86, 97, 100–102, 112
Border Brujo, 2, 17, 22, 226, 230, 233
See also Gómez-Peña
Borderland identities, 6, 20, 21, 125, 242
Borderlands, 9, 20, 23, 27, 34, 36, 53, 68, 71, 73, 75–78, 83, 85–88, 92, 93, 96, 97, 105, 111, 115, 116, 125, 126, 131, 152, 173, 194, 215–217, 220, 223, 224, 231–233, 268, 269, 272, 296, 309, 312, 313, 315, 317, 324, 327, 328, 340, 355, 359, 361, 364, 366, 370, 371
Borderlands consciousness, 304
Borderlands/La Frontera, 70, 77, 216, 309
Borders and boundaries, 1, 4, 10
Border theories, 73, 242
Borges, Jorge Luis, 51, 134, 358
Botts, Tina Fernandes, 71, 73, 74
Boundary, 1, 6, 33, 34, 58, 68, 69, 71, 74, 75, 77, 81, 82, 85, 86, 89, 91, 95, 97, 100, 112, 117, 265, 289, 292, 302, 303, 306,

308, 310, 326, 328, 329, 334, 338, 353, 356, 360–363, 365, 366, 369
Braidotti, Rosi, 2, 5, 14, 52, 68, 74, 75, 77–84, 86, 91, 93–97, 99, 105, 106, 110, 117, 242, 257, 260, 274, 275, 292, 299, 305, 307, 324–329, 333, 337, 343
Brazilian Baroque, *see* Baroque
Bridges, 81, 312, 336
This Bridge We Call Home (2002), 312
Brown, Andrew, 208
Buddhism, 359
Buenos Aires, 161, 162, 162n12, 167, 168n14, 169, 170n18, 191n25, 233–236, 234n46
Burgos, Fernando, 53
Busato, Susanna, 96, 264
Bustamante, Nao, 70
Bustillo, Carmen, 53, 66, 66n12, 133, 354
Butler, Judith, 73, 93, 118, 257, 258, 267, 282, 285, 303, 329

C

Cabrera Infante, Guillermo, 61, 133
Calabrese, Omar, 55
Cámara, Gabriela Cabezón, 355–356
Canclini, Néstor García, 5, 10
Cangi, Adrián, 298, 338
Caribbean, 8, 10, 17, 29, 37, 40, 43, 46, 47, 59, 65, 67, 127, 133, 242
Carilla, Emilio, 54
Carnival, 177, 178, 235, 261, 285
Carnival of Oruro, 177
Carpentier, Alejo, 56n5, 61, 62n9, 62n10, 65, 66, 133, 250n5
Cartography, 360
Casas, Francisco, 154–161, 154n9
Castillo, Ana, 70
Castro, Fidel, 204

376 INDEX

Categories of identity, 241, 253
Category, 257, 279, 280, 282, 283, 285, 288–291, 300, 305, 306, 322, 334
Cervantes, Miguel de
Don Quijote, 60
Charrúa, 189
Chaves, Jose Ricardo, 294
Chiampi, Irlemar, 56, 58n7, 62n10, 63, 63n11, 65, 67, 242, 324
Chicana, 68, 69, 75, 77, 78, 84, 92, 242, 310, 312, 313, 315–317, 340
Chicana border studies, 3, 6, 22
Chicana border theories, 68, 69, 78
See also Chicana border studies
Chican*e* identity, 317
Chicanes, 8, 131, 217, 309
Chilean dictatorship, 263
Chinese, 203
Ch'ixi, 3, 78, 309–320, 357, 358
Ch'ixinakax utxiwa, 77
See also Rivera Cusicanqui
Cisneros, Sandra, 70
Coatlicue, 217, 220, 221, 304
Cobra, 2, 17, 22, 26, 244, 247–249, 251, 253, 254, 264, 272, 323
See also Sarduy
Coincidentia oppositorum, 293
Colibrí, 142, 142n5, 143, 151, 247, 249, 251, 254, 254n7, 272, 323
See also Sarduy
Colonial Baroque, 7, 19, 23
Colonialism, 128
Colonial legacy, 128
Colonization, 39, 41–43, 63n11, 72, 73, 77, 85
Communicative act, 267
Community-building, 362
Conceptismo, 55, 243, 243n2, 244
Consciousness of the Borderlands, 221

Contact zone, 2, 13, 53, 69, 77, 84–86, 357
Continuadísimo, see Naty Menstrual
Copello, Francisco, 14, 116, 264, 355
Cornejo Polar, Antonio, 5, 9, 38, 45, 319
Writing in the Air, 45
Cortázar, Julio, 134
Counter-conquest, 18, 23, 63, 133
Creative leprosy, 65, 67, 323, 355
Criollo, 43
Crisis, 17, 22, 55, 57, 58n7, 60, 67, 98
Cross-dresser, 151, 157, 158, 174, 176, 182, 280, 281, 283, 303, 335
See also Transvestism
Cross-dressing, 13, 20, 22, 38, 69, 70, 76, 87, 88, 113, 117, 125, 134, 136, 146, 151, 153, 154, 154n9, 174, 218, 245, 264, 267, 272, 274, 276, 285–287, 291, 292, 300, 328, 337, 353, 360
See also Transvestism
Cuban Revolution, 129, 204
Cucurto, Washington, 14, 17, 26, 188, 233–236, 234n46, 234n47, 355
Culteranismo, 55, 243, 243n2, 244
Cultural anthropophagy, 49
Cultural hegemony, 18
Cybernetic body, 215
Cyber-punk, 85
Cyberspace, 339
Cyber-tech, 85
Cyborg, 6, 18, 22, 26, 54, 70, 71, 86, 88, 90, 189, 208, 212–215, 230, 231, 260, 272, 294, 298, 305–309, 334, 343
A Cyborg Manifesto, 305
Cyborgs, Sexuality and the Undead (2020), 36

INDEX 377

D
D'Angelo, Biagio, 257, 290
Dangerous beasts, 310–320, 358
Dangerous beasts poetics, 316, 317
Danna Galán, 174, 178, 183, 281, 282, 336
Dávila, Juan, 91, 186, 187
de Andrade, Mário, 135
de Certeau, Michel, 5
de la Pedraja, René, 42
de Lauretis, Teresa, 87, 104, 277
de Toro, Alfonso, 356, 356n2
Death, 97, 144, 163, 192, 195–198, 207, 213, 215, 220
Decategorization, 172, 173
Decentered sign, 16
Decentering, 243, 245, 246, 248, 253, 255, 258, 267, 268, 271, 274, 289, 311, 324, 342
Decentering identity, 3, 20, 125, 245
Decolonization, 272
Deconstructive techniques, 241
Del Paso, Fernando, 134
Deleuze, Gilles, 2, 12, 20, 39, 57, 59, 75, 78, 92, 96, 97, 106, 109, 117, 118, 118n20, 242, 255, 258, 259, 272–274, 276, 307, 308, 323, 327, 329, 335
Derrida, Jacques, 101, 101n15, 102, 107, 107n16, 335
Desire, 15, 21, 179, 212, 244, 260, 272–275, 278, 283, 285, 287, 289, 292–294, 298, 308, 326, 328–330, 334, 337, 338
Destabilization, 3, 241, 242, 244, 245, 247, 251, 253, 256, 266, 268, 275, 285, 288, 289, 300, 303, 317, 327, 330, 331, 334–336, 338, 358, 366, 368, 370
Destabilizing, 2, 5, 16, 17, 19, 20, 22, 24, 27, 136, 143, 146, 181, 207, 218, 234

Deterritorialization, 34, 51, 106, 224, 258–261, 263, 274, 326, 328
Devenir, 18, 20, 75, 78, 109, 119, 242, 267, 272–276, 279, 323, 358
Diablo en el pelo (2005), 294
Difference, 320
Diniz, Cristiano, 92n14
Discourse, 19, 21, 27, 33, 44
Disidentification, 15, 267, 273, 276–285, 358, 360
Disidentifications (1999), 89, 114, 282
Dispersed identities, 245
Dispersion, 118, 244, 245, 284, 307, 333
Displaced meaning, 270
Dissidence, 367
Dissolution, 265, 266, 289, 298, 326
Distortion, 56, 266
Diversity, 36, 38, 41, 45, 82, 97
Don Quijote de la Mancha, see Cervantes
Donoso, José, 134, 137
The Doors, 190, 192, 324
Dorfman, Ariel, 354
Drag, 136, 138, 155, 157, 160, 174, 176, 180, 183, 192, 230

E
Echavarren, Roberto, 14, 17, 20, 22, 88, 92, 116, 129, 130, 134, 150, 184, 189–191, 191n25, 194, 242, 291, 294–297, 299, 304, 324, 338, 340, 355, 357, 359, 366, 367, 369
Arte andrógino, 191
Ave Roc, 189
El diablo en el pelo, 189

378   INDEX

Echeverría, Bolívar, 6, 18, 20, 23, 36,
  48, 49, 58, 68, 75, 76, 322,
  341, 342
Eco-philosophy, 97
Edwards, Jorge, 134
El cuarto mundo, see Eltit
Eliade, Mircea, 293
Eltit, Diamela, 4, 14, 16, 21, 26,
  55n4, 59, 65, 66, 91, 133, 134,
  151–153, 152n8, 180, 200–202,
  200n29, 228, 255, 263, 266,
  281, 299, 301, 326,
  330–332, 335
E. Luminata, 200
Emo, 297, 298, 343, 369
Ena Lucía Portela, 355
Entre-lugar, 291, 309, 320–324, 321n19
Erotic-bodily act, 201
Eroticism, 18, 20–22, 24, 53, 58n7,
  59–61, 63, 67, 82, 86, 89, 90,
  93–97, 103, 104, 107, 108, 110,
  111, 117, 118, 244, 245, 247,
  249, 250, 256, 260–267, 261n9,
  262n11, 277, 280, 287, 294,
  324, 330, 342, 358, 367
Eschatological language, 303
Estar sendo. Ter sido, 264, 280
Estéticas Galán, *see* Danna Galán
Estrangement, 245
Estrella de Diego, 292
  El andrógino sexuado, 292
Ethno-cyborgs, 232
Eurocentrism, 40
Exaggeration, 293
Excess, 358, 366
Experimental narrative, 241, 264
Exuberance, 2, 6, 22, 26, 161, 197,
  201, 235, 242, 243, 243n1, 245,
  253, 257, 262, 263, 265, 290, 292,
  324, 330, 335, 344, 356, 366, 367
Exuberant style, *see* Baroque;
  Neobaroque

F
Familia Galan, 173–177, 174n20,
  174n21, 180, 181, 255, 264,
  272, 281, 336
Fashion, 150, 162, 191, 194, 260,
  287, 298, 331
Faulkner, William,
  134, 250n5
Feminism, 242, 258, 274, 300, 307,
  327, 332
Feminist border thought, 72
Fernández, Josefina, 286
Fernández Moreno, César, 39,
  39n2, 41, 42
Fetish, 250
Figueroa, Cristo, 22, 55, 56,
  58n8, 67, 242, 243,
  251, 252n6
Figuration, *see* Neobaroque
Flores, Juan, 131
Flows, 47, 77, 92, 94, 105, 110,
  260, 276, 307, 309–328,
  334, 337, 362,
  363, 365
Flux, *see* Flows
Fluxo-Floema, 357
The Fold: Leibniz and the Baroque,
  see Deleuze
Foster, David Wiliam, 25
Foucault, Michel, 73, 96, 282,
  305, 333n20
The Fourth World,
  326, 332
Fox, Arturo, 39, 69
Fragmentation, 3, 14, 16
Franca, Rodrigues, 260
Freud, 109
From Cuba with a Song, 248
Fuentes, Carlos, 134
Fugue, 39, 107, 112, 259, 262, 295,
  298, 301, 357
Fusco, Coco, 70, 112, 225, 226

INDEX 379

G

Galans, 178, 180, 181
Gálvez Acero, Marina, 331
Garabato, Sandra, 331, 332
Garber, Marjorie, 242, 286–291, 294, 321, 322, 334, 338n21
García Canclini, Néstor, 38, 49–51, 53, 85, 296, 319, 325
García Márquez, Gabriel, 233
Gay and lesbian, 88
Gender and sexuality, 174, 182, 189, 193, 217
Gender bending, 136, 137, 285, 289, 353
Gender Trouble, 329
Generation Z, 8
Gino Germani, 42
Ginway, Elizabeth, 36, 98, 341, 342
Glissant, Edouard, 11, 19, 29, 38
Globalization, 52, 53, 72
Gómez-Peña, Guillermo, 2, 4, 14, 17, 19, 21, 70, 71, 112, 131, 224–233, 224n39, 225n40, 233n45, 264, 309, 318, 332, 339, 340, 366, 367, 369
González Echevarría, Roberto, 133
Gosser-Esquilín, Mary Ann, 253
Goytisolo, Juan, 259
Gracian, Baltasar, 166
Gramsci, Antonio, 114
Grosz, Elizabeth, 101, 108, 109, 109n17, 263
Grotesque, 260, 265, 307
Guattari, Félix, 255, 307, 308
Guerrero, Gustavo, 62n9, 133
Guido, Angel, 65
Guimarães Rosa, João, 135
Gutiérrez, José Ismael, 357
Gynesis (1985), 101, 101n15, 107, 109

H

Haiti, 127
Halberstam, Jack, 2, 14, 20, 54, 88, 90, 93, 109, 109n18, 113, 115, 116, 242, 277–280, 283, 355n1, 363, 364, 371
Haptics, 116, 277, 278
Haraway, Donna J., 213, 305, 306
Haroldo, de Campos, 247, 356
Hatzfeld, Helmut, 54
Hawley, Daniel, 261n9, 262, 264, 266
Hayles, N. Katherine, 208, 306–308, 343
Hegemony, 353, 360, 363, 366, 368
Hembros, 18, 22, 208–212, 209n32, 209n33, 212n35, 294, 306–308, 333
Henríquez Ureña, Pedro, 11, 38
Hermaphrodite, 137, 197, 293, 294, 334
Hernández, Felisberto, 134
Herrera y Reissig, 137
Heterogeneity, 36, 38, 40, 45, 47, 49, 50, 52, 53, 59, 67, 125, 126
Latin America, 1, 5, 7, 10, 11, 14, 19, 24, 29
Heterosexual binarism, 368
Heterosexuality, 149, 198, 222
Hilst, Hilda, 59, 92n14, 96, 255, 260, 261, 264, 265, 280, 283, 355–357, 359, 361n4, 367, 369
Qadós, 89, 135, 197–199, 197n26, 198n27
Hind, Emily, 302
Hispanic or Latino population, 132
Hispanics, 131
Hispanics in the US, 131
Historical determinants, 126–136
Homosexuality, 134, 142, 143, 147, 149, 176, 182, 219, 222, 264, 280, 311, 322, 335
Hooks, bell, 81

380 INDEX

Hopi, 193, 194
Horror vacui, 173, 223, 250,
250n5, 296
Hybrid contexts, *see* Hybridity
Hybrid Cultures, see García Canclini
Hybrid identity, 354
Hybridity, 34, 36, 38, 45, 49, 52, 53,
59, 67, 68, 76, 83, 177, 208,
218, 228, 229, 242, 276, 292,
295, 304, 305, 307, 309, 315,
317–320, 324, 325, 329, 335,
339–341, 343, 365
hybridization, 5, 24, 26, 29
Latin America, 1, 11, 14, 19, 20, 28
Hybridization, 50, 51, 54, 57, 76–78,
85, 125, 126, 130, 169, 188,
226, 296, 319, 325, 326, 338
Hybrid spaces, 51
Hyperbole, 76, 235, 289, 293, 301
Hyperbolizing, 289
Hypertelic, 113, 113n19

I
Identity, 33, 34, 37, 40, 44, 53, 68,
69, 83, 95, 100, 110, 118
Illusionism, 242, 243, 311
Imagination, 56, 63n11, 69, 80, 82,
94, 98, 103, 105, 110, 112
Immigration, 129, 131, 168n13, 226,
227, 233, 235
In-betweenness, 68, 90, 119, 150, 255,
279, 298, 309–313, 321, 337
Independence Wars, 128, 188,
233, 234
Indigenous, 8, 9, 11, 15, 29, 36, 37,
40, 78, 84, 132, 177, 181, 184,
192, 218, 219, 309–311, 315,
318, 320, 324, 340
Instability, 242–266
Installation, 85
Interpellation, *see* Althusser

Interpretant, 15, 22, 25, 100, 104,
108, 109, 268–272, 288,
315, 318
Intersectionality, 6, 20, 52, 70, 71, 73,
74, 80, 81, 100, 105, 106, 112,
267, 268, 296, 311, 329, 340,
355, 365
Irigaray, Luce, 80, 92, 96, 97, 106,
107, 117

J
Jagose, Annamarie, 87, 88, 242,
276, 277
Jakobson, 245
Jameson, Frederic, 66
Jardine, Alice, 101, 101n15, 102, 107,
107n16, 109
Jouissance, 246, 333
Juana Aguilar, 137, 137n3

K
Kaup, Monika, 55, 55n4, 56, 63, 66,
242, 243n2, 250, 250n5, 324
Keating, AnaLouise, 216n38, 218
Kiremidjian, David, 254
Kombucha, 165
Kondori, 127
Kosofsky Sedgwick, Eve, 88
Kristeva, Julia, 12, 21, 254, 303
Kulawik, K. A., 65, 85, 309
Kulick, Don, 89, 280, 283, 338
Kushigian, Julia A., 118, 267

L
La Avanzada, 186
Lacan, 101n15
Laclau, Ernesto, 5
La esquina es mi corazon (1995), 335
See also Lemebel

INDEX 381

La estrategia neobarroca, see Guerrero
La expression americana, see Lezama
La Familia Galán, 4, 14
Lágrima Ríos, 295, 296, 338
La Malinche, 217
Lamborghini, Osvaldo, 355
La Monja Alférez, 136
La Paz, Bolivia, 174n20, 176
La petite mort, 264
Laqueur, Thomas, 356
Larrain, Jorge, 43–45
Latin American identity, 34, 36–38,
    44, 51, 52
Latin American Neobaroque, 28, 83
Latin American Neobaroque arch, 17
Latin American Trans Theory, 284
Latine and Chicane identities, 131
Laughter, 256
Lecciones para una liebre muerta,
    252, 301
    See also Bellatin
Lechner, Norbert, 52
Lego, 279
Lemebel, Pedro, 4, 14, 16, 17, 21, 91,
    154–161, 154n9, 357,
    366n5, 369
Leminsky, Paulo, 356
Leppe, Carlos, 91
Lepra creadora, 4
L'érotisme (1957), 266
Lesbian, 222
The Lettered City, see Rama
Lewis, Vek, 283, 333
Lezama Lima, José, 4, 16, 20, 23,
    56n5, 58n8, 61, 62, 62n9, 127,
    133, 137
LGBTQ, 292, 336
LGBTQ activism, 174, 177, 217, 233
LGBTQ-I, 8
LGBTQ-I community, 292
Libertella, Héctor, 355
Lins, Osman, 135

Lispector, Clarice, 135, 255, 356
Living otherwise, 369
Lóbulo, 308
Logocentrism, 272, 328, 339, 355,
    356, 364, 367, 371
Logos, 116, 265, 305, 331, 353
López Alfonso, Francisco José, 252
Los ríos profundos, 47
    See also Arguedas
Lumpérica, 255, 263, 272
Lyotard, Jean François, 17,
    267n12, 342
    The Postmodern Condition,
    60, 66

M
Macedonio Fernández, 134
Madureira, Carlos, 49
Magical realism, 133, 134, 233
Malamud, Carlos, 126, 129
Mano de obra (Eltit), 331
Mapping, 360
Marinello, Pedro, 155, 156
Martínez, Ariel, 169, 169n16,
    172, 173
Masculinity and femininity, 169
Masiello, Francine, 187
Mask, 252, 253, 260, 260n8, 292
Mateo del Pino, Ángeles, 335
Menstrual, 162–166, 174, 180, 290,
    291, 302, 303, 338
Menstrual, Naty, 4, 14, 17, 355
Mercado, Tununa, 103
Mestiza, 319
Mestiza consciousness, 309, 311, 317,
    340, 358
Mestizaje, 11, 36, 38, 43, 46, 48–50,
    53, 58n8, 67, 69, 75, 78, 83,
    310, 315, 318, 319, 341
Mestizo, 15, 25, 29, 43, 48, 84, 127,
    184, 188, 189, 217, 234, 235

382 INDEX

Metadiscourse, 60, 87, 99–101, 103, 107, 108, 146, 204, 206, 207, 241, 254, 264, 301
Metafiction, 244, 302
Metalhead, 369
Metamorfosis, 20, 22, 95, 125, 138, 139, 143, 150, 165, 177, 203–215, 220, 221, 246, 247, 251, 267, 272, 280, 285–309, 311, 331, 358
Metanarrative, 143, 147, 199, 200, 208, 213, 301, 302, 335
Metaphor, 247, 265, 271, 292, 319
Metonymy, 139, 201, 247, 249, 250, 280
Mexterminator, 226, 230, 231
Miki, 183, 183n24, 184, 186
Mimesis, 300
Mimetism, 355, 356, 367
Mirko Lauer, 355
Modernity, 6, 7, 14, 17, 49, 52, 55n4, 57, 58n7, 60, 66, 67, 72, 128, 266, 267n12, 324, 342, 366
Monsiváis, Carlos, 332, 335
Monsters, 172, 173, 294, 298, 303, 317, 358
Monstrosity, 171–173, 180
Monstrous, 55, 298, 302–304, 307, 338
Monstrous identity, 303
Montalbán, *see La Monja Alférez*
Mora, Ana Sabrina, 169, 169n16, 172, 173
Moraes, Eliane Robert, 92n14, 96, 261, 264
Moraga, Cherríe, 12, 69, 70, 75, 78, 102, 131, 242, 313–316, 340
Morris, Charles, 268, 271
Morrison, Jim, 190, 192, 196, 298, 324
Motley mix, 3
Mulato, 127

Muller, Alfredo, 179, 181–186, 367
Multiplicity, 5, 11
Muñoz, José Esteban, 15, 20, 21, 88, 89, 93, 114, 282, 283, 285, 360, 361n3, 363
Mutants, 8, 13, 24, 59, 61, 71, 107, 136–140, 143, 150, 165, 172, 181, 189, 193, 195, 198, 203, 206, 207, 230, 284, 291, 294–296, 298, 300, 302–304, 317, 324, 326, 331, 336, 338, 343, 355, 357, 368–370
Mutation, 307, 325, 338
Myth-making, 80

N
NAFTA, 227
Naftazteca, 226, 231, 232, 340
Nahuatl, 217, 218, 220, 304, 310, 315
Native Americans, 68–70, 77, 192, 226, 262, 315, 325
See also Indigenous
Native Andean, 182
Neoavant-garde, 56, 66, 80, 151, 186, 244, 368
Neobaroque, 1–29, 3n1, 33, 34, 36, 40, 48, 51, 53–56, 55n4, 56n5, 58–61, 58n7, 58n8, 62n9, 63, 65–68, 66n12, 71, 76, 79–83, 86–88, 92, 93, 95, 96, 98, 99, 106–108, 110, 111, 116, 117, 119, 125, 126, 128, 130, 132–134, 136, 137, 140, 143, 147, 152, 154, 157, 158, 160, 162, 172, 173, 180–182, 184, 185, 188, 193, 198, 199, 207, 208, 218, 229, 233, 234, 236, 241–268, 246n3, 272, 275, 277, 285, 299, 302, 307, 310, 315, 321, 323–325, 327–344, 353–360, 363, 365–371

INDEX 383

style, 40
exuberance, 2
poetics, 242, 315
Neocolonialism, 328, 339
Neoliberalism, 151, 154, 157, 158
Nepantla, 12, 68, 75, 77, 78, 115,
    304, 310–320, 324, 326, 343,
    354, 357, 358, 360, 364, 366,
    368, 370, 371
Nepantlera, 313–317
Nepantlism, 2, 12, 14, 20, 24, 77, 90,
    242, 310, 315, 316, 340
New *mestiza*, 217–220, 222, 223
New *mestiza* consciousness, 75, 77, 83
New Narrative, 134
New World Border, 226, 227n43,
    228, 233
    See also Gómez-Peña
New York City, 256
Nietzsche, 107n16, 109
Noll, João Gilberto, 135
Nomad, 213, 355, 359, 361, 369, 371
Nomadic
    identity, 173, 180, 182, 189, 190,
        205, 208, 225, 226, 361, 362
    plurality of selves, 167
    selfhood, 354, 365, 371
    subjects, 3, 25, 75, 78, 80–82, 84,
        92, 98, 99, 119, 125,
        160, 224
    transgressions, 136–236
    transits, 68, 94
    See also Nomadism
Nomadic Subjects (1994), 79, 80
Nomadism, 2, 4, 6–8, 14, 19–21, 26,
    33, 34, 36, 40, 71, 75, 77–83,
    86, 95, 97, 99, 100, 111, 112,
    118n20, 125, 132, 178, 223,
    241, 242, 258–261, 266–311,
    317, 324–331, 336–344, 354,
    358, 360–363, 366, 368, 369
Norat, Gisela, 332

O
"Object," 268, 288
A obscena senhora D, see Hilst
Oiticica, Hélio, 356
Onetti, Juan Carlos, 134
Open sign, 266–272
Opulence, 63, 67, 87, 96
Ortiz, Fernando, 10, 38, 46, 46n3,
    47, 53, 85, 126, 189
Oscar Wilde, 367
Other, 35, 36, 39, 43–46, 52, 53,
    58n8, 60–62, 62n9, 65, 68–71,
    74, 76, 78–82, 84, 85, 87, 88,
    92, 94, 95, 98, 100, 103, 106,
    113, 117
Otherness, 7, 8, 10, 15, 18, 24,
    26–28, 53, 70, 93–95, 111, 117,
    248, 252, 257, 261, 267, 273,
    275–277, 281, 286, 293,
    298–300, 304, 307, 311, 313,
    315–317, 320, 324, 325,
    328–344, 358, 359, 361, 364,
    365, 368–370
Overcodification, 246, 251

P
Palaversich, Diana, 144, 146, 207
Palinuro de México, see del Paso,
    Fernando
Panesi, 295
Parody, 2, 6, 18, 20, 22, 243–260,
    247n4, 265, 266, 285, 290, 301,
    321, 330–332, 339, 358, 367
Part maudite, 261
Patriarchal categories, 244, 306
Patriarchal logocentrism, 23
Patriarchal system, 210, 211
Paul Rivet, 41
Peirce, Charles S., 15, 22, 25, 100,
    104, 108, 241, 268–272, 288,
    294, 315, 318

384 INDEX

Peralta, Jorge Luis, 161–164, 161n11, 167, 290, 291n16, 302, 303
Performance, 33, 55, 58, 60, 68, 70, 71, 82, 85, 86, 89, 93, 96–98, 101, 106, 107, 110, 112, 114–117, 136–236, 171n19, 255, 258, 272, 283, 290, 294, 296, 298, 332, 339, 353–355, 361, 363, 365, 367, 368
Performance novel, 209, 209n33
Peri Rossi, Cristina, 134, 332
Perlongher, Néstor, 2, 14, 16, 20, 21, 29, 65, 67, 109, 118, 118n20, 133, 189, 242, 273, 274, 296, 298, 309, 320–324
  Prosa plebeya, 273, 323, 332, 335, 336
Pharies, David A., 269
Philosophical implications, 353, 364
Philosophical nomadism, 361
Picón Salas, Mariano, 38, 48
Plaza Atenas, Dino, 335
Poblete, Nicolás, 308
Pocha Nostra, 70, 225, 231
Poemario Trans Pirado
  Shock, Susy, 169, 170
Points of passage, 2, 24, 68, 189
Poland, 66
Political dissidence, 329
Political engagement, *see* Political implications
Political implications, 242, 257, 274, 344, 353, 355, 357, 361–367, 369
Politics, 53, 73, 82, 89, 97, 98, 130, 135, 147, 156, 177, 227, 256–258, 277–279, 297, 298, 307, 320–322, 329–334, 360
Polyphony, 47, 52, 53, 301, 333, 354
Positionality, 73, 79, 80, 106
Post-Boom, 134, 152, 242

Postcolonial, 6, 12, 14, 17, 18, 20, 23, 24, 36, 45, 56n5, 64, 66, 67, 85, 91
Postcolonialism, 273, 289, 324, 329, 330, 337, 339, 343, 364, 366, 368
Posthuman, 267, 272, 285–309, 327, 333, 343, 360, 361, 369, 370
  cyborgs, 267, 285–309
  identity, 208
  subject, 306, 333
Posthumanity, 126
Postmodern, 17, 27, 53, 57, 60, 66, 67, 79, 80, 91, 119, 242, 244, 251, 267n12, 341, 356, 357, 359, 366, 368, 369, 371
  condition, 17
  crisis, 359
  See also Postmodernity
The Postmodern Condition (1984), 356
Postmodernity, 17, 23, 52, 356n2, 358, 364
Poststructuralism, 242, 274
Potentia, 95, 275, 333
Potlatch, 261, 261n10
Potosí, 127
Prado, Eugenia, 4, 14, 18, 21, 59, 91, 208–215, 209n33, 212n35, 213n36
  Lóbulo, 213, 213n36
Pragmatic dimension of the sign, 271
Pratt, Mary Louise, 2, 84, 85, 228, 274, 329
Prieto, René, 103
Proliferation, 58n8, 76, 82, 247, 247n4, 249, 251, 255, 257, 258, 261, 299, 311
Proliferation of genders, 257
Puig, Manuel, 135
Punks, 343, 369
Puntos de pasaje, 309, 320–324
Purity, 5, 16, 27, 28, 222, 362

INDEX 385

Q

Qadós, 255, 264, 266, 272, 280, 283
  See also Hilst
Queer, 3, 4, 6, 14, 18, 20, 22, 24, 25,
  27, 38, 73, 77, 80, 87, 88, 92,
  93, 96, 114–116, 125, 130, 134,
  135, 147, 157, 165, 172, 198,
  218, 219, 222, 233, 241, 244,
  276–280, 282, 284, 296, 300,
  304, 316, 321, 322, 332, 336,
  339, 341, 342, 354, 355,
  363–365, 367, 368, 371
  and border theory, 3
  becomings, 354
  identity, 28
  studies, 25
  theory, 6, 25, 27, 73, 77, 88, 93
Queering, 267, 276, 277, 292
Queerness, 4, 17, 20, 22, 24, 25, 27,
  69, 83, 86–88, 91, 93, 95, 115,
  117, 189–203, 220, 242, 272,
  276, 277, 283, 292, 299, 300,
  304, 336, 353, 355, 369
Quevedo, Francisco de, 166
Quinlan, Susan Canty, 321–323

R

Rama, Angel, 8, 10, 18, 29, 35, 38,
  42, 46, 46n3, 53, 63
Rivera, Alex, 70, 71
Real maravilloso, 61, 133
Representamen, 268–272, 288
Resistance, 6, 7, 18, 20, 22,
  23, 28, 366
Restrepo, Luis Fernando, 41–43
Reyes, Alfonso, 243, 243n2
Rhizome, 2, 109, 255, 273, 327
Richard, Nelly, 90, 187, 275, 330–333
Rincón, Carlos, 14, 23, 51–53, 58, 81,
  296, 325
Río de la Plata, 61, 67, 355, 366n5

Rivera Cusicanqui, Silvia, 3, 5, 77,
  309, 318
Rodríguez Juliá, Edgardo, 335
Roth, Joseph, 302
Rousset, Jean, 55
Ruiz-Aho, Elena, 71–73, 242
Rulfo, Juan, 134
Russian formalists, 245

S

Salón de belleza, 252, 301
  See also Bellatin
San Martín, José de, 188, 234
Sandoval, Chela, 69, 78
Santiago, Silviano, 2, 14, 16, 20, 135,
  147, 147n7, 242, 255, 256, 281,
  291, 309, 320–324, 321n19,
  330, 335
Santos-Febres, Mayra, 355, 357
Sarduy, Severo, 2, 4, 14, 16, 17, 20,
  21, 35, 57–61, 58n8, 62n9, 63,
  65–67, 66n12, 76, 82, 92, 93,
  95, 96, 108, 111–113, 116, 133,
  137, 138n4, 141, 142n5, 203,
  203n30, 242, 244–248, 247n4,
  250, 251, 253, 254, 254n7, 257,
  259, 260, 262, 262n11, 263,
  265, 267, 291, 292, 296,
  299–301, 311, 317, 322, 323,
  330–332, 343
  Cobra, 60, 61, 89
  Colibrí, 60
  De donde son los cantantes, 60
Saussure, Ferdinand de, 15, 268,
  269, 271
Scarpetta, Guy, 246, 246n3
Schultz, Bruno, 66
Sedgwick, Eve Kosofsky, 73, 88
Sedition, 328–344
  See also Politics
Seduction, 6, 22, 320, 328–344, 367

386 INDEX

Self, 6, 14, 15, 22, 67, 95, 221, 286, 293, 311–312, 328–344, 358
Selfhood, 1, 2, 4–7, 13, 21, 24, 25, 27, 34, 35, 38, 49, 53, 68, 72–75, 79, 85, 94, 100, 102, 111, 115, 117, 119, 125, 127, 131, 136, 140, 150, 153, 163, 171, 172, 195, 214, 223, 224, 236, 242, 258, 267, 268, 272, 273, 278, 283, 289, 299, 305, 309, 310, 318, 328, 337, 339, 343, 353, 355, 357–360, 362, 364, 365, 368, 370
  See also Self; Transitive selfhood
Self-mutilation, 263
Semiosis, 258–261, 269, 270, 272
Semiotics, 241, 267–272, 315
Semiotic triad, 268
Señor Barroco, 62, 62n9, 127, 235
Serpent, 304
Sexualities, trans-gressive/-itive, 149
Shadow-Beast, 218, 304
Shock, Susy, 4, 14, 17, 167, 168, 168n15, 170, 170n17, 172, 173, 272, 284, 290, 301, 303, 304, 332, 355
Sifuentes-Jáuregui, Ben, 286
Simulacra and Simulation (1994), 251
Simulation, 61, 76, 99, 112, 113, 242–258, 252n6, 260, 266, 284–287, 290, 292, 294, 299, 301, 308, 311, 321, 330
Simultaneity, 5, 11, 12, 51–53, 81, 83
Sleep Dealer, 70, 71
Socio-critical theories of literature, 271n13
Soich, Matías, 23
Sor Juana Inés de la Cruz, 137
Space of contact, 6
  See also Contact zone
Space-in-between, 12

Spaces of in-between, 242, 310–320, 323
Spanglish, 2
Speech act, 264
Squandering, 111, 117, 246, 247, 249, 257, 261, 263, 330
Stella Manhattan, see Santiago
Strategy, destabilization, 3
Stylization, 56, 57, 61, 62n9, 63
Subalternity, 42
Subject, 101n15, 102, 118
Subject-as-becoming, 242
Subject-in-process, 5, 18, 20, 77
Subject without center, 273
Subversion, *see* Identity
Sutherland, Juan Pablo, 208, 298
Syncretism, 34, 43, 45, 53, 54

T
Tattooing, 101, 109
Technologies of Gender, 104
Technology, 208, 209, 211, 212
Tengo miedo torero, 357
  See also Lemebel
Tepotzotlán, 358
Textuality, 33
"Third" element, 269, 288
"Third" sex, 151, 288, 291, 294, 321
The Three Fridas, 231
Tokyo Hotel, 298
Toro, 14
Trans, 1–8, 12, 14, 16, 18, 20–29 transiting, 2, 8, 15, 23, 24, 27
Trans*, 2, 14, 25, 54, 69, 89, 90, 93, 109, 114–116, 242, 273, 277–280, 283, 284, 295, 311, 327, 353–355, 355n1, 358–366, 368, 370, 371
Trans*: a Quick and Quirky Account of Gender Variability, *see* Halberstam

Transcendence, 261, 264, 274
Transcendental, 359
Transcultural, 251, 309, 335
Transculturation, 10, 11, 19, 24, 38,
    43, 45–47, 53, 67, 85, 131, 296
Transentity, 1, 7, 8, 24, 241, 276,
    280, 325, 355, 359, 363
Transexuality, 285
Trans Formaciones, see Shock
Transformation, 2, 4, 7, 12, 15, 27,
    28, 33–35, 43, 48–50, 57, 61,
    68, 75–78, 82, 86, 90, 94, 95,
    97–100, 116
Transformative effects, 242
Transformism, 144, 146, 173, 174,
    177, 179–181, 207
Transformist, 145, 173, 174, 178, 180,
    183, 281, 301, 311, 336, 344
Transgression, 1, 3, 6, 7, 10, 21, 26–28,
    33–36, 70, 75, 77, 84–86, 92, 95,
    96, 98–101, 106, 111, 125, 136,
    149, 151, 177, 178, 180, 191,
    201, 202, 242, 245–258, 260,
    263–272, 274, 276, 277, 289,
    291, 292, 301, 316, 321–323,
    328, 330, 331, 333, 338, 339,
    342, 354, 358, 366, 369
Transgressive characters, 241, 242,
    244, 272
Trans-identity, 1, 3, 4, 6–8, 12, 14,
    18, 21–25, 27, 54, 88–90, 93,
    98, 100, 101, 114, 115, 153,
    167, 168, 185, 197, 226, 241,
    242, 261, 267, 274, 277, 278,
    283, 310, 311, 344
Transit, 1, 3, 10, 25, 29, 126, 131, 151,
    154, 168, 188, 197, 198, 213,
    226, 242, 252, 257, 273,
    297–299, 310, 316, 320, 322–325,
    329, 336, 344, 359, 361, 363, 365
Transitive identities, 1, 13, 24, 27,
    265, 284

Transitive self, 5, 19
Transitive selfhood, 3, 22, 241, 272, 310
Transitivity, 3, 4, 6, 7, 11, 19–23, 27,
    28, 33, 36, 38, 50, 52, 53, 68,
    75, 82, 83, 86, 89, 90, 95, 99,
    101, 110, 111, 115, 126, 147,
    149, 192, 198, 199, 217, 222,
    242, 252, 262, 274, 278, 280,
    283, 289, 296, 303, 308, 321,
    324, 325, 327, 329, 335, 337,
    344, 353, 359, 363, 368–370
Transits, 93, 94
Transmerica, 1, 3, 7, 9, 10, 23–29, 40,
    71, 93, 242, 276, 360, 371
Transnationalization, 50
Transplatinian Caribbean, 17
Trans-self, 1, 4–6, 8, 14, 18, 23–25,
    27, 28, 33, 38, 68, 86, 90, 93,
    98, 100, 109, 111, 117–119, 126,
    136, 143, 173, 179, 215, 223,
    236, 242, 261, 267, 282, 297,
    324, 326–328, 337, 339, 344
Transvestism, 242, 245, 276, 277,
    280, 282–309, 311, 322, 331,
    334, 335, 355, 357, 358
Transvestite, 137, 145, 146, 153,
    155–158, 162–166, 168n13, 169,
    171, 174, 178, 180, 188, 190,
    197, 198, 204, 206, 230, 249,
    253, 254, 256, 280, 281,
    283–285, 287–292, 296,
    299–301, 303, 332, 334, 335, 338
*Travesti/Una teoría lo suficientemente
    buena*, 145, 161n11, 164, 167,
    168, 168n13, 170, 173, 281
    See also Wayar
Triadic sign, 22, 25, 241, 266,
    268–270, 288, 294
Trompe-l'oeil, 300, 301
Tropicana, 70
The Two Fridas, 326
    See also Lemebel

388 INDEX

U

Urban cliques, 8, 343, 369
Urbanski, 36, 39, 40
US-Latinos, 3, 14, 70, 71
  US Latine, 3
US-Mexican border, 216, 226
US-Mexico border, 363

V

Vaggione, Alicia, 145, 146, 252
Valenzuela, Luisa, 135
Velvet Underground, 190
Versátegui, Peruvian Enrique, 134
Vested Interests, 286, 338n21
Villada, Camila Sosa, 355
Violence, 354, 361n4
Virginia Woolf, 93, 207
Virgin of Guadalupe, 217
Vivancos Pérez, Ricardo F., 75, 78,
  216, 242, 312–314, 316, 317
Vodanovic, Sergio, 91
Volpi, Jorge, 134

W

Waphuri, 177, 178
Waste, *see* Squandering
Wayar, Marlene, 89, 93, 167, 170,
  170n18, 281, 284

Williamson, Edwin, 126, 128,
  130, 131
Writing, 220, 250
Writing across Cultures, *see* Rama
Writing the Body, 21, 24

X

*A Xicana Codex of Changing
  Consciousness*, 313, 314

Y

Yeguas del Apocalipsis, 154, 156,
  159, 160
Yin and yang, 359
Yin-yang, 368
Yo era una brasa, 294, 295n17, 357
Yo, yegua, 335
  See also Casas

Z

Zamora, Lois Parkinson, 22, 56,
  56n5, 57n6, 67, 242, 243n1,
  243n2, 250, 250n5, 324,
  344, 358
Zavaleta, René, 10
Zimmerman, Marc, 18, 22, 25
Zurbarán, Francisco de, 182